D1485683

101 134 640 BX

Two Young Men See the World

By Stanley Unwin

The Truth About Publishing

"It is the most candid, informing and interesting book on these matters I have ever read, and everyone any way concerned with the book trade will be the wiser for reading it." *Bookman*

"Mr. Unwin, at any rate, sets an example to authors in readability." *Manchester Guardian*

"The Aristotle of publishing!" HOUGHTON MIFFLIN COMPANY

"This admirably clear, reasonable and constructive study of modern publishing conditions. . . . He must be a very learned publisher indeed who does not find something to learn in the fruits of Mr. Unwin's wide experience." *Daily Telegraph*

"I place it among the two or three textbooks I know which are as fascinating to read as novels." A MUSIC PUBLISHER

"I have learnt about five hundred things from it." ARNOLD BENNETT

1 The Two Young Men

2 "Mosi-oa-tunya"—The Smoke that Sounds

Frontispiece

Two Young Men See the World

by

Stanley Unwin

and

Severn Storr

133 Illustrations

London

George Allen & Unwin Ltd

Museum Street

PRINTED IN GREAT BRITAIN
by
Unwin Brothers, Woking
on paper supplied by
Spalding & Hodge
The illustrations reproduced by
the Collographic Art Printers
Bound by Key & Whiting in
Morton Sundour fabric
fadeless & washable

FIRST PUBLISHED IN 1934

To

OUR HOSTS AND HOSTESSES
THROUGHOUT THE WORLD
TO WHOM WE OWE
SO MUCH

Prefatory Note

"TUSITALA," the Writer of Tales, as the Samoans called their beloved Robert Louis Stevenson, has said that the best way of writing a good book is to write it first in the form of letters to someone you care for. This book was compiled unconsciously in just such a way in letters written at odd moments from odd corners of the world to the family circle in the Homeland.

After our return from eighteen months of wandering, and during the lapse of twenty successive years, the many friends who read our letters insisted that we should make them into a book, "because," they said, "they contain much that others might like to know."

We have all been travellers, and all the world is "written up," but we feel that our book, while it paints a picture of the world that is to some extent changed, yet gives an impression of Colonial life that will for many years to come remain a truthful one. Our Colonial communities are too nearly democratic to be threatened by the sudden changes which menace our older civilizations; and although roads, railways, and aeroplanes have done much to open up what was practically undeveloped country twenty years ago, and skyscrapers and cinemas may have altered the outlook of city dwellers, yet the "atmosphere," we feel sure, is still the same. And it is with the Colonial "atmosphere" that we are most concerned; if bungalows have been replaced by skyscrapers in the cities, the dry warmth of the South African high veld remains, the mauves of sunset are unaltered by the zoom of record-breaking planes. The limitless blue gum forests of Australia and the wellnigh two-thousand-mile-long banks of the Murray River are perhaps as sparsely populated now as they were then, and still await the hand of man to turn them into a productive paradise.

We can imagine little Tasmania just the same, her delightful pastures and orchards, hedgerows, streams, and hills clothed in a dappled quilt of shadow and sunshine as the great white clouds go rolling by. So with New Zealand: the majestic heights of Mount Cook, the beautiful shores of the Southern Lakes, the windswept Canterbury plains, and the restlessly palpitating thermal region of the North Island are still free for those who wish to roam there. In Polynesia and Melanesia unimagined political changes have taken place, and the Natives no doubt are slightly more Europeanized; but in Samoa let us hope they still sing the same sweet songs, and no doubt in New Guinea they still have cut-throat expressions on their faces.

Japan, perhaps, is where we shall see most change, Tokyo having been almost entirely rebuilt since the disastrous earthquake of 1923. But the upheavals of Nature and the ravages of Time appear to give additional charm to what has and will always be a land of perfect countryside visions.

We hope our book may encourage emigration when the good times return, as they surely will, and that it will give our readers some idea of what the countries described herein are really like; of their general atmosphere and individuality; of their everyday life, and what work is done and under what conditions.

If the following pages can do anything to decide the man of capital or the man of brawn to decentralize himself from the overcrowded British Isles and take his place in the great open spaces beneath the vast clear skies overseas, then we shall feel that the labour involved in selecting the most suitable passages from our letters and uniting them in the form of a continuous narrative has not been labour in vain.

In almost every Colonial city and in many of the smaller towns will be found a society of cultivated men and women in which anyone will feel at home; and Colonial hospitality is proverbial.

If we have dwelt at some length on our sojourning with various kinsfolk, it is in the hope that the reader may obtain from these artless records a truer impression of what life overseas really means than he might derive from a book written with more care and more deliberate purpose.

Our endeavours to abridge the book have not proved as successful as we could have wished. We submitted the MS. to several competent readers, but the suggested deletions of one were reinstated by another, together with portions which we ourselves had definitely excluded, and in the end the length remained unchanged.

The title has been criticized on the ground that we did not see the entire world. Who has? Our idea was to see as much as we could in the eighteen months at our disposal and whether our eyes were opened or not by what we saw, we will leave our indulgent readers to judge.

In conclusion we would like to say that we undertook this journey primarily to study bookselling conditions in the countries visited, and secondly to study the conditions under which the peoples of those countries have to live. We were not out to write a story or to seek adventure, but we enjoyed the latter when, as is inevitable on such a journey, it came our way.

Our readers must remember that extracts have been made from the letters of two different writers; sometimes "Stan" and sometimes "Johnnie" takes up the tale, but in most cases we have endeavoured, though it has not always been possible, to talk about ourselves as "we"!

Contents

JAPAN

List of Illustrations

Two Young Men See the World

AFRICA

What do we know (and what do we care) of Time
and his silver scythe?
Since there is always time to spare so long as a man's
alive:
The world may come, and the world may go, and the
world may whistle by,
But the Pace of the Ox is steady (and slow), and life
is a lullaby.

CULLEN GOULDSBURY

Chapter I

OUTWARD BOUND

A STRONG stale smell of whisky permeated the passages and cabins; at least Huxley, our cabin steward, told us that it was whisky when we complained to him about it. "We've a large cargo of whisky on board," he explained, "destined for South Africa and Australia. The smell will wear off in a day or two," he added with a knowing grin. Little did we realize then how extraordinarily cheap whisky was—I believe 3s. 6d. a bottle, for I am talking of the month of July 1912. Little did we know then of that great power for good *and evil* that was being borne southwards with us over the tossing seas, to be hailed by white man and black alike as a demi-god, in the vast, parched, dusty plateaux of the veld, the palatial bars of Jo'burg, or by the bush whackers and sundowners of Australia's blue gum wildernesses. As the good ship *Anchises* rolled and pitched down the Irish Channel, I lay in my bunk and wondered—wondered if I was going to be sick, wondered if I should ever see Home again, and if I had really made a good decision in accepting my Father's generous advice and financial assistance, to complete my education by this trip round the world.

My companion Stanley, fellow collaborator in the pages that follow, who was groaning in the bunk below me, had already seen something of the New World, and had worked long enough in the Old to pay his own way without paternal assistance; and the third occupant of our cabin, my brother (Wilfred R. Storr), who had amassed a moderate fortune in the City, was eating a hearty breakfast with the hardened travellers of the deep in the saloon, and was just going as far as Las Palmas to see us on our way and enjoy his few days at sea. Those who have travelled the high seas know how wearisome these long voyages can be, and those who have not done so are always envious of those who have. Stan and I were no lovers of the sea, except when it was dead calm, but there were moments when even land-lubbers like ourselves could revel in this first step on the long journey we had planned.

At night, as we drew near the Line, we stood in the prow of our ship clad only in pyjamas, and by day, from the same place, we looked down upon the shoals of flying fish, pink nautilus, porpoises, and sharks. The uninitiated males spent much time speculating as to what was to become of them when we crossed the Line, and Father Neptune and his Court came aboard with their horrid gear of soft soap and vinegar, tridents, razors, and syringes. The catalogue of tortures we were about to endure grew in length and gruesomeness as the distance between us and our fate was steadily decreased by thumping engines, lashing propellers, bugles calling us to meals, and kindly stewards (our enemies-to-be) poking us in the ribs to wake us, to bathe, to biscuits and inevitable tea!

Friends returning to the Antipodes told us on melting moonlit nights of the approaching glories of the Southern Cross, and the wonders of Sydney Harbour, beyond compare. We criticized Mrs. This and Mr. That, gossiped, scandalized, slept, confided, shocked, and sometimes apologized. We played chess with the serious and flirted with the frivolous, played deck games and danced with those we favoured most.

I was elected entertainment secretary because I was green and fell into the trap; I also fell into many others, and was always paying for drinks for this section of the crew or that. I found out how many talented people we had on board who were travelling incognito, and how many more there were who thought they were talented but were not. I also discovered that if you are lucky enough to win the sweep on the day's run, it is best to keep away from the smoke-room that evening. Ingratiate yourself rather with the Commander, and pace his favourite stretch of deck with him; no one will molest you there, your money is safe, and you are forgotten at noon the following day.

Thus we slid through the oily seas, which at night our propellers lashed into a lace-work phosphorescent train; by day squadrons of shining flying fish led us on and on, springing from the cleaving waters at our prow in tireless relays, whilst we sat and sweltered in the awning's shade.

Everyone knows or has read of King Neptune's time-honoured but graceless ways. He boarded us one night after dinner, he and his oily courtiers horrid in their regalia of engine grease and soot. There was a stampede for the cabins and oldest clothes; some emerged in pyjamas, others in bathing suits, and others again in underpants and socks. One might have thought from the excitement that our vessel was about to sink, but for the amusement and merry banter that was shouted all around. First the members of the crew and then the passengers were hunted out by name as Neptune's scouts scoured the ship for their victims. It is astounding how these shrewd detectives of the high seas know who has crossed the Line before and who has not, in spite of the clever lies they are told; and, with one exception, we all went through the mill and duly revenged ourselves on the Royal Court and the King of the Mighty Deep himself in a most spectacular rough and tumble in and around the swimming bath on the well-deck forward.

Such was the excitement that we all forgot to look for the Southern Cross until next evening after dinner, when, resting our bruised bodies against the promenade deck rail, we pointed it out with much pride to our favourite companions, who were invariably the most charming ladies figuring on our passenger list!

It was some two or three days after this when a rumour went round the ship that a certain Mr. X had escaped King Neptune's benediction. A meeting was called immediately in the smoke-room; Mr. A was elected to the chair, because he was the man who had crossed the Line more often than anyone else among the passengers, because he always liked to be foremost in making things uncomfortable for everyone else but himself, because in fact he saw to it that we *made* him chairman. It was decided after much argument that Mr. X must stand his trial at the Supreme Court of Justice of the High Seas, which was to sit for this special purpose in three days' time. Judge, jury, prosecuting counsel, and witnesses were easily obtained, but no one would act as counsel for the defence until my companion, Stan, said he would willingly undertake that duty. People looked at him askance, although the whole thing was a joke, during those intervening days; but when the time came for him to address the jury, after the prosecution had made out a flawless case against the prisoner, the packed Court House was genuinely thrilled by a speech which was delivered in all seriousness and with much oratorical skill. Even the judge saw it would be hopeless to convict the defendant in the face of such a just and loudly applauded pleader. In his summing-up he indicated that Mr. X should be acquitted, and this was done, but the poor fellow had behaved in such a stupid way throughout the whole affair that he remained the blacksheep of the ship's company for the remainder of the voyage, whilst his counsel rose high in the estimation of his fellow passengers.

In such ways as these and in pleasant games and conversations is the boredom of a long voyage dissipated. Our ship drew out of the tropic seas and soon was tossing in the troubled waters off the Cape of Good Hope, where Atlantic and Indian Oceans wrestle for supremacy and the cold Antarctic keeps breaking them asunder like a watchful referee.

At last, after a somewhat riotous Sunday evening, knowing that the morrow would see us ashore, we turned into our bunks early, but to little avail. No sooner were we asleep than we were awakened by the steward and told the immigration officer wanted to see us. And later we were disturbed again, to visit the same official, but this time in error. The donkey engine above our heads began to work, and we heard some say that the pilot had brought letters aboard. To make matters worse they put the clock on an hour and called us accordingly, so that, as Johnnie said, "You could hardly call it a night."

What a wonderful sight greeted us next morning as we came on deck!

Two Rooineks* *Arrive at The Cape*

If the heart of the Englishman who has been long absent from Home thumps within him when he sees the white cliffs of Dover once again, and that of the Australian when he beholds the puny Heads of Sydney Harbour, the heartstrings of the South African must wellnigh break when he rushes on deck to gaze on his "Mountain" and its attendants, the Lion's Head and the Devil's Peak. Bathed in the red light of early morning, its lower limbs beskirted by an opalescent, hovering veil of mist, set in a background of topaz sky where rare stars linger, here is Table Mountain, two miles broad, 4,000 feet high, the colossal black guard of Africa, whose magic spell remains with a man throughout his life! How the stout hearts of Saldanha's scurvy-ridden and verminous crews must have been awed by the sight of this gigantic wall of precipitous rock towering above their pigmy ships when they came here in 1503! How they must have longed to get ashore to explore the unknown land spread temptingly at this giant's feet and about the immense perimeter of the curving bay! Fresh water and fresh food were worth risking life to find, and what was life to them who knew all the horrors of the Great Unknown? A Hottentot in pursuit of game on one of the bush-clad foothills, which composed this monster's toes, looked down a moment on the wide expanse of bay. What were those great white birds he saw, skimming the water towards the shore? He knew them to be enormous birds, yet at this distance, and from the height where he stood, they looked like newborn clouds in the vastness of an azure alpine sky. To him, and

* *Rooinek* (=red-neck), Cape Dutch for an "inexperienced person," a "muff."

those of his race to come after him, these ships proved to be a newborn cloud!

Thus came the Portuguese officer, Antonio de Saldanha, and his men, the first white men to enter Table Bay and to set foot on the Cape Peninsula, and thus we had come many centuries later fearful of finding a cockroach in our cabin, disgusted and demoralized by the bite of a bug; fat, well, and clean from the luxuries enjoyed on our voyage to the Cape.

During our ten days' stay in Cape Town we were the guests of friends and relations whose almost excessive hospitality was but a prelude to that which we were to receive in every other land we visited. In England we hardly know the meaning of the word "hospitality"; in our Colonies and dependencies the word has outgrown its meaning! In this way we were treated as one of the family in every home we went to, and we had every opportunity, not only of studying the conditions of living at first hand, but of being taken on numberless excursions into the country and learning many of its problems and successes.

The vast majority of houses in South Africa are of the bungalow type with broad stoeps or verandas around them. Upon these stoeps passes much of the family life of townsfolk and country people alike. Here we often sat in our shirt-sleeves, basking in the grilling winter sunshine, writing letters home, raising our eyes from time to time to marvel at the deep purple of the mountain's flanks, the bright ultramarine of Table Bay, or the brilliance of some quaint flower. Our hostess would arrive with the inevitable cup of tea, and a great grey-backed red-tailed parrot, swinging in its cage, would keep calling: "Come on! Come on!" But we just did *not* want to "Come on" so long as we could sit there and swelter in that mellow sunshine. Here on the stoep we often took our meals, entertained our callers, and at sunset, when the great red disc plunged abruptly behind the purple mountains, we sipped our "sundowner" of whisky or lime juice and watched the dazzling stars as they crowded into the swiftly darkening night. Except for its situation and surroundings, which are magnificent, Cape Town could not be called an imposing city. During our stay we saw everything there was to see, or nearly so.

We were "personally conducted" over the Houses of Parliament by Dr. Flint, Librarian to the House of Assembly. It was as we were passing through the Library that we came across the Hon. W. P. Schreiner, an ex-Premier and brother of Olive Schreiner, the famous authoress of *The Story of an African Farm*. Dr. Flint at once introduced us, and we had a very interesting half-an-hour's conversation.

We were shown round the Museum by its amiable Director, M. Peringuey, who explained the most interesting collection of bushman drawings. These are native pictures, mostly of animals, that have been found on the walls of caves up country, and of which we were to learn more when we came to Bulawayo. We visited the editors of the local Press, and were shown over their printing establishments; Stan called upon all the booksellers, and I called upon a few tobacconists with a line of cigarettes, from the commission on the sale of which I hoped to help pay my expenses. Unfortunately my expectations were doomed to disappointment, for, on unpacking my samples, I found most of the cigarettes had grown mouldy beards in the tropics, the manufacturers having disregarded my instructions to pack them in airtight tins! We sometimes took lunch with our friends on the first-floor veranda restaurants that overlooked Table Bay. This was another delightful innovation to a Londoner used to taking his hurried midday meals of roast beef and boiled, with compressed squares of cabbage, in some glittering underground smoking hell.

One morning we took train for Kenilworth, a suburb of Cape Town. We were invited to lunch with Dr. and Mrs. Murray, a charming couple, who had a delightful house in an entrancing situation. Here we met quite a large party of distinguished residents, and we were entertained in a liberal manner. For the first time we tasted the flesh of springbok and some wonderful orange syrup.

We talked with Dr. Murray, who was a keen eugenist, and later to Mrs. Murray, who was a friend of Olive Schreiner. It was very interesting to hear something other than the Imperialistic anti-Dutch point of view which we had heard on practically all sides. We did not find ourselves wholly in sympathy with either party out here. We held no brief for the Dutchman, for some of the few we had then met had not proved very lovable or very "straight," according to English ideas. But we could well understand and appreciate his desire to preserve his national traditions. "Punishment is lame, but it comes," and it seemed to us that the British were paying somewhat heavily for the South African war. But the jingoes did not look upon it at all in this light, they laid the blame entirely upon Gladstone's surrender after Majuba. Superficially, there seems to be a good deal to be said for this line of argument, but although these questions interested us above all others, space does not allow us to go into them here.

After tea at the home of some other friends we had a walk through the beautiful Wynberg Park, and then we hurried back to "Town" as we had to be astir early next morning to climb the "Mountain." Table Mountain may be scaled in various ways, and since we were there, a way up has been made for "infants and invalids" by means of an aerial cableway. In our day, thank goodness, no such monstrosity existed; either you went the easy way up by Kasteel's Poort, or, if you were an expert rock climber, you went up as a fly walks up a wall, hanging on to the slightest projections of the rock by your eyebrows, your finger-nails, and the clouts in your boots.

Unfortunately for the readers of these lines we were not experts, and so we went the easy way up, but even this proved almost too much for one member of our party in a subsequent ascent. This time, however, Mr. Townshend took charge, for he had been up the "Mountain" hundreds of times. We had intended starting out early in order to make the climb in cool morning air, but the day broke with the weather vane pointing to the south-east, an evil omen our leader told us, for at any

3 Cock fighting on board the *Anchises*

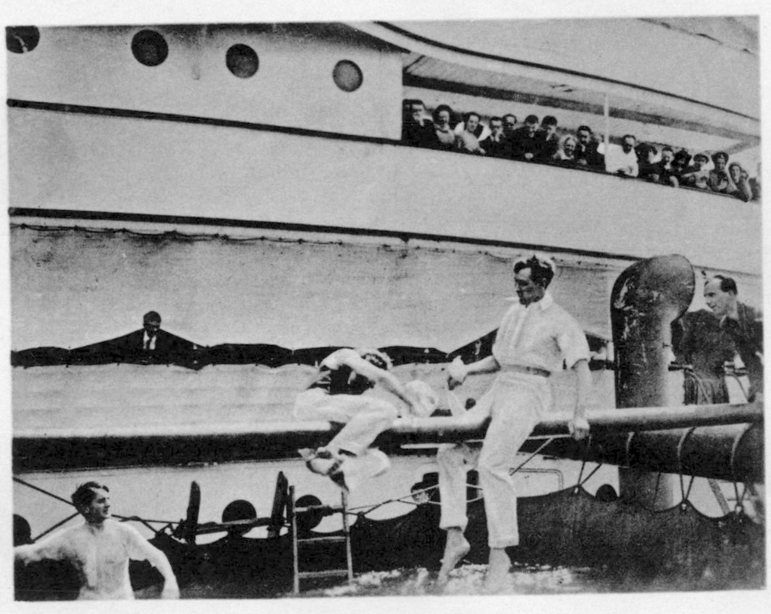

4 John Stead disposes of Stanley Unwin

5 Atlantic Breakers and The Apostles, Camps Bay

6 The Lion's Head from Camps Bay

moment, and in spite of cloudless skies, the famous "Tablecloth" might be flung over the mountain-top and hang its even-edged folds of dense vapour into space and so obliterate the summit ridge from view.

Not a few unwary mountaineers have been trapped on Table Mountain in this way. Some sat still for many weary hours waiting for the clouds to lift, chilled to the bone and without food, and others, groping their way through the dense fog in search of the Platte Klip Gorge, have stepped into space and been shattered to pieces on the rocks at the end of a 4,000-foot fall! As our disappointment would have been great if we had not made the climb, and as our guide knew his ground so well, we decided to start. It was 11.30 a.m. when we arrived at Kasteel's Poort, the place where those leaving "Town" at 5.30 a.m. stop to rest and breakfast. Here the mist began to blow up from the sea, but we still hoped that it was only "morning glory" and would clear away, so we decided to go on as we had planned, and return by the gorge. But the mist became thicker and thicker, and although we could see little of the beauties that surrounded us, it was clear enough to find our way easily to the Reservoir. At this point we got on a false track, and in a few seconds we could hardly see our feet in the denseness of the fog. Just at the critical moment the clouds lifted a little and showed us that we were going away from our objective, but before we could take our bearings properly we were enveloped once more, and our path again lost to sight, "though to memory dear." Thus we wandered hither and thither in the ever-thickening mist that seemed to soak its way through our clothing and chill us through and through.

Mr. Townshend was not a young man, nor very thin; in his youth he had been in many a worse scrape than this; he had fought in the Zulu wars as well as in the more recent campaign against the Boers. Since those days, however, he had taken unto himself a wife and child, and although he would be the last man to admit it, I could see he was thinking of their anxiety when he confessed, a little later on, that he was completely lost! The summit of Table Mountain is not one of those knife-edge concerns where a man has scarcely room to stand on his two feet; it is in reality a large undulating plateau, rock strewn and seamed with little boggy dales bedecked with most magnificent flora at nearly every season, a place where anyone might wander for days when the "Table-cloth" is neatly laid.

Mr. Townshend suggested that we should shelter under a nearby rock and eat our lunch and wait for a possible clearing of the mist, but Stan and I were eager to press on to the gorge, if it could be found; we were wet and cold, and preferred to keep on the move.

Since boyhood, when I spent much of my time wandering about some of the wildest parts of the Surrey hills, which were often wrapt in mists such as the one we found ourselves in now, I had always been known for my extraordinary "bump of locality." After a little discussion I managed to get myself elected guide, and we set off again in Indian file. I had no idea how far we were away from the Platte Klip Gorge, or what it looked like when we got there; I only had my host's assurance that it was on the brink of the 4,000-foot precipice, over which I might go at any moment if I did not exercise the greatest care.

I felt a distinct sense of direction, a very uncanny positive feeling; I doubt if I have ever been so sure of myself before or since. We had no compass, the sun was obscured, we had turned this way and that so many times that none of us knew which was the north. The wind was rising every minute, and blew uncertainly among the high rocks that towered about us in all directions. I went forward as quickly as I could to keep the blood circulating in our veins, for nothing is likely to dispirit a man more than a creeping chill crawling into his body. With my eyes glued to the ground searching for the sight of the slightest track, we scrambled onward over rocks and bogs, tripping up in the low scrub and slipping over loose stones. Once or twice I glanced over my shoulder and could

7 A ruffled "Table Cloth"

8 Rock strewn and seamed with little boggy dales

9 Crossing a Spruit on Stellenbosch road

10 "The Mountain of the Winds"

Photo by N. G. Unwin

just see the form of Mr. Townshend following on my heels, but Stan was obscured from my sight by the density of the fog; only his footsteps and an occasional remark assured me that he was still in touch with us. We had been on the move, one could scarcely call it walking, for some time when suddenly I heard a dull thud behind me and a hoarse exclamation from Stan. Turning quickly I could no longer see the shadow of Mr. Townshend, who had dropped some yards behind in negotiating a rather large boulder, and Stan was also out of sight, yet he, it proved, was the most terrified of any of us by what had happened. Emerging in his turn from behind the boulder, he was just in time to see Mr. Townshend stumble, lurch forward and disappear into the mist, his arms waving wildly above his head. Stan could not see me of course, and for a moment he was petrified with the thought that we had both gone over that precipice to a sickening death below! A few seconds later we were all roaring with laughter over the incident, whilst tears of mirth streamed down Mr. Townshend's cheeks. It appeared that he had tripped over a small hole covered with rushes and fallen heavily into the bog surrounding it, and when Stan came up to assist him he in his turn went into the hole and was up to his knees in icy-cold water!

This little mishap, combined with my gift of an extra sense, seemed to bring us good luck, for shortly afterwards I struck a distinct track which enabled us to get along more quickly. Mr. Townshend was a bit shaken up by his fall, so I told him to come along gently with Stan whilst I went ahead to investigate, and if I came to any branch path I would wait for them. I had not gone very far when I noticed the wind was still increasing in force, and as well as blowing horizontally it appeared to be blowing upwards, while the wall of cloud packed itself more closely and swirled about my head. I stopped and listened; a dull moaning noise rose from almost under my feet, and mingled with it, yet faint, a short shrill note that came and came again. Just as I was puzzling to make it out, the cloud suddenly rent itself and I saw with feelings of genuine horror that not four yards from where I stood the earth came to an abrupt end and complete emptiness lay beyond!

This I knew to be the treacherous "face of the Mountain," the noises I heard were the sirens of shipping in the bay mingled with the roaring of the wind against the precipice, a sound so awe-inspiring as to give the name of Devil's Peak to the eastern sentinel of this lofty range; it bore the more poetic title of "Mountain of the Winds" in van Riebeek's day. I hastened back along the path to warn the others of our proximity to the only real danger of climbing Table Mountain, and a few minutes later, wet, cold, and weary, we were munching our sandwiches behind a sheltering rock at the head of the gorge.

The descent is at the best of times a somewhat troublesome, not to say wearisome, performance, but, in the thick mist that still prevailed, it was additionally difficult. It was a case of clambering from boulder to boulder and doing your best not to sit down too suddenly. In due time we reached our homes, much to the relief of anxious friends and relatives, but it was a bitter disappointment to us not to have seen the superb view from the top of the "Mountain."

Next morning our good friend Mr. Jack Rose and his wife turned up in their car, and, after passing Somerset West, in about an hour we were climbing to the top of Sir Lowry's Pass. Our view was somewhat spoiled by the south-easter of the day before, mist and clouds still enveloped the higher mountain peaks, but the panorama was magnificent nevertheless. After a good scramble up a mountain side where we gathered armfuls of gladioli, protea, heath, and Africander, until the car was full of blooms, we turned back to Stellenbosch, the centre of Dutch learning and second oldest settlement in South Africa. Here in this peaceful old dorp were to be seen beautiful Dutch houses with their gables and thatch, many paned windows, and wide stoeps supported by tall white columns, dating from the end of the seventeenth century.

Avenues of oak trees lined the roadways, where water-courses rippled along bringing shade and freshness to the hottest day. But in contrast to these beauties of an age gone by, the architecture of some of the houses put up to-day is a positive eyesore.

About ten miles out of Stellenbosch we picnicked out on the open veld at a spot where we had a superb view of False Bay, and the ride from this point onwards through Paarl and Huguenot was a gradual unfolding of delightful Dutch villages, farms, and vineyards, all of course in their naked midwinter glory. And so on over the Drakenstein Mountains, past the Rhodes fruit farms to Merriman's and to Smartt's, who was then leader of the Opposition. Much of the best South African wine comes from Stellenbosch and Paarl, and likewise from Constantia on the Peninsula nearer to Cape Town. The first-named place was laid out by an early Dutch Governor, Simon van der Stel, in 1681, who, adding the maiden name of his wife, Bosch, to his own, called the place Stellenbosch, and the same lady's Christian name was Constance, hence Constantia.

Our friend drove skilfully over most atrociously bumpy roads that were often crossed by deep streams or "spruits," so that it was impossible to keep up much of a speed. In spite of this we covered a distance of about 135 miles on our day's drive, and came back by way of the Blue Berg Mountains, on the opposite side of Table Bay to Cape Town, where Mrs. Rose's mother had a farm of some 2,000 acres. To get there we had to climb over a steep hill, the road consisted of damp red clay, and although we were in bottom gear the car had the utmost difficulty in reaching the summit!

We came to the farm at last, a pretty old Dutch house with a row of eucalyptus trees standing guard in front. It lay in a fertile "daal," a lonely valley, looking out over the Atlantic, and some eighteen miles from Cape Town. An exquisite mauve and red sunset greeted our arrival there, and pale flashes came from the lighthouses along the distant coastline. Native boys were running hither and thither driving the sheep and goats into the kraal for the night, whilst Mrs. Rose and her mother were loading the car with cakes and chickens and legs of mutton to be taken away with a maternal blessing!

When we drove back round the bay at dark it was a wonderful sight to see the continuous curving line of lights dotted like fairy lamps all along the wide lap of this gigantic sitting monster, Table Mountain.

Thus the days sped by all too quickly; we wished for more time in which to revisit the many beautiful places in this winter paradise; but in five months' time we should be back again after our extensive tour up country and then we should be able to see Cape Town and its beautiful suburbs in their midsummer dress.

"If you venture to travel second class on the railways," said our kind friends at the Cape, "you will have a most unpleasant time; indeed one hardly ever sees white men, except 'poor whites,' travelling in this way." They did their best to dissuade us,* but we were poor enough not to be able to afford a first class fare for the long journey we had planned, so one morning we gave our friends the slight indignity of seeing off their poor relations second class, on the first stage of their journey, to Kimberley.

To Kimberley and its Diamond Mines

We had heard on all sides that the South African railways were very competently and successfully run by the State. Where traffic was comparatively light and distances great, as in such a country as South Africa, every possible economy had to be effected in the laying of the track. Instead of chairs and sleepers, all carefully wedged and bolted, the rails were just pegged down to the sleepers, and it was extraordinary to what a pitch of perfection they had brought this system, though the results were naturally not to be compared with a G.W.R. or L.M.S. track. The line was narrow-gauge, and

* This was over twenty years ago!

did not, therefore, permit of the huge 50-ton freight cars used in the States. But they made up for this in length, nearly three times the length of our trucks at home, and also by letting the cars project on either side. They would thus carry nearly forty tons. There were scarcely any tunnels, it was easier and cheaper to go round the hills; and the line was a "single track," except of course at sidings. The main difficulty out here was the question of gradients, and that fact alone prevented a faster service.

We spent many nights on these trains, and ate innumerable meals in the restaurant cars, and we found everything astonishingly well managed considering the distances run and the intensity of the heat by day and the density of the dust at times.

We soon left Cape Town behind, and the large townships or "dorps" of Paarl, Wellington, and Worcester, after which we passed through bleak and lonely valleys with long ranges of bare mountains on either side. There was little to see but a sort of scrub, though in places the colouring of the rocks was very wonderful, with here a homestead and there a Native kraal.

At sunset we came to the Hex River Pass, of which South Africans think a lot, as we can well understand. Personally, we had heard so much about it that we were disappointed, particularly after having visited Switzerland so often. For nearly twenty miles the railway line was laid at a gradient of 1 in 40, the great climb up to the enormous plateau 2 to 6,000 feet above sea-level, of which the South African continent consists.

We whiled away the dark evening hours by playing whist with two men in our compartment, having first made it clear to them that we were not prepared to play for money. Betting and gambling is as rife in South Africa as in any other part of the world, and the keenest interest was taken by all English and many Dutch men in the classic racing events at Home.

When the time came to go to bed an attendant brought us as many blankets as we needed for 2s. 6d.; windows had to be kept shut on account of the dust, and hot-water pipes were turned on to keep out the cold—it often freezes on winter nights on the Karroo. It was not an easy matter getting to bed! Six men wrestling with braces and bootlaces, belts, baggage, and collar studs which would roll under the long table running down the centre of the compartment or under the lower bunks! The back of the seat lifted up to make a middle bunk, and the luggage rack was transformed into another bed, so we were three on each side. What ladies there were on the train had all been herded together in special compartments, and, if unaccompanied by their husbands, they always travel thus during the day. We did not have the unpleasant time our friends foretold, but four drunken Scotchmen in the next compartment made the night hideous with their noise, and sleep became impossible. "Sons of Empire"—our Cape friends would doubtless have called them!

The next morning we looked out to see the Karroo in all its barrenness. It seemed marvellous that sheep could thrive here without a sign of grass, among those scrubby little bushes. Every now and then we saw some ostriches, but it was not until near the end of our travels in this country that we came into the heart of the ostrich-farming district.

By midday we were passing through the scenes of countless skirmishes and many battles. At Deelfontein, for instance, we saw the remains of a hospital and a little cemetery near by. Many of the blockhouses still lined the route, and it was difficult to go far without seeing a grave. It was a bare, lonely part of the world, with occasional kopjes, and one could easily understand how vital it was in those days of war to keep the railway line as a base. We crossed both the Orange River and the Modder River, on the banks of which how many lives were wasted!

A Boer farmer was one of our travelling companions, and he kept us refreshed during the heat of the day with *naartjes* grown on his own farm, which he extracted from a large basket under the seat, and from him we learned much of interest concerning the country through which we were passing.

As we came into Kimberley at 6 p.m. we could not help contrasting the view from the two carriage windows. On the one side a racecourse, well fenced and well kept; on the other the Kaffir Location, ill-kept and dirty, the kraals consisting of a patchwork of odd bits of galvanized iron and rusty tin. Kimberley itself did not impress us very favourably. It was particularly dusty owing to the drought, but weather conditions apart it offered no attractions—what else can be expected of a town that is solely absorbed in diamond getting and drinking bars!

At Kimberley is to be seen "the biggest hole ever dug by man." The superficial area at the surface is 38 acres! Originally it consisted of hundreds of diamond diggers' claims, but the deeper they dug the more the intervening walls began to fall in, until it was eventually one huge pit with as many as 10,000 men grubbing in it!

We wrote to the Secretary of De Beers asking permission to see the diamond mines, and our permit to view the "Pulsator" duly arrived at our hotel, so we set out thither one morning. "Although on pleasure we were bent," as we continually reminded one another, "we had a frugal mind"; accordingly we did not "jump into a cab," as they suggested in the Secretarial Offices of the Company, but trudged out along the Boshof Road.

It was a weird place, this Kimberley: barbed-wire entanglements 10 feet high, dust, and drinking bars were the things that made the greatest impression on us. Being a Saturday, the Natives had just received their pay, and the boot shops in particular were doing a roaring trade. It was too absurd to see these Kaffirs with their own highly satisfactory footgear, their own good hard skin, investing their wages in thick, bright yellowy-brown boots, in which they were obviously uncomfortable. Their clothing, too, was a sight to behold. Bits of blanket pinned round the top, and perhaps a dilapidated pair of trousers below. The most ingenious garment we saw was cut out of a sack, and it really looked quite smart.

Before describing the "Pulsator" it would be as well to say something of the first steps involved in diamond mining. The "blue ground" in which the diamonds are found is blasted and then brought to the surface in the usual way. Instead of being "crushed" immediately in the old style, the earth is laid out on specially enclosed areas and exposed to the sun and the rain. The weather breaks up the "ground" most effectively, and thus saves the necessity for anything much in the way of crushing. After three to nine months of this exposure the "ground" is taken in little trucks to undergo its first washing.

The trucks are drawn up an inclined plane in batches of three or four to the top of an enormous structure. Here they are tipped out into revolving circular tanks.

The process is a long and continuous one. The diamonds and hard stones, being heavy, have a tendency to fall to the bottom of the tanks, and the earth is washed off the top and centre, for in revolving the heavy objects work to the outside. Lumps that do not go through a certain mesh are sent along moving belts to be crushed in another part of the structure. Only 1 to 1½ per cent. of what comes in goes on to the "Pulsator," and it is sent there in carefully enclosed trucks like large tanks, so that nothing can be lost. The "tailings," as the refuse is called, are disposed of with great rapidity. Huge tanks filled at the rate of three a minute are whisked up two or three sets of rails by powerful machinery and emptied into a huge pile. On coming into Kimberley by rail one sees these "tailings" from a long way off. Selections from the "tailings" are constantly set aside and examined carefully to make quite certain that no leakage is occurring.

The "Pulsator" is a mile or so away from the first washing place, and two or three miles out of Kimberley. Before we were allowed through the barbed-wire entanglements we had to produce our permits, but once in the manager's presence we were treated with the utmost courtesy. As the guide was not available, the assistant manager himself took us round and explained this part of the process, which is perhaps the most important.

It is, of course, a continuation of the washing process, and it is really extremely ingenious. The movement of the long trays in which the material is now washed is more like that of a sieve. Hence the word "Pulsator." The lighter material is washed away again till nothing but diamonds and hard pebbles remain. These are again washed over a *greasy* inclined plane—the diamonds stick to the grease, the pebbles roll down. The man who made this discovery saved De Beers thousands.

The pebbles are looked through to prevent any leakage. The diamonds, which are now easily discernible, are scraped off the oscillating band, grease and all, and placed in perforated iron drums. These are dropped into boiling water, and subsequently into paraffin, and the grease is thus removed. The gems are then taken to the office and carefully gone through, one at a time, by Natives working under the supervision of a white man.

We were surprised to find Natives handling the actual diamonds at this stage; still more so to notice the broad arrow on their clothes. We enquired of the manager and found they employed no less than 1,200 convicts, and paid the Government 1s. 4d. per head per day for their use. From some points of view these prisoners were actually preferred! The Company had even more control over them than over the Natives, who only remained, or rather bound themselves to remain, three months at a time in the compounds. The convicts, of course, had their own quarters, from which they were not allowed to go; whereas the other Natives were free to come and go anywhere within the compounds—a pretty extensive area. On the whole the advantages of the compound system seemed to outweigh the temporary loss of liberty, for, in the case of De Beers, no alcohol is supplied in their canteens or is allowed in the compounds.

The diamonds are finally handed over to one or two experts in an adjoining room, and here we had the opportunity of examining them. Some of the black ones we should never have thought to be diamonds. We were very much taken with heliotrope stones, though they are seldom as well formed or as good.

The country between Kimberley and Immigrant, where we were to spend some time on a real South African farm, was very barc, with the invariable kopjes rising from the red dusty plain here and there. Paardeberg was about half-way, but there was nothing special to be seen from the train to remind one of its war-time associations.

"*Karreerand*"

Our train crept along past several little sheds, called stations, and after stopping at one of these the guard requested us to move into another compartment, in order that a well-dressed Native chief and his attendants, who were travelling second class, should have a carriage to themselves, and not "contaminate" the white people.

At last we pulled up at a siding labelled "Immigrant—4,500 feet above sea-level" in very large letters. Our luggage was dumped by the side of the track, and the train, a collection of passenger coaches, horse-boxes, cattle-trucks, and goods wagons, went rumbling off on its leisurely and apparently never-ending way.

We found ourselves alone, except for a dark-skinned damsel with very prominent lips. No other passengers had descended from the train, and no living soul seemed to be in charge of the station. Not far away was a shed made of galvanized iron and dried mud, and here we found two or three Kaffirs squatting on their haunches in the shade, and the place bore a notice which read "Sub Post Office"; it was also a primitive general stores. Presently an individual, known in these parts as a "Jew-boy," appeared from behind a huge packing-case. He informed us that "Mr. Percy," our host, usually drove in to get his letters on this particular day and might arrive at any minute. We collected our baggage in a heap and I sat on the top and scanned the vast plain with my glasses in an endeavour to pick out any moving objects on the veld.

Away in the far distance I saw a tiny buggy drawn by a tiny white horse, and I could just make out the figure of a man seated inside the vehicle; he was wearing a broad-brimmed felt hat and shirt with sleeves rolled up. As the buggy drew nearer I saw it was followed by a crazy-looking cart drawn by two donkeys and driven by a Kaffir "boy." Closer still they came, and I could recognize the features of my cousin, our host-to-be, and soon we were grasping his great horny hand and admiring his shaggy beard and bronzed, honest, care-worn face.

We piled our luggage into the Cape cart, sat on top of it, and off we went, jogging along the sandy track that wound across the limitless plain. In the trail of red dust behind came the dark-skinned damsel with the prominent lips, our host's new cook, in her donkey chaise. Not a house was to be seen, only the two little sheds, away back there, marked where the station was; just a flat wilderness of brown grass and tufts of dry bush, some like old decayed gooseberry bushes, others more like bog myrtle, heather, or broom, but none exactly like our own British plants, not even the grass!

After a mile or so we came to a barbed-wire fence, with a loose gate made of wire and poles without a framework. The whole thing collapsed when unfastened and had to be dragged across the road before we could pass by. This was the kind of gate mostly used out here, where wood is very scarce. Indeed, no tree was visible anywhere; but later on we drove past a small farmhouse, near which there was a large dam of water, and here stood the usual sign of human habitation, a handful of tall eucalyptus trees. After an hour's drive over a very rutty track, during which our cart pitched from side to side and appeared to be in constant danger of capsizing, we arrived at a small galvanized house with a stoep along one side of it. This was to be our home for a few weeks. Nearby, a small iron windmill pumped water from a borehole into a large corrugated-iron tank: from this a pipe led into the kitchen; and ours was the only house for miles around with "water laid on." All our neighbours, none of whom were nearer to us than four miles, had to fetch their water "from outside."

Water is the great problem of this arid, thirsty land. With an adequate supply the veld can be turned into a Garden of Eden; without it no very useful vegetation will live. No rain had fallen for over three months. The farm was entirely dependent on the wind for its water supply, and when the wind failed us for several days our stock of liquid dwindled dangerously low. It was no uncommon thing for the Natives to walk miles to buy our water, either by giving us so much of their labour for so much water, or by paying a *tikkie* (3d.) for a large bucketful. Out here water was a marketable commodity, and because there was no currency in circulation of less value than the threepenny bit, the Native women carried home their bargains in large iron pots on their heads!

We brought good luck with us to "Karreerand," for, although the moon was bright in the heavens when we turned in for the night, snow fell about midnight with frost, and in the early hours a short but rather alarming thunderstorm brought welcome rain. Sometimes they would get as much as from 3 to 6 inches in a few hours, and the water rushes along over the open ground, tearing deep gullies in the soil. If it can be caught behind a dam there will often be a supply large enough to last for six months or more, that is if the dam does not leak—often there is a crevasse in the rock, or the sub-soil is porous. It seemed to us a great life this, farming out on the open veld, though a mighty lonely one. Unless this country has been seen, it is difficult to form any conception of it. When we visited "Karreerand" a few young trees were growing up round the homestead, and there were a few out-houses, but when Percy came here some years ago there was only a three-roomed galvanized-iron shack dumped down in the middle of the Karroo: no trees, no water, and no other homesteads to be seen!

Anthills, about 18 inches high, dotted the ground by the hundred in every direction, but as they were more or less the same colour as the sandy soil it could hardly be said that they brightened up the landscape. A faint tinge of green was given to the veld in places, not by the dried tufts of grass, but by a little green bush about 9 inches in height, which was the one thing the sheep and cattle did not seem to be enthusiastic about, though they ate it at a pinch we were told.

On the morning after our arrival we had a look round Percy's 3,000-acre holding. The thunderstorm had unsettled the weather, and the great altitude of the place made us feel so chilly that we were glad to return to the homestead and talk around a fire, where dried cakes of sheep and goat dung, the coal of the Karroo, were emitting a cheerful warmth and a fragrant odour not unlike the peat fires of the Homeland. One of the chief crops grown out on the Karroo farms is maize, but as this may be devoured by locusts or spoiled by drought, stock rearing is the principal source of income. Sheep, goats, donkeys, horses, cattle, and poultry of all kinds thrive well on the coarse herbage of the veld, and are allowed to wander as they like, and live entirely in the open. As jackals were abundant the sheep and goats were driven into wired enclosures at night time, otherwise the flocks would soon diminish.

The black people, or "boys" as they were called, lived in mud huts roofed over with old sacks, skins, bits of petrol tins, reeds, or anything they could lay hands on; and these "boys" (male adults) and "picannins" (children) provided the labour for the farm, and their womenfolk helped with the housework. They were content with very little in the way of wages, the average being from 10s. to 15s. a month, with 80 lb. of maize and a little tea, coffee, sugar, and tobacco. Sometimes a Native family will come and squat on a farm, and then the farmer can make a bargain with them to his advantage. Such a family was on Percy's farm when we were there. They were going to plough a certain piece of land, sow the seed Percy provided, reap the corn, and give half the produce to him; he, of course, paid them nothing, but one of the sons was engaged to build a stable on the farm.

We went up to the little hill where these Natives were living in a rough tent. One old woman was crushing coffee with an oval stone on a large flat one, the father was mending harness, and the son was building the stone walls of their future home. There were plenty of good, flat stones for this purpose to be had for the digging and picking on the little hill where they were living, and it was wonderful how well they built without the aid of mortar. The stones were chipped fairly square on the front surface, and the whole wall was carefully built with the stones "bonding" together with no joints one above the other. When finished, the surface was plastered with clay and cow manure, and this strange but practical mixture formed the floor of our kitchen down at the homestead, and can be used as roughcast for walls and threshing floors. When spring-cleaning time came round, or whenever the kitchen floor got worn into potholes by the constant tread of domestic service, the Kaffir girl was told to renew it, and the ingredients being readily available in the farmyard, she would squat on her haunches on the floor and smear the mixture on with her hands!

It is amazing how little it requires to keep these Natives. Their food is chiefly Indian corn cooked in various ways; meat is a luxury for them. Percy provided them sometimes with separated milk and occasional tit-bits, such as a lick of jam left in a jam dish, or the half-picked chicken bones from our dinner, or a little porridge scrapings. Indeed, what we threw away they often appreciated; and one day Lil, our hostess, found some cream had gone mouldy on top, so she scraped it off and placed it on a saucer and left it in the kitchen. Later

11 The Baas, "Mr. Percy"

12 A Visitor arrives at "Karreerand"

Photos by N. G. Unwin

13 A three roomed galvanized iron shack dumped down in the Karroo

14 Farm hands and housemaids

Photo by N. G. Unwin

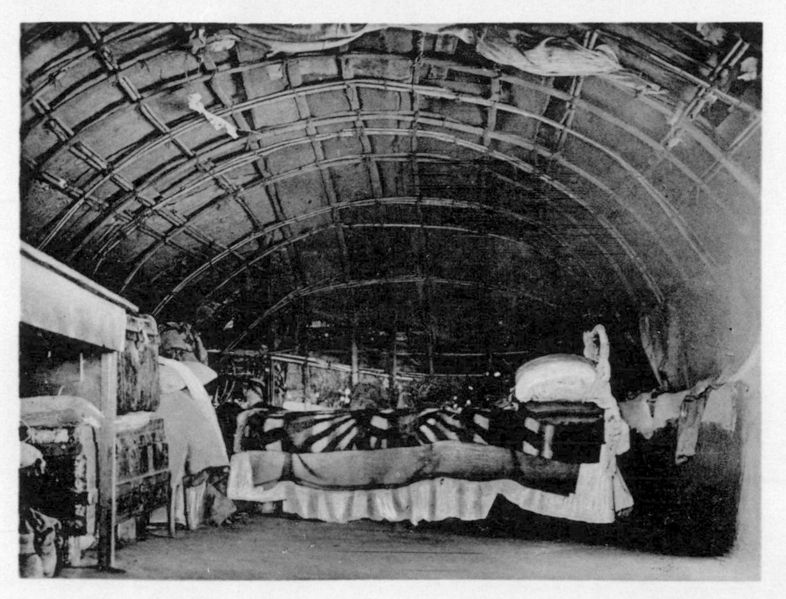

15 A big double bed covered with gaudy blankets

16 Are *you* a wheelwright?
Photo by N. G. Unwin

17 A delightful occupation

18 Dipping sheep at "Karreerand"
Photo by N. G. Unwin

on Lil found the Kaffir girl singing lustily whilst she whipped up the mouldy cream with some sugar in our egg beater; she was as happy as a princess! Her sister was nearby dancing for joy; in the oven they had two small loaves of bread for the party that was to be held at their hut on the morrow. Doubtless the mouldy cream was handed round as the *pièce de résistance* of the feast; it *looked* quite appetising anyway. These girls lived in a hut about a quarter of a mile away; it was about the size of an average room, and in it lived two grown women, one man, two babies, two small boys, and four girls aged nine, thirteen, fifteen, and eighteen respectively. In the evenings, when the day's work is done, they light a fire of sheep's droppings inside and fix a sheet of corrugated iron in front of the doorway; there is no window and no chimney. The fire burns in an old petrol tin punched all round with holes; little wonder these huts have their own peculiar reek, yet it would be hard to credit from their ramshackle exterior how clean they are inside, at least the few we inspected appeared so; and in some huts we saw big double beds covered with gaudy blankets or patchwork bedspreads.

It is not surprising if there are sometimes family "dust-ups" under these overcrowded conditions of living, and now and again a servant will suddenly disappear without giving notice to her mistress. This had happened to Lil on more than one occasion, but the employer can get the girl imprisoned if she breaks her monthly contract before the time is up, and often they can be persuaded to come back when the family quarrel has had time to simmer down.

It does not do for a farmer out here to be too critical about his labourers, who only get such small wages, and who can obtain as good or better easily elsewhere. There have been times when Percy has been entirely without Native labour, which means no one to look after the sheep and drive them into the kraal at night, no one to keep the calves from sucking all the milk from the cows, no one to help milk and labour and assist in the house. It often takes an hour to find the cows on such a holding as this and drive them home at milking time, and often longer to round up the fourteen donkeys and yoke them to the plough! So a good deal of tact is required to keep off unnecessary rows with one's staff, the juvenile members of which, the picannins, are often the most useful of all, as they do all sorts of odd jobs almost for nothing.

There was a big solitary kopje a little distance from Percy's house, and one morning before breakfast we climbed to the top of it just to show *how* energetic we could be when we wanted. It was extraordinary what a tremendous distance one could see in this rarefied air, and our view was bounded by a long range of curiously shaped hills that were, at that moment, under the spell of a weird phenomenon—a mirage. At the foot of these hills were large lakes that we knew did not exist, and on the summits stood other hills inverted, peak touching peak, with long spiky pieces sticking out from their sides. When we returned to the homestead with our appetites well sharpened for breakfast, we found Lil and Percy having a regular *indaba* (serious conversation). The "boy" was late and there was no milk! Percy had been politely asked by his wife to get a little—such a simple process on a farm, you have only got to milk a cow. Yes—only! Well, we fetched the cow and got her into the yard, we fastened her up, but as she had been separated from her calf, she was in no pleasant frame of mind. It was more than five minutes before we could get a noose over her horns, nor were our difficulties ended when we got her two hind legs lashed. For our trouble she splashed us all over with the farmyard mire attached to the end of her tail. After considerable effort, and one or two upsets, Percy managed to extract a tumblerful of milk, and then that Kaffir "boy," supposed to be without brains, arrived with the calf, and so long as her baby was near her the milk came forth in a warm, gushing torrent!

We Plough with Fourteen Donkeys

After breakfast we often went ploughing, having first of all rounded up and in-spanned the fourteen recalcitrant donkeys. This was a rough-and-tumble experience, guaranteed to warm up both heart and language on the coolest of Karroo mornings. It generally meant that if you escaped being hurled into the air by the hind hoofs of the beasts, you found yourself embracing them, with your arms round their necks, in accordance with official instructions from the *baas*, so that donkey and man were suspended lip to lip, swaying this way and that, treading on each other's corns in an absurd pantomimic fashion. But once the team was set the task proved a most delightful occupation and the donkeys a willing mob. The great thing to do was to keep shouting at them, so as to let them know that you were there, otherwise they might go to sleep. As Percy said: "Anything does: the name of the girl you dislike most, for preference." It was quite useless to have a "runner" with a whip to urge on any particular span, for as one passed along one side or other of the team the donkeys would make a mighty swerve in the opposite direction, which generally ended up in an inextricable tangle of harness. So we just crept along and kept shouting, whilst the foals gambolled alongside, or tried to thrust their heads under the protruding bellies of their mothers. The furrow was one thousand yards long, and by the time we had been to the end of it and back we might be interrupted by the arrival of a neighbouring farmer and his wife, who had dropped in for morning tea.

The cattle on their farm, which is one of the most beautifully situated in the whole district, and well supplied with trees and water, had been badly affected, together with those on many other farms, by a disease called *lamziekte*. Great efforts have been made to trace the cause of this mysterious complaint, a kind of paralysis, but so far with little result. It seems to be a form of poisoning, but whence it comes nobody can tell.

The joints of the beast stiffen, it collapses, and finds it is nearly impossible to rise again. Their jaws move, but the cattle are no longer able to feed or chew. They sicken and die, and nothing can be done to help them or prevent the recurrence of the disease. The sheep suffer from illnesses called *jagziekte* and *geilziekte*. The first is a form of consumption, and the second a sudden sickness and rapid decomposition. Then, of course, there is scab, a dreaded foe to all sheep farmers.

Fortunately the great loneliness of these far-separated farms is almost forgotten in constant toil, and the social side of life is not entirely absent. When a neighbour calls for morning tea, the *baas* and his wife cease their toil, and local gossip and local problems are discussed at length. Sometimes a half-day off is taken, and during our stay at "Karreerand" we went with Percy and Lil to visit many of the surrounding farms, run by Dutch or English, some of many years' standing, others that had been just started.

During these parties politics were discussed and heated arguments arose, but these were tempered by songs, accompanied at piano or on mouth-organ. Here we were in the heart of the Orange River Colony, half-way between Bloemfontein and Kimberley, where British troops had destroyed Boer farms and war had raged not many years before. Racial hatred still lingered under a smiling face, yet we always came away from these parties with a present, either a bunch of young onion plants for the garden or a large basket of oranges freshly culled, or maybe a home-made cake or loaf. We received kindness everywhere, from Briton and Boer alike, and we came back with only one regret, that the fruits of Peace could not mature more rapidly in the heart of Man. "Boer and Briton, each had shed his blood amongst the sparse Karroo bush and the crimson aloes. These things came into my heart, and I longed to see some way whereby Boer and Briton might, now, after they had fought their inevitable fight, pull wisely and wholly together to free themselves of the black cancer that ate at their vitals, weakening, dividing, threatening."*

Sometimes we would walk home to "Karreerand" at sunset, across the endless tufts of grass and scraggy bush. The air was keen and clear, the sky all shades from brilliant orange to darkest blue, and the distant kopjes stood out, around the horizon, in a jagged purple line. Perhaps a flock of sheep would be moving along the hillside to the kraal that showed up black against the flaming sky, and smoke arose from the homestead chimney that looked so far away. Then a hungry cry pierced the silence of the veld, half bark, half call; it was an evil sound, this eerie cry of the jackal, the farmer's most bitter foe. Woe unto any stray ewe or lamb that was not within the sheltering walls of its kraal at nightfall, for next day it might be found dead, or wandering the parched veld with its entrails dangling beneath it.

Meerkats can be seen at any time on the veld; they are not unlike a weasel, and they destroy the corn. We once saw a small tortoise; whilst birds, both large and small, are in great quantities, comparatively tame and beautifully coloured. Buck, hares, and partridges occasionally graced our table, but our meat diet consisted mainly of mutton, which we killed as wanted on the farm. One sheep lasted about three weeks if it was well salted, but by the end of the second week it was very tough and dry, and, in spite of days of soaking in fresh water, tasted very salt. We imagine the "salt junk" which Nelson's sailors lived on must have been very similar stuff. Our own bread was baked and our own porridge ground on the farm, and our butter, of course, was also home-made. As we were forty miles from the nearest town and five miles from the nearest store, we had to be content with very simple fare, and if we forgot to order in advance, when stores were low, we had to go without. But an old garden on the farm produced quinces and figs in abundance, and these were made into jam and also dried in the sun. The new

* *The Autobiography of Kingsley Fairbridge.* Oxford University Press, 1927, pp. 125–6.

garden was scientifically riddled with irrigation channels, and so long as the wind turned the sails of the mill our vegetables flourished there. What wonders water can create out of this barren soil can be learnt from a visit we paid to a neighbour's farm, where we saw peaches, violets, and narcissi growing in profusion in the garden. Oh! it was good to see a violet and *smell* it; but what labour it involved to produce it—endless irrigation all the year round!

One day Percy suggested jokingly that we should take unto ourselves a Kaffir wife each. He said we could pick up a good Hottentot or Kaffir woman in exchange for six oxen, and if we offered some old goats, or a few sheep, as well, we might have the pick of the Colony for the asking. But we replied with a cunning grin, "Ikona," which in Native language means, "I don't think."

It is not often that a mere visitor to a farm has the chance of being a witness of the ceremony of engaging a new shepherd "boy." Yet this was our good fortune one day, and Percy's mother-in-law, a Mrs. Smith, acted as interpreter. The shepherd was an elderly man, and he brought his son with him to help him in his negotiations with his prospective *baas*. The old fellow sat on a mud wall and his son squatted on his heels on the ground. Mrs. Smith reclined on one of the best chairs which we had brought out from the house, and Percy stood by, and we helped to make the *indaba* look a very important affair.

Mrs. Smith began in Dutch: "Die Baas say he give you one sheep and half a crown one month and 15s. the next month." The old Native repeated, holding his fingers and checking off the bargain: "One scap and haff kroon and vivteer sheelling." Then father and son talked in Kaffir for a few minutes, and finally he gave Mrs. Smith to understand that he usually wanted a sheep and half a crown, but if he wanted cash instead, would the *baas* be willing to give it? This was agreed to.

The next matter was the question of rations, and Mrs. Smith

again translated Percy's remarks on the subject: "Die Baas say twenty pounds mealies a week, one pound sugar, and six ounces coffee and tobacco a week." The old man did not know what a pound was, so we had to weigh out the quantities and place them in pans and dishes. He was very anxious to have a bucketful of mealies instead of 20 lb., and a long discussion with his son followed. Finally he gave us to understand that he wanted to know how much coffee it would be per month, so we showed him 1½ lb. compared with 6 ounces; then he was of the opinion that he got more by having 6 ounces at a time! He agreed as to his food, and we fixed up when he should build his hut, and told him that if he lost sheep during the day he would be responsible and have to pay. We promised to give him a new pair of boots if he stayed on the farm one year, and also to give him old clothes from time to time. We thought that was all he wanted, but oh! no, it was not. He lingered on, and asked after the health of the "Missis," and then wanted to know if we had any brandy. We told him "No," but promised him he should have some land of his own, and our plough and donkeys to cultivate it. This pleased him mightily, and he soon forgot his disappointment at not having any brandy, and, beaming all over his face, he bade us good-bye until Monday. The whole discussion had lasted an hour and a half, so slow but sure and cunning the Natives are.

A few days later we made the acquaintance of the white ants which inhabit the millions of ant-hills all over the veld. They are very destructive brutes, and one morning, as we were getting up, we noticed a dirty mark of earth half-way up the bedroom wall. This was the trade-mark of the white ants, who always work under a covering of sand or earth; they are never seen unless the earth is knocked away. In this case they were making up the wall to the ceiling joists, and had we not disturbed their progress they would not have taken very long to eat the roof supports right through.

Ants and flies were among the minor worries of a farmer on the Karroo, but they were an ever-present pestilence;

many were the pats of butter and dishes of jam and pieces of meat that we ate hungrily and thankfully at times, riddled as they were with half-dead ants and flies! In the dairy at "Karreerand" Percy had fitted up a small table or stand on a shelf; the legs of this stand rested in four tins of water, and on it was kept the butter and cream, safely ant-proof, though these wretched insects climbed about everywhere else. Occasionally the water tins had to be cleared, for in time they became choked up with the corpses of those hero ants who thought they had been born with webbed feet!

When we came to this vast, parched, dreary-looking sandy wilderness called the Karroo, we were just two soft-handed, rather disgusted and disappointed *rooineks*. For the first few days we could see little to charm us in this life on the veld; we were nauseated by the sight of ants in our food and the smells that arose from the sheep kraals. But after serving our apprenticeship for a few weeks at "Karreerand," we came away gripped by, and converts to, the charm that is "Africa." Looking back through the years to those days of our initiation, we still yearn for that wonderful open country, treeless and without streams, its sunsets and its great stars, shimmering beside the gaunt summits of kopjes, black and erect, in a sky whence came the colour of a peacock's plume. We still yearn for the cattle and the sheep, the black Natives, the smell of the burning fuel, the Kaffir corn porridge, the rides over the sandy tracks, the cry of the jackal—the solitude, the great peace of its silence.

When the time for our departure came, we drove down to the railway in solemn state, in the old Scotch cart drawn by two oxen. On our way back to Kimberley we stopped at a suburb to have tea with some friends. Our host was a pioneer in the diamond fields, and one of the last to give up his claim, and at the time of our visit he was a large shareholder in De Beers, Ltd. Yet there he remained in his poky little house, furnished with scraps of cheap and gaudy ornaments. He would not travel, nor would he allow his sons to see anything of the world, so they all sat there, dry-rotting in this dusty dorp, waiting for their father to die. That evening we took tram to Alexandersfontein, some seven miles out of Kimberley. Here De Beers had erected a large hotel and laid out an extensive pleasure garden of ponds and shady walks, tennis courts and swimming baths, where the jaded folks of the town came to seek refreshment and amusement in summer time. We had high tea in the Arcade, and whiled away an hour in a neatly furnished room, where Stan played to me on the piano snatches of old ditties and old tunes.

Chapter II

BULAWAYO AND THE VICTORIA FALLS

THE next morning we took train for Bulawayo and were fortunate enough to have a little coupé to ourselves. The coach was a brand-new one, and our compartment was built for three, and had its own little arrangement in the corner so that without moving from the seat we could wash our hands and sponge our faces every hour, a very necessary proceeding as will be learnt later!

After studying Bryce's account of this part of his journey*—the railway did not go farther than Mafeking then—I was ready to have my bed made up. We were really, or should have been, very comfortable, but suffered from an excess of ventilation. On the fringe of the Kalahari Desert ventilation means clouds of dust; and an excess of lung power on the part of some infants in the adjoining compartment, who literally howled and screamed as if they were being throttled the greater part of the journey, did not add to our peace. Johnnie would have liked to have wrung their necks, and got so exasperated that I could not help laughing each time they started afresh.

In the middle of the night we passed through Vryburg, and at seven in the morning we woke up to find ourselves at Mafeking. It was certainly from outward appearances a flat, uninteresting place, but it was a joy to see a few more trees about. It is true that these trees were of a rather scrubby, uninspiring type—a species of mimosa, I believe—and seldom much more than bushes, but they served to break the monotony of the landscape.

As we passed northward we had the Kalahari Desert on our left. The dust was so thick as almost to choke us. When the train travelled at any speed we simply dared not open

* *Impressions of South Africa.* (Macmillan.)

a window. English settlers seemed to be few and far between in these parts, but there were plenty of Native children, with an extremely modest amount of clothing, at most of the halting-places. We occasionally saw a few of their kraals, but there were doubtless plenty more a little farther from the line, particularly at places like Palapye (pronounced pa-la-tchwy), an important Native centre. Our second night in the train was highly satisfactory, thanks to the window being closed and the babies temporarily exhausted. By 6 a.m. we were passing through such places as Plumtree and Figtree, and shortly after 7 a.m. we steamed into Bulawayo, "The Place of the Killing." This name was given by the Matabele to their capital or seat of government and residence of the king, a fresh site being chosen as each new king came into power. Death was the only penalty meted out for crime; hence this gruesome name for what is now a very law-abiding place.

It was a cold windy morning, and I felt quite sorry for our friends having to turn out so early to meet us, but there sure enough was Arnold on the platform. We mounted the cart, and, entrusting ourselves to Muriel and their pony "Bobby," we drove out of Bulawayo in a hurricane of dust; we could not have seen the town under more unfavourable circumstances.

Life in a Rhodesian Suburb

The veld outside Bulawayo was very different from the O.R.C. in that it was covered with large bushes, mostly rather scraggy. We did not find it as fascinating as the more open expanse of the Karroo. In due course we arrived at Hillside, about 4 miles from "Town," and then we passed the home windmill, which, at that time, pumped up no water, and finally our destination, "St. Cyrus," came into view. The children and Mrs. Carnegie were out on the stoep to meet us. Mrs. Carnegie gave us the genial welcome one would always expect from her. The guest chamber in which we were quartered was built specially for our advent and was just finished in time! It had brick walls, corrugated-iron roof and a floor of beaten earth covered with matting, and three little windows. Some of the panes got broken in course of construction, and one of the window frames was not yet properly secured. But perhaps the most interesting item of the whole apartment was the door, which was an ordinary stable door, with bolt and latch complete. Ours made a very comfortable bedroom when some of the draughts were cut out by means of stuffing our correspondence file in the place where a pane of glass once was, and local skin rugs took the place of eiderdowns.

The view from our stoep extended for some miles across wooded lands interspersed with tall grasses. Half-way between us and the town rose the grandstand of the racecourse.

There was nothing very impressive about the town of Bulawayo itself, except the extraordinary wide streets (broader than Kingsway in London) and the *dust*. The corner plots at street crossings, being much more expensive sites, had seldom been built upon, thus giving the town a very unfinished appearance. There will be no need of expensive street-widening schemes, and the long teams of oxen that drew the great wagons of farmer, trader, and prospector had ample room to turn round with ease.

The influence of Cecil Rhodes could, of course, be seen everywhere. In Rhodesia, as at Kimberley, they had no use for anything less than a *tikkie* (3d.), and they carry their contempt for a mere penny still farther. For instance, I tendered 8s. for a 7s. 10d. ticket and I was given 3d. change. This arrangement pleased me exceedingly until the tables were turned and I found myself receiving 3d. when I was entitled to 4d.!

Water was again the coveted element here. Our friends had sunk one borehole without result, 5 feet of it was through solid granite at a cost of £5 per foot. During our stay with them they were sinking another well with more hopeful prospects, for the granite they were blasting was coming out quite wet, and the diggers had already sent up one bucketful of water! What that meant in this dry and thirsty land it is difficult to convey. Every drop of water had to be fetched from a neighbour's house a quarter of an hour's walk away, and a nice flower and vegetable garden that once flourished in front of the house had been burnt to a cinder owing to lack of rain and a proper water supply.

Water winning was not wrought without misfortune, however. Native "boys" were employed on this task at "St. Cyrus," and one morning we were alarmed by the cries of one of them, who came running to the house, shouting, "Baas! Baas! Nigger boy dead bottom well!" He told us how the big galvanized-iron well-bucket, with a 2-inch flange round its base, and full of blocks of granite, had slipped from the hands of his mate and himself as they were unhooking it from the chain at the mouth of the well. It had fallen 15 feet down the shaft, with a sickening crash, onto the head of the third "boy," who was acting as filler at the bottom. The two "boys" who were acting as hauliers promptly "presumed" their mate to be dead and ran to the house to tell us so!

We hastened to the well and Arnold slid down the chain, quickly ran a noose under the dead man's armpits, and we hauled him to the top. To our astonishment he was not dead at all, not even unconscious; he merely rolled his great black eyes and sighed and crooned to himself, in spite of the fact that he had a good deep cut on the top of his head 4 inches long, a curve-shaped cut made by the bucket's flanged bottom. A white man would have received his ticket for the next world from such a blow, but these Kaffirs have such terribly thick skulls!

We gave first-aid to the poor fellow and drove him to Bulawayo to see a doctor, who said he could do nothing more for him than we had already done. If the "boy" had a week's rest and we saw that the wound was kept clean "he would be all right." So he sat in his hut, over a wood fire, and being near the house we could hear him sighing and crooning to himself all that night and the whole of the following day and night. The next day we heard our "boy" singing, and towards evening he was singing and laughing to himself. The fourth day after his accident he was back at his job at the bottom of the well, with a beautifully clean, well-healed scar on the top of his woolly head.

Many years ago the warlike Matabele had enslaved the pastoral tribes of Mashonaland, farther to the north-east. White settlers found that the peaceful nature of the Mashona made him fairly useful as a servant, and to us they seemed more lithe and childish than the Kaffirs of the Karroo. Little incidents tickled them tremendously, and our servant Umzindo was an excellent example of this childish light-heartedness. If the dishes and plates that he brought to table were too hot, he would pass them rapidly over the tips of his agile fingers, like some professional juggler. At the same time he would hold his head to one side, utter excited little exclamations, with a rapid intake of his breath, "Eh! Eh!" his white teeth showing between his thick, smiling lips and his tongue darting in and out of his mouth like a serpent's.

Once a month he received his wages, and his mistress always impressed on Umzindo the virtues of saving his money and the folly of spending it unwisely on clothes and beer in the town. He always promised his "Missis" to do as she bade him, but when he went to "Town" his childish vanity always overcame him.

One evening Umzindo was trudging back along the four miles of dusty road from Bulawayo, singing like a lark in spring. We were sitting on the stoep, sipping our "sun-downers" and watching the little whirlwinds raising red dust spouts over the town. Presently we heard our Umzindo chanting lustily to himself as he came up the drive. As he rounded the corner of the stoep to go to his hut we saw to our amazement that he was clad in immaculate new clothes from head to foot: a large-peaked doggie cap was perched at a daring angle on his woolly pate, and besides a new Norfolk

19 "St. Cyrus"

20 The Euphorbia tree

21 The naked shining limbs of the giant baobab trees

22 We crossed the famous bridge over the gorge

jacket, large-checked riding breeches, woollen stockings with brightly coloured tops, he carried a pair of bright yellow boots coyly in his hands. These he would only put on when in "Town." No wonder Umzindo sang; how happy he was and how proud! His poor mistress was outraged to think that he could have wasted his money so foolishly, but Umzindo sang and laughed, laughed and sang, almost ceaselessly through three days and three nights, and all the songs he sang were composed of three quavering notes!

How we used to long for a few of the sweet smells of the Old Country, the flowers and trees and damp odours after rain! Here there were few scents and few blooms; everything was as dry and parched as a long-buried bone. But as we sat on the shady stoep in the midday heat, writing or reading, there was always something going on to distract our attention. The late winter sun beat down fiercely from a cloudless sky; not a breath of wind stirred the scanty foliage; flies, forerunners of summer, began to tease and taunt; whilst far in the distance rose the blue height of Taba s'Induna—The Hill of Chiefs. Suddenly a miniature whirlwind would pass, churning up the dust, bending the trees low, and any movable thing, like a sheet of corrugated iron, or an old hen strutting across the yard, would be lifted upwards with a rattle and a cackle in an agitated flutter of feathers, leaves, and paper, then, as suddenly, came peace again.

Looking towards the town it appeared as if the entire place was on fire, for the wind was racing across the wide streets and raising the red dust in gigantic clouds like thick flame-reflected smoke. We were in the month of August, spring was not far away, and our hens were mostly through the moult, but we had not had an egg for many weeks. One morning we saw to our astonishment an elderly biddy busy in the yard with what we thought was a piece of rope. On closer inspection it proved to be a small snake, about 18 inches long! After playing about with it for some minutes, and tripping up over it as she carried it across the yard in her beak, she then proceeded to swallow it tail first as a python swallows a buck. Inch by inch she managed to jerk the reptile down, but we could see by the expression on her face that it was a bigger worm than she had bargained for, and we grew anxious for her safety.

But biddy was not going to be done! Her dignity and even her life were at stake. She seemed to be going purple in the face, and the old rooster came running up to help her; but seeing the fangs of the snake he shook his head, ruffled his wings, and called up the remainder of his concubines. By dint of twisting her neck round in a succession of spiral curves and rotating her crop, the old hen finished her meal at last, and standing with her legs wide apart for a moment or two, and swaying unsteadily from side to side, she finally waddled off under the bushes. Next day we found a beautiful double-yoked egg in the nest box!

The Victoria Falls

We had slept soundly, half smothered in dust, and our train was gradually slowing down and creeping along a hillside that gave us a magnificent view over sloping wooded country. Now that the noise of beating wheels upon the metals had subsided an unfamiliar sound came to our ears. It was the distant roar of the Victoria Falls!

The sun had risen but an hour, the sky was pale gold and blue, and here was a trainload of excited, dusty travellers all dishevelled from their sleeping bunks, eagerly straining their eyes for a glimpse of the great falling waters of the Zambesi—"Mosi-oa-tunya," The Smoke that Sounds.

Some looked towards the horizon, as if they expected to see volumes of water pouring from the sky; others, craning their necks out of the windows, peered under the very railway embankment, for the noise seemed to come from there. Somewhere in that forest on which we were gazing was a gigantic gorge about 400 feet deep and a mile wide into which the

23 Before us lay the great chasm of the Victoria Falls
Photo by M. Carnegie.

24 We shot silently through the broad, eddying stream

25 This ceaseless and stupendous strife of water against rock

26 The Spirits of the Falls, the rainbows!

waters of the river went thundering down, to be carried away between the winding walls of a cañon for forty miles or more.

Presently our train stopped at the Falls station, and as we busied ourselves with throwing our luggage out of the compartment window and putting it in charge of the hotel people, we could hear the increasing booming of "The Smoke that Sounds."

We had decided to go on with the train to Livingstone, capital of N.W. Rhodesia, and perhaps canoe back down the Zambesi in the evening. As we were eating our porridge in the restaurant car we crossed the famous bridge over the gorge; it is said to be the highest bridge in the world; it is built in one span of 500 feet, a total length of 650 feet, and is 350 feet above the seething torrent. But we paid little attention to this triumph of human skill that had been made possible by flying a kite, attached to a light string, across this chasm some years before. We all jumped to our feet to obtain a brief glimpse of the greatest of Nature's waterfalls, before the train plunged into a cutting on the farther side, and we were soon traversing the thin forest again. Here palms and the naked shining limbs of the giant baobab trees stood about the forest clearings like huge prehistoric monsters. They are known by the Natives of some parts of Africa as the "Kerramatata" trees, and from the acid powder with which their fruit is filled comes our cream of tartar, a curious similarity of sound. Many of the trees are 100 feet in girth, and the recesses of their massive trunks often contain large quantities of rain-water. The fruit when mixed with this stagnant water makes a safe and welcome drink for the thirsty hunter or prospector, and it is also said to be valued by the Boers as a specific against fever.

On arrival at Livingstone it did not take us long to find the office of Muriel's friend, Mr. Elliot, who was quite a high official in these parts. As it was barely 9 a.m. Mr. Elliot had not yet arrived, but we did not have long to wait. He at once placed his trolley at our disposal, and said in about half an hour he would himself escort us.

Johnnie and I came to the conclusion that this was the right country to live in, where you can take a Saturday morning off the moment any friends turn up to see you. It was a great ride on that trolley, the only means, I may say, of getting to the river side unless you wanted to walk, which one was not anxious to do in that tropical sun. It was about four miles downhill practically all the way to the river, so that on this journey the Native runners had very little to do, and, in fact, sat on behind part of the way while the trolley careered along, jolting and bumping all the time as it sped over the rails.

On our arrival at the river Mr. Elliot found the canoes locked up in the boathouse, but, being on the Livingstone Rowing Club committee, he gave instructions for the padlock to be broken and, in a few minutes, we were comfortably settled in our canoe with two Natives at each end paddling for all they were worth, and one in the stern as cox. There was a lethargic sensation of satisfaction in being on the water again after our long and dusty journey of nearly 2,000 miles from the Cape. As we shot silently through the broad, eddying stream, urged on by the rapid driving blades of our paddlers, and as the hot sun poured down its warmth upon us, long-legged cranes and long-necked divers peered at us with unconcerned curiosity from their rocky midstream perches or from among the palms and rushes on the river banks. Our coloured crew chatted and laughed, and the musky smell of Native mingled with the slight fanning breeze, while our six-foot blue-eyed English host spun yarns to us of adventures with hippos and crocodiles, and of the disasters they caused in these strange yet peaceful-looking waters. He explained to us that this stretch of water was, in all probability, the finest regatta course in the world, and sculling competitions had been held on this beautiful reach ever since 1910. We thought of far-distant Henley, and what the aged rowing Blues, in their gay caps and blazers, would say if a hippo suddenly rose up from the depths of the Thames and capsized a Committee launch!

Mr. Elliot had worked us up to such a pitch of excitement with his yarns that when he accidentally hit me on the back of my head with a paddle he was using I thought for a moment that his words had come true and that a hippo was "having a game of water polo with the heads of our capsized crew." But instead our Native paddlers were making good headway against the stream; with a swift plunge of a shining blade here and a backwater there our "boys" guided the canoe through narrow channels, where the oily whirl of water revealed the sharp edge of an almost hidden rock. On our left was Loando Island, where the oxen spent their days of quarantine when on their way from Southern into Northern Rhodesia, and a little farther on we came to the Island of the Seven (Palm) Sisters.

On our way farther upstream to Kandahar Island we saw some crocodiles basking on the limbs of trees that lay out low over the water; it was difficult to see which was croc and which was wood until our "boys" shouted in a peculiar way, and in a flash the beasts were gone, leaving hardly a ripple on the surface of the stream.

We also saw a hippo or two fully submerged except for their great ugly snouts, like a rounded rock, moving about imperceptibly near the banks.

There was little to see on Kandahar Island beyond a few interesting examples of tropical vegetation and hippo spoor in the mud. Hither come visitors from the Falls and residents from Livingstone to picnic, the hippos sometimes creating a mild diversion from the picking of chicken bones, as a herd of cows or a pair of swans will do sometimes at Home! As we ate our lunch the canoe "boys" lay about in the deep shade cast by the palm fronds reading a Native translation of Bunyan's *Pilgrim's Progress*.

We were soon drifting back downstream towards the falls again. Ere long we could see their spray rising above the trees in great clouds, and, as the breeze caught them and cast them towards the sun, its beams turned the vapour into a great curtain of beautifully shot colourings.

Mr. Elliot told us that on windless days, especially during the rainy season, the vapour from the falls rises in columns, sometimes known as the "Five Fingers," and it serves, like the pillar of smoke which preceded the Israelites in the wilderness, to guide travellers from spots even more remote than the old hunting halts at Deka, seventy miles away, and Panda-ma-tenka, on the Bechuanaland border.

After landing from the broad river of islands and rocks and a short walk through dried scrub, we turned a corner suddenly, and before us lay the great chasm of the Victoria Falls, nearly 400 feet deep and a mile long. The two sides of this enormous fissure are almost exactly on a level and in places less than 400 feet apart, so that they give the impression of a gigantic cut, or split, that has cloven the earth asunder. Into this deep mile-long cañon the river, which flows quietly almost to the brink, suddenly plunges in a series of remarkable and terrifying cascades. The waters sweep down with a noise like the crash of thunder and with such force that the spray rises high into the air and is carried, in the form of light showers or heavy rain, hither and thither by the wind.

If one stands on the opposite edge of cliff one is in what is known as the Rain Forest; here it is nearly always raining in heavy showers or driving spray, and the glories of the vegetation bear witness to the fact. From these bowers of fairy-like greenery one looks right into the very entrails of this ceaseless and stupendous strife of water against rock.

It was the season of low water; each fall was separated from its neighbour by some show of substantial rock, and each group of falling water could be studied in its own particular beauty. Some fell sheer into the abyss, others leapt from rock to rock in a fanciful display of feathered froth and foam; others tumbled in a clear green stream, the colour always intensified by the hot rays of the sun. All thundered down upon the almost invisible rocks below, where the waters pounded and churned, in so terrible a turmoil as to resemble the breath of some hideous monster which might be lurking in the black recess of this apparently bottomless and awful ravine.

Then there were the wonderfully delicate Spirits of the Falls, the rainbows! These varied with the position of the sun, but at all times they were excessively brilliant. Here they were traced across the face of rock, there they rose from the very heart of that grim inferno and arched clear of the chasm high into the azure sky. Sometimes they seemed so close as to be touched by the hand, and always there was a curious movement among the colours as the sunbeams caressed the driving spray.

From Cataract and Livingstone Islands the falls look even more imposing than from the Rain Forest, for here we were on the very lip of the falling water, and one false step would have sent us to a horrible death below.

The water being so low, we were able to scramble over the rocks and wade up to our knees across the actual bed of the rapids, and so arrive at a spot *below* the level where the waters began to descend. In the rainy season it is impossible to get to these islands on the edge of the falls owing to the tremendous volume of water in the river, so we were fortunate to be able to clamber around as we did.

One of the most remarkable things about the Victoria Falls is the way in which the Zambesi, a mile wide before it takes its plunge into the ravine, forces its way out from the gigantic trap that Nature has prepared for it, through an opening but 100 yards wide! On the ravine side of this opening is a ghastly maelstrom of tossing water called, very appropriately, the Boiling Pot, whilst on the other side is the Whirlpool, a much more serene but infinitely more sinister turmoil.

It is not surprising that the Victoria Falls have been placed among the Wonders of the World. Only those who have seen them, and heard the thunder of their glory, can realize their magnificence. The gay plumage of the birds, the matchless butterflies and evergreen foliage of palm, fern, and tree, the brilliance of the rainbows by day and their phantom-like appearance in the moonlight, the sparkling rush of "Leaping Water" and crashing headlong flight of "Devil's Cataract," who can forget these once they have seen and heard? Little wonder that the Arabs, when they came that way, called the place "Musa-i-nunya," "The End of the World." We could approve the advice given by an American who, asked by a friend at Buffalo to let him know whether the Victoria Falls really were so wonderful, cabled after he had seen them, "Sell Niagara."

We met some exceptionally interesting people among our fellow guests at the hotel, one of whom, a Mr. Rosazza, a Swiss, educated in Italy, who subsequently worked in Paris and America, came to Africa some years ago for his health. He was delightfully international in his point of view; he seemed rather "fed up" with the Chartered Company and their ways, but had a high opinion of Crown Colony Government.

He was not so bitter against the Belgians as Colonists as many I have met. He admitted their inexperience as colonizers, but individually they were good enough fellows for the most part, though their continental training offended the susceptibilities and prejudices of the average Britisher. We had many bonds in common. He was an ardent Socialist, a very rare bird in these parts, and it was refreshing to both of us to yarn on social questions. For him it was very unusual to meet anyone in Northern Rhodesia, where he was then working, who would even approach such matters without violent prejudice.

On our return to Bulawayo we busied ourselves with preparations for our journey to the famous Zimbabwe ruins. The late Mr. R. N. Hall, who had written many books on Rhodesian archaeology and had done much excavating work

27 We were on the very lip of the falling water

28 The Zambesi forces its way out from the gigantic trap

29 His garden was a blaze of whitewashed stones

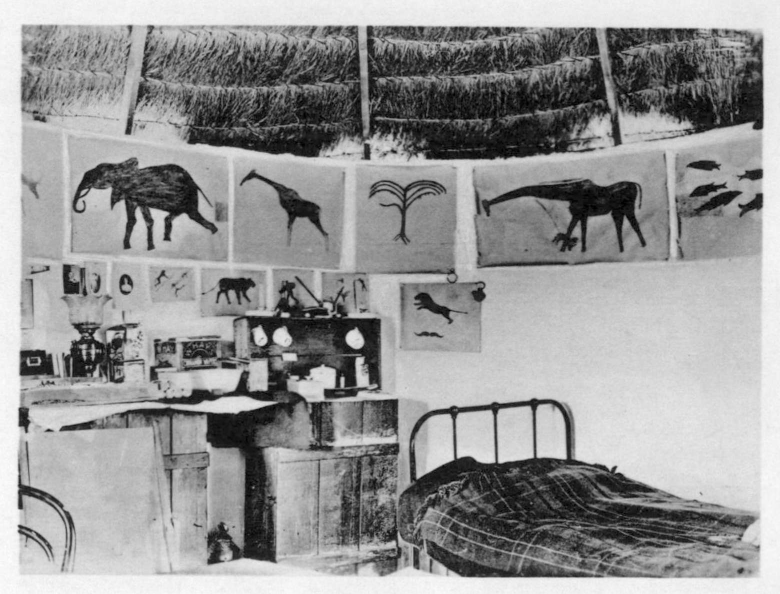

30 Interesting specimens of rock painting

at Zimbabwe, was (then) living not far from "St. Cyrus." His home, which consisted of several circular white-walled thatched-roofed *kaytor* and *kia* huts, was situated on the summit of one of the many picturesque, boulder-strewn kopjes in the neighbourhood. His garden was a blaze of whitewashed stones, among which euphorbia and other trees and cactus plants grew in quaint profusion. On our way thither to see him we passed the great dams which held in normal times Bulawayo's water supply, but on that particular day they were as dry as a bone, and had been so for many weeks.

We found Mr. Hall busy with incubators and chickens, but with the usual courtesy of all Colonials he ceased his work to show us round his little estate and entertained us to tea. His dining-room was also his bedroom, and the white-washed walls were decorated with tracings he had taken of most interesting specimens of rock paintings, done by the Bushmen on the walls of caves many years ago, and which are still to be seen here and there in this fascinating land. Mr. Hall had coloured these tracings as near as possible to the original drawings, and the yellows, browns, and reds, combined with the naïveté of the designs, made an unusual form of decoration to his apartment.* When he was not out on one of his frequent expeditions of exploration into the many mysteries which lie hidden in the history of Rhodesia's past, Mr. Hall lived here alone in company with an old pioneer who acted as handyman, gardener, and cook. Mr. Hall gave additional zest to our enthusiasm to see the ruins, over which so much speculation still exists as to their origin and purpose, and recommended us first of all to pay a visit to the Khami ruins, which lie some fourteen miles W.N.W. from Bulawayo. Meanwhile we had made arrangements with two gentlemen, Messrs. Cauler and Trump, to go with us to Zimbabwe and

* The drawings in yellow pigment are probably the oldest, as in some cases other pictures in browns and reds have been superimposed at a later date. It is thought that none of these paintings date back farther than the eighteenth or nineteenth century, but the engraved pictures found in similar places are decidedly older.

spend a week or more camping there, as we felt it was an experience not to be missed and a unique opportunity of getting right away from civilization; the ruins were (then) about 100 miles from the nearest railhead, in a district where big game was still abundant.

The Khami Ruins

Though spoken of rather contemptuously by some, we found the Khami ruins extremely interesting, and from every point of view well worth visiting. They were supposed to be neither so ancient nor so extensive nor so important as the Zimbabwe ruins. Their construction, though extraordinarily good in parts, was thrown into the shade by the latter's exceptional brilliance. Some authorities on the subject say that Khami was almost certainly built as a stronghold to store grain and gold; there is evidence of an extensive trade with Persia and the East, and, as far as can be seen, the place was quite unconnected with any religious observances. When one reads of the Queen of Sheba and her wealth, one little realizes that it almost certainly came from Rhodesia, for the dominion of the Kings of Sheba extended far into Africa. In addition to this evidence of the storage and transport of gold, in most of the richest Rhodesian gold mines there were traces of earlier workings, perfectly carried out, and showing that the ancients had tapped the most profitable surface veins ages ago.

The ruins were wonderfully situated, mostly on the top of kopjes, and in many cases no more than the building of one wall, or perhaps two, was necessary to form an impenetrable stronghold. It was a unique position, for there was in the immediate neighbourhood *the* essential requirement of these parts—an unfailing water supply. The view from the top of some of the kopjes was wonderful: it was a most wild and desolate country, where huge boulders abound. Some groups of these enormous rocks were perched high up in such a position that it seemed as if the slightest breath of wind might send them hurtling down into the valley below, and at times they assumed the most fantastic forms, scattered indiscriminately here and there and often quite indistinguishable one from another. The whole neighbourhood was a happy hunting ground for animals, but at midday when we were there there was little to be seen beyond the spoor of baboons and various kinds of buck, with which one soon becomes familiar.

The sight of these ruins was sufficiently interesting to whet our appetites for the larger remains at Zimbabwe, and it was extraordinary to think that these neatly cut granite blocks might possibly have been placed in position by a busy population that, as some people presume, inhabited all this region some centuries before A.D. 915.*

Our cycle ride back along the fourteen miles to Hillside, beneath a sweltering sun, against a hot head wind, with our front wheels skidding almost continuously in the thick sand which composed the road, gave us a thirst the like of which we had never experienced before. As soon as we arrived in Bulawayo we rushed into the first bar we came across, and whilst Stan imbibed iced lime juice, Alfred and I made the most of two iced lagers, and small ones at that, that cost us 1s. 2d. each. It was the first drink of this character that I had had since leaving Kimberley nearly three weeks previously, and how good it was!

The Native well-diggers, on a neighbour's land, had again been indulging in attempts at murder during our absence. This time they thought it would be interesting to see how quickly they could lower their comrade in the bucket to the bottom of the well, with the result that long before the bucket arrived at its destination the two "boys" at the top lost control of the windlass, and their luckless companion went hurtling down to an almost certain death. Again the butter-fingered

* The most recent discoveries seem to confirm the theory that Khami and Zimbabwe were constructed in mediaeval times. See *Zimbabwe Culture*, G. Caton-Thompson.

Kaffirs ran to the homestead with their sorrowful tale of a brother's death, but fortunately the undertaker was once more cheated out of a job, for his client was found later sitting in a pool of dirty water and mumbling to himself as he rubbed his bruised and battered shins.

By Bicycle to the Matopos

Early one morning Johnnie and I, mounted on borrowed bicycles, started off for the Matopo Hills. It was a hot and rather exhausting experience, the numerous sandy patches on the bumpy road would pull one up quite suddenly, and to push the machine, heavily laden with cameras and knapsacks, was almost equally tiring.

Just beyond Hillside I had my first encounter with a large snake. It went whistling across the track in front of me, and I was so excited that, only armed as I was with a lady's bicycle, I dismounted and gave chase, but I soon lost it in the long grass. But the creatures of which we saw most in these parts were lizards of all varieties and hues, besides a pretty little animal like a shrew mouse, and of course endless rock rabbits.

The country was now becoming exceedingly beautiful. From the flat, undulating, bushy veld we were gradually climbing up among the huge rocky spurs of the Matopos, and presently we cried a halt near the Dam Hotel, a delightful spot where, even in that very dry season, one looked down on a considerable sheet of water. We seated ourselves in a patch of scanty shade and imbibed the cool water from Stan's thermos with avidity, ate "love and kisses" biscuits and *naartjes*, parting gifts that the young ladies of "St. Cyrus" had stuffed into our knapsacks.

Then we pushed on again, dodging projecting rocks and broken bunches of thorns 6 inches long that lay, a half-hidden menace to our tyres, in the sand drifts. Now and again we passed an almost naked Native woman trudging into

"Town," stripped to the waist and carrying an incredibly heavy load on her head. Her baby was slung on her back, where it either slept or fretted at the flies which hung about its eyelids and lips as it sucked from the great black elongated breast which was slung over its mother's shoulder or passed under her arm.

It was the custom with the village women here to don clean apparel on entering the town. Of course they did not wear it along the dusty roads and paths, but carried it with them, and when close to the town it was a common sight to see them putting on their clothes by the wayside, with a simple modesty that was charming to behold.

Our own raiment became more and more scanty at every mile, until I suggested that Johnnie should abandon his shirt altogether, as it was next to useless in the *négligé* manner he was wearing it! Happily he did not follow my advice, as he would have been skinned by the burning heat of the sun.

We soon came to a signpost that directed us by one way to the World's View and by the other route to the Terminus Hotel. We chose the latter way, and presently we crossed a stream by means of awkward stepping-stones, balancing our bicycles on our shoulders as we went. I made a *faux pas* at the last stone, and stepped very gracefully into the first mud we had seen since leaving the falls about two weeks previously!

The sight of running stream water always made us feel horribly homesick, and we could hardly believe the yarns we heard on every side of horses, buggies, and men being swept away when endeavouring to cross a spruit that had been bone dry an hour or so before. To us *rooineks* these tales of the great 1912 drought always appeared as incredible fabrications, yet the roads themselves lent some truth to these statements, for in places they had been completely washed out by the rains of previous years, and new tracks, often making a wide detour, had had to be struck.

After we had satisfied our hunger and only temporarily

satiated our terrible thirst at the Terminus Hotel, we rested in deck-chairs on the veranda that overlooked a wide and pleasant stretch of veld surrounded by blue hills. Then we mounted our machines once more for a further seven miles' sandy struggle to the famous World's View.

Our road took us past the Nursery, for, in accordance with Rhodes' will, the whole district was being extensively planted with trees of every species; by now these trees must be a sight to behold. At last we passed through some large iron gates marked "Rhodes Matopos Park" into a narrow gorge with huge kopjes on either side and the inevitable boulders perched on top. These enormous boulders were *the* feature of the Matopos, and were both larger and more pervasive than those at Khami. Before we had got far along the gorge I heard a weird noise on my left, and turning round found I was within 30 yards of a herd of baboons who were making a meal of wild oranges that grew by the roadside. I yelled to Johnnie but, before he came up, they had made off. We clambered up the rocks and gave chase and saw them disappearing in the distance. Later in the day on our return we saw any number of them again perched high up on the rocks, making the most of the setting sun and spanking the young ones before putting them to bed!

We had been told many things about these animals. One man related how impossible it was for his wife to go outside the lonely homestead where he lived without being molested by the brutes. So long as he was about the place the baboons kept well away, for they knew he carried a gun, but as soon as they saw him go off on a round of his farm, or away to market, they would come and surround the house and make it unsafe for his wife to venture forth.

The path from the "Outspan Halt" up to Rhodes' grave was, for the most part, over gently sloping rock, but in some places was quite steep, and how the oxen succeeded in dragging up a gun-carriage with a coffin upon it I fail to understand. The grave itself was unpretentious enough: just a large brass tablet with a very brief inscription, "Here lie the remains of Cecil Rhodes," let into the rock in a clear space between the seven or eight huge boulders that crown the flat stone summit of this kopje.

In one corner, right at the edge of the little plateau, was the large granite memorial to Alan Wilson and his men who were killed on the Shangani River during the Matabele wars in 1893. It was dedicated, "To Brave Men. There was no Survivor." Round the side were life-size bas-reliefs of all the men very well executed in bronze. But there were too many unpleasing incidents, to put it mildly, about our wars with the Matabele to make me desire to ponder upon them.

The boulders surrounding Rhodes' grave were covered by lichen of many colours, some of it of the most brilliant emerald hue, though there was no moisture about to encourage its growth.

The view from the top was wonderful, enormous kopjes appearing in every direction. It was unique and yet, at the same time, characteristic of South Africa in its vastness, its loneliness, and its silence. I may be wrong, but I cannot forget "Trooper Peter Halkett of Mashonaland" when I think of Rhodes. He was without doubt a great man. One feels that when he camped on the top of the Matopos and saw South Africa spread out before him, he was very literally taken up into a high mountain and faced with the eternal question, "all this shall be thine *if* . . ." I believe that he honestly felt it was worth the price, but such a bargain can never be accepted with impunity. It does seem to me necessary to remember this when listening to the perpetual chorus of glorification of his every act, word, and deed that one hears on all sides out here morning, noon, and night. For in Rhodes' case, though "the evil that he did lives after him," there is no fear of "the good being interred with his bones." In South Africa (as elsewhere) there was, it seemed to us, too much of the feeling that, if a man is successful, it matters little *how* he was successful.

We stayed on top until the sun was getting low on the horizon and the boulders stood silhouetted against the sky. It was a joy to be up there quite alone. The moon had risen by the time we reached the Terminus Hotel again, and we certainly felt we had done enough for that day. We found the manager and his wife extremely kind and attentive. He made arrangements for rooms for our friends who were coming from Bulawayo to join us, and reserved a Cape cart and four mules to drive the girls the seven miles to the foot of the Sansom's kopje.

Next morning brought another of those perfect days which we had come to look upon as a matter of course, and we strolled out to climb some of the kopjes. We passed a Native village and admired the cleanliness of the kraals. The headmen and their wives came out and wished us many "sa-go-bonas" (good mornings), the picannins were just driving the cattle out to feed and carried the newborn lambs and kids in their arms as they followed the flocks and herds, and then, fastening upon the tallest kopje in sight, we proceeded to climb it. It was hot work clambering up, and we were glad to reach the top and lie on our backs in the sun. The view was delightful, and the time slipped by as we drank in the fresh breeze and talked of everything from "cabbages to kings." We visited a little local store and post office combined, owned, I believe, by a Chinaman who employs a peer's son to serve at the counter for him! Some younger son down on his luck, I suppose! At 4 p.m. *the* event of the week took place, the little train arrived, bringing our friends from Bulawayo. As old habitués of the place, Johnnie and I strolled along the siding in our shirt-sleeves to meet them, our linen bags of Boer tobacco dangling from our belts.

The Terminus Hotel had a most delightful stoep, and here tea was ready for our four guests, all of whom were, I am sure, very relieved to be away from the dust of Bulawayo. After tea we strolled along the river-bed together, Arnold going ahead with a little rifle he had brought with him. We saw a pigeon, and that he promptly brought down at the first shot. We struck nothing else until I spied a giraffe in the distance just on the edge of the big-game enclosure. We had great fun stalking along until we got up quite close. There were two of them, not 20 yards away from us, together with their constant attendant, an eland, the largest of all the buck. It was delightful to see them in the open, and we were all very excited, but alas! the light was beginning to fail, so that Johnnie was prevented from securing an excellent photograph.

On our way home we saw a sable buck and got within a yard of a water-buck, and as we were nearing the hotel we spied a "Go-away" bird, and proceeded to shoot at it. The amazing thing was that it did not "go away," and in the twilight it took twenty-three shots to bring it down. Arnold said that the first shot must have killed it, and that its body was held by a fork in the branch. Let us hope it was so, for the "Go-away's" sake as well as for our own repute as marksmen, for we all six had several shots at it! To look at, the "Go-away" bird is like our wooden toys, for he has a crest on his head and a wide flat tail that he raises up and down in spasmodic jerks whenever he is alarmed.

That evening we learnt that our Native waiter at the hotel, who was very proficient and who pattered to and fro on his naked feet, was reputed to be worth some thousands of pounds in cattle. He was nevertheless very gratified by a 2s. tip for attending on six of us for two days. To press 2s. into the palm of a bare-footed black man whom you know to be infinitely more wealthy than yourself takes a bit of doing, especially when he can live on a few handfuls of mealies a day which cost him almost nothing, whereas every farthing is precious to an impecunious World Traveller! Next day we spent several hours at the World's View again and had a picnic lunch. The hotel people had forgotten to put any spoons in our hamper, so when we came to the tinned apricots we had to eat them with our fingers and lick the juice off the plates with our tongues, but who cared so long as the sun shone down from an azure sky.

We had the good fortune to see a troop of some fifty baboons come down from the nearby hills and cross an open valley to water on the banks of a shady stream. We could see them quite plainly with the naked eye, but with the assistance of field-glasses we could observe every antic as the little ones chased and tumbled over each other and the elders walked sedately behind like the congregation returning homewards from a village church. Their coming was heralded by a curious bark, evidently emanating from one big fellow who was acting as leader and walked on the flank of the party. His duties appeared to include those of scout and guide, for every now and then he paused and had a good look round, sniffed into the wind, barked, and then went on again. So long as they are not molested these animals are harmless enough, but if you wound one then there is the devil to pay. We were sorry to leave those sun-scorched granite rocks, but at 5 p.m. the one and only train started back to Bulawayo, and if we had missed it we should have had to wait six days for the next!

Folks were beginning to talk about summer, and the weather was becoming decidedly warmer, although it was but the first week in September. All kinds of strange insects were already making their appearance: bumble bees about six times as large as those in England, and enormous flying ants that seemed to wear their bodies about a foot away from their heads, the two being joined together by means of a wire-like apparatus, delighted to perform a kind of ungainly two-step around the lampshade every evening, and finally drove us shuddering to bed. At the falls a species of black beetle had got into the drawer of my wardrobe and consumed a cork out of one of my medicine bottles and nearly the whole of one of my best handkerchiefs! But all these were as nothing compared with the ravages of the jigger flea and the sheep tick. The former lay their eggs under one's toe-nails,

31 We found the Khami ruins extremely interesting

32 "Here lie the remains of Cecil Rhodes"

33 Voor-looper and aachter osse

34 Wagons laden with sacks of grain

the big toe-nail for preference; in due course the young jiggers hatch out, and then the fun begins! The unfortunate victim, their host, is treated to all the finest forms of torture known to that King of Fiends—Irritation—until, driven to the verge of madness, the toe-nail is forcibly removed by a Native servant, fortunately expert in the art, and all the young jiggers have a speedy end put to their promising careers.

One evening we went over *en masse* to the Howard Moffats* for a sing-song. We had a very jolly time, and were enjoying ourselves so thoroughly that it was 11.30 before we left and took our moonlight stroll back. Another evening we discussed with Mr. F. Eyles, a farmer from the Mazoe, and one of the elected members of the Rhodesian Assembly, Rhodesia's most pressing problems, viz.: the high cost of living, which he had come to Bulawayo to investigate. Roughly speaking most things cost at least twice and sometimes three times as much as in London.

There was packing to be done and vast preparations to be made for our journey to Zimbabwe, acetylene lamps and rifles to be cleaned, and another visit to the Howard Moffats to be worked in, for this was the nearest place where we could get a last hot bath, a very useless proceeding as will be learnt hereafter! Muriel had made us both wonderful sleeping bags of rugs, and generally "mothered" us. We were still hard at it when supper was announced and our friend, Mr. Trump, arrived. At 9 p.m. we set out for the Suburbs Halt Station with the Natives carrying our kit, a knapsack, a rug roll each, the lamp, the camera, rifles, etc. It was a beautiful starlight evening, so Jessie, Muriel, and Arthur accompanied us a little part of the way. I may say at this juncture that I had no great confidence in Mr. Trump's management of the expedition; he was really quite nice and amusing, but I felt sure we should soon have to take things into our own hands. It was a relief therefore to find that the fourth member of our

* Mr. Howard Moffat was until recently Premier of Rhodesia.

party, Mr. Cauler, who was already in the train with the tent and other paraphernalia, was one of those quiet individuals who, although they won't take charge of affairs, know what they are about. It was obvious he had camped out before, and his rough features and horny hands contrasted oddly with Trump's somewhat ecclesiastical appearance.

Chapter III

WE TREK TO THE GREAT ZIMBABWE

AS the train went lumbering off into the night, and after we had arranged our beds and baggage and praised the beauty of guns and cameras, we went to the refreshment saloon and had a drink, for the night was oppressively hot. Stan produced his pipe, always a rare event with him, but considered a good omen by his friends, and we set to talking about snakes and lions and things. For some days before our expedition started, Trump had implored us "to get hard feet," and already he was bemoaning the fact that his own were blistered through walking the short distance from Hillside to the Suburbs Halt in riding-boots. "It will be impossible for me to walk another step for days," said he, and he seemed distinctly nervous about the possibilities of meeting with snakes and lions, good shot though he was!

That night was one of the bumpiest I ever remember spending in a South African train, we might just as well have been in a goods wagon, so it was with a feeling of great relief that we arrived at Gwelo at 6.30 next morning. Here, after breakfast, we purchased a canvas bottle for our kit; these bags leak abominably until they are broken in, and this one made a disgusting swamp as we carried it along the corridor of the train that was to take us up to the railhead at Umvuma.

At Umvuma our troubles began. No vehicles, mules, or horses were procurable for love or money to take us the eighty miles to Victoria. The contract for the coach that carries the mails had just expired, and, with only four days' notice, Zeedebergs were maintaining a service. Their vehicle would take three passengers only. One man, who had been sitting at Umvuma four days waiting for the privilege, had booked the first seat. There were thus two available seats and four passengers. What was to be done? We thought of going back and trying Selukwe, but learnt that Zeedeberg's man had commandeered all the mules from that district he could lay his hands upon. We thought of tramping, despite the fact that Trump had blistered his heel walking to the Suburbs Halt, but we found that Native carriers would be exceedingly difficult to obtain. Anyway it was piping hot, and the accounts of the road were depressing. An immediate decision was essential, for the coach was on the point of leaving. Trump was prepared to go straight home. I was *not*, after coming all that way. It was finally decided that Johnnie and I should go on ahead and that the others should follow by the next coach three days later. What they would find to do in Umvuma Heaven alone knew, I didn't!*

After hastily gulping down some food we took our seats. We little knew what was ahead of us.

In Quest of Victoria

I think we should hesitate to call such a trail a road in England. It was more like the loose sand at the top of a beach than anything else, except that it was loose black dust instead of sand. At times our eight mules found considerable difficulty in dragging us through it, and for quite a long period at the beginning of our journey we left the "road" for a cart track across the veld. This involved a painful amount of jolting, but was a welcome change from the inferno of dust. Any dust which the thirty-two legs of the mules did not stir up the four wheels of the coach did, and thanks to a slight following breeze we seemed to get the benefit of the lot. I thought we had served our apprenticeship to dust in Kimberley and Bulawayo, not to mention the railway journey to the falls, but that was all child's play compared to this. Time and time again all eight mules were out of sight, enveloped in

* At this point it will be noticed that the leadership of our expedition had slipped, without argument, into Stan's hands.—[S. S.]

a cloud of dust, and we could barely see the half-caste driver and his Kaffir "boy" on the seat in front of us.

On such a journey the driver carries a whip, an instrument with a handle 12 feet long and a lash 20 feet long, used with both hands after the manner of a rod in fly-fishing, and terribly punishing in the hands of an expert. The Dutch make lashes for these whips from giraffe hide, for it is possible to cut a single strip 20 feet long down the back portion. The driver urges on his team with yells and curses, accentuated with cuts from his enormous whip, which fall on the beasts' hides with cracks like pistol shots. A thick, heavy "sjambok" of hippopotamus hide is also carried for the benefit of the *aachter osse*, or wheelers. These, with the span in front of them, being well within reach, come in for the most generous share of encouragement, and it is rarely that, in an up-country Boer's team, one of this unfortunate quartette does not rejoice in the name of the "Englishman." The second "boy," generally a picannin, is known as the *voor-looper*, or fore-runner, his duty being to lead the front span (in the case of a team of oxen) by means of a strip of green hide (reim) attached to their horns. Occasionally, when the driver's throat has temporarily succumbed to gutturals unapproachable by an Englishman, the *voor-looper* takes a turn at the whip and shouting.*

We could quite understand the relief of the mules when we came at last to a relay station and the joy with which they celebrated their freedom by a thorough roll in the dust.

It was very pleasant after we left Umvuma to see some green again, where water had collected at the bottom of one or two of the valleys, or *vleis*. At the moment there was not much water, and the *vleis* presented the appearance of marsh-land. Soon afterwards we came to a place where the land sloped away for miles in front of us and then rose again beyond. The sun had just disappeared behind the hills, and all the land ahead seemed like a huge lake around the shores

* *Guide to South Africa*, 1911–12 Edition. A. S. Brown and G. G. Brown, Ed.

of which clustered hundreds of little white villas. It was a joyful and refreshing sight coming at the end of such a hot and tedious day, but alas! the lake was nothing more than a wide expanse of young green grass, and the white villas but hundreds of grey granite boulders caught in the dying rays of sunset. Just after nightfall we reached a little place called Felixburg and made sure we should be stopping there for the night, but learnt, to our surprise, that we had another fourteen miles to drive to a place called Makoweries. To ensure our having something to eat, I purchased one of the few things they had at the little local store and post office, a very excellent tinned cake "made in Australia." On we went again into the darkness of the night which was acceptable if only for the fact that we could not *see* the clouds of dust that surrounded us. Talking was reduced to a minimum, as every time we opened our mouths they were filled with dirt; if there were boulders in the way we had to go over them; if there were ditches we had to go into them. We had held on to that wretched cart, that called itself a coach, like grim death ever since the early afternoon, often being hurled against one another with some violence. Little wonder that we became drowsy, our heads would droop, and our grip on the sides of the cart relax, but only for a moment or two; the next instant we were brought to our senses with a start, as the coach gave a violent lurch and nearly capsized. There was no moon, but the road being so sandy was just distinguishable, in spite of the fact that we carried no lights on the vehicle. Every now and then the driver had to get down and strike matches close to the ground to make certain that we *were* on the road at all!

Just as we were dozing off again we went crashing through the overhanging branches of a tree, and Johnnie made sure that we were being attacked by lions! The next moment the mules evidently caught sight of something, for, with a united leap, they swerved off into the veld in a state of panic. It was at this juncture that our half-caste driver turned round and, in broken English, explained that he had never been along this way in the dark before, and *could we tell him if we were on the right road!* Our stolid Scotch companion remarked, "That's guid!" We were too knocked all of a heap to do anything but roar with laughter! Our only surprise was that the driver did not hand us the reins! Our leader mules showed much nervousness for some time after this, and the whole team was pulling in so uneven a manner that we had to stop and rearrange the beasts and mend much broken harness by candle-light.

Then we went ploughing on again. Wearily the miles went by; we saw no light but that of the stars; we met no living thing. Suddenly, just as I roused myself from a short dream of being lost in a trackless wilderness, I thought I saw a faint glimmer ahead. It might have been the glare of a wild beast's eye, or the glint of a will-o'-the-wisp, but no! it was a little flame, and it was moving about. We stopped the cart and watched, listening. Our driver was so worked up that he would not go and see what it was unless I went with him, and, as we watched, the light went out. That was a most forlorn moment for us all, and it was almost with a shout of joy that we hailed its reappearance. The driver and I now went forward; at first we thought it was the fire by an outspanned wagon, but soon we found ourselves among a herd of mules gathered round a Native hut. Some Kaffirs now appeared, aroused by the barking of their mongrel dogs, and told us we were on the right road for Victoria and had struck a relay station, but they were indisposed to give us fresh mules at so late an hour; it was nearly 9 p.m.

However, after our driver had sworn at them in some of the choicest of King's English, we were soon out- and inspanning by the light of the candle sheltered from the breeze by my old brown hat. When all was ready we took our seats and plunged into the night once more with renewed hopes of getting to a resting-place sometime! We were so worn out and saddle sore from all this jolting that we just sat and hung our heads and slept until more fires beside outspanned wagons awoke us and our hopes rose yet once again. At length a light came into view shining through some tall gum trees. This we learnt was Makoweries, and here we should find scoff* and beds awaiting us. Our worthy postmaster, agent, chief official, farmer, host came out to greet us, lantern in hand, and conducted us straight to the office-dining-room, where three hot plates of steaming soup were placed before us. He had heard by telephone—oh, blessed instrument!—of our coming, and without waiting even to remove the top layer of dust we settled down to one of the best meals a hungry man could wish for. A chicken, unrivalled in size and flavour, followed the soup, and besides potatoes our astonished eyes fell upon a dish of *greens*, a thing we had not tasted for many a long day! Soon after our weary bodies had forgotten the discomforts of our primitive journey through the wilds and were resting on clean beds, in round thatched *kaytor* huts, that made blessed the civilizing hand of man.

We were due to leave again at 5 a.m., but I am glad to say that our host and driver overslept themselves, and it was not till 6 a.m. that we left. My alarm watch went off all right, and *we* knew the time, but I'm afraid we had no qualms about delaying His Majesty's mails for an hour. There is no hurry in Rhodesia, and it was far more important that we should have a little extra rest! Thanks to our later departure, we were enabled to see the homestead by daylight. When the railway to Victoria is built (it had already been surveyed) the line will pass close by.† The construction was only being held up by a few farmers who refused to give the free grant of 50 yards on either side of the line for which the railway company stipulated.

With a cup of coffee to stimulate us, and the previous day's dirt still hanging to our clothes, we started once more on our dusty drive. The surrounding country was more thickly

* Food.

† To-day this picturesque journey is done by rail and in comfort, and motor-cars pass along this road, which is improved beyond recognition. At the time of which we write, cars were not to be seen in Victoria.

covered with wood, and distant blue hills rose on the horizon and were a welcome sight indeed in the early-morning sunlight. At 9 a.m. we reached another relay station (from first to last we must have used some forty mules), where an amusing old Native with spectacles informed us that he had "tea, coffee, cocoa, bread-butter, all ready, sirs!" We were very relieved to get anything, and gladly followed him to a neat little hut while the mules were being changed. A box with a dish-cloth over it formed a table about 9 inches high, and three little boxes formed our seats. The old Native stood in our presence and bent from the middle as he poured our coffee into the cups on the low table. We made a hearty meal, spreading our bread with "Dorset" butter that was preserved in a cardboard box and into which more ants than butter had accumulated during the course of time, but ants make a tasty potted meat to eat with bread and butter! As we went to join our cart again we met a huge Dutchman under the enormous fig tree that spread its branches over the collection of Native huts. We learnt from him that his name was Rubenheimer, that he dealt in cattle, and that he weighed 270 lb.; his kindly shadow was to cross our path on more occasions than this; beside him we looked like three ants regarding a hippopotamus. He told us how the old Kaffir who had supplied us with breakfast had given him a similar meal one day that consisted of a scrap of bacon and two bantams' eggs, and when asked the cost the old fellow had replied "5s. 6d.," and on another occasion he had charged 2s. 6d. for boiling some water!

In two hours' time, he said, we should be in Victoria, and apart from the fact that we were all becoming more and more unrecognizable in our coatings of dust, nothing marred our progress except the usual entanglement of the team whenever we charged some rocky spruit. This always necessitated constant delays to pull the traces from between the mules' legs, or to give some of them a merciless thrashing for not pulling properly. We have seen beasts thrashed in our time, on the

Continent and elsewhere, but none so inhumanely as these poor South African animals. As previously explained, all the driving of these teams is done with the whip, the reins are only for lugging the mules back on to the road, or to have something to hang on to if the team should bolt. The whip-boy picks out the tips of the unfortunate beast's ears; this is the mule's one and only tender spot, for they are nearly all "buttoned," or pierced, for identification purposes. Presently we came over the shoulder of a hill, and there at last lay Victoria, nestling among the spurs of some big blue hills that rose from a wide, long valley. All we could see were a few white and iron houses peeping from among the tall blue-gum trees, and this oldest township of Rhodesia looked no larger than the smallest of English villages.

In another hour came signs of civilization; many wagons laden with sacks of grain were outspanned by the roadside, and here and there lay the corpse of a dead mule or horse upon which flocks of crows were feeding greedily. Then just one more shaking across a wide dry river-bed and we were rattling through the apparently deserted streets of Victoria. It certainly gave one the appearance of being at the end of the world.

A group of men were standing round the Post Office awaiting the bi-weekly mail—the only event of the place, I imagine—and one of the older settlers, whom I noticed the others called "Daddy," was particularly warm in his greeting to me: "Hullo! Are *you* back again?" "Hardly," I replied; "I don't recollect ever having struck these parts before."

A Night in Strange Company

A few moments later, when we were in our room at the Thatched House Hotel, I could easily understand anyone mis-taking us for anybody else, since we couldn't be seen for the layers of dust that had accumulated on us. After a hot bath and some lunch, Johnnie lay down while I sat in the shade and did a little writing. In a weak moment we had promised Trump to be in Victoria on Sunday to meet their coach, but to sit around until then was quite impossible, as the bar and the billiard-room were the only places where any business was done or pleasure taken. We decided, therefore, to get out to Zimbabwe in the morning and return two days later to Victoria to meet our friends. Once more the difficulty was transport. The distance was about seventeen miles, and we felt too exhausted to tramp it in the heat. Whilst Johnnie rested I bustled round the town to see what form of conveyance I could get for the morrow. Everywhere I went I was told that Mr. So-and-so was up at the hotel—at the bar, of course—and I got very fed up with tracking people thither, and generally I managed to get to the bar door and *no* farther!

We had heard that it was a fairly good road, so tried to borrow cycles. One man undertook to provide them; he would be along, he said, between seven and eight in the morning. We thought we would make sure of a good night's rest, so retired at 8.30. At 9.30, just as we were getting nicely off to sleep—it was so close that we had only a sheet over us—a messenger came in with a note for us to say that a small vehicle was available and two mules to start at 5.30, and could we drive it ourselves? I replied that it must wait till the morning. I couldn't deal with correspondence in bed. At 10 p.m. I was again awakened by a visitor, but this time of the most objectionable species. Thanks to my electric flash-lamp, the insect was speedily traced, crushed, and immortalized on the wall beside my bed. This necessitated a thorough inspection, but nothing else was revealed. The bar, which was *the* rendezvous of the place, had been going strong all the evening, and at this point some of the men and two rowdy, though sober, females appeared to settle themselves on the stoep outside our door. After a vigorous protest from the nineteen-stone Dutchman, Rubenheimer, who had a room next door to us and wanted some sleep, peace reigned, and we dozed off once more, until our door was opened suddenly and a drunken man staggered in on the arm of his friend. After I had succeeded in impressing upon him that it was not his room, he withdrew, but not before giving us some good advice and putting the key of our room on our table, "Just ter shatishfy" himself, as he somewhat vaguely put it. The cats then started a chorus with an obbligato accompaniment from our drunken friend, who had now found his room, where he raised hell for some considerable time, snarling at his boots and sighing most distractedly when he was not yelling like a demon. Before we had barely got to sleep it was time for our Dutch friend to start, and owing to his immense weight he could not dress and pack his belongings quietly. Then a deputation of friends visited the drunken fellow in the other room to tell him there was "plenty of whisky left." The "boy" then brought morning tea; this generally arrived about 4 or 5 a.m.; I had to get up and unwedge the door, and *that* night was over!

At breakfast time we had the drunken intruder at our table of course. Even at that early hour he had been going the pace in the bar, and when the "boy" brought him the menu he just gaped at it. The "boy" very intelligently concluded that porridge was wanted, and when this was placed before our table companion it was quite a time before he could realize what it was, and then he ate it as if in a dream. He was not the only incapable man to sit down to breakfast that morning, and later he called me to his room to know if some enormous collars on his dressing-table were mine. As I wore size 13½ and these were 17's, I had reluctantly to disclaim ownership. He became confidential and told me he had been Native Commissioner in the Jo'burg district, and was now employed in recruiting Native police for the Chartered Company. He lamented the indolence of the Makalanga, in whose country the Victoria district lies. He also kept repeating how much he regretted the hospitality of the people of that town—they were so generous with their drinks, and he *had* to treat them all in return; and he spoke of his wife and child who were in camp on the veld some miles away. I could but feel profoundly sorry for the man; he had come to town to see a little life, perhaps after working for months in the wilds, and *what* a town to come to, and what else *was* there to do but drink!

Meanwhile Stan, who had slipped away to make final arrangements for a conveyance to Zimbabwe, now returned with a two-mule gig and a Cape Hottentot "boy" to drive them. The trap had only seating room for two, with a narrow plank at the back for luggage, but we quickly devised a luxurious hammock sling seat by means of ox-hide reins, a cushion, and a door-mat. It fell to my lot to occupy this novel contrivance, suspended in a half-reclining position between the two back wheels, a little above axle-level, with my feet under the seat of the vehicle and nothing below me but the cushion, the mat, the reins, and space! In this somewhat degrading and farcical manner, and to the amusement of the bar loungers, we clattered away from the Thatched House Hotel, out over the veld to the Great Zimbabwe. Stan peered down at me over the back of the gig as I half lay, half sat, suspended between the wheels, breathing in the thick clouds of red dust stirred up by the hoofs of the mules; this position was quite a comfortable one so long as I did not contemplate too much the possibilities of falling backwards. Thus we journeyed for an hour or so until we came under a hill, where we found water, a distant kraal, and a large thatched farmhouse. Here we outspanned and ate our lunch of bread and cheese, and the Hottentot cooked us some eggs to perfection in an old tin he found in a bush near by whilst looking for ox dung for the fire.

This Hottentot was a stumpy man, strong and square, with a few tufts of hair on his chin, a big flat nose, and a very evil eye. He had a large rent in his trousers where covering was most needed, and although he could cook eggs to a turn he was to prove the stormy petrel of our expedition.

After lunch Stan took the hammock seat and I sat beside the driver, and helped him with shout and sjambok to stir our lazy mules into some semblance of pace; but the whole outfit was decrepit, the harness kept breaking, and likewise the whip. "Knifes pleases Baas," said the Hottentot as he clambered down to do the repairs; indeed, he seemed too proud of my knife and took an endless time to cut a stick or divide a reim. Poor Stan had worked himself back into an almost recumbent position in his hammock seat. I knew too well how those thongs were cutting into him, in spite of cushion and mat, and to make matters worse for him, all that vile dust and the heat of the sun beating on his head had brought on a severe attack of nose bleeding.

First Sight of the Ruins

A few hours later, feeling somewhat exhausted, we drove up to Mr. Mundell's huts at Zimbabwe. He had built them on a ridge, a beautiful situation, overlooking the valley of the ruins. The country around was almost mountainous and of impressive beauty. It was still terribly hot, but we felt we could not let another moment pass before seeing something of the ruins that had drawn us from afar. Leaving Mundell's by a rocky track we passed down a valley strewn with great boulders and covered with long, dry grass. It was in this valley, about half a mile from the ridge and under the shelter of an enormous rock, that our camp was to be pitched a few days later. On our left towered the steep Acropolis Hill, upon the summit of which many of the ruins were situated, while the Temple ruins lay in the vale at our feet, where it opened out and fell farther away to the south. The Temple remains were enclosed in a gigantic elliptical wall, of small and evenly faced granite blocks, about 40 feet high and 15 to 20 feet thick. Inside this was a huge conical-shaped tower, most perfectly constructed, and a maze of passage-ways, just wide enough to allow one person to pass along at a time between their colossal walls. Steps leading through doorways and the rounded jambs of these entrances were all constructed with these small stone blocks, which must have necessitated an enormous amount of labour and patience, spread over a long period of time, to hew from the granite rocks that lay piled on every side.

Many relics have been unearthed here, including gold ornaments, soapstone effigies, and articles of phallic worship, all of which, and especially the aspect of the ruins themselves, lead the uninitiated to support Hall's theory as to their great antiquity.

We were too tired to do more than sit about on the piles of stones and gaze with wonder on those amazing dry-built walls, the rough beauty of their strength, the mystic loneliness of their surroundings, where the scarlet flowers of the kaffir-boom tree made magnificent contrast with grey stone and azure sky. On our return to the very large and comfortable huts a wonderful sight greeted us. We had noticed the veld fires, both while driving along from Victoria and while sitting at the ruins, but from Mundell's ridge the whole countryside seemed to be ablaze. It was now dark, and the flames could be seen extending in straight lines for miles. It was as if some Mercury with winged feet had encircled the hills with a flaming torch, setting fire to the tall, dry grass as he sped along. They were not accidental fires, for we had watched them springing up almost instantaneously at wide intervals. Mr. Mundell explained to us at dinner that evening, when his wife and Mr. Wallis, the curator of the ruins, and the local policeman were also of our company, that the fires were started by the Natives in order to obtain sweet, young grass for their cattle. Too much new grass, after the long drought of fifteen months that they had just experienced in that district, was really a danger to the cattle, as they often gorged on it and died. The Natives themselves, he explained, were starving, and the Government was rushing wagon-loads of grain into the Zimbabwe and Chibi districts to their relief. It was not a charitable but a business proposition on behalf of the Company, however, for that part of the country was so suitable to cattle raising that the supply, it was said, was almost inexhaustible. The Natives, of course, were big owners of cattle, and the Government gave them three sacks of grain in exchange for each beast. The high price of 25s. per sack was being paid for mealies at that time, as against the ordinary price of 5s. or 6s., so it was obvious that the position was a serious one, especially if no rain came to make the new grass grow now that the countryside was burnt up. Mr. Mundell added that a Mr. Brown, one of two youths, the eldest aged twenty-one, who were farming near here, had had to ride miles out of his way that evening, because of these fires, to fetch his letters. He had reported that a lion had killed a cow and calf of his a few days before, whereat we pricked up our ears!

That night was so hot we could scarcely breathe, and as we lay naked on our beds we prayed for something cool to look at or to touch. But in spite of the intense heat we slept as it is good to sleep at times, in a heavy lethargy, enhanced by cleanliness and peace. At Mundell's we had both cleanliness and peace, and there was no risk of our night's rest being disturbed by "drunks," but the morning brought us a rude awakening, a sudden answer to our prayer: we found the countryside enveloped in a thick, chilling Scotch mist, "Gooti" weather, as our host called it at breakfast time, "and," he added, "it invariably lasts three days."

We had packed our knapsacks as lightly as possible, thinking that we should be cycling. We had thus no change of outer garments with us. The day before any clothes felt oppressive; now, even with our never-failing Shetland wool waistcoats, we were cold. All our plans of spending a long day among the ruins and climbing up to the Acropolis were knocked on the head. There was nothing for it but to accept the inevitable and sit on the stoep or in the hut. We had been so spoiled by the weather in South Africa that we could not complain. In the afternoon Mr. Mundell and Mr. Wallis lent us coats and we wandered round the Temple, but it was cold work and we were glad to get back. That evening Rubenheimer, the weighty Dutchman, turned up with his wife, weather-

35 Acropolis Hill with our tent among the boulders at Zimbabwe

36 Eastern Wall of Temple Ruins

37 A wonderfully constructed entrance to the Temple

38 Natural entrance through the solid rock on Acropolis Hill

bound from a cattle-purchasing expedition, and he kept us all amused by his tales. He told us how he and four companions once sat down to breakfast, and their average weight per man was about 306 lb., nearly 22 stone apiece! "That," he added, "was in my youth, when I weighed very much more than I do now."

Next morning we were up at 5.30 so as to be back in Victoria to meet the others, and we ate our breakfast, which consisted of dry bread three days old, an egg, and some impossible cheese, as we drove along in our four-wheel gig! As a matter of fact, our two friends did not arrive until 2 p.m., for they had an even worse time than we did. They got hopelessly lost in the mist and were out all night in it, and arrived at Makoweries at 8 a.m. that morning instead of 10 p.m. the previous night. They never got to Felixburg at all with the mails, so had to send them back by runner from one of the relay stations. Being Sunday we all took it easy that afternoon, and at tea time we were asked into the sitting-room of the Thatched House Hotel, where the barmaid, chaperoned by her aunt, gave us a jolly good tea in celebration of her birthday! They were the only ladies present, their guests were twelve or fourteen men. Our hostesses, if typical of their profession, were jolly good sorts, and the elder woman was considered the "Mother of Victoria," and kept the whole town supplied with bread, no one else being capable of baking.

We went early to bed to get a good rest before our tramp back to Zimbabwe next day, and after listening to Cauler's yarns of his experiences in the Boer War we fell into a light slumber. At 10 p.m. a gramophone concert started on the stoep outside our window, together with songs and dancing, and these final celebrations of the barmaid's birthday went on far into the night, and soon after they ceased Stan was bitten again and awoke disgusted.

Next morning we hustled round buying provisions and making arrangements for our little gig to take our kit out to Zimbabwe, as carriers were not procurable; but it was nearly noon before we got away. Johnnie and Trump went on ahead, while Cauler and I stacked the cart. At the seven-mile outspan we caught them up. Here in an inspired moment I suggested to Johnnie that he and I might endeavour to procure some bread from the thatched farmhouse we had seen on our previous journey, for we had been unsuccessful in obtaining any in Victoria. The farmer at once asked if we would have some tea; he would not take "No" for an answer, and in five minutes we were sitting down, not merely to tea, but cold meat, bread and jam, and chatting to a fever-stricken comrade who was squatting in his blankets on the floor, with his back propped up against the wall. In twenty-five minutes, greatly refreshed, we decamped with a half-loaf under my arm! We found the others had walked slowly on, so we hurried after them with the bread. Trump was of opinion that "man cannot live by bread alone," but they had not bothered to unpack the scoff boxes, beyond getting out a little chocolate. Both men were already showing signs of weariness, and Cauler, having raised a blister, was walking barefoot!

The water at the next stream was not appetizing, so it was decided to proceed to an oasis three miles farther ahead. Neither Trump nor Cauler breathed a word to us that they had told our driver to outspan for scoff at this same stream we were leaving behind. After walking two miles we saw a buck in the distance, a "duiker." Cauler was carrying his gun and, although the buck was well on the move, brought it down first shot. It ran about 40 yards after being shot, climbed to the top of a large ant-hill, surveyed the charred and shelterless veld for the last time, and then disappeared from sight. Thinking it was getting away wounded, we chased after it, but found it expiring on the other side of the mound.

There was great rejoicing amongst the carnivorous campers at the thought of fresh meat. Trump and Johnnie walked slowly on while Cauler and I waited for the gig that never came. After sitting on the veld for half an hour we came to the conclusion that we had better walk on, so we carried that buck between us, no light weight, for quite a mile.

At this point Mr. Palgrave, the local Assistant Native Commissioner, drove by on his way to collect the hut taxes from the four or five hundred Makalangas living round the Zimbabwe district. I had made his acquaintance at Victoria, so stopped him to enquire after our gig. He told me it was outspanned for the night, and the camp-fire made at the stream three miles back! There was nothing for it but to chase back those long three miles and leave Cauler and his blistered foot with the buck.

The mules had wandered in search of the fresh pasture that is not easily found at this season, and it was dark before the driver had inspanned them again and we had rejoined Cauler. There was no room on the gig for either of us, so when the road permitted we stood on the back axle and got a lift that way. Meanwhile Johnnie and Trump had taken refuge at Mundell's, and were refreshing themselves with tea. Trump was in a state of collapse, and but for Johnnie would never have got there. What would have happened to him if we had adopted his suggestion of walking the additional seventy to eighty miles from Umvuma at the rate of twenty miles a day I cannot imagine.

It was just sunset when Trump and I arrived at Mundell's; the "Gooti" weather had cleansed the air of veld fire smoke, and soon the great flaming disc slipped down behind the blue hills. On the rocks of the ridge, silhouetted against the bright evening sky, squatted hundreds of Natives in their quaint garments, waiting to receive their Commissioner. At that moment Palgrave drove up in his gig, and the great assembly moved forward to the edge of the road with a dull cheer of greeting and a curious clapping of hands which was the customary expression of Native pleasure. Palgrave had come to collect their taxes: £1 from the owner of each hut, and 10s. for every additional wife, if the husband had more than one. Stan and I thought it over afterwards and came to the conclusion that it would be almost worth while "turning Native" and having half a dozen wives apiece at that price, for, it must be remembered, the Native wife does all the work in Africa! Just fancy what might happen if we in England were to welcome our income-tax collector with cheers and applause; but, as I have said before, these Mashonas or Makalangas are but children—"Children of the Sun" as their name implies!

Big Boulder Camp

The next morning we climbed up to the Acropolis, and what a wonderful place it proved to be! It was infinitely more extensive than we had ever supposed, and much more wonderful than the Temple ruins. Like the Victoria Falls, Zimbabwe was unique; it was on the outskirts of a mountainous region. Wherever one looked were granite rocks; in fact the whole countryside seemed to consist of granite. One walked 100 yards through the tall, dry grass and then 50 across flat, bare granite. The Acropolis Hill was a large kopje standing out from the rest with huge boulders upon it, some of them as big as a house and having perpendicular sides impossible for man to climb. A fissure extending for hundreds of yards between the rocks formed a natural entrance to this otherwise impregnable stronghold. Nature's work had been completed by the addition of a number of those dry-built walls of solid granite blocks that we have already described. The extent of the walls, their construction, their size and situation were alike marvellous. Every peculiarity of the formation of the rocks had been taken advantage of, and nothing appeared to have been overlooked. The ruins were so extensive that one could wander about them the whole morning and yet miss many passages and walls. And, despite its size, a handful of men could hold this Acropolis against unnumbered foes. The view from the top was magnificent, and one could see right into the Temple, with its extraordinary conical tower and parallel passages down in the valley. To me it is an inexhaustible subject, but I dare not enlarge upon it. Little is certainly known about the ruins; practically everything is surmise; so that one is free to let one's imagination run riot.

H. Rider Haggard's *She* and *King Solomon's Mines* are books written about the mysteries of these curious remains, and whether the great treasure that is supposed to be hidden there will ever be discovered is mere conjecture. A Mr. Wilson, an old prospector in this country, remembered the gold seekers turning up the soil around the Great Zimbabwe ruins, and he himself found many ornaments of gold on the margin of the spring whence we obtained our water; trinkets that had slipped from the bosoms of fair water-carriers, how many centuries ago? Mr. Wilson also prevented some ruthless prospectors from blowing up the unique conical tower, where they hoped to find the treasure hidden in its solid interior. The granite blocks show signs of damage still where the charge of dynamite was inserted!

Whilst at Zimbabwe we had some wonderful tramps and scrambles over the surrounding rugged country after game for our larder, and before long we had quite a bountiful supply of biltong hung out on a reim line near the tent. We always carried a piece of this sun-dried meat in our pockets, and whenever we felt hungry we scraped some into the palms of our hands with a penknife and tossed it into our mouths.

It was glorious to sit round the camp-fire in the evenings and watch the shooting stars and vie with each other in the telling of yarns about reptiles and other horrid things. There was the 15-foot-long python that had been found in the bush near Bulawayo not many weeks before. He had collared his buck by the head instead of the tail—oh, gluttonous and ill-bred serpent!—with fatal results to himself. He had managed to get the buck completely inside him, and the antelope's head had travelled three-quarters the length of the python's body, but then the horns pierced through this creature's skin, and he had died a slow, agonizing death that lasted a good three weeks, whilst sightseers came from afar to witness this rare spectacle, and even brought their children to give them a moral nature-study lesson. Trump taught us the first principles in attack and defence against lions; he told us why travellers and hunters always kept their camp-fire burning at night and placed their transport animals in a circle around it, any ass or mule in the team being kept well on the outside, for a lion prefers ass flesh to any other form of diet. And if when walking through the tall Zimbabwe grass you suddenly come face to face with a lion and his wife, always pot at the lioness first; if you kill or wound her the lion will slope off, but if you shoot the lion his wife will do her best to make short work of you. It is somewhat similar with human beings: if you see a man knocking his wife about and you intervene in her interests, she will often turn and rend you!

With thoughts such as these running in our minds we would lay ourselves down to sleep; sometimes sleep did not come easily, especially if one had the outside berth beside the carcass of buck that was covered with a towel and pegged to the ground to keep the wild dogs and other prowling beasts from running off with it. When I lay in this berth I often stayed awake wondering if the hungry scavengers of the night might not prefer warm, living, human flesh to that of cold buck. I was aroused in the early hours one morning by a curious noise as of a reptile opening and shutting its jaws, a weird sucking and snapping sound; I listened intently and a cold sweat began to moisten my brow; I stretched out my hand cautiously for my gun, but my wrist was caught in an iron grip! Our indolent Cape driver "boy" had stolen a haunch from that buck only the day before, and I thought of him and his evil eye, his almost cannibalistic eye. My trousers hung above my head, and my jack-knife dangled from the brace button; I groped for it in the darkness with my free hand. Suddenly there was a gurgling noise, the hand that held my wrist began to jerk from side to side, someone started tittering, and then Trump lisped out: "It's all right, Johnnie, I was only *pretending* to be a python!" "If you go on like that," I growled, "you'll blinking well wake up in the morning with its mate curled up on your chest!" With that we both relapsed into slumber again.

Early next morning we walked across the hills to Dr. Helm's mission station, only to find the bird had flown. As luck would have it he had gone into "Town" that very morning; however, Miss Myburg, a trained nurse, who was one of his assistants, gave us tea and took us round. The scenery was very beautiful, and it was worth going there for the sake of the walk alone. The kaffir boom, with its brilliant scarlet blossoms and leafless boughs, quite lit up the landscape at this time of year and made vivid contrast with the azure sky and the browns and greys of the parched and rocky countryside. The Helms had a very prolific orchard of oranges, lemons, bananas, *naartjes*, and pineapples. There were so many huge lemons that they veritably littered the ground under the trees. We took all that we could carry in our pockets, but wished we had brought a knapsack. The air was heavy with the scent of carnations and orange blossom and many other flowers that grew in profusion in this pleasant corner of the wilderness. The Helms had a number of lepers under their charge, and were soon likely to have more. On our return to camp we paid another visit to the Acropolis, and at 3.30 we had to take our departure in our old friend, the two-seater gig, Johnnie being strapped on behind on top of the rug rolls this time!

There was a somewhat unpleasant incident in connection with our departure. We sent one of our Mashona "boys" to fetch our Cape driver. On returning to camp the latter started to abuse our Mashona "boy" for carrying out our instructions, and commenced to knock him about. Here we intervened, and Cauler told the Cape "boy" that if he struck the Mashona we should thrash him. A lot of abusive language followed, in Dutch, and the Cape "boy" was most insolent. Had not

Trump intervened Cauler would have gone for the chap there and then, for he was a thorough old rascal and had absolutely deserted us most of the time. A little later he came to me for some scoff. We were not responsible for his food, and Cauler said if he didn't do any work he couldn't expect us to give him food, and seeing that he had already stolen a leg of venison he would jolly well see that he got nothing else! This led to further insolence, and as the "boy" used some very unpleasant epithets Cauler went for him. A conflict ensued in which the "boy" got some hard knocks and Cauler had his old pair of trousers ripped up. Trump separated the combatants, and we started off wondering whether *we* were going to come in for trouble. But he did not give us any further cause for complaint.

Rough Roads and Rough Manners

We got back to that terrible place Victoria just after dusk, and rather than spend another night there we decided to start for Selukwe right away. Groman, the contractor, who was himself coming with us, was quite agreeable, and it was arranged we should start at 9 p.m. and do the first stage that night.

As I had experienced before, all roads lead to the bar in Victoria, Rhodesia, and if you want to find anyone you are more likely to do so by stopping at the Thatched House Hotel than by visiting their place of business or private residence. I tried the experiment several times, but the result was always the same. It seems hardly necessary to add that if you hear of a man's "roof being lifted," or his house being broken into and his furniture smashed to bits, or of the entire contents—bed, bedding, chairs, washstand, and carpet—of the room adjoining yours being burnt to ashes, it is at the bar that you will find the delinquents, and even if it be 7.45 in the morning you must not expect to find them sober. The deliberate firing of a bedroom actually took place the first night we were up at Zimbabwe. I spoke to the manageress about it, and to quote her words: "You can't say anything. They have paid up the £30 and we have replaced everything better than it was before."

I could give many other and still less pleasant incidents of the way they "enjoy themselves" in these parts, but I have said enough to show that we shed no tears when we mounted Groman's coach at 9 p.m. and left Victoria behind.

It was pitch dark and we could only proceed slowly, so that it must have been after midnight by the time we reached the first outspan. Here we lay on mother-earth "under the wide and starry sky" for a few hours' rest until the dawn.

Another traveller was sleeping there, with his mules tied up to a tree where a lighted lantern swung. We hitched our beasts up close to his and flopped down on the ground between them and the fire. Dead tired as I was I could not get warm, and could not therefore get to sleep, so I sat up on my kit and wearily watched the meteors and the stars as they flickered and blinked and skimmed along the dark ridges of the hills. The "boys" were busy preparing the mealies for the mules, whose acrid odours mingled with the pleasant scent of burning blue gum boughs. Then, their work completed, the "boys" wrapped themselves up in their blankets and fell asleep; the mules crunched away at their mealies and fought and squealed the while. Now and again the Natives would rouse themselves to curse at the mules or throw more boughs on the dying fire. Presently the animals ceased eating and quarrelling, the fire burnt down to a glowing ember, and there was no sound save the heavy breathing of my companions and an occasional sigh of satisfaction from the tired-out beasts. Hardly a breath of wind stirred across the veld, yet I was cold, and weary at last of gazing at the stars I slipped into my bag and lay there, half shivering and half sleeping, until the first faint light—the coming of another day.

When we arranged to return via Selukwe we thought nothing could be worse than the road from Umvuma. We little knew! I really think it was five times worse. In places we had the same trouble with the dust, and for the rest it was more like a washed-out river-bed than anything else. The thing that amazed us most was the way the coach held together. Any ordinary vehicle would have been smashed to pieces. And the larger the boulders and the bigger the ditches, the more these wretched mules were whipped up. But our remorseless driver (a Cape "boy") did not confine his lashes to the mules. Before we had time to realize what he was doing he was applying the heavy thonged *aachter osse* sjambok to the little picannin who was assisting him with the reins. Groman intervened and a moment later the piccaninny, who was of course crying for all he was worth, got off to do something. We waited, but the kid stayed behind and refused to come on. An altercation ensued, and finally the Cape "boy" got off the driver's seat and gave chase. Needless to say, I was on the side of the young 'un, and I told Groman, who was quite indignant, that he couldn't expect anything else to happen. For a solid hour were we stuck in that road, and Groman, fearing lest the driver was lost on the veld, fired his gun off twice to indicate our whereabouts. In due course the driver returned, complaining that the piccaninny had the legs of a buck and had got away, for which I thanked Heaven. I veritably believe that had that Cape "boy" caught him he would have killed him.

Our first halt after this little incident was the Shasi, where a Jew-boy, who had a store, provided us with an indifferent but costly breakfast. We were already tired with the terrible jolting, and we were not through a third of the journey. We had to hold on to the sides of the coach like grim death, and the strain of it all just wore us out. We were at it all that day, from five in the morning until seven that night, with outspans to rest the mules—seven mules and one horse, to be accurate—every twelve or fifteen miles. We had nearly ten rivers to cross, for, unlike the Umvuma Road, there was plenty of water, and these crossings sometimes proved the most trying of all. Johnnie got some excellent snapshots, but even they gave no adequate idea of the absurd angles at which we got tipped up. I still fail to understand how it was that we were preserved from capsizing on several occasions.

At 7 p.m. we reached "Mumford's," a wayside farm, still thirty odd miles from Selukwe, where we were put up for the night. We were on our way again shortly after 5 a.m., but it was not until 11 a.m. that we reached Selukwe, for it was a long climb uphill, and our whip was not functioning properly for some reason or other and the team slackened its efforts in consequence.

Selukwe itself is beautifully situated, and from all accounts quite one of the prettiest of the mining centres. It was certainly a great contrast to Umvuma, for, instead of being flat, it was surrounded by well-wooded hills. The last ten miles as we neared Selukwe were very beautiful, and it was delightful to see a buck bounding across the road in front of us.

Although we had had no breakfast, we had to hold on till 1 p.m. for a meal. I was feeling very snappy, for my thermos had been broken by the jolting, my overcoat lost but subsequently recovered, and we were thoroughly worn out. However, I bethought me of my youth, and purchased a tin of something that, in a cattle-raising district like this, one would imagine would not be required, a tin of condensed milk, and I was greatly comforted.

There was little to choose between the bar at Selukwe and the bar at Victoria. The extraordinary thing was the difficulty that I had in escaping "drunks." They amused Johnnie, but they filled me with loathing, and it was always to me that they came. No sooner was lunch over at the hotel than a huge, fat, drunken chap swooped down upon me. I escaped twice, but the third time he got a chair alongside of mine before I knew it, and his great beery face was within half an inch of mine. There was plenty of room next to Johnnie, but not a bit of it—he had heard I was a missionary! . . . I told him that he had heard wrong. Well, then, was I buying or selling cattle? When I told him I had never owned a cow in my life and was nevertheless not a missionary, that was too much for him. But it did not prevent him from holding forth at great length about the missionaries and the Natives. He thought that it was absolutely wrong to educate the Natives, forgetting that to live in the same country with them is to educate them, that to be drunk in their presence is to make an ineradicable impression upon them.

Our train did not leave until after four, so I was glad to find a refuge from the Selukwe Hotel with the local chemist, who was, at the same time, the local bookseller. When we got down to the station I said to Johnnie, "We are not likely to be troubled by our fat friend here." "No," he replied, "he is not likely to go so far away from the bar." Now *the* thing to do in Selukwe was to see the train off, and to our dismay we saw our huge beery friend, who was called most appropriately Bill Firkin, heading the procession of the inhabitants down to the station, on the arm of a companion, with two Natives in advance, each carrying a case of bottled beer on his head! Bill Firkin was bringing the bar on to the platform, where eventually the two cases were finally deposited, and he started to treat all and sundry to a farewell glass. The sight was not a very edifying one, but we could not help smiling when the huge form of Bill Firkin reeled to the edge of the platform, and, waving a foaming bottle of beer above his head, he pointed wildly at Stan, who was some way off, and shouted at the top of his voice, so that all could hear, "There's that *damned* missionary man that wanted me to sign the pledge!" This last because Stan had politely declined to have a drink with him.

We had learnt during our short stay in Selukwe that Bill Firkin was the owner of a small gold mine away out on the veld, who had "turned Native" and owned a number of wives. He was said on one occasion to have slung a "boy" to the branch of a tree and lit a fire beneath him. Fortunately a missionary heard of his doings and exposed him; hence his hatred of missionaries. During our travels we heard a great deal about the excesses of the Natives; we also heard of, and saw with our own eyes, the excesses of the white man, who too often proved a poor example to the races he had subdued.

Just outside Selukwe I was surprised to see some very well-cultivated ground, and found it consisted of market gardens run by coolies. They brought us strawberries at the next halt, rather tasteless and very dirty, but I had no hesitation in assisting my neighbour in eating the bagful he had purchased, so welcome was the sight of them. Just as we were leaving Selukwe a tall gentleman with moustache and beard came to our compartment and asked whether we could find room for him. I took a fancy to him at once, he had such an exceptionally kind face, and soon got into conversation with him. Both Johnnie and I were delighted to hear what he had to say on the Native question in a general discussion which followed. It was not until we were nearing our destination (Gwelo) that we exchanged cards, and I discovered that he was a missionary. I found that his station was precisely in that part of the Matopos which I most wanted to see. His name was Steigerwald, and he was connected with some American mission. They appear to give the Natives who come to them a most excellent and practical training. He invited us out to his place, about twenty-five miles from Bulawayo, and offered to send his mules to fetch us if we would let him know in advance. Had we only known earlier we might easily have arranged it, but it was unfortunately no longer practicable.

Johnnie was too exhausted with the Zimbabwe trip to come on with me to Que Que to spend the week-end with Alfred Carnegie, who was working on the Gaika Mine, so he returned direct to Bulawayo.

Alfred was at Que Que Station to meet me, and on arrival at his *kia*, a square brick-built thatched hut which he shared with his senior assayer, Mr. Bellasis, we had the good fortune to run into Colonel Heyman, who, besides being at the top of the tree in the Rhodesian mining world, is one of the seven elected members of the Rhodesian Assembly. We sat on the beds in the hut (chairs are apt to be a rarity even in some of the Rhodesian hotels!) and for an hour and a half we four yarned away. It was most interesting to me, and he was quite amused about our Zimbabwe experiences. He was most anxious that I should write a letter to the paper warning tourists what they must expect, and that the much advertised "facilities" for getting there simply did not exist. This I subsequently did, and the letter which duly appeared in the *Bulawayo Chronicle* was apparently not without effect.

After Colonel Heyman left, Alfred and I had a picnic lunch and talked over his affairs. The tennis court is just outside their *kia*, and we joined in for occasional sets during the afternoon.

After supper we strolled along to the little Congregational Chapel, of which Mr. Lunn was the minister in charge. The congregation numbered about thirty-five, which, out of a population of only two hundred, doesn't seem bad.

We were indeed glad to get back to Bulawayo and the homely companionship at "St. Cyrus" for three or four days, which were spent in many pleasant ways, and it was with much regret that we bade all our kind friends farewell and took train for Salisbury, the capital of Southern Rhodesia.

Salisbury, Umtali, and Beira

Here, as elsewhere, we were fortunate in having the hospitality of friends who included Mr. (now Sir) Clarkson Tredgold, at that time Attorney-General for Rhodesia.

The first evening after our arrival in the capital I accompanied Mr. and Mrs. Tredgold to a flower-show at the Drill Hall, and I took the opportunity of having a chat with C. T. about the Chartered Company's affairs. I had heard quite sufficient criticism of the Chartered Company to enable me to draw him out, and I thoroughly enjoyed myself. I knew the important office he held, of course, but did not realize what a much more important position it was here than at Home, and how much wider the functions were. He was an administrator as well as a barrister and legal adviser. For instance, the entire police and prison services were directly under him.

We climbed to the top of the kopje that overlooked the town, attended an "At Home" and a musical evening, where we saw something of Salisbury Society, and one afternoon C. T. motored us off towards Mount Hampden, the first intended site for the town of Salisbury.

We visited a friend's farm there and indulged in an afternoon's shooting; it was an interesting experience, and we were glad to see a Rhodesian farm. A Cape cart was inspanned and we drove off across the veld, over ant-heaps and into ant-bear holes. We had not gone far before we spied a buck grazing in the distance. C. T. fired, and the shot must have whistled between its ears, for it just shook its head and remained stationary. His friend fired and hit its back leg, and it was off like the wind. A long chase followed, but unfortunately the animal got away wounded, but our friends said they would probably get it on the morrow. The next thing we saw was a jackal; it was a long way off, and much to our grief C. T. missed it. We must have started quite a dozen other buck of various species before we got back.

Next morning early we left for Umtali by the goods train, to which one passenger coach is attached. Johnnie chose the coupé, and when I sat down I noticed to my dismay no less than six bottles of beer under the opposite seat. I knew what that would mean.

The owner of the beer soon put in an appearance, and it did not require much observation to know what he had been doing the night before. He soon dozed off, but the sleep which we hoped would bring *us* peace did not unfortunately last for long. He woke with a desire for further liquid refreshment and an opportunity to air his views. Needless to say, although I was at the opposite end of the compartment and had remained discreetly silent, he fastened upon me. I have no objection to listening to anyone who is reasonably coherent in the expression of his views, but when this factor is missing it is really too exhausting.

Our respective hostesses had provided us with scoff, and on the whole the journey passed pleasantly enough. Our drunken friend, a Canadian by birth and a handsome chap in his time, removed himself occasionally to the seat in the open air which is always attached to the end of the coaches.

As we dropped down from Salisbury to Umtali the country became greener, better wooded, and, thanks to innumerable kopjes with the inevitable huge granite boulders, more attractive from the scenic point of view. Umtali, although only third in importance of the towns in Rhodesia, is certainly first in the beauty of its situation. Our first view of it was by the light of a full moon which had risen just before our arrival, and mountains were to be seen in almost every direction. As we walked along the one interminable street of which the town consists, we vowed that the morrow should see us upon the top of Cecil Kopje—the highest peak near by.

A man whom Johnnie had met in Salisbury had undertaken to see that we were put up at the Club at Umtali, and we were congratulating ourselves on our good fortune. On our arrival we found the "Court" was there, some Judge and suite, and there were no rooms available, so we retraced our steps to the Hotel Cecil. We could find no one to show us a room, and had perforce to leave our things in the hall while we went to dinner. Just as we were finishing the manager sent word that he had had our things taken to No. 3 Room. We were very tired and glad to retire at once. We did not observe that our hats which we had hung up just above the luggage had not been brought along. We were too occupied with the discovery that Johnnie's bed had been slept in the night before and that some of the gentleman's belongings were still in the room, which the aforesaid gentleman turned up in half an hour's time to claim! We were very busy next morning getting our mail letters off, and it was not until

39 The Conical Tower, Zimbabwe Ruins

40 The Conical Tower and portion of decorated wall

41 Johnnie was strapped on behind on top of the rug rolls

42 The Acropolis Hill Ruins at Zimbabwe

we strolled out to see the gentleman who was putting us up for the Club that I observed that half of my double grey hat had been removed and, of course, the half that was left was the half that is useless by itself. I at once complained to the barman, who replied, "Oh, that must have been Andy Johnson; he was very well oiled last night, and was boasting he had got a new hat, and now I come to think of it I saw him with it on." He was sure "A. J." would return at lunch time and he would get it back for me. So there the matter was left while we adjourned to the Club to finish our letters. At lunch time the hat was not forthcoming, but they were sure that they would catch A. J. on the train.

After calling upon Mr. Barnard, one of the local magistrates, to whom C. T. had given us an introduction, we set out to climb Cecil Kopje. It was hot work, but we were rewarded by one of the most beautiful views we have seen in Rhodesia—range upon range of mountains on all sides, and even though the ground was parched and burnt in places it was a fine sight.

On our way down we noticed a snake just a foot away from the path. In the uncertain light of sunset we thought it had its head in a tin, it was so puffed out, but we soon realized our mistake. We had unfortunately no stick with us, but we were nevertheless determined to "blot that puff adder out," to use the local phraseology. It was a good 3 feet in length, but I had puttees on and felt fairly safe from the knee downwards. I got round behind it and heaved some substantial boulders at it, but I missed owing to the failing light, and it moved on. I renewed the attack and hit it, but not very seriously. It was not at all pleasant to behold when it reared itself up and turned round to see what was happening, so I fled hastily for further ammunition, returned, and gave it some parting shots. By this time it had got some way from the path, the sun had set, and it seemed foolish to pursue the chase. I was reluctant to depart, for I should have liked to add a snake-skin to our collection of curios. It was the first snake Johnnie had seen . . . he hoped it would be the last. To my mind snake killing is far more sporting than shooting buck.

The following morning, after a few calls, we walked to the top of Christmas Pass and back. It was rather an effort in the heat, and *after* Cecil Kopje the view was disappointing, but to those who had not climbed higher it would seem unique.

On our way I was reminded of one of the fairy stories in De Morgan's *On a Pincushion* by the pods of a tree that we kept passing, which burst with a report like that of a pistol. In the fairy story they were called Zirbal nuts.

At lunch we were each presented with an envelope. Imagine the shock which we received when we found inside a printed letter to the effect that we had been approved as temporary members of the Club; *that the subscription of 10s. 6d. for 3 days, or a guinea for 7 days, was payable in advance, and they would be glad to receive our cheque!* A curious sort of hospitality! I have been put up for honorary membership for a few clubs in my time—I was a member of five in New York—but have never been treated like that before. Beyond writing a few letters there one morning we had not been inside the place, but there was nothing for it but to pay for our experience. We found they had the same arrangement at the Bulawayo and Salisbury Clubs, so we were thankful we did not accept offers to put us up for membership there. It would have been different had we slept or even fed there.

We visited the Turner Memorial Library and the Public Gardens. The latter were particularly attractive, and there were some excellent tennis courts adjoining. By this time I had made a few more enquiries regarding Andy Johnson, to see whether he was worth powder and shot. He appeared to be a red-faced Scotsman who owned a mine out at Odzi and only visited Umtali when there was a prospect of getting drunk at somebody else's expense. He had left his own hat behind and had only taken mine out of "drunken devilment."

It seemed to me only reasonable that *he* should pay for his amusement and not I. Were he hard up and in need of a hat I should have looked at it very differently. I accordingly adjourned across the way with the hotel manager to the police quarters and laid a formal charge against Mr. Andy Johnson. The police wanted me to stop and give evidence. I told them that if they would stop the boat for me at Beira nothing would give me greater pleasure. I pointed out that the hotel manager was responsible, and that he must prosecute. He agreed to do so, though he repudiated responsibility. The police at once wired to their man at Odzi, and I awaited the result with interest.

An hour later our train left for Beira.

The whole time we were in Rhodesia people condoled with us for being there in the dry season, forgetting that we had seen enough rain in England to last us a lifetime, and that we just worshipped the sun. It was quite true, however, that from the point of view of the vegetation it was a very unfavourable time. It was the end of an exceptionally dry season. Some places didn't have as much rain the whole year as Manchester gets, at times, in four days! The country was parched everywhere, and in the places where the grass had been burnt off it looked very bleak and bare. But from what we saw of the wonderful fertility of the soil and the rapidity at which things grow when they once have water, it did not require much imagination to realize what a picture the country must be after a week's rain. I always long to see it all again at another season, because, to form a really adequate conception of the country, two trips are necessary, the change is so great. The insect life, too, which is such a feature, is practically non-existent until the rains begin. The butterflies were wonderful, and at Umtali we saw some of the biggest I have ever come across. The ants would require a book unto themselves. What impressed me most was the variety in the types of ant-hill. In the O.R.C. they were like large beehives, and up towards the falls they resembled pointed pyramids

8 or 10 feet high. North of Salisbury they took the form of wide, flat cones, and covered enormous areas. I was disappointed never to see an ant-bear, for to judge by their holes there must have been a great number about. They only come out at night, and when I recall that Mr. Howard Moffat had only seen about two in a lifetime spent in the country, it is not surprising that we did not come upon any. The Native beehives were also a curious feature of this interesting land, and I remember the first we saw one evening gave us quite a start—it looked so like an animal crouched up in the tree. It is really only a sort of primitive box which the Natives put up in the hope that the bees will use it.

The effect of dropping 5,000 feet from the high plateau of Rhodesia to the muggy atmosphere of Beira is depressing. It was piping hot when we arrived about 9.30 one Sunday morning, and after passing through the Customs we were glad to take a seat in an absurd little trolley and be pushed to the Savoy Hotel, for there were no roads, merely hard cement pavements and loose sand between them. All the transport of the place was effected on trolleys pushed by Natives along rails laid down on the sand. The Savoy Hotel was a palatial and expensive establishment, and a great contrast to some of the places we had lately been patronizing, but we were not slow to settle down to hot baths and slip into our tropical suits. There was a violent bell-ringing at 11.30, and we thought it must be for some service; it was not till 12.25, still just in time, that we discovered it was the lunch bell we had heard, and woke up to the fact that we were in a continental town. Everyone appeared to go to sleep from 12.30 to 3 p.m., and if it was always as hot as it was on that day it is the very best thing one can do. We sat in our respective rooms, opening on the balcony and next door to one another, in our shirt-sleeves, indulging in our usual occupation—writing!

After a *small* cup of tea, which was brought to us in our rooms, we braced ourselves for the effort of inspecting Beira. To our minds it was not much of a place: the sandy beach was very muddy in parts and the surrounding country quite flat. On the way down from Umtali we had passed through forests and thick undergrowth, but as we neared the coast it was bare, uninteresting country, which in the rainy season must form one large swamp. There were plenty of buck about of all sorts, some quite close to the railway line.

The best thing about Beira is, we understand, its golf-links, but all we saw was the very fine avenue of palms leading thither.

The Natives in these parts struck us very favourably; they had a better physique, looked cleaner, and appeared more intelligent than, say, the Mashonas. A very large number of "coloured" folk were to be seen.

We were very pleased to find on our return to the hotel that the Rev. W. F. Lack, for whom we had enquired at Selukwe and elsewhere, was stopping at the same hotel as us. He had noticed our names and joined us at dinner. He proved very pleasant company, and I attended his service in one of the rooms belonging to the Bank of Africa. He invited us to accompany him to an "At Home" given by the Portuguese Governor. It would have been great fun, but as our "wedding garments" (i.e. evening dress) were at the Cape we could not accept.

Chapter IV

INTRODUCING THE *EAST AFRICAN*

THE next morning we felt we did not mind how soon we got on board the *East African*,* or how soon we got away. We did not know then what a small boat she was, what company we should find on board, or how long we should be destined to be on board in sight of Beira. It was not until four o'clock in the afternoon, after messing about for a long time on the quay, that we were taken off in a motor-boat to the *East African*. Our advent was not encouraging. She proved a small tub with very little accommodation, and that nearly all occupied. The second class accommodation had been filled up with steerage passengers, so that, although our tickets were only second class, we were at once shown to the saloon. The first class accommodation consisted of six cabins, each containing two berths and a sofa. After considerable delay we were shown to our apartments and offered the sofas of two otherwise full cabins. We protested violently at being separated, even refused for some time to have our luggage taken along, but all to no avail, for there simply was no other vacancy. Another passenger, who arrived later, shared the First Officer's cabin.

We tossed up for cabins, quite a useless proceeding, for we had noticed the bunks in one of the cabins were occupied by two unkempt, unshaven, unpleasant-looking apparitions who seemed to be drunk, and *I*, of course, got them as my companions.

Although the Indian steward swore that he was only asking us to share cabins with *Englishmen*, my unkempt sallow companions turned out to be Portuguese divers who could not speak a word of any other language. I have no grievance against them on the score of nationality. For that matter they

* This is, of course, a pseudonym. The actual vessel no longer exists.

were harmless enough creatures, except that they would spit noisily and continuously anywhere and everywhere in the cabin. When they were in the cabin, and one stayed in his bunk practically all the time, they did little else but spit, and they wasted few precious moments either in washing or undressing! One of Johnnie's companions, a fat old Dutch padre, who had been in their cabin up to Beira, simply could not stick it, and had made the Chief Officer promise to move him the moment anyone left.

So much for our cabins. As for our fellow travellers, they included one of the most degraded and foul-mouthed specimens of womanhood one could possible encounter. I was awfully sorry for the woman, but one could do nothing. Johnnie's two companions, the old Dutch padre and a Yorkshireman, had tried to help her, and the Captain had given the strictest instructions that she was not to be supplied with liquor at the bar. But, although they kept her all right for a few days, she got round some wretched engineer who joined the ship at one of the smaller ports, and who had not seen a white woman for months, and they both went to pieces. She made herself so objectionable that there was nothing for it but to boycott her. They tried to leave her behind at each of the ports, but without success. She was always brought back —no, carried back—by the Native police. Of the other four womenfolk, one was the little worn-out wife of a prospector, whom we called "Auntie" straight away, another was a distant relative of a famous naval officer; she had gone up Umtali way to take the post of barmaid, but finding a great deal else was expected of her, wisely returned. About the last two—a señorita and a Colonial—the less said the better.

The menfolk were a very mixed assortment, and included a music-hall artist with long hair and a game leg, who called himself Professor Mac. The officers were infinitely too fond of liquid refreshment, and, though he was never actually drunk, the First Officer was very near it every night. We describe the passengers and officers in detail, because instead of getting over the journey in thirty-six hours, we were destined to spend a week in the closest association with them.

So far from sailing on the Sunday as advertised in Bulawayo, or Monday as advertised in Salisbury, or Tuesday as we were informed by the agents at Beira, it was Wednesday morning before we got away. There was a lot of rice to be loaded and some sugar to be taken on board, besides some goods to be transhipped from another boat lying alongside. Never, I think, could more noise have been made in the process of loading and off-loading. I do not refer to the donkey engines, for they were quiet by comparison, but to the babel that proceeded from the motley array of Indian coolies, Kaffirs, and Arabs, all shouting and gesticulating at the same time, and above all to the hoarse voices of foreign officers, compelled, of course, to give their commands in the universal language—English. It was a wonderful scene, especially at night, with the brilliant arc lamp at the masthead. The Arabs with their turbans, the Kaffirs with their woolly pates, clad in all sorts and conditions of clothing, running hither and thither or perched in absurd positions, made a picture one would have laughed at on the stage as something altogether too grotesque and absurd, and the sing-song of the Kaffirs as they hauled in a rope, and the systematic clapping in time, and for a definite period, when they had completed a job, added to the weirdness of the effect. How we managed to sleep at all through the hubbub I cannot think. The funniest sight was to watch them all feeding, were it not at times so revolting. But after all, our hands were made to eat with, and why shouldn't we seize our boiled rice or mealies in them, roll it up like bread pellets, and eat it that way?

Before our boat sailed on what was to be an ever-memorable voyage for all the passengers, we managed to mail our reply to an advertisement that had just appeared in the Personal column of the *Salisbury Herald*, which read as follows: "Heavenly Twins: Will the disappointing, much travelled, mysterious pair please communicate with 'X,' this office."

We thought the advertisement must refer to ourselves; perhaps unconsciously we had overlooked the languishing attentions of some fair damsel up country, or possibly there was news of the missing portion of Stan's hat, but, like so many incidents in life that begin under such romantic circumstances, we heard no more about it; and besides, Fate was at that very moment weaving a much more dangerous web of adventure about us.

The ancient port of Sofala lies about thirty miles south of Beira as the crow flies, and unfortunately, owing to its present-day insignificance and silted harbour, it was impossible for the *East African* to call there. But to us Sofala had a special interest, as it was supposed to be closely connected with the ancient trade in gold at Zimbabwe. Some thousand years ago one Massoude, an Arabian, visited the port and describes its immense trade in ivory, amber, and gold with Persia, India, and China. In 1505 the Portuguese planted their first settlement here and commenced the great fortress of San Gaetano, which endured until the beginning of this century, when the inroads of the sea caused the massive walls to crumble.

Inhambane

We had been told that our steamer would put in at Inhambane on the way down to Delagoa Bay, and, as we were out to see as much of the world as we could for our money, we had no objection. Our second morning at sea we got up to find our vessel steaming along the large river estuary that leads to the little port. Were this properly dredged it would form a magnificent harbour. As it is, it was a most tricky channel, and we had to go dead-slow, taking soundings all the time. One great trouble about the Portuguese, apart from their Southern lethargy, is that they never have any money for development work. In the case of Inhambane it is true that no considerable expenditure on the harbour would be justified for a long time to come. A small railway runs for a short distance thence to the interior, and, except for passing ships, it is quite isolated. The commodities exported, such as sugar, tobacco, and coco-nut fibre, could only be drawn from the country in the immediate vicinity, and, although this was very fertile, the source was limited.

Inhambane is a pretty little place. I should think it must be quite one of the cleanest, best kept small ports in the Portuguese possessions. The buildings are nearly all of brick, colour-washed, and make a pleasing contrast to some of the galvanized-iron shanties at Beira. The streets are macadamized and lined with trees, and there are palm trees galore, and enough coco-nuts to sink a ship. In some of the taller palms, steps had been cut up the trunk, and we induced a picannin to climb up and kick some coco-nuts down for us. As we were returning to the ship a picturesque sight greeted us: hundreds of Natives, men and women and children, wading out to sea to unload cargo from two or three Arabian dhows. Needless to say, most of the carrying was done on their heads. We entered a pretty little mosque at the invitation of the priest, and watched the Arabs at their devotions.

On arriving at the jetty we heard from a fellow passenger that the degraded specimen of womanhood, whom we had dubbed "Saidee," had divested herself of all her clothes the moment she had landed from the steamer. The miscellaneous collection of Natives on the jetty were much amused of course, but the disgust of the few white people who happened to be there can well be imagined. Saidee was speedily arrested by the Native police and hustled into a motor-boat and taken back to the ill-fated *East African*.

It was as well Stan went to bed early that evening, for he would not have been an appreciative spectator of everything that took place between 9 p.m. and 4 a.m. that night. I was determined to see the matter through, knowing full well that there would be little sleep for me if I *did* go to bed.

It was customary for most of us to have a night-cap, after

the usual dance round the little saloon, before turning into our bunks, but that particular night someone suggested a sing-song, as we were lying peacefully at anchor and the stars were gleaming with their usual brilliance. Professor Mac, whose long hair, scoop-shaped mouth, and goggly eyes were typical of his trade, strummed on his banjo and strained his vocal chords to such an extent that he nearly blew us all through the smoke-room port-holes. Then the continental lady produced her guitar and sang songs whilst we all sat round drinking, smoking, admiring. She had no voice, and they were just languid little ditties that required no great talent, little *chansons familières* sung in Portuguese, dainty and fascinating, so that poor Lance, who was on his way to British Columbia to seek the fortune he had lost in Northern Rhodesia, kept raising his glass to her, and shouted: "Heresh to your vurry good health," and then he turned to me and, in a confiding tone, said how much those songs reminded him "of Venice."

As the night drew on, people gradually retired to their cabins, until there were only five or six of us men left, leering over the brims of our glasses as the continental lady became increasingly confidential and told us something about her past. Once she had been left to bleed to death, and she showed us the marks on her wrists; and often she had been nearly murdered. She was in the middle of one of these dramatic tales, half whispering with suppressed emotion, the First and Second Officers were leaning forward in their chairs eager not to miss a single word, when the white-uniformed, stocky figure of the Captain stumbled into the doorway. He had evidently been having a *very* good time ashore; he gave us all a surly look, and took his departure. Our self-styled "married lady" companion now became alarmed to think that the Captain had found her still up talking to six men at that time of night, for in those days such things simply were not "done," but we assured her there was safety in numbers, and we carried on with our talk. After the Captain sent a steward to inform us that we were keeping other passengers awake, I took the tip and slipped off to my cabin, but the others became hilarious, and presently I heard the Captain bawling through the skylight and abusing the Second Officer for not going to bed. For some reason or other the continental lady now became hysterical, and, accompanied by the Second Officer, Second Engineer, and one or two other men, paced up and down the deck for the remainder of the night, wondering how they would meet the Captain's ire in the morning.

In the middle of all this Saidee, who had managed to get ashore again, was being bundled up the ship's ladder by the Native police, struggling and swearing as she came. Once aboard she started shaking all the doors of the cabins, and, finding one unlocked, she blundered in in drunken error. Ejected from there by the indignant occupants, she was at last piloted down to the third class quarters, and, being unable to find her bunk, she finished up by sleeping in a heap on the bathroom floor! Her arrival on board had so thoroughly aroused the "lady" passengers sleeping in our part of the ship that they kept awake the remainder of the night, giggling and chattering to each other through their cabin ventilators.

We are Nearly Shipwrecked

Daylight was never more welcome than the following morning, and at 8 a.m. we left the shelter of Inhambane with the certainty of making Delagoa Bay that night or very early next day. That evening Professor Mac gave us his "highly instructive and refined" one-man show, a portion of the deck having been turned into a magic chamber, gaily decorated with bunting. We hardly recognized him in his immaculate evening clothes, and the missing upper section of his right index finger proved an invaluable tool of deception when he performed his card tricks.

Previously we had been watching an uncanny display of "summer lightning, of quite the harmless variety," as Stan explained, and somewhere about midnight I had to go into the passage-way, in my pyjamas, to coax the gigantic Dutch Reform padre back to bed, as he would insist in standing there talking to the ladies through their cabin ventilator. It was rather like a flea coaxing an elephant, and I had no success until Stan emerged from his cabin, and with ashen and weary face demanded: "Silence and a *little* slumber, *please*!" We could not have been asleep more than two hours when I was aroused by the howling wind and the heavy rolling of the ship. I could hear the crew busy about the deck and the officers blowing their whistles incessantly. With the dawn the wind increased in violence, the *East African* heeled more steeply, and "Daddy," as we all called the padre, who had been up and down this coast a great number of times, declared that he had never experienced such a storm. He confessed to the Yorkshireman and myself that he thought we were going the way the *Waratah* went some few years before, lost with all hands and without a trace remaining, in just such a storm as this, and not very far away from our position at that time. He became so agitated that he got up and went out to have a look and soon returned with a very alarming report.

I got up about 10 a.m., but I could find nothing to interest me in the huge seas that were running, nor in the alarming list our vessel had developed. Three sails had been hoisted to steady her, and her single propeller kept racing dangerously as she dipped her nose into the roaring trough and flying spume of the sea. We all hoped that we might still be able to make the shelter of Delagoa Bay before nightfall, but as the day went on the storm grew steadily worse. Stan and I found it impossible to leave our bunks, where we had to hang on to straps fixed to the wall of the cabins to keep ourselves from being hurled to the floor. Our experiences on the road to Victoria and Selukwe were as nothing compared to this. A few passengers who were still able to crawl about the decks brought still more alarming reports every hour. The stout old Arab bo'sun had been seen to spread his mat on the deck at midday and pray fervently to Allah, whilst the Captain, purple in the face, blew his whistle frantically at him from the bridge. Later many of the ship's officers had been observed drinking heavily in their cabins, one of them with a lady passenger. Late in the afternoon a particularly heavy sea struck our vessel amidships; my side of the cabin went up in the air, Daddy and the Yorkshireman seemed to disappear beneath me, and everything that was movable and many things that were fixed fell like an avalanche upon them. In spite of the screeching of the hurricane and the crash of the waves, we heard a general smashing up of crockery coming from below. The boat shivered in that uncanny way boats have; her timbers moaned in the agony of extreme torture; she remained in that alarming position. "Just too far, *just too far to come back!*" I thought, as I hung like a spider to the end of my strap. Recalling what slight rudiments of mountaineering I knew, I spread my legs and arched my back, and made a feeble resistance to the horrible slide into the great maw of the ocean that was now inevitable. I screwed my eyes up tight and clenched my teeth: "Too far, just too far to come back!" the words ran again and again through my mind. Yes, we were going, we were sliding, with gathering speed we went; the tension on my strap had gone, yet the end still remained in my hands; I was flying through space, down, down; the gruesome sound of the sucking, satisfied waters gurgled about my muffled ears. In desperation I opened my eyes in an endeavour to meet death with some form of courage; to my amazement, in the dim light that prevailed, I perceived the padre and the Yorkshireman hanging on to their bunks and leering *down* at me with terror in their eyes. Undoubtedly our ship had foundered with all hands, and we were turning over and over as we descended in this maelstrom of the seas.

Suddenly something hit me in the stomach, and there was the sound of breaking glass; water came rushing in under the cabin door. "Now for it!" I thought, and I calmly closed my eyes and held my precious breath for quite a record number of seconds. When I could hold it no longer, and no water rose to stifle me, I half opened my eyes again sufficiently to see that the little window that gave on to the side passage leading to our cabin had been blown clean out and had fallen on me on its way to the floor, where it lay now shattered, the pieces being carried hither and thither in a goodly wash of seawater.

"That was a near one," muttered the Yorkshireman between his teeth, as we regained the horizontal, and a stifled moan came from the padre, whose huge stomach rose up and down in spasmodic jerks beneath his ample nightshirt.

But the night brought even worse horrors than the day had done. There were no dramatic moments when it was a relief to feel that the end was at hand; it was one never-ending buffeting this way and that, just as if one lay on some super-crazy floor in some ultra-modern fair. An earthquake would be child's play to what we went through that night, and, although I had eaten nothing for twenty-four hours, my stomach seemed as if it were filled to bursting point with an enormous stone. The boat was rolling and pitching to such an extent that it was impossible for Stan and me to keep on our sofa bunks; we were so worn out that we could no longer hang on to our straps. Stan was hurled to the floor of his cabin time and time again, until in the end he pulled his bedding after him and lay there in spite of thc filth from the expectorating Portuguese; one of whom had been trying to solace himself by drinking beer fairly continuously and bringing it up with constant regularity all over the floor, where it was swung to and fro, mingled with the seawater that surrounded Stan's little island of bedding.

We learnt afterwards that all the officers and crew were standing by all that night ready for any eventuality. Some of the former were, according to the last reports we had, too intoxicated to be fit for duty, and it had been said that even Saidee had been admitted to the Captain's cabin to shelter from the horrors of the storm! Apparently we had turned back on our course to run with the wind and so ease the strain on our propeller, and although the weather moderated somewhat the following day, it was still blowing half a gale, and the sea running too high to permit our passage of the narrow Inyack entrance to Delagoa Bay.

What food there was, and nobody wanted it, consisted of grease and onions and weevilled ship's biscuits, and only whisky to drink. It was not until dawn on the Monday morning, five days after sailing from Beira, and after eight miserable days on board, that the ringing of engine-room bells and the deathly silence of stilled machinery told us that we were safely over the bar and riding the quiet waters of the bay.

As soon as our boat was moored to the quayside at Lourenço Marques, and without waiting for anything else, we dashed off to the post office. The way in which it lurched about while we were waiting for our letters was distinctly unpleasant. We hurried back to the ship to look after our luggage, and then strolled round the town. We had been so delayed that we felt it wiser to press forward at once and catch that day's train to Pretoria. The difficulties and expense of transport, and the lack of time, precluded our making a trip to Swaziland, a very bitter disappointment.

An Interview with General Smuts

Delagoa Bay is a place of marvellous possibilities, or would be were it in British hands. It is a wonderful natural harbour, and Lourenço Marques is a well-laid-out town. It was one of those perfect cloudless days which we had got quite accustomed to expect, and, as the sun was mightily hot, Johnnie and I were glad to sit quietly outside one of the cafés and watch the life of the place. I had a very pleasant interview with Mr. A. W. Bayly, who was then editor and proprietor of the *Lourenço Marques Guardian*, and he was greatly disappointed we were not making a longer stay.

The country between Lourenço Marques and Pretoria was very attractive in parts. Near the coast it was very flat, and the

43 We had nearly ten rivers to cross

44 A Rhodesian highway

45 Street scene at Inhambane

46 Oh, these South African stoeps, what a joy they are!

railway ran alongside the shallow waters of the Komati River, but we soon began to climb, and at Pretoria, where we arrived after a fairly peaceful night in the train, we were once more 4,000 feet above sea-level. It was exceedingly pleasant to be back in a really civilized British community, and the Transvaal Hotel, where we put up, was very comfortable. At breakfast next day the hotel proprietor, bowing very low, informed us that General Smuts, then Minister of Finance for the Union of South Africa, had telephoned through to say that he would be pleased to see us any time that morning. This in reply to a very carefully worded letter dispatched the previous day with Mr. John A. Hobson's introduction.

The great man was engaged when we called, but his secretary was amiability itself, and enquired whether he could be of assistance to us. We told him what other calls we had to make, and, as one official whom I wanted to see for the Eugenics Education Society was quite handy, he suggested our making that call, by which time he was sure the General would be free.

On our return we were at once shown into his sumptuous bureau, and he came forward to greet us. He was most affable, and we were at once at our ease and deep in conversation. I told him how greatly the country had impressed us, and quickly plunged him into controversial topics by asking him what the Government was doing to encourage immigration. As a matter of fact they were doing nothing! His reply was most instructive. In the first place, he pointed out, they could not make a wide appeal like the Canadians, for there was no opening in South Africa for agricultural labour: all such work being done by the Natives. That ruled out nearly everyone except the settler with some capital at his disposal. Him they welcomed, but experience had shown that it was unwise to attract him by giving too rosy a picture of conditions in the Union. South Africa is a land of disappointment as well as a land of promise. It is no uncommon thing, in a year of drought, for instance, to sow and to reap nothing. If a man has capital and can afford to go on and wait, he will undoubtedly "come out on top," and eventually reap a hundredfold. But how many can afford to hold on? In the case of many, their little all would be wiped out by two bad years.

General Smuts pointed out that, although enormous progress had been made, agriculture was then still in the experimental stage in South Africa, for the experience gained in other countries was often of no value there. The greater part of the country was from 3,000 to 6,000 feet above sea-level, and thus it was a case of farming on a mountain all the time, though people did not always realize it.

I mentioned the cattle-sickness known as *lamziekte*, and he told me that the latest research work of Dr. Theiler pointed conclusively to its being a form of vegetable poisoning which could only be remedied by winter feeding.

We discussed the possibilities of farming without irrigation in places where the annual rainfall is only 10 to 20 inches in the year: "dry" farming, as they call it in the Western States. In fact, we had a *long* talk about anything and everything, and a most interesting one at that. We had taken so much of his time that I rose to go, but not a bit. How was Mr. Hobson, and what about affairs in England and Home Rule? And we were off again! He was not impressed by the Ulster agitation and the efforts to coerce the majority.

The General was a fascinating man to talk to, with charm of manner as well as of appearance, and we thoroughly enjoyed ourselves.

From the old Government buildings we walked to the new ones then in course of construction. These made an imposing structure on the side of the hill at the "Sunnyside" end of the town; they cost, when finished, nearly £2,000,000, I believe. I am all in favour of a far-sighted policy in the erection of Government buildings, but it does seem to me that they could have built something equally effective and efficient for half the cost. The total white population of South Africa was at that time not a quarter of that of London, yet they were spending two millions on one building, and that merely Government offices. It seemed to be out of all proportion and grossly extravagant. Apparently the idea at the back of all this expenditure on Pretoria was to ensure its retention as the executive capital of the Union. As the railway system was then, it was not an altogether satisfactory centre, but if ever the North Transvaal line were carried through to West Nicholson in Southern Rhodesia the situation would be different.

One afternoon we drove out by motor-bus to Water Kloof, where a friend of ours was sharing a house with three other men. It was a solidly built little bungalow, and they all kept horses to ride the five miles to and from town. You could get a horse for £25, and they told us the keep cost little more than they would otherwise expend on omnibus fares. They had three Native "boys" to look after them, and their rent was £2 10s. each, or £10 per month. I told our friend that if four bank clerks in England could do themselves as well, they would think they were in Paradise. Round their bungalow they had a delightful stoep. Oh, these South African stoeps, what a joy they are! There is a peace and a quiet about them, a sense of repose one could never feel indoors. Inside of four walls one felt ashamed to sit still and do nothing, but on the stoep, in the heat of the day, in the cool of its closing hours, alone with the evening star, one knew what true contentment was.

As I lay in bed one morning, after having been disturbed three times for morning tea that I didn't want, and for clean boots and hot water, I said to myself:

"Give me the open veld I love,
The silent peaceful *vlei* [flay];
Give me a cloudless sky above
The narrow tortuous way
That leads me to a Kopje's peak
Whence I can see afar;
Give me the wider view I seek,
Give me the evening star."

But, as I remarked to Johnnie, morning tea is a bad thing when it leads one to write "poetry," let alone crib and adapt other people's!

I paid calls all the following day; the only one of special interest was to the late Lord Methuen's son, to whom I had an introduction. He was in charge of the scientific side of the Museum, and proved a most charming and delightful host.

The Witswatersrand

Next day we took our seats in the restaurant car and left for the hub of industrial South Africa—Johannesburg.

What a vile place it is to approach! Forty miles of black chimney-stacks, endless uninteresting machinery, and innumerable great mounds of dirty white tailings or "dump." Occasionally, where the dump-heap was still fresh and clean, it looked like a snow peak in the distance, but this was only a fleeting impression. At Germiston I thought I was on the South-Eastern entering London, so unsavoury did some of the buildings look. But we were soon at Park Station in the heart of the town.

"I am happy enough for myself. Joy comes streaming in upon me from every side. Only, for others, I am not happy." I think these words of Goethe's described very much what I felt in Johannesburg. It is one thing to flit through and sip the honey as one passes. It is another to be caught in the soul-crushing tentacles of "Corner House" and Throgmorton Street. For it is a soulless place. Ostentatious luxury and all that gold can buy were there in abundance. But of any "vision" other than of gold there seemed little enough evidence.

"It is a remarkable thing," I was told on every side, "that all this is the product of less than thirty years." "Much more remarkable," I wanted to reply, "that thirty years, or at most fifty, may see the end of it!"

On our arrival at Park Station we hired a rickshaw for the first time since our arrival in Africa, but it was to carry our luggage, not ourselves. The Langham Hotel proved a palatial establishment, but much more homely than *the* hotel of Jo'burg—the Carlton. It was certainly a contrast to anything we had hitherto struck. After our stay in Rhodesia we felt like country cousins come to Town. To have a band playing really good music to us during dinner; to sit in the lounge and drink coffee afterwards, took us right back to those distant times when we were in the Old Country!

To me Jo'burg was an extraordinary place. Modern eight-story American buildings stood alongside very indifferently built stores; there was plenty of hurry and bustle, in this the biggest town in South Africa. It was strange to come back to fashionably dressed women, but in Jo'burg men predominated, of course, and the shops that impressed one most were the men's outfitters, many of them magnificent stores.

We wandered into the Art Gallery—one of the few collections then worth looking at in this country—but were made uncomfortably conscious that if Mrs. A had not presented this or that particular picture, Mr. B had.

In the afternoon we received calls from Mr. L. B. Chesterton (uncle of the great G. K. C.) and Mr. John Stead. We gave them both tea in the lounge, and had a pleasant chat. Mr. Chesterton very kindly invited us both to the Country Club to lunch on the morrow. Johnnie was, however, not feeling very grand, and, when Sunday came, felt it wise to remain quiet. I met Mr. Chesterton at the Rand Club, and we drove to the Country Club via Park Town, the fashionable residential quarter of Johannesburg. The Country Club is situated in a veritable oasis, on the site of an old farm, and shut in on all sides by trees, so that one forgot in a moment the very existence of those fifty miles of black chimneys and dirty white dump-heaps. It was quite a fashionable resort—nay, *the* fashionable resort—and our table on the stoep outside was one of the many thronged with people, ladies as well as men. It was quite a fascinating scene. The brilliant sun lighting up the trees, the well-kept lawn, the willows overhanging the lake, the little yellow weaver-birds flitting in and out of their "bottle" nests, literally woven onto the tips of the willow branches, the black and white swans on the lake, and the sparkling fountain, were among the many things that contributed to the delights of the place.

We sat out under the shade of the trees, and I learnt something of the ways of Johannesburg. We strolled round the grounds, and visited the excellent golf course, the fourteen magnificent tennis courts, the croquet lawns, the squash racket court, and the swimming bath, which were all that money could buy. A friend of Mr. Chesterton's joined us at lunch; he was the secretary of a large gold-mining company, and as pleasant a villain as you could desire to meet. He gave one the impression of being one of those dilettante financiers one reads of in novels, who would rob you of your last farthing with the same innocent grace with which they would receive a charming young damsel in a drawing-room. I must confess that he amused me immensely. He was exceedingly kind to me, and at once promised to arrange for me to see over a mine when I expressed a wish to do so; "though why anybody, who wasn't paid handsomely to do it, should ever want to go underground and get himself in a filthy, dirty mess passed the wit of man to comprehend!"

He lived at the Country Club, and showed me his rooms; he collected books (a sign of grace!), but I noticed that they were nearly all of the Rackham picture book variety.

After tea under the trees I hastened back to the Langham to see how the world went with Johnnie, who seemed to have either contracted a chill or eaten some bad food.*

Down a Gold Mine

Next day I went by taxi to the Witwatersrand Mine and found that the manager, Mr. F. B. Lewis, was an old schoolfellow

* I had consumed too much good food and drink in celebration of my escape from death on board the *East African*.—[J.]

of my brother Sid. It was very disappointing that Johnnie was not sufficiently up to the mark to accompany me. Mr. M——, who kindly made the arrangement, had told me that a taxi was the only way to get there. When I discovered subsequently that "he really hadn't the ghost of an idea where the mine was, he hadn't seen it, and hoped he never would," I quite understood the advice, but it cost me 25s., and it was worth it. The driver of my taxi was an intelligent Swiss, Johannesburg being about as cosmopolitan a place as could be found. Mine after mine slipped by as we motored along, each with its tall black chimneys, its ungainly machinery, and its great white dump-heap. The "Rose Deep" followed hard on the "Simmer and Jack," and the "Glen Deep" and the "Knight Deep" adjoined, their boundaries defined to an inch. So close were the mines to one another that, with very little boring, the reef could be followed underground for fifty or sixty miles.

We were soon at the offices of the Witwatersrand Mine, and I was given a very warm welcome by Mr. F. B. Lewis, the manager. Much to my relief, he told me that I might safely dismiss my taxi as, when the time came, he would have me driven to Drifontein Station, no great distance away.

We at once adjourned to the changing room, where I donned some khaki slacks and an old coat. While I was putting them on, Mr. Lewis suggested that before seeing the mine I might care to inspect a new shaft which they were sinking. The old Cornish miner in charge of the shaft warned us that owing to a "break" in the granite they were being drenched with water. If we were going below we must put on "oilies." He had a new pair that would just fit me. They certainly enveloped me so that I could scarcely move in them. They would have fitted G. K. Chesterton.

We scrambled into the large bucket and were lowered into the darkness. This was worse than an American thirty-story lift, for I could not see what was happening, I could only guess from certain weird sensations at the pit of my stomach!

At first I had no doubt that we were dropping, but there soon came a time when I felt confident that we were going upwards with great rapidity. Then I began to believe we were going both ways at once, when a great spray of water suddenly brought me to my senses. The next moment I was dazzled by the glare of acetylene lamps, and deafened by the noise of running water and incessant hammering. We were pulled up suddenly, and had arrived at the bottom of the shaft. When my senses had accustomed themselves to their new surroundings I was able to discern an engineer and a gang of Natives all up to their knees in water and working, with oilies on, in a veritable shower-bath. The ventilation was excellent, whilst the water was being pumped up continuously; as water was a precious commodity even in these parts, it was carried off in pipes for use in different places in the mine. Specially long drills were being used so that the tops were clear of the water. The Natives seemed happy enough; it was much healthier than working in a dusty atmosphere, and the old Cornishman, a quaint card in his way, pointed out several to me who had come back four or five times to work for him. However well treated, Natives never seem to stick to any form of town work for more than about six months on end, if they can avoid it: wherein they show good sense.

The shaft was being sunk through solid rock, and, owing to a break in its formation which it was impossible to foresee, there had very nearly been a disaster; but fortunately the mass of rock that fell away did so during a change of shifts. We ascended once more into the sunshine, and, having discarded our oilies, motored off to a different part of the mine, where I examined all the new machinery. Here we went underground in earnest, and it was three hours before I saw daylight again. Instead of dropping down vertically, we slid down an inclined plane into the abyss. We clambered into one of the huge wet, dirty, empty skips which, only a few moments before, had brought up several tons of "slack." I skidded down to the bottom of it, acetylene lamp and all, and felt like a glow-worm at the bottom of a well. Mr. Lewis gave some signals on an electric bell, and down, down, we went. About every 50 yards we were conscious of a fine spray of water, just sufficient to lay any dust. We dropped to about 1,500 feet below the surface level. In many of the mines you would go straight down 4,500 feet, and would still be above sea-level, for Johannesburg is at an altitude of nearly 6,000 feet. The depth naturally depends upon the exact location of the reef. This reef is the all-important factor, it is the life-blood of Johannesburg, and I will try to give some idea of it.

Imagine, in the first place, a stratum of gold-bearing rock varying from a few inches to a few yards in thickness, and covering an area of 60 or 70 miles by 6 or 7 miles. Picture this same stratum no longer level, but broken up and disturbed by innumerable upheavals, sometimes extending for thousands of feet at an angle of 45 degrees, sometimes breaking off abruptly, sometimes almost vertical, occasionally almost horizontal. Where that stratum goes there the miner follows, for it is this thin layer of rock, and this only, that possesses any value. Even this thin layer varies again in value according to the percentage of gold that can be extracted from it. But so long as it contains gold in payable quantities, it is blasted out and carried to the surface, for further treatment, in the enormous skips which I have described.

The blasting process is quite interesting. The holes are bored with compressed-air drills; the noise is deafening, and, as I was standing with my head close to the exhaust when one of the drills was started, I was nearly blown over. Under the Miners' Phthisis Act water is laid on everywhere: there are fine sprays in every passage-way, and in places it was like being in the rain forest at the Victoria Falls once more, but without the aesthetic compensations. Even when they were drilling, a hose had to be applied to the hole; it was all very necessary, but it seemed to me they will develop some new form of disease instead. Anyhow, it was killing work, and the men were correspondingly paid. A man in charge of the drilling would in those days think nothing of drawing £80–£90 a month. It often came to over £100.

These men were supplied with a gang of "boys," and paid so much per foot. It cost the mine-owners just as much for water, compressed air, labour, etc., per day, whether the man in charge was competent or not: the more expert he was at the game the better it paid them, for speed was half the battle. There were, of course, endless lines of trolleys underground, running to and from the spots which were being blasted—literally miles of trolleys and at different levels, for the mine was a big one and covered a T-shaped area. I noticed its capital was £450,000, and, after I had been all over the mine, I realized how easy it would be to sink all that money and possibly have nothing to show for it. The reef might start well and come to an abrupt finish. It is of necessity a highly speculative business. The mine I am describing had regularly paid dividends of 35 per cent., but even so its £1 shares stood at under £3, for the mine was said to have but twenty years to live. The life of a gold mine was one of the chief factors that governed the price: one could buy shares that would yield 30 per cent. on one's money, but in three to four years they might be worthless.

The ventilation down below I found for the most part quite excellent. Things are very different from what they used to be, and the whole process is reduced to a fine art; for instance, there were staircases running alongside the inclined shaft up and down which the skips ran. It can be readily understood that even a small piece of rock commencing to roll down these stairs would soon gather a great momentum; this was a continuous source of danger, and every now and then someone got killed. A foreman was killed on the staircase I went down only fourteen days before, but they now have what they call "breaks" every hundred steps or so.

Mr. Lewis showed me their extensive electrical pumping plant, for in some places they would be soon swamped if they did not keep the water under.

Finally, after apparently wandering miles, we were driven to the surface by the pangs of hunger. Mr. Lewis gave his private signal along the wires and, after we had waited five minutes, an empty skip mysteriously stopped just where we were standing, and we were whisked up into the daylight.

The engineer at the works could tell exactly where each skip was at any moment by means of little indicators beside him, but one day, forgetting that he had human freight on board, he tipped the poor unfortunates, nine in number, I believe, right over the top like so much rock. The amazing thing was that nobody was killed, and only one arm and one leg were broken in the process. After changing, and enjoying the luxury of a bath, Mr. Lewis motored me off to his home near the mine, and we had lunch under the trees with his charming wife. A place had been laid for Johnnie, for whose absence I had once more to apologize.

After lunch we returned to the mine, and went over the enormous surface workings, of which I had seen something at the Globe and Phoenix Mine in Rhodesia. The process was even more complicated than in the case of diamonds, and even were I competent to give a detailed description, it would be too technical to be of interest. The enormous stamps for crushing the rock, the endless arrangements for "washing," the furnaces, and, perhaps most important of all, the cyanide process were very interesting to watch. And finally the unending procession of trolleys, each adding its quota to the enormous white heaps of "dump." The cyanide process, introduced, I believe, in 1895, by a man named McArthur, has been the making of modern gold mining; but for it, few of the mines would pay.

At a quarter to four, Mr. Lewis placed a carriage and pair at my disposal, so that I might drive in comfort to Drifontein Station.

It really was a most interesting experience, infinitely better than going over a "show" mine with a *blasé* guide. I could not have had anyone better to explain things, for Mr. Lewis was an enthusiast, and I clambered around anywhere and everywhere with him.

Next morning I was busy paying calls, and amongst others I visited was a young fellow named V——, whom Dr. Burford Hooke had particularly mentioned to me. He was exceedingly nice, most interesting to talk to, and told me a good deal about municipal affairs in Johannesburg and the P.W.D. (Public Works Department): America did not seem to have a monopoly in the matter of corruption.

We were due to lunch with Mr. Chesterton, so I called for him at his office and accompanied him to the Rand Club. The great feature of the Rand Club, apart from its outward display of opulence, is the bar. It was *the* business rendezvous of the town, and its size had to correspond. At 11 a.m. the great magnates feel the need of a whisky and soda. At five minutes to one nothing but a gin and bitters (did you say two?) will save them, and at 5.30 it is whisky and soda again, until the time arrives for their 7 p.m. cocktail. At all the times I have mentioned they could be found standing three deep at the bar, and the fact was pointed out to me with pride! How they ever got through any work I don't know. My own little theory is that some more abstemious person did it for them!

Accompanied by Mr. Marshall, we drove to the Athenaeum Club (did you say another cocktail?); this was where Mr. Chesterton lived. It was a much more homely place than the Rand Club, and he had two very comfortable rooms; in fact, everything that any aged widower could desire, including a drawing-room in which he could entertain his lady friends.

Unfortunately for us these South African hotels nearly always charged you so much per day (12s. 6d. or 15s.), whether you were there for meals or not. At the Langham, where everything was tip-top, Johnnie was ill and could eat nothing, and I was nearly always invited out to lunch and dinner, so that we got poor value for our money.

One night I was leaving the writing-room when Johnnie

came up in his dressing-gown, looking very pale, and said: "I suppose you know the hotel is on fire." I am afraid I was not a bit enthusiastic, but merely yawned and said, "No." However, I promised to make enquiries, for there was endless rushing about going on upstairs. Johnnie thought we might as well save our trunks—he said nothing about women and children! So I adjourned to the hall and found that fat old Mr. L—— (with a sixth crease on the back of his neck) was having a quiet talk on the phone with the fire brigade. Would they "mind sending a couple of firemen at once? No, no, no, not the fire brigade, the hotel was on fire . . . ," but at that point I felt I might safely go to bed and hear the details in the morning. This amounted to a theory that the heat of the sun, shining through a hole in the roof, had ignited some already heated woodwork.

Johnnie, who was now feeling himself again, joined me one day, and together with Mr. M—— we visited the head office of the Standard Bank. Here we were shown a special reserve of £1,000,000 in gold, which they always kept on hand, and we examined the bags, containing one thousand sovereigns each. But our mission was to see the bars of gold as sent in from the mine—the finished article, so to speak—so we were taken to the Gold Department. The bars for the most part were just too heavy to handle with any comfort, but at the same time not hopelessly unmanageable, and were worth about £4,000 each. They were brought into the Standard Bank by the various mines, and were carefully packed and dispatched by each mail to London, where they were sold by the bullion brokers. The Bank had its own excellently equipped assay office.

Through Natal to Durban

We said good-bye to Johannesburg one evening, and when we awoke next morning it was to find ourselves at Majuba, and an hour or so later we were at Ladysmith, but war, battles, sieges, and soldiers evoke no great enthusiasm in this child's breast.

We had planned to put in a couple of days at Ladysmith. We made the most careful enquiries, but found that there was little to be seen save bare veld and tombstones. Bare veld we could see without taking long, expensive carriage drives, and as to tombstones there were enough along the railway line to last us for eternity. We steamed through Colenso railway station with its neat little white-stone-bordered flower-beds, and then along the banks of the ill-fated Tugela River. Every fifty yards there was a grave, sometimes a group of them. Oh, the futility of it all! Nothing impressed me more than this during our stay in Africa, and the irony of the situation. We objected to the Boers governing the Transvaal in the way they did, we fought and conquered them at endless expense, both of money and of lives, and they were now governing the whole of South Africa. The Jingo said: "Rotten Liberal Government." The Philosopher replied: "The inevitable and logical consequence!"

Quite an hour before we arrived there we could see Pietermaritzburg with its solid red-brick buildings lying in the hollow beneath us. The line twisted in and out like a Swiss mountain railway or the coils of a serpent, particularly as we drew near Durban.

At Pietermaritzburg, Johnnie and I parted for a few hours; we felt it was better for him to go right through to Durban, where he could settle down. It was about 3.30 p.m., and by a little hustling I managed to see the Librarian and all my important customers that same night, winding up by calling on Mr. Horace Rose, the editor of the *Natal Witness*, with whom I attended a most amusing political meeting.

In its way, 'Maritzburg was quite an imposing town, and before the Union was the capital of Natal, though second in size to Durban. Its buildings were all well constructed, someone called it a red-brick sepulchre, but that is libellous. It is an educational centre of some importance, and, as a further sign of intelligence, had, for its size, more reputable booksellers than any other place in South Africa.

As one left the Transvaal behind and entered Natal, I think what impressed one most was the much more English appearance of the landscape. I should say British, for it is a very Scotch Colony. It was nice to see grass again that wasn't merely dry stalks, and it was a joy to observe wild flowers once more growing by the railway side.

I found Johnnie at the Royal Hotel. They charged 15s. per day, and, as it was already obvious that we should be out for all meals, we approached the manager for his terms for bed and breakfast. The assistant said: "Seven and six," but the manager said: "We never do it now!" "Then out we go," I said. "We have been paying 15s. for bed and breakfast at Jo'burg, and we don't intend being bitten that way again." We tried the Marine Hotel, but they also were obdurate. We took a tram to the beach and walked into the newest and best hotel there, the Edward, where, as it happened, General Botha was stopping. We explained the situation. "Why, certainly." They would give us bed and breakfast for 6s. 6d. or 7s. 6d., according to rooms. Would they fetch our luggage from the Royal? With pleasure! Thus it befell that we took up our abode at the seaside, and very thankful we were for the salt sea breeze, as the humid air of Durban was very depressing after the exhilarating atmosphere of Johannesburg.

The next few days were spent chiefly in business calls and the enjoyment of the generous hospitality of the multifarious branches of the Green family. One day, Mr. Sidney Green had very kindly invited me to lunch at the Durban Club; he plunged me with great rapidity into a warm political discussion. On our way to the Club we met Senator Churchill, a very charming gentleman, to whom I had been introduced after church one evening.

He asked me whether I had been out to the Trappist Monastery, or the Mount Edgcombe sugar factory, both of which I am sorry to say we missed, owing partly to Johnnie's indisposition. There was one thing which, he said, he would be glad to show me personally if I would come back at 5 p.m., and that was an interesting experiment which the municipality was making.

A Municipal Experiment with Beer

We drove in a pony rickshaw to the scene of this interesting undertaking in the poorer part of the town. The experiment might almost be called a municipal public-house for Natives. It sounds rather extraordinary, particularly when you hear that they sell beer because in Rhodesia, the Transvaal, the Orange River Colony, and Natal it is not permissible to sell any form of alcohol to the Natives. The fines are heavy —£50 or more—but the profits of illicit trading are so enormous that a good deal goes on. In Cape Colony, which leads the way in so many other respects, no such prohibition exists, thanks to the vested interests of wine growers, who to this day pay part of the wages of their Native labourers in wine (of sorts). The Orange River Colony, on the other hand, grants no licences of any sort outside the few large towns, so that the country districts are, what they would term in New Zealand, "dry."

After the Boer War things were temporarily in a very bad way in Durban; the police were corrupt; drunkenness amongst the Natives was rife, and there was any amount of illicit selling going on, and the stuff that was being sold then as spirits was little short of poison. It was suggested that an alternative method be tried as an experiment.

The alternative method was for the Municipality of Durban itself to undertake the business and make a monopoly of it. They analysed and examined various samples of the Native beers to which the Kaffirs were accustomed, even before the advent of the white man. They set up their own brewery and experimented with the production of Native beer until they could turn out a wholesome and satisfactory beverage of the same character, at the same time reducing the percentage content of alcohol to a minimum. Even so they arranged that

47 Martha and Mary dominated the horizon

48 "Quaggas' Kerk"

49 The Two Young Men at Quaggas' Kerk

50 Panorama from the summit of Quaggas' Kerk

it should only be sold at their one place, that it should be consumed on the premises, and that no Native should be allowed more than a certain quantity. The management was entirely disinterested, and furthermore the regulations provided that all profits should be kept distinct from the municipal accounts and devoted to the benefit of the Natives themselves. They carried the scheme yet farther by adding a large wing adjoining the other, and separated only by a sort of grille, in which tea, coffee, non-alcoholic liquors, and *food* could be obtained at moderate prices.

The womenfolk were allowed to join the men on this side, but on this side only, with the result that it was far more extensively patronized than the side where only beer was to be obtained. The beer was sold in large tins, price 3d., 6d., and 1s., and tickets had to be obtained for the amount required as the customers passed through a turnstile into the hall.

The Natives were very sociable in their habits, and, if four friends went in together, they would often order one large tin between the four of them instead of four smaller ones. It was really rather quaint to see them sitting in a group with one large round tin in front of them, about two-thirds the size of a Huntley & Palmer biscuit tin.

There is always a danger with these Native beers that in great heat, or if they are kept any time, the percentage of alcohol will increase. To avoid possible trouble on this score, all beer not consumed the same day is thrown away. It is queer-looking stuff, rather like *café au lait* in appearance. I tasted it and found it not undrinkable. In fact, on a really hot day, I think it would be quite acceptable to the ordinary run of mankind. Personally I disliked the taste it left in one's mouth afterwards.

The arrangements on the other side of the grille were very interesting. They wanted to encourage the Natives to do their own catering instead of getting into the hands of the low-class coolie and Jew. They accordingly arranged the hall with separate long tables, which they let out at 1s. per diem, just as is done in a market. The shilling included the use for the day of a definite section of the kitchen, facilities for washing up, etc. Only Natives were allowed to hire a table, and they were not permitted to have more than one each. Naturally those tables were patronized most where the owner gave the best value and attention, and competition had become quite keen. The result was that instead of being supplied with bad food at exorbitant prices by coolies and Jews, they obtained really cheap and wholesome food. I cannot say I should have sat down to it with enthusiasm myself, but it was infinitely superior to what I had seen them consuming elsewhere.

The profits of the first year, amounting to about £1,200, were devoted to the building near by of a hostel where Natives coming into Durban to find work could obtain accommodation at 1d. per night. The profits of the second year were being devoted to the construction of a similar hostel for Native women. Unfortunately, time did not permit of my seeing these, as Senator Churchill had to hurry off to the station to bid farewell to General Botha, and I thought I, too, might as well pay my respects to the Premier of this fascinating country, as I had met him previously at a reception in London.

It was very disappointing that we could not enter more fully into the life of Durban as a seaside resort. But the renewal of Johnnie's indisposition and the weather were both against us. They had the most wonderful facilities for bathing—mixed bathing, of course! It was far too dangerous in the open sea, so they had enclosed part of it for those who desired to indulge in surf bathing. One was out of doors, but safe from the backwash of the Indian Ocean rollers and such trifles as sharks and whales. There was an extensive whaling industry at Durban. For those who desired to swim there was a magnificent swimming bath on the beach, three times the size of any ordinary bath, with diving boards, water shutes, etc. In none of these delights were we able to participate, save that we enjoyed watching the goings-on the first afternoon of our stay. There were many good cafés and restaurants down on the front, which

I patronized on the few occasions on which I was not dining out. Johnnie was at this time still imbibing beef tea and Vichy and milk alternately, with various medicines thrown in, but fortunately Dr. McKenzie pronounced him well enough to proceed by the *Walmer Castle*.

On our last day I had the opportunity of watching Mr. Sidney Green conduct an auction at Reed & Acutts' Wool Mart. Prior to the sale I had been round and examined all the various wools. They were in enormous bales, and quite a large proportion would be pressed and done up ready for shipment by the mail-boat next morning.

A rickshaw, with a most wonderfully and fearfully attired Zulu to draw it, was requisitioned so that we might go to the docks in comfort, and once aboard the *Walmer Castle* we were, of course, quite all right. The dividing of the deck into two parts incensed me after the freedom we had enjoyed on the *Anchises*, but, as we were only aboard from 4 p.m. until 8 the next morning, it did not seriously affect us. The band played *Auld Lang Syne*, and a few minutes later we were steaming steadily down the coast. Boats of even 8,000 tons could safely enter East London, but as the *Walmer Castle* was 12,000 tons we stopped outside.

There is nearly always a heavy swell in this roadstead, so that landing on a tender is apt to prove dangerous. The method adopted, if humorous, was both expeditious and safe. As many as eight or nine people enter a large basket, which is attached to one of the derricks, and lifted up like so many tons of goods and carefully deposited on the tug alongside.

East London, when looked at from the sea, would not appear to be a particularly attractive place in which to spend four idle days, but at the Beach Hotel one would have to look far, even amongst English seaside resorts, to find a more pleasant place. There is very little that is artificial beyond a liberal supply of comfortable seats and free bathing shelters, for Natives as well as Europeans. There were artificial swimming baths, very well arranged, on the beach, and beyond the breakwater were the harbour and the docks, and the tracks along the sandy hills that border the shore towards the Bat's Cave bring back memories of Devon and Cornwall; whilst just at the back of the beach there were most beautiful sylvan walks and a sort of inland sea or salt lake. Our long peaceful week-end and the bracing sea breeze certainly did us both good and quite restored Johnnie to his wonted good health and spirits. East London is thrice blessed, for, apart from its sea coast scenery, it has the Buffalo River with its well-wooded banks and Queen's Park with its 80 acres of beautiful trees and winding walks.

Chapter V

BACK TO THE HIGH VELD

I SELDOM remember enjoying a day in a train more than I did that up-country journey from East London to Queenstown, the first few miles of which is a steep climb among rounded down-like hills and around the sides of sloping valleys, where cattle browsed and scattered villages lay nestling in the fresh green grass, with the blue ocean bounding the horizon. The rich brown earth bore abundant crops of other refreshing verdure, and here and there a group of Native women could be seen in their curious orange-red coloured garments, from which protruded their chocolate-coloured arms, breasts, and legs; whilst up among those breezy downlands the wind swept savagely along, bending the blue gum trees and combing through the corn.

It was good to be alive that morning and feeling fit again, good to know that we were gradually climbing back to the dry, health-giving heat of the high veld. As the train bore us on past Blaney Junction, the lower spurs of the great Amatola Mountains stood out above us along the sky-line. They were not like the ordinary rock-strewn ridges of the Karroo, for these hillsides were covered with the great dark green patches made by gum and wattle plantations, and on the foothills, around which we were creeping in swinging curves, the thorny mimosa grew sparsely here and there.

At Peelton is a large mission village, charmingly situated on a long low ridge of productive land, surrounded by cactus hedges. The little white church stood in the centre of a cluster of tall gum trees, and the whole place gave one the impression of a model village.

As we toiled up the steep rise of 1 in 30 or 40, a common gradient on South African railroads, we were much amused by the Native children of both sexes and all ages, many clothed in a piece of string, who ran beside the train waving their hands and calling for bread. At a place called Stutterheim Road we came right to the foot of the Amatola Mountains, and passed along thickly wooded hillsides, whence tumbled tiny streams down imposing watercourses. Few people can imagine with what joy we looked upon these dense plantations hanging from the mountain sides: green and glorious they were to eyes that had beheld nothing of the kind for so many months! Then we climbed still higher and passed along a great cutting in the hillside overlooking a plateau of enormous width. Native kraals could be seen dotted about, and flocks of sheep and cattle with their herdsmen appeared like midget toys in the great dry plain below. This was considered grand sheep country, and though patched with green in places, even then after more rain the whole countryside would be covered with verdure; at the worst of times there was enough pasturage on every three acres for *two* sheep, which was thought *excellent*! On the opposite hillside a wool wash was pointed out to us, where an acre or two of fleece was drying in the sunshine.

At Imvani we were much amused by a number of quaintly clad Natives, whose womenfolk had smeared their faces with a kind of light-coloured clay. At first we thought the ladies of this district were suffering from some ghastly disease, but we were assured that this was not the case. Another "belle" had placed a reaping sickle blade downwards through her short curly hair as an ornament; we had never seen a more grotesque assembly during our travels through this land.

One of our fellow passengers was a pleasant young German who had been born in South Africa. When Stan addressed him in German he replied at first with blushes of embarrassment. Another was a gnarled old transport rider, born here to Essex parents. He told us many interesting yarns of his experiences before the railways came; how it took as many *days* as it now takes *hours* to get from one town to another; how the Orange River once held him up for twenty-four days before he and his wagons could cross in safety. According to him the rainfall of the country becomes more and more scanty every year, and he smiled with childish delight at our *Guide Book to South Africa* and how it told us "everything we wanted to know about every place we came to."

Queenstown and Tarkastad

An hour later we arrived at Queenstown, and were once more over 3,000 feet above sea-level. It would be hard to imagine a warmer welcome than that accorded to us by our host, Mr. Malcolm Moffat, and his family. Mr. Moffat was on holiday from his mission station at Serenje in Northern Rhodesia, where his three bonny sons were born under circumstances which would astonish most English mothers at Home. Their nearest railway station was *two weeks' walk* away, and their letters were brought by Native runners, who cover about one hundred miles in three days! Mrs. Moffat told us that she did not like Queenstown, as it was not so civilized as England nor so wild as Serenje.

During our short stay in Queenstown, or "Queen" as it is called locally, we met some very nice people and enjoyed a few hours of real home life, which included some excellent piano playing by a young lady just back from her studies in England. She charmed us for an hour or more with Dvořák, Debussy, Brahms, and Beethoven, and as she played we dreamed of Home. We climbed a kopje one afternoon and studied the layout of "Queen," spread at our feet. Defence against possible Native attacks governed the ideas of those who originally planned it; the town was designed in the form of a hexagon, the market place in the centre being six-sided, and a main street radiating from each angle. From this centre, which formed a rallying place, the streets could be easily raked with fire, but at the time of our visit they were lined with oaks, beefwoods, gums, and pepper trees, growing there contentedly in the piping days of peace. Queenstown folks were so persistent in their praise of the great Bongolo Dam, that held their water-supply of some 1,500 million gallons, that it was imperative we should walk there to see it, and a very fine walk it was.

We were early astir next morning, and a very curious caravan started out to catch the 7.25 train for Tarkastad. Mr. Moffat headed the procession, carrying Stan's Gladstone bag and a rug roll containing a very heavy miscellaneous cargo. Stan and I followed with knapsacks on our backs and my valise between us suspended from a broom handle, our free arms laden with overcoats and sundries, whilst young Moffat brought up the rear bearing huge bows and arrows and Native spears, decorations for our future host's new house at Quaggas' Kerk; my glasses and camera dangled from the boy's shoulders, and sticking out from under my coat was a large bundle of enormous thorns, curiosities I had gathered from the commonage around "Queen."

The three hours' journey on to Tarkastad passed quickly enough, owing to the volubility of a pianoforte tuner, to whom I had been introduced by one of my customers. He pointed out historic spots to us, for even down here in Cape Colony we were still on the scene of recent conflict. He also showed us an interesting rubber-like liquid, which some local speculators were extracting from the pincushion cactus, and which when injected into bicycle tyres would prevent punctures for several months.

Our new host, Mr. Livingstone Moffat, was at the station to meet us, and, after breakfast at a local hotel, when we ate more house-flies than mutton, we tied up our luggage and drove off in a couple of very comfortable buggies, each with its pair of excellent horses, on our thirty-two miles' journey to Quaggas' Kerk. Stan rode in Mr. Moffat's cart, and I in the other which was driven by an Argyllshire Scot, recently immigrated with his family into our host's employ. My feet rested on a curious oblong box, not unlike a baby's coffin. "That contains the pipes," explained Sandy, when I asked what was in it; these pipes would one day curdle the bushes on yonder innocent veld.

All the petty little inconveniences of this style of travel troubled us no more; if the horses dashed down the sides of some rocky spruit, and if there were no brakes on the cart, what matter? If the road was dusty and bumpy and the sun was hot, why, this was just paradise, and life a slow, passing dream with nothing to worry about except the dryness of the veld, the deplorable condition of cattle and sheep, and the long tarrying of the rain. The sky was clear and blue, the sun beat down fiercely on the brown hillsides that culminated in flat or conical peaks, and as we passed a Native hut a curl of blue smoke would be wafted across our way, smelling sweetly of burnt sheep dung. For long, two flat-topped hills called Martha and Mary dominated the horizon, and presently our road passed close by them and we noted their huge caps of precipitous rock.

We went on and on, circling among the beautiful hills, and then along a well-watered valley where homesteads nestled among the trees and large fields of lucerne and young wheat lay here and there. We saw a few ostriches apparently in fine condition, but most of the sheep that farmers had brought from many miles away in search of "something" for them to eat made a pitiable sight indeed! At about four o'clock that afternoon we arrived at Spring Valley, where stood one house which was store and post office and farm as well. Here we outspanned for an hour to rest our horses and refresh ourselves with a pipe and a cup of tea, after which we sat in the stable to get out of a big wind that had suddenly sprung up. A Boer farmer came in as we were sitting there and shook hands all round, as is the custom. He talked with Mr. Moffat in Dutch, and told how he had been forced to trek many miles with his sheep in search of food for them, and how he had at last been able to hire grazing for them on an adjoining farm.

When only half an hour's drive from our destination, we came across an ox wagon stuck fast in a spruit and right in the middle of our way. Stan and I were left in charge of our respective vehicles, whilst Mr. Moffat and the Scot went to the assistance of the two "boys," who were endeavouring to get their wagon out of the spruit by hitching their team to the tailboard. The position did not appear to be a difficult one, but we soon discovered that the oxen were tired and "rough," not good team oxen. The Kaffirs told us that they had been stuck there since noon, and after they—the Scot and Mr. Moffat—had thrashed, "hollared," and yelled, and shoved for twenty minutes and the beasts had pulled in every direction *except* forward and *together*, it was resolved to outspan our horses and see if we could not pull our carts through a narrow place between the wagon and the rocks. After a delay of half an hour and a manœuvre of considerable difficulty we were successful, and we were able to proceed on our way.

Quaggas' Kerk

Soon after, we arrived at the modern, yet original and charming bungalow homestead, Quaggas' Kerk, so called after a large hill that rises behind it. The Quagga, which is now extinct, was a beautiful animal, often confounded with Burchell's Zebra, but striped to the centre of the body only. Two generations ago it was found in immense numbers on the plains of the O.R.C. Kerk means a "gathering place," and in days now passed, when there were a number of quaggas in this district, they always used to collect in this kind of mountain stronghold whenever the settlers went forth on a shooting expedition.

The homestead had been built of stone quarried from the Kerk and prettily designed by the same architect who had charge of the Union Government Buildings at Pretoria. To step into this charming modern home after such a drive, to have soft carpets beneath our feet and beds beyond the dreams of luxury, was a surprise as well as a joy to find in this land "on the edge of beyond." To be surrounded by trees such as fir, oak, and poplar, to be greeted by the homely and almost heart-breaking scent of roses and wisteria, that clung in masses to the stoep of the old homestead near by, gave us an immediate sensation of welcome, of peace, and of good will. Few people can imagine *how* sweet a fresh bright bloom smells to those who have breathed South African dust for many tedious hours on the road.

The hills and the veld around were very bare, there was scarcely a bush or an ant-heap, yet, with all their barrenness, they were very beautiful. It was just typical African scenery, especially when viewed from the top of one of the hills whence we could see, in every direction, range after range fading away into the distance. The veld in this neighbourhood was best suited to sheep farming, and, though Mr. Livingstone Moffat had some prize bulls and a goodly herd of cattle, sheep were his main standby. He had 6,500 of them, and their wool brought in 6s. or 7s. apiece, so it will be seen that there *was something* in it. But their wool was not the only source of profit: a greater one was the way in which they increased in numbers. Thanks to thirty-eight miles of jackal-proof fencing, costing £60 per mile, that he had erected round his farm of 2,850 morgen (about 6,000 acres), he was able to let his sheep run day and night in the various camps into which his farm was divided. This saved endless labour, and the sheep were healthier and bred more rapidly.

Our chief occupation whilst we were at Quaggas' Kerk was walking and riding. The latter was a great joy; we took the post to Spring Valley one day, mounted on Dingaan and Chum. Perhaps I am wrong in saying that riding was *my* chief occupation; Johnnie would say it was talking, for Livingstone and I were always at it! He had all the good qualities and all the prejudices of a follower of that highly respectable and excellent paper, St. Loe Strachey's *Spectator*.

Life on a farm, particularly a South African farm, has a joy of its own. We had to be up with the sun, it is true, but isn't the early morning the best time of all in the country? We heard our hostess apologizing for the sameness of the diet, the unvarying mutton and lamb, but had we ever tasted such mutton and lamb in a town? Was there any restaurant, French, English, or German, that could give anything one half as good as simple homely farmhouse fare? And the outdoor life, that glorious gallop across the veld on a fresh and spirited horse, that made one feel the sheer exhilaration of just living. And that quiet hour after lunch as we sat in the shade of some friendly neighbour's stoep, did not that bring visions and an inward peace that town life can never give? The peace of Yeats' *Lake Isle of Innisfree*. Oh, yes, there are plenty of prosaic things to do on a farm. For instance, catching a sheep by its hind leg, carrying it to the shearing machine, dumping it down on its hind quarters in a most ludicrous and inconvenient position from the point of view of the sheep, with its head tucked between your legs, and then proceeding to act the barber with the aid of a pair of automatic clippers attached to a noisy oil engine, clippers that have an unhappy knack of clipping the unfortunate sheep's skin when one ceases to give the matter one's undivided attention.

Livingstone had the Pringles as neighbours; Mr. Willie Pringle on the Spring Valley side, and their cousin, Mr. Robert Pringle, over at Clifton. The latter farm was a charming place, and we spent the greater part of our last Saturday there. It was very nice to find a house full of children, and it did Stan's eugenic heart good to see them growing up under such ideal conditions. The eldest son was at Cambridge.

Beyond Clifton, down the Bavin's River, there are endless other Pringles, all descendants of one good Scotsman and his large family of sturdy sons. At Baaken Kop, to which we went for our first ride, seven farms met, and three of them belonged to members of the Pringle family. Talking of Baaken Kop reminds me of a curious thing I noticed there; although the valleys are 5,000 feet above sea-level, the sheep apparently always go to the highest point to sleep. The tops of all the kopjes are worn bare, and on several occasions we noticed them trooping up of an evening. This is explained by the fact that the top of the hill is the warmest place at night, free from the frosts and valley mists, and the last and first place to be warmed by the sun's rays.

Seeing how cold it can be there, I was surprised by the number of canaries to be seen about Quaggas' Kerk; they were not quite so bright as those one would see in hotter parts, but they were nevertheless beautifully coloured. I was surprised, too, to see such a number of cranes, whilst meerkats were everywhere in great numbers, and it was a pretty sight to see them perched on an ant-heap enjoying a sunbath.

Onward to Cradock

It was November 11th when we said good-bye to our kind hostess at Quaggas' Kerk after a very happy and interesting ten days' visit; we did not even get to the foot of the Winterberg, much as we desired to climb there. All along the road back to Tarkastad I was busy with my cameras; it was a day such as South Africa alone can supply, radiant with sunlight, and soft shadows draping the steep krantzs of the hills. A Kaffir was driving my buggy, and as we journeyed along I carried on a conversation with him as best I could. He wanted to know if we were returning to England, and as he could only understand one or two English words, I tried to explain to him how we were going on to Australia and New Zealand. The "boy" was dumbfounded when I told him we were going still farther; he opened his big mouth and rolled his eyes in a dazed manner, and exclaimed his long-drawn-out Native sigh of wonderment, "E-e-e-eh!"

While we were having lunch among the flies at the hotel at Tarkastad we heard the car drive up that had come from Cradock to fetch us, but when we went out at 2 p.m. to take our departure thither the blessed thing had vanished. After making a fruitless search of the town, we ascertained that the chauffeur had gone "out to Mundell's farm, about eight miles off, on business; but he'll be back *just now*." "Just now" is a fatal South African expression, it means anything from an hour to a *day* hence. My cousin, Mr. Storr Garlake, was expecting us in Cradock to tea, but it was 4.30 before the driver, "a son of the soil," returned, and we received him very ill.

The effects of the great drought became more and more evident on our fifty-mile drive to Cradock. The situation was daily growing more serious; the ostriches we passed were in very poor condition, but the sheep, poor things, were worse; everything was dried up, and in many districts the stock was nearly starved. I shall never forget the look of one sheep we saw by the roadside; nowhere in sight was a blade of grass or a Karroo bush at which it could nibble, and for that day, at any rate, it had given up hope; it was little more than a skeleton. It stood gazing vacantly into space, dreaming perchance of green pastures and refreshing rain; it had no strength to move, not even to turn its head, though the car whizzed by within a couple of feet of it.

All the rivers we passed, with the exception of one small sluit, were absolutely dry. Fortunately, there was still some water in many of the dams, but all too little.

We passed acres and acres of dry brown mother-earth, and of stones there were plenty, of grass not a sign. A few withered twigs showed where bushes might have been had drought and starving cattle permitted. Only two things seemed to thrive —the thorn bush and the prickly pear. It was strange amidst all this parched and desolate veld that the prickly pear, with its thick, green, cactus-like leaves, should be able to produce those beautiful orange-coloured blossoms that reminded me almost as much of an arbutilon as of a cactus. It was difficult to imagine what the country could be like after rain, for even at this dry time it was wonderfully beautiful, a beauty that was unique; a beauty that held and fascinated one. But it was in the silence of the evening that one felt it most; the vast distances, the wonderful colour effects, the gorgeous sunsets, the brilliant starlight are alike almost overwhelming. On our motor ride across the veld we were exceptionally well favoured. Here and there groups of springbok were out feeding at their favourite hour, and, though only a few yards from the road, they would turn round to look us squarely in the face before leaping away to a more safe distance. We were driving westward, and had the joy of seeing the sun set three, if not four, times, and each time the colours seemed more gorgeous, more wonderful than the last. We were passing alongside the dried-up Tarka river-bed. It was a lonely narrow valley at this point and presented quite a romantic appearance as the sun dropped behind the kopje ahead of us. In another seven or eight minutes we were at the top of the rise and had the sun once more in view as we crossed the broad plain beyond. Any description of the colouring would seem exaggerated, any painting that reproduced these colours would be deemed impossible. Never have I seen such deep and impenetrable blues, such rich orange effects, and they were not confined to the west. The very veld around us was lit up with a deep purple, and, most wonderful of all, the kopjes far behind us glowed with a salmon pink that surpassed even that of the Alps at sundown. A new moon, the evening star, and yet another planet added a finishing touch to the picture and shone out brightly as we mounted the next rise and saw the sun once more. A sunset on the veld is a perpetual joy, a living memory that leaves one richer so long as life lasts.

After getting out of the car to open the gate to Cradock "commonage," which extends for some miles, it was some time before we saw the lights of the town. Our host and hostess, Mr. and Mrs. Storr Garlake, were wondering what had become of us, and had already instituted enquiries.

Our first day in Cradock was a scorcher, and I am afraid we did little but write a few letters, interview the editor of the *Midland News*, and stroll through the park. In the afternoon a terrific duststorm sprang up, the worst our host had seen for years, and we were glad to take shelter. The following morning we were energetic once more; we rose before six and drove off with Mr. Storr Garlake to a natural sulphur water bath about three miles away. It was a beautiful day, and we thoroughly enjoyed our morning swim, despite the objectionable smell of that health-giving spring—H_2S is never pleasing, but we did our best to forget its presence. The two main springs were walled in with stone to form a natural outdoor swimming bath about half the size of an ordinary one; the water was quite warm, and bubbled up continually. It was a diver's paradise, for the whole bath was over 6 feet deep.

"*Krantz Plaats*"

Mr. Garlake had arranged to devote his half holiday to taking us some twelve miles out of "Town" to Mr. Harry Barber's farm. We saw innumerable buck, springbok in particular, and we passed one of the crack farms of the district, Mr. Hilton Barber's, where there were about 1,200 ostriches. The birds were fed almost exclusively on lucerne, which can only be grown successfully on land that is irrigated. As a result, all the progressive farmers, such as Mr. Hilton Barber and his sons, Harry and Gray, have gone in for extensive irrigation works and steam ploughs. When the rivers are in flood the water is carefully led off instead of being wasted.

After outspanning and drinking the inevitable cup of tea, we commenced our tour of inspection of Mr. Harry Barber's farm. We began with white Angora goats, of which he had over a thousand, to say nothing of legions of beautiful white kids, hundreds of which had never left their kraals, thanks to the hopeless state of the veld.

We then had an adventure with a pair of ostriches and a flock of thirty-seven chicks. Now ostriches are at all times tricky things to deal with, but a cock bird that is mating, or a bird of either sex when it has chicks, is positively dangerous. We wanted to photograph the happy family in question in their kraal, but they had broken into another enclosure. Telling

51 We visited a neighbour's farm

52 Mr. Harry Barber with his white Angora kids

53 A brood of thirty-seven, by no means all their own

54 "Krantz Plaats" and the kopje where Olive Schreiner was buried

the others to walk round, Mr. Barber invited me to "come along, we'll turn them out," and the next moment I was over the fence and in the enclosure. I knew that I was with an old hand at the game, but was quite glad to get behind him as he suggested. Scarcely had we got in sight of the birds when the cock ostrich made a charge. Mr. Barber had armed himself with a *tak* (a branch of a thorn bush) and held it out at arm's length. It looked a very weak defence against such an onslaught, but it proved wonderfully effective. The cock bird in this instance soon gave in, but not so the hen. Time after time she charged in a most reckless manner, beak open and wings half outstretched. The others thought we were in for trouble, but no; each time, though she charged right on to it and pricked herself badly, the thorn branch brought her up short, like a fence, which she, foolish creature, probably thought it was.

The absurd part of the whole performance was that one kick would have sent even Mr. Harry Barber (6 feet 1 inch, and broad in proportion) to eternal rest, and he was well within reach! He admitted that he wouldn't dare tackle some of the cock birds which were red about the beak and legs (a sign that they are mating) with such a small *tak*. They would go on charging until the blood was streaming from their necks. The moment we had driven the birds into the kraal they gave in and were quite docile, and Johnnie secured a good snapshot. I mentioned their having a brood of thirty-seven, but these were by no means all their own. The average size of their families is fifteen to eighteen, and an egg is laid every alternate day by each of the two hens which a cock bird is allowed; but, after the eggs are hatched out, other chicks are introduced into the family. In this respect the parent birds are extraordinarily good-natured, for, so long as the incubator chicks are smaller than their own offspring, they will take them under their wing. The birds that are mating have to be double-fenced apart with a clear yard between to prevent them from fighting.

While we were standing by the fence one of the cock birds rushed up to us. Mr. Barber said: "Would you like to see how we catch them?" and, without more ado, seized the bird with one hand by its neck and gripped it like a vice. By bending its head down you get the bird pretty well in your power, but I should want to do a lot of Sandow exercises before I started tackling ostriches!

Our next interview was with a flock of young birds, "first after chick," which are quite harmless, and were running about the veld. In this part of the world "flappers" are called "first after chick," and young men in love are told they are looking red about the legs!

The day was drawing to a close, the little white Angora kids were bleating pitifully for their mothers, and it was time for us to be going, when I discovered the most interesting thing of all: the farm we were visiting used to be called "Kraantz Plaats," and it was here that Olive Schreiner lived when she wrote the *Story of an African Farm*. Fancy visiting *the* "South African Farm," and only finding it out by accident! They seemed to think nothing of Olive Schreiner here. "She wrote that awful book" (which they had *not* read!) "called *Trooper Peter Halkett*, didn't she? When we took the farm we altered that horrid Dutch name to 'Riverview.'"

On a kopje behind the house Olive Schreiner's little child was buried, and, long before Rhodes was laid to rest on the top of the Matopos, an acre had been purchased and enclosed by Olive Schreiner on the summit of this kopje for her own last resting place. How I would have loved to climb that peak and listen to the silence of the veld by day, or harken to the shrillness of its night music as the insects play to the stars!

The drive back was very beautiful: the sunlight on the hills, the crimson clouds, the graceful buck grazing in the twilight. Once more I thought of Goethe's words, "Joy comes streaming in upon me from every side."

We had a most interesting walk round the town the next

55 A 15 ft. python skin owned by Mr. Grattan

56 The Victoria Hotel, George

57 The Commonage at George

58 Breakfast on the way to the Wilderness

afternoon. It is really very well laid out, and any number of trees have been planted. For a small place it seems to have been particularly well managed, except for its water-supply. We climbed up some hills overlooking the town and saw where they were fortified during the war. Ninety per cent. of the people we met out here had been through the Boer War, and had had some experience of what war means. I wish I could say that 90 or even 9 per cent. had profited by that experience! Our host, Mr. Storr Garlake, appeared to be a popular hero in Cradock, with Briton and Boer alike. On all sides he was spoken of as "a friend of the poor," whilst during the war he defended many Dutchmen who had been condemned to death.

The proprietor of a big Dutch store here (a Mr. de Kock) was one of the Commandants who was present at the signing of the peace of Vereeniging. It was most interesting to cross-examine him as to the source of origin of all the goods in his store. In quite a number of lines America and Germany took the lead, but in the majority of instances Great Britain held the field. Then again, though he dealt direct with Germany, there were some things—toys "made in Germany," for example—which it paid him better to buy through London.

Grahamstown and Port Elizabeth

That evening we entrained for Grahamstown. Our night journey, about the fourteenth we had had, was very comfortable, and before Grahamstown was awake we were having a two hours' walk around the neighbouring woods and hills. The town was charmingly situated and the countryside was very English in appearance; it was nice to walk on grass once more, and we noticed some of Kipling's "flannelled fools" at cricket later in the day. Very isolated and bearing the appearance of a sleepy but pleasant provincial "burg," and an important educational centre, Grahamstown was the ancient capital of the Eastern Province; in fact, the only source of information regarding much of the early history of the Colony is the file of the *Journal*, the earliest paper published in this town, not as a daily in those times, but "whenever there was any news!"

In 1885 Kingsley Fairbridge was born in Grahamstown. As a boy of twelve he had "a vision of waste land filled with homesteads," and, when later he went to Oxford University, his lifelong dream became realized, and with the assistance of many of his fellow students the Child Emigration Society was founded. His autobiography, published by the Oxford University Press in 1927, should be read by all who love South Africa.

There was nothing to keep us in Grahamstown, and, as we did not wish to spend a whole day travelling, we passed another night in the train and arrived at Port Elizabeth early next morning. We stayed at the Beach Hotel, which was much nicer than being in the town.

Port Elizabeth is quite an imposing place, though I should put it after Durban, and its trade is chiefly wholesale.

Like many others that we had seen in the larger South African towns, its park was well arranged and was, in places, a natural zoological garden; there were some beautiful specimens of buck, and some emus and kangaroos disporting themselves in the most happy way. Just outside the park there was a most beautiful Boer War memorial, representing a trooper giving water to his horse, and it was inscribed with these very significant words: "The greatness of a nation consists not so much in the number of its people or the extent of its territory as in the extent and justice of its compassion." On the drinking trough below were these words: "Erected by public subscription in recognition of the services of the gallant animals which perished in the Anglo-Boer War, 1899–1902."

At noon next day I had a glorious bathe. Mixed bathing was, of course, the thing here, and the costumes certainly were very mixed too; three ladies I noticed were sitting in the water with their hats on, and enormous erections at that!

Practically the whole of the day following was occupied in seeing people, and many of the calls proved very interesting. Amongst others I saw Sir Edgar Walton, editor-in-chief of the *Eastern Province Herald*, late Treasurer-General, and President of the Rhodesian High Cost of Living Commission. He spoke most enthusiastically of Bruce Moffat as the ablest administrator they had in South Africa; and I also saw Mr. Fitzsimons, Director of the Museum, author of important works on the snakes and monkeys of South Africa.

Last but not least we met Mr. W. C. Scully, the magistrate, and probably one of the most accomplished literary craftsmen in South Africa. He took me along to have tea at his house, and I spent over two hours with him listening to extracts from the book he was writing at that time entitled *Lodges in the Wilderness*, and discussing anything from publishing to Natives. Many of his experiences were unique, as he had been in the most out-of-the-way parts. He was considered a crank because he was a man of original ideas who had always had the courage of his convictions. He was a pro-Boer, and his views regarding the Natives were too humanitarian to be popular.

The next morning at nine we joined Mr. Scully at the railway station, for he had kindly promised to take us to New Brighton. The name does not sound prepossessing, but New Brighton, the Port Elizabeth Native Location, interested me.

Every South African town has its Native Location. Many of them are a disgrace—just patchwork shanties and hopelessly unsanitary. Port Elizabeth was no exception when Mr. Scully volunteered as magistrate to take entire charge of the place, provided he was given a free hand. He undertook also to go out there every week and try any cases in person. He was on his regular visit when we accompanied him.

There was a population of over five thousand Natives of all

types and conditions, but that week there had been no breach of the peace, there was not a single case to try. A Native Location is usually a place to be shunned; it was a pleasure to go through this one. They are nearly always filthy; this one was clean. I remembered certain rows of dwellings at home (in South-East London, for instance), and I thought of the condition of the children, the dirt, the squalor, the hopelessness of it all, and I felt ashamed of my country.*

It would take too long to give a detailed account of all that had been done at this Location, but there are a few facts I should like to put on record. The type of dwelling had been steadily improved. They had tried well-built Native huts, but these were not a success for two reasons: the most suitable materials were not obtainable locally, and the Natives preferred a more European abode. The latest type, specially designed for coolness, was semi-detached three-room dwellings constructed of galvanized iron and wood at a cost of £138 the pair. Only a nominal rent was charged, about 7s. per *month*, which included free water-supply and sanitary services, but even so the Government obtained 9 per cent. on their monetary outlay.

The better-class Natives secured the better-class houses. We visited a Native bootmaker's and a Native policeman's house: both spotlessly clean. There were, of course, most stringent regulations against the introduction of alcohol. The lower-class Natives were allowed, under certain restrictions, to brew their own Native beer in small quantities. If a better-class Native wished to brew beer, he would be told he must go and live in the lower-class quarters. They quite understood and stopped where they were!

The land used for the Location was a Government reserve, too stony to be serviceable for agriculture. Curiously enough,

* Kingsley Fairbridge was similarly impressed. In his autobiography, which we have mentioned before, he describes his disgust on seeing the rows of squalid London houses, and adds: "Not far off a bully was knocking his wife about. The negroid races are not supposed to hold women in respect, but such an incident as this I have never seen in Africa" (p. 130).

it was on some of this land about one hundred years ago that "Downing Street" wanted settlers to take up small holdings! There was no water, and it is doubtful whether one sheep could find grazing on five acres of it.

There were still over a thousand Natives waiting for accommodation in the Location, but Mr. Scully had had an uphill fight and found great difficulty in getting further Government grants. He had an excellent man in charge, a descendant of the famous Henry Grattan, and after inspecting a most successful Ethiopian school we had morning tea with him. We were very pleased with the school, and the teacher had the most perfect control, though the class must have numbered seventy or eighty and contained children of all ages and sizes.

There were plenty of snakes about, even round Port Elizabeth, and Mr. Grattan's abode seemed peculiarly favoured. He was standing by his door only a night or two before our visit when he heard a slight rustle. He turned to see what it was and, before he knew it, a large puff adder had bitten him. Fortunately its fangs closed on his trousers and not his leg. He had no stick with him, so had to go indoors to get one, dragging the snake after him. The house was in darkness, but he found a stick and then proceeded to go outdoors again into the moonlight. Directly he stopped, the snake released itself and scuttled off, but he succeeded in killing it before it escaped, and the skin was decorating the wall of his room. Not a pleasing experience! "When it was all over and I had time to think about it, it made me feel positively sick," added Mr. Grattan. Scully capped this story with another. One day he was walking across the veld when he nearly trod on a particularly venomous reptile about 6 feet long. The brute made off with Scully in pursuit, though unarmed. The snake was disappearing down its hole when Scully grabbed at its tail, dragged it out, and flung it some distance away. Again the snake made for its hole, and again Scully meted out the same treatment to it. This procedure went on for seventeen times, but on approaching its hole for the eighteenth time the brute looked sideways, winked its eye at Scully, and started going down the hole tail first! A certain amount of truth can be given to this yarn, for snakes *do* go through holes in walls or in the ground tail first when they are pursued.

Some time ago there was a bad case of rape by a Native at Port Elizabeth. Of course Scully was blamed and the Kaffir was nearly lynched by the white population. Ultimately he was hanged, but feeling was running so high in the town that the white people took every opportunity they could of kicking the Natives off the footways. Scully waited and ere long a deputation of Natives came to him. They said they did not come to complain of how they were being treated, they knew too well that one of their people had committed a great crime; they simply came, they said, to explain that they, as a race, were willing to tolerate this brutality in consequence of what their fellow Kaffir had done!

There are many laws among some South African Native tribes which put our European moral code to shame; for example, it is not very generally known that if a Native seduces a virgin he suffers the death penalty if he is found out.

The Golden Feather

Next morning our train was approaching Oudtshoorn. The countryside was pretty if unprofitable, for prickly pears, thorn bushes, and euphorbias were growing in great profusion everywhere. As we drew near Oudtshoorn the scenery changed considerably. Fields of lucerne were in evidence on all sides, and any number of ungainly ostriches feeding upon them.

Oudtshoorn itself we reached about midday. The heat was intense; the distance to the town considerable, so for once we patronized a hotel bus. The town was blessed with the most beautiful flowering trees; one that pleased us particularly had a foliage like the decorative asparagus and a mauve blossom like a spiraea. But I am afraid its fragrance was wasted on the desert air, for the majority of people in Oudtshoorn did not think much of anything but ostrich feathers and motor-cars! It was in these days an enormously wealthy district; many of the people were ignorant of how much money they were worth, and the worst of it was that they had made their money so easily, thanks to the whims of fashion. Illiterate Dutch farmers, who could barely write their own names and lived in a sparsely furnished homestead, had incomes of ten thousand a year. Two brothers, who owned eight thousand birds, were said to have an income of well over £40,000 a year! And most of them had no idea what to do with it, except buy more land and rear more ostriches. The result was to send up the price of land in these districts to fabulous figures. Some of the farmers had given their children a good education, and when the present generation drop out there will be a change. But in contrast to all this wealth we gathered from Mr. Phillpots, the magistrate, to whom we had an introduction from Mr. Storr Garlake, that there was plenty of abject poverty, and nowhere in South Africa was it *more* difficult to raise money for any public purpose.

We quote the following interesting information about ostrich farming from *The African Handbook* for 1932, published by George Allen & Unwin Ltd.: "In 1913 the total of domesticated birds reached 776,000. . . . The profits during the years from 1900 to the fatal slump of 1913 were quite astonishing; the values of suitable farms rocketted sky-high. In 1913 the industry reached its apogee. Feathers were exported to a total value of £2,953,587; unheard-of prices were given for breeding pairs or even for scarcely hatched chicks of prize strains. Then came the catastrophe, brought about by over-production and a change in fashion enhanced by the outbreak of war. Numerous bankruptcies resulted; on all sides retrenchment or total abandonment of the industry was the order of the day. Nor has the position since changed to any noteworthy extent. The number of ostriches had fallen by 1926 to 103,688; the value of exports from

£2,953,587 in 1913 to £31,458 in 1928. In 1930 it amounted to 86,000 lb. of feathers, valued at £42,478. Since the slump, however, the inhabitants have readjusted themselves to the changed conditions, and, where ostriches flourished before, valuable crops of fruit, grain, and tobacco enable this district to share again in the general prosperity of the country."

We were very tired after our night's travel, and it was so fearfully hot that we indulged in an afternoon siesta in a state of *déshabillé*. Thus were we two found when the magistrate walked in to make our acquaintance and to invite us to call after dinner that night. We spent two pleasant hours on his stoep, but his fair daughter, who had been instructed by Mrs. Storr Garlake "to be sweet to us," was unfortunately rehearsing and did not turn up till late.

During our stay at Oudtshoorn we made *the* excursion—a trip to the Cango Caves. Mr. Phillpots very kindly motored us thither, and we also had the pleasure of the company of his daughter. On the outward trip I sat in front, and I was rewarded for doing so by discovering in the flesh the chauffeur of *Man and Superman*, with this difference, that he had a slight stutter instead of a Cockney accent. He came out with the most original things in such an extraordinarily funny way.

The road to the caves was very pretty, and in parts reminded me once more of Corsica, though a baboon crossed our path just to impress upon me that I was still in South Africa. The caves themselves were marvellous. The entrance was high up on a mountain side. After following a slightly winding passage some 400 yards and climbing down some steps, we found ourselves in a gigantic hall. Darkness reigned supreme; gross darkness, I believe, is the expression, and it wants to be seen to be felt. There was scarcely a sound to be heard, for, as a result of the drought, the caves were unusually dry. In the ordinary way we should have heard on all sides the drip, drip of the water that forms the marvellous stalactites and stalagmites with which the caves abound. Here and there complete columns had been formed, and most beautiful pillars decorated at the top with a row of smaller stalactites like the fringe of a curtain or a piece of lace. We lit up our candles, they did little beyond show up our immediate surroundings. We ignited some magnesium ribbon, and in a flash we realized the immensity of these underground palaces. We followed the guide yet deeper, down a winding passage, where gigantic halls, fantastic forms, and immense pillars followed one another in bewildering succession. We came to a solid pulpit of stone. I climbed into it and looked down into a space more than half the size of the Queen's Hall, and close by there was a thin projecting layer of stone that resounded like a gong when I struck it with my fist. It was possible to wander on for miles and yet find no end to these caves, and new discoveries were constantly being made.

In addition to ostrich farms there were extensive tobacco and whip-stick plantations at Oudtshoorn which gave their owners substantial revenues. The water was conserved everywhere, and it was, of course, due to irrigation that such wonderful crops were secured.

In these parts even the despised prickly pear has its uses, because a special machine had been invented to cut it up for food for the stock.

In Search of the Wilderness

The drive from Oudtshoorn to George over the Montagu Pass was very beautiful, but I must confess I found these long post-cart journeys over indifferent roads extremely fatiguing. The weather was rainy and cold, a great contrast to the day we arrived at Oudtshoorn, and many of the magnificent peaks that surrounded us were capped with snow! The railway was being pushed forward, and the most difficult part had already been constructed; when finished it would form quite an important connecting link.

On the Oudtshoorn side of the pass the country was rather bare, but the road down into George Town wound in and out amid the most luxuriant undergrowth and green trees. We arrived just after 9 p.m. by the light of the moon, but were too tired to do more than notice that it was a pretty place. We had the novel experience of finding an hotel that was too full to take us in, but the Victoria, to which we were originally recommended, had room enough and to spare.

Next morning, when we walked out on to the hotel stoep, we realized to what a charming spot we had come. Extending straight ahead of us for nearly a mile was the broad main street of George. None of your busy shop-lined thoroughfares, but a quiet, peaceful avenue of trees with an occasional cow grazing on the delicious green turf which lined the road for a good thirty yards on either side. Here and there a few buildings were scattered, a few pleasant villas, a church, an occasional store, and farther on some farms, but they contributed to the homely effect, for they had gardens and the gardens were full of flowers. Behind us was the most gorgeous row of mountain peaks, beckoning us to climb them.

But our meditations were interrupted. A man approached whose face was of a suspicious colour. A broad white band which stretched across his chest bore the legend, "B——, the World Walker."

"Pleased to meet you, gentlemen. I am walking round the world. I'm a Yank! Shake!"

His clammy hand told the same story as his face, and it was quite unnecessary for him to confide in us that he had been imbibing too freely. I beat a hasty retreat and left him to Johnnie! It ended in his inviting Johnnie to take a seat on the platform at a lecture he intended giving (alcohol permitting!) on the following night.

We had set our hearts upon visiting the Knysna Forest, but it takes at least twelve hours each way by cart; and by motor-car? well, they wanted more than we could afford.

We had heard a great deal about a beautiful spot called the "Wilderness" by the seaside, some fourteen miles along the Knysna road. At this stage of the proceedings who should turn up at the Victoria Hotel, George, but mine host from the Wilderness Hotel, a genial Irishman of the name of Cox. We were carried right away by his eloquence, and decided to walk out first thing next morning. We were eager for the walk, and were up and afoot before breakfast. Our energy was well rewarded, for the road proved exceptionally picturesque. Just before the fourth milestone we called a halt, for we had arrived at an ideal spot for a picnic breakfast. The view ahead of us down a broad ravine, both sides of which were covered with luxuriant undergrowth and flowering bushes, was extremely charming. To sit on a pleasant band of turf with bracken and arum lilies growing in profusion all around was in itself a joy, and to see one flowering in some unexpected spot made my heart leap with pleasure. "Proteas" of all sorts and wild flowers of every variety, including violets, were to be seen on all sides; but I think the trees gave us the greatest delight of the walk. We did not realize how we had missed them until we were amongst them again.

It was somewhat of a shock to encounter a toll-gate, but it had its uses, for the Dutchman in charge put us on to a short cut, a bridle-path across the fields to Kaaiman's Drift. It was quite a toss up whether we should take it, for were the tide up we should have to wade across the river. Thanks to our early start, we were just in time. In less than a quarter of an hour after we had crossed on the stepping-stones Nature has so kindly provided we watched the first wave race in from the sea.

Kaaiman's Drift is a very pretty spot, not unlike, and yet if possible even more beautiful than, the Lyn at Lynmouth. Once across we found a footpath through the thick undergrowth leading us up the hillside and round the coast. The path was for the most part entirely shut in by the overhanging branches of the trees and the "rope" creepers that dangled from them like festoons.

The track led on around the contour of the hill, and gave us from time to time unique glimpses of sandy beaches and foaming sea, whilst brightly coloured birds and insects flitted hither and thither from tree and flower. Suddenly we burst from the wood into an open clearing, where stood our little unpretentious hotel. We were soon partaking of a plain but very acceptable meal, and discovered that our hotel had no licence, not even to sell *lemonade*—a welcome change for this country!

A grassy slope led down to the river or the sea; we had our choice! On every other side we were surrounded by trees or bushes, many of them plumbago in full blossom, so that we fell in love with the place at first sight.

Next day, with a perfect blue sky and a brilliant sun to cheer us, we set out with Andraas, the Native boatman, to visit the Kaaiman Falls. Our way led us back through the woodland glades we had traversed the day before, and then a very short row brought us to the falls. It was a most wonderful spot, almost completely enclosed by precipitous rocks and, at times, I imagine it might be impossible to enter the boiling cauldron into which the water drops.

In the afternoon we rowed up the Touws River (touw=rope) to the "ebb and flow." I can only say I have never seen anything more perfect in the way of river scenery. The steep banks on either side, in many places rising high above us, were covered with trees and dense foliage—a veritable paradise for birds. The river twisted in and out like the coils of a rope, and each bend hid a more perfect view. And the amazing part of this wonderful river was that it had no apparent outlet! It flowed to within a hundred yards or so of the seashore and there came to a dead end, for the sea has washed up a bank of sand. Doubtless the water slowly percolated through, but there was no evidence of this to be seen. At high tide, on the contrary, the waves often washed over into the river, which at this place was quite salt. At flood time, when the swollen waters became a menace, the farmers would turn out and dig an outlet for the river through the sand bar, but it would soon silt up again.

The following day we seemed to do nothing but bathe. We bathed before breakfast, bathed before lunch, and again after tea, and between whiles we lay out in the sun on the hot sand and got cooked. Our shoulders were so badly caught by the sun that it was a perfect misery to lie down that night. It was a divine place for a holiday, and as usual we were sorry to move on, but before leaving our host arranged a delightful drive for us up the mountain side, whence the most perfect views could be obtained: views of the mountains, lakes, meadows, rivers, trees, with the deep blue sea as a background in every case.

Two days later we left George for Cape Town, more than sorry that our wanderings in South Africa were at length drawing to a close.

We could not have had a more delightful finish to our trip than our stay at the Wilderness, and to crown it all our good-natured Irish host never charged us for the three excursions and only 8s. per day for our board and lodging.

Last Days at The Cape

Our journey back to the Cape was uneventful, save that we made the acquaintance of the nephew of the late Sir Redvers Buller, who had been stopping with his wife at the Wilderness. We left the train at Mossel Bay, Riversdale, and Swellendam to get meals, as there were no restaurant cars on this line—the only one not owned by the Government at that time. The scenery was not exceptionally interesting, neither did the farms in this district count amongst the best.

Our little train sauntered along, and at seven next morning, after a sixteenth night in a railway carriage, we found ourselves once more under the shadow of Table Mountain. It was as perfect a day as one could desire, and Cape Town looked its best, and it is, without doubt, *the* town in South Africa.

We found Mr. Townshend on his way to meet us, and a genial welcome awaited us from his wife at their home, which on this occasion was to be our joint headquarters.

The day after our return to Cape Town Col. Inglesby took us for a motor drive round the mountain. We were delighted to see it once more and at a different time of year. I can only reiterate that for beauty and variety of scenery combined I cannot conceive of any more perfect drive.

On this occasion we had the added pleasure of visiting the memorial at Groote Schuur and seeing the view from the top. In the front of the memorial stands the original statue, Physical Energy, by G. F. Watts. The view over the plains below, to the various beautiful suburbs of Newlands, Claremont, Mowbray, Wynberg, and Kenilworth, and of the hills and seas beyond was just superb, and one can readily understand Rhodes' joy in the place.

Life in Cape Town was too much of a rush to leave us any adequate opportunity for letter writing. Most of my very hurried Christmas mail was written on the stoep, in the front of the house, behind the shade of honeysuckle, the scent from which was almost overpowering. My eyes were apt to wander from my writing to the honeysuckle and from the honeysuckle to the blaze of flowers below me, and beyond them to the cool blue sea.

We motored out to Caledon Sanatorium, some eighty miles away, where we spent one night at the invitation of our kind friends, Mr. and Mrs. Rose. We went by way of Stellenbosch, a detour of quite ten miles. Our first stop was at Sir Thos. Smartt's most beautiful house. We knew that Dr. Smartt himself was at Grahamstown speaking at a by-election, but Mr. Rose, who was a great friend of his and was particularly anxious I should meet them, hoped to find Lady Smartt at home. But our luck was out; we found she was away from home at some function at Stellenbosch. We therefore drove once more through the glorious avenue of trees that led to their house, past well-kept vineyards and fruit farms, to Caledon via Somerset West.

Some time later we were speeding through the famous Houw Hoek Gorge, with high rocky cliffs on one side and, far below,

59 Kaaiman's Drift

60 We watched the first wave race in from the sea

61 With Andraas to the Kaaiman Falls

62 The surf at the Wilderness

the Bot River tumbling over the stones in its deep ravine. A little later, just at sundown, we came to the wooden bridge that spanned this stream, and on a sandy patch by the roadside, shaded by oak trees, we spread our rugs, set the kettle to boil, and prepared our meal. It was about seven o'clock and a beautiful summer evening, so difficult to believe it was the month of December! We thought of the dear folks at home, and imagined them hugging a roaring fire, sipping their afternoon tea, and looking out upon the darkness, or at street lamps gleaming through the fog perhaps, whilst here we sat beside this dark brown stream, and sunlight still lingered on the hills around us, turning their slopes from golden to purple, from purple to an opalescent grey.

The heat of the day being over, we lowered the hood of the car and set out across the darkening land on the last few miles of our journey, and arrived at the Sanatorium Hotel at Caledon at about 9 p.m. The heat was very intense, but it was good to sit on the balcony outside our bedrooms and watch the stars and the dim outlines of the Zwaartberg and Hartebeest Ranges, until our eyelids drooped with healthy weariness.

After breakfast next day we climbed up to the spring to imbibe some of the healing waters that an American was pleased to describe as the "Volcanic Juice." It really was wonderful water, clear as crystal and rather hotter than you could comfortably bear it in your mouth. It was full of iron, and the rock through which it flowed and the channel of the stream were alike orange-yellow.

We went to Hermanus past that fine hill called Babylon's Tower. The Caledon district is renowned for wild flowers, and although September is the best month they were still a wonderful sight. Every here and there we stopped to gather them until the car was literally packed with flowers.

Hermanus was some way along the coast in Walker Bay. It is really a little fishing village in a wild and picturesque spot with mile after mile, acre after acre, of white sand. The Riviera Hotel, where we went to lunch, was another three or four miles away, and was just above an enormous *vlei*, in reality the mouth of the Klein River, which, as at the Wilderness, the silting up of the sand by the breakers has effectually dammed.

The first person we noticed on the hotel stoep was the Hon. W. P. Schreiner, K.C. It was curious that I should run across him again, though on this occasion I only had a few minutes with him.

From Hermanus it must be nearly a hundred miles to Cape Town, rather more, in fact, via Durbanville and Koeberg, the route we took in order to visit once again the farm belonging to Mrs. Rose's mother. At 9 p.m. we were once more in Cape Town thanking Mr. and Mrs. Rose for a most perfect glimpse of yet another part of the Colony.

Another day we were due out at Kenilworth to lunch with Lady Innes at her house "Karatara," and a beautiful place it is.

We found Lady Innes both exceptionally cultivated and charming, one of those delightful people who always say and do the right thing and at the right time. She had offered to take us for a drive in her car and, like Mr. Rose, suggested of her own accord the one place to which we desired to go, which was along the coast of False Bay to Millers Point. We passed through Wynberg, Muizenberg, St. James, Kalk Bay, and Simons Town (the naval base), skirting the sea nearly all the way. At Millers Point the wild flowers were strictly preserved and grew in great profusion. A road was being made which will be carried right round the peninsula to Hout Bay, and it will then, without doubt, be the finest and most beautiful drive in the world. On the return trip we drove through the Government plantation at Tokai, where a most picturesque old Dutch house, with its high stoep and white pillars, situated as it should be amongst the pine, blue gum, and oak trees, was used as a reformatory, and appeared to be run on very sensible lines. There was a large farm attached where the inmates were made to work, and if environment counts for anything the reforming process ought to be both complete and enduring. As in Rhodesia, we found convict labour was constantly used for the benefit of the community. For instance, the Victoria Drive and the beautiful walk round the Devil's Peak were both largely, if not entirely, constructed by convict labour. It certainly seems the most intelligent way of dealing with those whose action has been detrimental to the well-being of the community.

Tea was awaiting our return, and after tea we adjourned to the beautiful garden that surrounds "Karatara," and here we were soon joined by Sir James Innes. He was a most interesting man to talk to, level-headed and humanitarian, and his judgments always impressed me as sound. I was sorry our time with him was so short, but when he returned from his work it was time for us to go.

The following afternoon we spent surf bathing at Muizen berg. You turn your back on the waves, shove off just before one comes along, and are carried to the shore on its crest, lying comfortably on your board like an expert on a luge.

The next day was our "Field Day." At 5 a.m. a party of us commenced the ascent of Table Mountain via Kasteel's Poort. After breakfast at the top of Kasteel's Poort we walked across the mountain to Platte Klip Gorge. On this occasion we managed to find our way, for instead of a sou'-easter to blot out our view we had the most perfect day imaginable. And what a glorious prospect there was from the top! In front Cape Town and Table Bay lay spread out before us; to the right the Devil's Peak looked a simple climb; to the left, a thousand feet below us, was the Lion's Head, and beyond it Hout Bay. Yet farther round, False Bay was to be seen in the distance. It was a gorgeous sight, and we spent some time walking along the face of the mountain. The descent of the gorge was quite an exciting, if exhausting, process, and when we did arrive at the bottom no one, besides Mr. Townshend, Johnnie, and myself, showed any intense desire to prolong the walk and go right round the Devil's Peak to Groote Schuur!

After a few sandwiches eaten under the trees by the side

of a mountain stream, we parted company, and together with our host we set off once more. I had been over part of the ground five months before, but I very much wanted to see it again, and I found it none the less beautiful for a second visit. The path was half-way up the Devil's Peak, and extended for some miles. Trees had been planted on either side, and formed a shady avenue, and here and there little streams trickled down the mountain side.

In our anxiety to keep sufficiently high up the mountain we overshot the mark, and after walking some way through extensive pine woods saw both Groote Schuur and the memorial in the distance, hundreds of feet below us. Our efforts to reach the spot were not rewarded with success, for after endless clambering about and some miles of tramping round the outskirts of the estate we found ourselves at Mowbray. It was then nearly 5 p.m. We had been on the go twelve hours, and somehow a tram home has its attractions at times! Weary and content we took our seats, and presently were once more in Adderley Street. The cries of "Botha's resignation!" greeted us. Was Hertzog to be jettisoned at last? *We* should not know for three weeks, and in Australia who would know or care?

Johnnie had calculated that we had travelled 5,000 miles by rail, 791 miles by steamer, 700 by wagon, car, or cart, and about 600 miles on foot during our five months' tour of South Africa, a total of about 7,500 miles.

Next morning our slumbers were disturbed by a voice calling through our window, "She's in!" (i.e. the *Anchises*), and shortly after breakfast we went to see her. She was just where we had left her five months before. The Captain, the Chief Steward, the Second Steward, our cabin steward, our saloon steward—all gave us the heartiest of welcomes. It was almost like returning home. Our night on board was brief, for at 4.30 a.m. we rose to bid adieu to Table Mountain. By the time Cape Point was passing out of sight the bugler was at work blowing the reveille.

Two Young Men See the World

AUSTRALIA

The narrow ways of English folk
Are not for such as we;
They bear the long-accustomed yoke
Of staid conservancy:
But all our roads are new and strange,
And through our blood there runs
The vagabonding love of change
That drove us westward of the range
And westward of the suns.

Our fathers came of roving stock
That could not fixed abide:
And we have followed field and flock
Since e'er we learnt to ride;
By miner's camp and shearing shed,
In land of heat and drought,
We followed where our fortunes led,
With fortune always on ahead
And always further out.

A. B. Paterson

Chapter VI

SOUTH AUSTRALIA AND VICTORIA

"SHAME, how *can* you! Do you know there is a poor man lying ill in that cabin?" We heard a shrill female voice utter these words above the din that a serenading party was making outside our quarters. It was New Year's Eve, and a large number of fellows we had on board were still so young as to think it manly to imbibe too freely. At the bar they had been making up for a particularly dull day, and now they had discovered the lair of the unfortunate "Missionary from Selukwe." I had previously had cause to address a few of them as politely as I could through our cabin ventilator, but this only fanned the flaming "oil" in the raucous throats of these Scotch nightingales who were migrating across the Southern Indian Ocean to Australia. Perhaps it was the sweet voice of the young New Year that had spoken, but, be it as it may, our tormentors flitted away on hearing it, leaving us to slumber peacefully. Perhaps they had been gathered up and carried off under the great wings of old Father Time.

On the whole our voyage to Adelaide passed pleasantly enough in the society of many new friends and many others who bored us to distraction. The outstanding figure of our own particular "circle," and indeed of the entire ship's company, was our excellent Commander, whose courtesy and friendship has been long remembered by the writers of these lines. It was a chilly voyage, with blustersome winds that swept up from the Antarctic, but we found our bunks were cosy places in which to spend much of our time reading, dozing, sucking peppermint lumps, smoking my favourite John Cotton tobacco that I had discovered at the Cape in a Christmas parcel from Home.

Late one afternoon I was busy packing in our cabin when suddenly one of our bright young fellows started shouting,

"Land! Land! Land on the starboard bow!" I popped my head out of the port-hole, and there, sure enough, was a faint, curious blue line along the south-eastern horizon. As we drew nearer we could make out the high cliffs of Kangaroo Island, bathed in the yellow sunlight of evening. I felt a particular interest in Kangaroo Island, for a great-uncle of mine, a Mr. Samuel Stephens, was the first adult colonist to put foot on South Australian soil. He came by the first vessel (the *Duke of York*) on July 27, 1836, and landed at Nepean Bay, Kangaroo Island. He was sent out by the South Australian Company as its first manager, to give the colony a start, and was the leading spirit at the Kangaroo Island settlement. After Colonel Light had pronounced against Kangaroo Island as a place of settlement, Samuel Stephens and other settlers removed to the mainland. He imported the first horse into the new colony. One of the pioneers (Pastor Jacob Abbot) has left upon record an account of his first meeting with the horse and its owner. Samuel Stephens was walking down the North Terrace of the embryo city of Adelaide, leading his newly imported horse. A short distance away was a group of black-people. Directly they caught sight of the animal "their expressions of astonishment and horror were indescribable." The men shouted; the lubras (Native women) screamed; the children sought refuge behind their parents. Gradually they became calmer, muttering, "Big kangaroo! Oh, big kangaroo!" I quote from the Rev. John Blacket's interesting book, *History of South Australia*, published by Hussey & Gillingham, Adelaide, 1911, page 448. Samuel had two brothers, John and Edward, who followed him out to this young colony. John founded one of the first newspapers, *The Adelaide Observer*, and later *The Register* came under his direction. Of him it has been said: "He was the unflinching and unvarying advocate of civil and religious liberty; the truthful and uncompromising exposer of every proved corruption and abuse." Edward was entrusted with the foundation of the pioneer bank, and he and his wife had to take up their abode in a tent not far from the beach at Holdfast Bay. Edward Stephens took a leading part in all public matters connected with the young colony, and when he was absent from the tent bank, interesting himself in the affairs of the new community, his wife told how she used to sit, in fear and trembling, on the chest that contained the £10,000 of capital the bank then possessed. Edward Stephens had a distinguished career of service to the State and his fellow men in Adelaide, and, together with his two brothers, did much to earn that respect in which their names are held to-day.

This digression would seem unpardonable, but it gives a scanty introduction to the new land we were rapidly approaching in our luxurious ship, as well as a glimpse of three of the many exceptional men who helped in the founding of Adelaide and gave South Australia such a magnificent start. Later on, when we arrived in the city, our presence there got noised abroad, how I know not, and it was not long before representatives of the *Adelaide Advertiser*, with which the paper my great-uncle founded about eighty years before is now merged, came to see us, and interesting interviews were published under snappy headlines, and the city librarians were kept busy delving among old records and stirring up the settled dust of bygone days.

First Impressions of Adelaide

The sudden silence of the engines awoke me next morning, and I heard the shrill whistle of the officer of the watch as he called up his quartermaster for orders. A grey light crept through the port-holes. We had dropped anchor in the roadstead off the Port River. Some time later the sound of the 6.30 bugle roused me from a heavy slumber, and a few moments after the quiet voice of Brownhill, our cabin steward, announced, "First bugle, Mr. Storr; bath ready, sir." He tapped me politely on the back with his finger-tips, and I rolled over in my bunk grunting a drowsy reply. As I climbed down from the upper berth I noticed the bright sunlight shining on the deck, and the silvery blue water of the distant anchorage where a fleet of frigates lay swinging with the tide. Stan was muttering in his bunk, growling at the shortness of the nights and cursing the doctor whose inspection we had to undergo in half an hour's time.

As soon as the doctor's inspection was over, we weighed anchor and crept up the narrow channel to our berth in the Outer Harbour. A handful of white labourers and a policeman manœuvred the hawsers as received from our great ship. The orderly way they went about their work was an immense contrast to the clumsy haste and laughable antics of the Kaffirs in African ports.

We were more than sorry to say good-bye to the old ship, her Commander and crew, and the friends with whom we had had such a good time, but Mr. J. S. Thompson had sent us a letter to say he and his wife would be glad to offer us hospitality for two or three nights. It was extraordinarily kind of them, especially as they had an infant aged fifteen months, and were temporarily without a domestic. I wondered how many English homes under such circumstances would add still further to their labours by welcoming two guests! It was marvellous how Mrs. Thompson managed. There was no fuss or worry, and somehow everything got done, and done well. Mr. Thompson was kindness itself, and was determined we should see as much of Adelaide and its "Garden Streets" as was possible in the time available. We accordingly set out at once to visit the sights.

The city of Adelaide, so far from growing in any haphazard way, was most carefully planned. The city proper can never be more nor less than one mile square, for outside that limit come the "Park Lands," a beneficent belt of fresh air ensuring for ever the healthy atmosphere in which Adelaide rejoices.

From the Cathedral we wandered on through the Zoological and Botanical Gardens, where the flowers did one's eyes good. The place was crowded with people, for it was Sunday afternoon; all were well dressed and very orderly, though obviously not of the élite. Near a beautiful avenue of plane trees, orators, religious and otherwise, had gathered small crowds together, and turned the place into a miniature Hyde Park, but at five o'clock the Gardens were closed. We were in Australia, and even park keepers were human beings and got their Sunday evening off.

We visited St. Peter's College, where Mr. Thompson was science master, and saw the bridge from which people committed suicide; we examined the place where a policeman was shot, and finally we were quite relieved to jump into a tram for Kensington Park, where our good friend resided. Adelaide is very proud of its tramway service—one of the most up-to-date systems to be found anywhere. All the "points" at important centres were controlled from little signal boxes, perched high up, whence a view of all the trams coming and going could be obtained. We were in a country where labour was top dog; accordingly no trams ran before 1 p.m. on Sundays. Highly inconvenient possibly, but an excellent arrangement none the less.

There was a homely sound about all the names in Adelaide, and it was certainly a very English town. We found ourselves passing through Croydon, or getting into a Hyde Park tram, and, but for that cloudless blue sky and blazing hot sun, we could have imagined we were at Home. Yet there were lots of differences.

There was an air of independence about the working classes and an entire absence of obvious destitution as one knows it in English towns.

We spent a pleasant evening sitting out in the cool of the veranda, and we were up betimes next morning to watch Mr. Thompson milk his cow, a process in which his cat took a profound interest. She nestled up alongside with open mouth ready to catch the stream of milk which he would turn at times in her direction!

My night was badly disturbed by a mosquito—an ill omen, for in South Africa they always preferred Johnnie!

I recalled that a distinguished Australian author, with whom I had always taken pleasure in corresponding, lived near Adelaide, and I found his house was no very great distance from where we were staying at "Mia Mia" (My My, i.e. home). Accordingly I called upon him the following morning on our way to the Burnside Waterfall. He was Mr. W. G. Hay, author of several novels of Australian life. Both he and his wife gave me a very warm welcome, and it ended in his driving the three of us to the waterfall—a very pretty spot—and inviting Johnnie and myself to spend a day or two with him on our return from Maclaren Vale.

Life on a Vineyard

We dined at the Grand Central Hotel, which is a palatial establishment owned by and situated above Messrs. Fay & Gibson's stores. In due course our friend Mr. Luke turned up at the hotel with two of his friends, and the following afternoon motored us out to the Tatachilla Vineyard. We went by way of the Coromandel Valley and Clarendon—a glorious ride. The countryside reminded us more of English park-lands after a hot summer than the South African veld. It was a joy to see plenty of trees again, even if 99 per cent. of them were Australian blue gums. We noticed apricots being picked in one orchard we passed, so promptly stopped and loaded the car up with a large box of them. On arrival at our destination we soon found ourselves seated once more in deck-chairs, alternately gazing into a brilliant blue sky and grappling with our Home mail. It was no longer the stoep of a South African farm; it was the veranda of Mr. Luke's charming homestead at the Tatachilla Vineyard, Maclaren Vale, about two miles from the sea and twenty-five miles from Adelaide. Our beloved South African veld was replaced by 400 acres of vines, which I must confess have a charm of their own, for, like Omar, I am a lover of the grape. I think I love it more in that I object to seeing it fermented!

It was a most comfortable house of the bungalow type, with tiled roof and fly-proof doors and windows, which were very necessary with a shade temperature of 99° and mosquitoes and flies buzzing all around.

These beautiful green vineyards were most refreshing to look upon, but I should have loved to see them a month later, when the grapes would be ripe. Acre after acre of small standard vines, planted in straight rows about 5 or 6 feet apart, led out in every direction around us. They looked almost like currant bushes. A huge building was in course of erection behind us to deal with that year's vintage, and we had already been initiated into the process of wine making. Never have I seen such enormous barrels, some of them holding 10,000 gallons. The whole process was carried out scientifically and with scrupulous cleanliness and care. The Australian Government had passed most stringent adulteration Acts, so that Australian wines are among the purest. That they were growing in favour was evidenced by the fact that they were the only wines on the London market the sale of which had increased in recent years.

Mr. Luke proved a most genial and jovial host; he was always full of fun, and we were a delightfully informal little party. "No swank about us," he would say, so we thoroughly enjoyed ourselves.

Mr. Patter, his book-keeper and accountant, who lived with him, was exceedingly interesting in that he had seen so much of life in the back blocks of Australia, whilst Mrs. Underwood and her little daughter "Jacky" completed this interesting household with their gaiety and charm. Mrs. Underwood was refreshingly cosmopolitan, being Spanish by birth, French by education, and speaking six or seven languages fluently. She had travelled widely, read extensively, lived in such remote parts as the Gulf of Carpentaria, and yet studied music with the best professors in London, Paris, and Germany. She was as vivacious as one would expect a Spanish or French woman to be, yet full of the solid common sense and wisdom wide experience brings. One evening we spoke German together, and every now and then we would break into French. They had a first-class Bechstein piano, so that we had plenty of music and an occasional impromptu dance. "Jacky" was the quaintest little thing, age about nine, full of personality, plenty of imagination, perfect little manners, but in appearance a trifle coy and affected. She told her mother she had come to the conclusion she liked us both, but that she wanted to sit next to the gentleman with the beard!

The temperature dropped one day from 100° to about 75° in the shade, and to celebrate the cool spell a picnic was arranged on the coast at Port Noarlunga. There was nothing remarkable about the scenery here; indeed, the yellow stubble fields, the low cliffs, and scattered homes were very like the south-eastern shores of England. So we were highly amused when a girl of our party asked us if we did not "feel strange, picnicking like this, *miles from anywhere*!" The child seemed to think this was the edge of beyond, whereas we were surrounded by well-cultivated fields and only twenty miles from the capital of South Australia, and hither came its inhabitants to get a breath of sea air and sail about the small bay in their yachts.

On our way back to Tatachilla a friend took Stan and "meself," as the Australians say, into the village pub for a drink. The bottled beer was labelled "bitter," but it tasted more like lemonade. I pointed this out to the publican, Mr. O'Neil by name, who handed me over a second bottle free of charge. Meanwhile two local harvesters, who had just come in for their after-work "boozer," overheard our friend introducing us to the landlord as "world travellers." "'E ain't never done no work, Bill," remarked one horny-fisted harvester to the other. "Look at 'ees 'ands!" But we were not slow to explain to them how we had probably done harder work, during longer hours, than they had ever done, but with our *brains*, and under very inferior conditions to those in which they had to work. They looked at their horny hands, *grand* hands and no mistake, as we continued to impress upon them the difference between a twelve-hour day in a stuffy London office, at from 10s. to 40s. a week, and their own outdoor life in a glorious climate, with an eight-hour day at 8s. a day, and, in many cases, with food thrown in as well. "That's right," they admitted at the close of our conversation, an expression that we found was very generally used in the Antipodes by those who were not entirely convinced by, or had not thoroughly understood, what had been said.

The following morning we mounted on to the top of a rumbling old coach and wended our way back to Adelaide, through the fields of standing corn and stubble and here and there a glimpse of the distant sea. The same afternoon, having made arrangements for our trip up the Murray River, we were due at the office of Mr. H. Phillips in Grenfell Street. Here we found Mr. Phillips himself and a very smart carriage and pair. Instead of taking us straight to his very charming house he kindly drove us round some of the most interesting parts of Adelaide, and we learnt much of the many benevolent institutions and trusts that make the life of the aged and infirm of Adelaide a very pleasant one. From all appearances it would seem difficult to find a city with less destitution or where, such as there is, it is better provided for.

Mr. Phillips' garden would have rejoiced some of our South African friends. It was an excellent example of what an efficient water-supply will do when coupled with semi-tropical sunshine.

Our visit to the Art Gallery proved that the pictures are of quality if not quantity, and the collection is most interesting. Later on we were the guests of Mr. Hay at his pleasant house, situated at the foot of the Mount Lofty Range. Mr. Hay was Scotch, and the upbringing of his three youthful sons was an agreeable contrast to what we had encountered elsewhere.

On retiring to rest I was appalled at the number of mosquitoes in our room.

> Say not the struggle naught availeth,
> The labour and the wounds are vain,

wrote A. H. Clough, and the lines brought comfort and encouragement to us in the ceaseless war we waged against flies and mosquitoes during our stay in Adelaide. Elusiveness, thy name is Mosquito! Persistency, thy name is Australian Fly! In South Africa we knew where we were. If there were any mosquitoes, they went for Johnnie; if there were any . . . . they came for me! But in Australia no such rule obtained; they one and all thirsted after my flesh, and even roused me from slumber with their self-satisfied humming. The noise was deafening. In despair I would seize my electric torch; probably there would not be a mosquito to be seen, and if there were it would be peacefully seated on the ceiling! But with the dawn came retribution! Their movements were now more lethargic, for they had drunk deeply of my life's blood! My hands moved slowly, "but they crushed exceeding small!"

It was oppressively hot again the morning we set out in a car with Mr. and Mrs. Hay for a day's tour of the countryside. A stifling wind was raising dust clouds over the city, which lay sweltering below us as our car climbed up the winding roadway of the Mount Lofty Range. The air was heavy with the scent of the "bush" from the ragged foliage of the shea oak, the sweet-briars growing in wild profusion, and the eucalyptus and Native cherry trees, densely branched like spruce, and peculiar for the fact that the cherry stone grows *outside* the fruit. Penfold's vineyards lay spreading up the hillside, a wealth of wonderful green, and olive groves and orchards clustered in the sheltering folds of the mountain side, contrasting oddly with the dried-up grass beneath the trees on the uncleared land. From the summit of Mount Lofty we drove down to Bellair and entered the

63 Adelaide Cathedral and the Torrens River

64 The cat nestled up alongside with open mouth

65 These green vineyards were most refreshing to look upon

66 The Christmas bees were singing

National Park, and glimpsed the well-wooded valley of Piccadilly on the way. The National Park is a large woodland area adapted to the requirements of the people, where streams and grassy glades abound and a large number of tennis courts, each with its shelter and water-supply attached, where folks can spend a long day in the open air. Except for these signs of civilization, we might have been in the back blocks of this great continent, and here we stopped to eat our luncheon, in the shade cast by the giant gum trees in whose branches the Christmas bees were singing their eerie raucous song. Later we walked up a pretty woodland dale where trickled a tiny stream, and suddenly we came upon an orchard kept by a picturesque old couple of Scots. After a sip of cool water in the shady parlour of their cottage we strolled out beneath the fruit trees and helped ourselves to peaches, plums, and nectarines, and finally took away with us a basket full of these fruits, together with a blessing from the old folks and the wish that we would go back to see them again soon. The branches of their fruit trees were so heavily laden that they were weighted to the ground and so densely packed with fruit along the boughs as to make their stems almost invisible!

We completed our drive by going to the coast at Brighton, where we had a refreshing bathe, and returned to spend our last night in the neighbourhood of Adelaide under the hospitable roof of Mr. and Mrs. Hay.

Away up the Murray River

A train journey of about 120 miles brought us to Morgan, on the Murray River. The line traversed leagues of undulating wheat-bearing country, which was of little interest except for its apparently limitless extent. As we approached the river flats beyond Endunda, what looked to be a distant view of the sea was in reality miles of "bush country" stretching away to the far horizon.

On our arrival at Morgan that evening the heat was still

very intense, so we were not sorry to go immediately on board the S.S. *Ruby*, and soon we were starting off on our 350-mile journey up the "Nile of Australia," as the Murray is sometimes called. From its source in the Snowy Mountains near Mount Kosciusko to its mouth, which is virtually the great Lake Alexandrina, whence an insignificant channel leads into Encounter Bay, the Murray has a total length of 1,719 miles. It is navigable by flat-bottomed paddle boats, such as the *Ruby*, for 1,589 miles, and, together with its huge tributaries the Darling, the Murrumbidgee, and the Lachlan, over 3,000 miles are open to water-borne transport of this description, a distance equal to that from Adelaide to Port Darwin and more than half-way back again!

The *Ruby* was a queer-looking craft with three decks. On the lowest one was carried a miscellaneous cargo of farm carts, building materials, and household furniture, and here were the engines and stacks of logs for fuelling. The middle deck was occupied by the cabins, saloons, and bathrooms. The cabins were fitted with spring wire berths, an excellent idea against vibration, and the doors and windows had mosquito-proof shutters which, according to our genial supercargo, Mr. Piggot, merely served to imprison those that had already got inside! The top deck gave access to the smoke-room, officers' quarters, and wheel house, wherein our Skipper spent most of his time. He was no beautifully gold-braided specimen, but clad in his shirt-sleeves and an old soft hat he steered skilfully around mud banks and snags, and would lend a hand when the time came, together with passengers and crew, in shifting the cargo or taking more fuel on board. The crew was a mixed-looking lot, clad in anything from a Sunday suit to a shirt without sleeves, and all smoked their pipes and lay on their backs among the cargo as we threaded our way up the winding stream.

The *Ruby* was built to carry about twenty-six passengers, but there were over fifty of us on board during the first twenty-four hours, so we had to take our meals in the little saloon in relays. Next day our passenger list was temporarily increased by meeting the *Ellen* coming downstream with a number of people on board taking a Sunday outing on the river. Many of them transferred to our boat for the return journey to their homes; they were mostly honest settlers, farmers, or fruit growers, of that magnificent horny-handed type.

Food and table manners were, of course, pretty rough, and we could not help smiling with surprise when one mighty "bush whacker" at our table started gathering up the green peas on his plate with the blade of his knife, a pretty dexterous balancing trick, but they "got there"—to his evident satisfaction. One or two others were apparently more familiar with chisels than table forks, for they treated them as such!

The sun went down behind the ragged gum trees that lined both banks, their fantastic boughs silhouetted against a background of blazing orange and tender green, and their great roots seemed all exposed to view in a weird tangle along the waterside, so that as our boat sped forward to the thumping of her paddles we were reminded of the old song:

> Her foot's as big as a gum-tree root,
> Such a *lovely* foot has Sally!

We sat on the fore-part of the upper deck in the delicious evening breeze, watching the moon and the stars and the reflections of the gum trees as we steamed slowly upstream. By moonlight the scenery was quite romantic. It was impossible to tell that the ground under the tall gum trees was in parts parched and bare; it looked like the green swards of English park-lands. Those trees that had recently shed their bark as the snake sheds its skin, shone a mysterious white, and every here and there the stumps of old trees startled one into believing that they were stealthily moving forms. The river itself twisted about like a serpent; at one moment the Southern Cross and the Pointers would be ahead, and a moment later they would have dodged behind us. It seemed a pity to turn into our bunks on such perfect nights; the moon and the stars, combined with the dazzle of our electric headlight, made such bizarre effects on the water, the root-bound banks, and among the gaunt branches of the trees that we were spellbound. It was a fantastic scene, so still, so quiet, as we travelled farther and farther along this great Australian waterway.

We were just listening for the cry of that peculiar Australian bird commonly called the Laughing Jackass when Mr. Piggot came up and mentioned that there was a lady on board who said she thought she knew me. I followed him below with no little fear and trepidation! It turned out to be a cousin of a lady we had met at Maclaren Vale, and a sister of Judge Herbert of Papua.

It was a fairly hot night and our cabin was very close, but we were better off than those who had to spend their night in the smoking-room and elsewhere. But fortunately, what with the movement of the steamer and the delicious cool breeze which sprang up, we were not so seriously troubled either by the mosquitoes or by the heat as our friends had confidently predicted.

Most of the following morning we sat under the awning on the upper deck watching for the change in the scenery which each bend in the river promised but never brought. To some it might have been monotonous; to us it was just delightful, for, after five months in South Africa, in a year of drought, what greater bliss than to see a river and trees and the fresh green of the water grass.

Say what you will, there is a fascination about the Australian gum trees. They may not compare with the oak and the beech, but they have a beauty of their own. It was interesting to notice traces of the Australian Aboriginal Natives, as, for instance, on the boles of certain gum trees there were scars still showing where canoes had been cut out of their bark half a century or more ago. Outside the Northern Territory there are now few Natives about, save in the northern part of Western Australia and Queensland. We passed one couple fishing on our way up, but I believe it was about the only family in that part of the river.

Occasionally we steamed close to a high cliff of soft sandstone, curiously worn by the action of the water in flood time, whilst the corresponding cliff was perhaps a mile or more away across the bush, and in times of great flood all the intervening country would be submerged, as the presence of vast quantities of lignum bushes and water grass bore evidence. On certain occasions, when the Darling has been in flood, steamers have been navigated for twenty or thirty miles, *away from the main stream*, on these inundating waters. About tea time that day we arrived at the prosperous little settlement of Loxton, largely peopled by German colonists.

We had some interesting fellow passengers on board. One man, who came from the Home county of Buckinghamshire and had been a clerk in the Bank of England, told us he was making more money at clearing land and tree-felling than he would ever have done at Home. It was a very rough life, but he hoped to be in a position to "chuck it" in ten years' time and return to England. The thing he missed most was music; he had always been accustomed to playing the violin or viola in a quartette, but now he seldom had a chance even to hear a note, "and as to my playing," he said, "look at my hands." They were certainly no longer suitable for the violin! There was another man whose mission was to inspect some three thousand sheep, which he hoped to buy at about 12s. a head. He intended fattening them up on lucerne and selling them a month or two later for double that price.

For many years the New South Wales, Victorian, and South Australian Governments were at loggerheads in regard to their respective riparian rights in the waters of the Murray and its lengthy tributaries, the Darling, the Murrumbidgee, and the Lachlan. During the consequent litigation the water was running to waste, but fortunately it has now been put under Federal control, and the day is not far distant when these rivers will be properly "locked" and their waters conserved.

When this task is accomplished a vast acreage will be opened up for the cultivation of fruit, rice, and forage crops. Some idea of the extent of these possibilities can be gleaned from the following quotation taken from *A Handbook of Information, Etc.*, Sydney, 1928, issued by the authority of the Hon. T. R. Bavin, K.C., B.A., Premier and Treasurer of New South Wales. "The largest irrigation settlement is in the Murrumbidgee area, on which there is a population of about 15,000. . . . The land is eminently suited for the cultivation of a wide variety of products, including apricots, nectarines, peaches, prunes, pears, melons, and citrus fruits; also wine and table grapes, currants, raisins, sultanas, figs, olives, and most varieties of vegetables and fodder crops. . . . Rice has been successfully cultivated in the last few years, the area under crop this season being 12,000 acres, which will supply about half the requirements of the Commonwealth. . . . The value of production for this area for the year ended June 30, 1927, was £884,000. Competent authorities have estimated that the ultimate annual production of the N.S.W. areas may reach £3,000,000."

The *Ruby* still panted and puffed and hooted as she drew in occasionally to the river bank, at such places as Overland Corner and The Devil's Elbow, to discharge her cargo or refuel with logs that lay ready stacked up by the woodman, who led an apparently solitary life in his "humpie" near by. Everyone gave a hand at passing these logs on board: many of the volunteers were immaculately dressed in their Sunday finery. At some of these halting-places no living soul appeared to exist, but we were informed that "some farmers would drive in in a day or so from their farms forty or fifty miles away up country to collect the merchandise" we had dumped for them on the forsaken river bank.

As we drew off into midstream again we watched the

woodman stroll away into the bush, his axe over his shoulder, and his blue trousers could be seen from afar, bright against the sombre background of dead grass in the evening sunshine, whilst his blue boat swung idly in the slow current of the stream.

All the way along the Murray, though sometimes miles apart, were the homesteads of squatters and farmers—comfortable-looking buildings standing beside the original dwelling of some fifteen years before—ample testimonials to success. Their "blocks" or farms would cover many square miles, and at many of these we stopped to deliver goods, from petrol and galvanized iron to provisions and household utensils. At one station called "Moorna," to give an example, the owner and his sons had their own electrical plant, their own pumping station, a motor-launch, and one or two cars, besides a nice house and garden. Their "station" or "block" extended for miles into the interior, and carried at least seventy thousand sheep. Seventy thousand sheep whose wool alone would bring them in those days anything from 7s. to 10s. apiece, and that with little trouble, for in Australia you can contract for all your shearing, baling, and carting to be done for you, and the branding as well if you want it. But it has its other side. In a year of drought half that flock may be wiped out. We made enquiries as to the land value of such stations. A fair basis seemed then to be £1 per sheep that the land will carry. This includes all improvements, and is, of course, only an average figure.

It was pleasant to see horses and sheep grazing contentedly on the river banks—all of them looking in excellent condition. Whenever we stopped for any length of time fishing was indulged in—a very simple process as far as we could see: just a piece of string with two or three hooks on and a bit of bait. The bait used was raw meat, and seemed to prove attractive, for not only were numerous Murray cod and bream caught, but of all things a turtle! Apparently these river turtles are not what Lord Mayors' are made of, so we had none of them.

On the following day we passed the inter-State boundary, and for a little while we were between Victoria and South Australia; but only an hour or two later we had left South Australia—the most aristocratic of the Australian States—behind, and on our left bank we had New South Wales and on the right, Victoria. The population of South Australia is comparatively small; the people have never made any great display, but the general level of well-being must be exceptionally high. There was a solid prosperity about the country which it did one good to see.

These boundaries are marked by a fence extending, in the case of Victoria, all the way from the Murray River to the sea coast. This is not a fence to keep out human beings, but a rabbit-proof fence hundreds and hundreds of miles in extent.

Rabbits are the scourge of every Australian state, and everything possible is done to keep down their numbers. Strychnine bait is used extensively for this purpose, and also to poison the wild dogs that do so much damage to the flocks of sheep. Unfortunately other animal and bird life suffers in consequence; nevertheless we saw many interesting specimens. There were a vast number of duck, including one variety that has entirely lost the use of its wings, yet it has been found at water-holes some miles away from the valley of the river. Flocks of white cockatoos with yellow crests made a fascinating sight as they crossed the river against the deep blue sky. Cranes flew from time to time off the many dead stumps of timber that lay dangling in the sluggish stream, where shag would also perch and watch for fish. Hawks were very numerous along the banks, and they were constantly harassed by very small birds whose courage evidently ran very high. Our friend the "bush whacker" told us that he had often been set upon by these small birds, not much bigger than a sparrow, when he had been at his work in the bush. We also had the good fortune to observe a few emu wandering about the bushes at the river side.

Irrigation Settlements

Very early next morning we arrived at the important irrigation settlement of Renmark, but we had not sufficient time to see anything of the orchards or raisin yards before we were off again on our upstream journey.

The country beyond the banks was still identically the same: the inevitable gum trees on either side, behind which stretched away dense patches of low polygnum bush over the river flats, interspersed with the harder, small timber known as box and bull oak. Where the sandy loam ridges came in close to the river side we could distinguish the hop bush and mallee bush that cover the country for mile upon mile, except where the great tracts of wheatlands have superseded them.

In the afternoon we were steaming up a long reach when suddenly a curious jar and bumping brought us to a standstill. We had run aground in midstream! After a great deal of engine work full astern, and soundings taken with an oar, which revealed that there was only a blade's length of water, we managed to get off, and jockeyed across into deeper water after a delay of fully thirty minutes. The Captain said it was lucky we had not stuck there for seven hours, and he recalled one voyage when the river was low when they had to haul the boat by means of steel ropes attached to the engine and the trunks of gum trees for a quarter of a mile over sandbanks; it took them twenty-two hours to accomplish that feat!

Towards dusk we reached the junction of the River Darling with the Murray, and, leaving the Murray for an hour or two, we steamed up the Darling to the important little settlement of Wentworth. An old wooden church with coloured glass windows stood side by side with a modern brick building, indicating perhaps the material progress of the community. A very fine bridge, with a centre that lifts up, now spans the Darling, and stationed on this we watched the *Ruby* being unloaded by the light of the moon. Although only a tributary of the Murray, the Darling is over a *thousand* miles long. Being the season of low water there was barely room for the *Ruby* to turn, when later in the evening she returned to join the Murray once more.

Early next morning we arrived at our destination, Mildura, the scene of one of the earliest irrigation settlements. Mildura has had a very chequered history since the days when the brothers Chaffey came from California and founded the fruit-growing industry on American lines.

Mildura, at the time of our visit, consisted of 12,000 acres of fertile land which, by means of pumps, aqueducts, and channels, were flooded three to four times a year with water from the Murray.

We have said enough about South African and Australian conditions to indicate the enormous possibilities of cultivation where both water and semi-tropical sunshine are present. But perhaps a few figures will illustrate this better. Twelve thousand acres would be a very small sheep station for these parts, and would bring in on the most favourable basis £8,000 a year and employ about half a dozen people. The value of the crop of the 12,000 acres at Mildura in 1912 exceeded £400,000, and employed a population of several thousand. As to the crops themselves, sultanas, raisins, and currants take the lead, but peaches, pears, and citrus fruits are grown in considerable quantities, and also lucerne. The land is divided into ten-acre plots, but the average holding was about twenty to twenty-five acres.

We saw the pumping stations where the river water is forced into the irrigation channels of varying levels, and we saw the water flowing along these miniature aqueducts for many miles, and we noticed how it was led off among the vines and orchards and fodder crops that were growing luxuriantly on the numerous holdings. We were shown over a packing shed by a courteous manager; here they were preparing for the rush of work which would commence as soon as the growers began to bring in their sun-dried raisins, peaches, and other fruits, which would be graded, packed, and exported from here. We were shown a machine that takes the stalks off the dried raisins and grades them into sizes, after which they are packed and dispatched all in a day.

We went over one twenty-acre holding, where we found the owner, a Mr. Cutts, irrigating his promising crop of sultanas and muscats. He spoke of the yield being worth about £75 to the acre. Two years previously he had paid £110 per acre for his land, and he was reckoning on making an easy profit of at least £1,000 a year clear. He had been earning a small income in an office at Melbourne and had cleared out and come up to Mildura, where he seemed happy in his work, contented, prosperous, and ambitious. "It is a pity more people do not realize that money is not made solely by working in the unhealthy atmosphere of a dingy office," said Mr. Cutts. "It can be made more rapidly perhaps, and certainly more joyfully, by applying water to an apparently arid soil, to which must be added some hard work out in the hot but healthy sunlight," and the many charming homesteads we saw, surrounded by semi-tropical trees and brilliant flowers, vouched for the prosperity of this place.

To-day nearly all these settlements are connected by rail with their capital cities, and the whole district must have progressed in the last few years beyond the dreams of any of the original settlers. The heat no doubt remains unaltered, and it was certainly too hot to be pleasant when we were there, especially as we were short of changes of raiment, having sent our main baggage on by sea from Adelaide to Melbourne. So we were not sorry when Friday morning came to say good-bye to our rather dirty coffee-palace hotel and take one of the "three times a week" trains to the capital of Victoria.

In and Around Melbourne

The line from Mildura to Melbourne runs through the heart of the country. It thus gave us an additional glimpse of the back blocks, and from a scenic point of view it was far from inspiring. Flat and monotonous would be the universal opinion of most of the country. For the first few hours it was covered with bush, but not the thick undergrowth one associates with semi-tropical countries—just endless mallee bushes with a few feet of bare soil between and occasional tufts of dry grass. In places it had been cleared (a much simpler process since the advent of the "stump jump" plough), and although the rainfall is poor (12 inches), wheat is grown in considerable quantities.

The farther we went towards the coast the greater the development, and at every siding we saw stacks and stacks of wheat waiting shipment, all carefully done up in sacks but lying out in the open, for there is little fear of rain. The growing of wheat has been vastly stimulated by the use of superphosphates and special manures. It is the old story of the application of science, and in this, as in so many other instances, it has made the apparently impossible both possible and profitable.

One must not tell the Australian that he has anything to learn, but in the matter of railway management the South Africans can give him many points. However, in due course we arrived fairly punctually at Melbourne; it was nearly eleven by the time we found ourselves in our rooms at the Grand Hotel.

The morrow was a Saturday and the Monday following Foundation Day, so if we wanted clean clothes—and there was nothing we desired more—it was imperative to make an early visit to the wharf side as all work would cease there at noon. Our baggage that had been discharged from the *Anchises* was too voluminous for any cab; we therefore hired a van from the local general carriers and drove in it to the docks.

As no Australian dock labourer is ever willing to assist one with one's luggage, especially during the time of his "smoke-o," we had to deal with it ourselves, and the van man helped us haul our boxes—one was so big we called it the "treasure chest"—from under a nearly immovable stack of colossal packing cases. Meanwhile several labourers were looking on, evidently enjoying the sight of someone else doing their work whilst they were smoking their pipes, and with folded arms lolled about, supporting themselves against the walls of the building or on other people's boxes. What a joy it was to get clean clothes at last after existing for two weeks in a grilling climate on a very limited supply of underwear!

As there was no business to be done on Foundation Day, we devoted the afternoon to watching some superb tennis. Lowe, Dunlop, N. E. Brookes, and J. C. Parke were the stars who entertained us with their magnificent play. It was quite impossible to obtain a seat, so we had to be content with standing in the blazing sunshine wedged in on all sides by an enormous crowd of spectators.

On returning to the hotel we ran across an old friend and invited him to accompany us to Luna Park and St. Kilda's Beach. We were anxious to see how Melbourne "enjoyed" itself. We found Luna Park was a second-rate White City crushed into about a third of the space. It was crammed with people, and the dust and the heat were stifling and oppressive in the extreme. There were two girls to every man, and many of them would have been better in bed; many were carrying babies. The inevitable side-shows were there in plenty, and among those that were the most popular were shies of various sorts. Some of them were quite ingenious, and others so disgusting that we took upon ourselves to lodge a complaint about one of them to the local Society for the Protection of Animals; it was called "Ringing the Duck." Four or five wretched, bedraggled, water-logged ducks had hard quoits flung at their heads all day long. *If* you got the quoit over the duck's head—a highly unlikely event—you were entitled to torture the duck yet further by carrying it off under your arm.

On the whole the people seemed exceptionally orderly and well behaved for a Bank Holiday night. We moved on to St.

Kilda's Beach in the hope of a breath of fresh air. We were not rewarded. There was no breeze, and after picking our way between couples strewn here, there, and everywhere, and lying in each other's arms, we found that even the seawater at that point did not seem too appetizing. A few folk were bathing in the semi-darkness, but it was too near the harbour to attract us. We must confess we were surprised at the number of young girls who were disporting themselves on their own of an evening. We noticed that a local schoolmaster suggested in one of the papers that the girls' sole aim in life, from the very juvenile age at which they develop here, was "scalp hunting." For the truth of this we are not in a position to vouchsafe, but the rapidity of the development of the girls presents problems that cannot be ignored.

We also visited the Museum, Picture Gallery, and Public Library, besides going to the Prahran Library and Art Gallery and going over the Observatory. The Museum proved very interesting; it has a very complete collection of ethnological subjects. The Picture Gallery contains many good paintings, but unfortunately they are swamped. The Gallery is heavily endowed and able to pay big figures, and they have travelling scholarships—an excellent idea if only they would burn some of the pictures that result!

After a week in Melbourne we fled awhile from the madding crowd to the peace and quiet of Warburton—the mountains and the trees. It was a joy to leave behind all thought of smoke and bustle, and to find ourselves walking quietly up Scotchman's Creek knee deep in bracken. Gum trees (red, white, and blue) were there in plenty, also "stringy barks," "messmates," and mountain ash, but most wonderful of all were the gorgeous tree ferns. Seldom had we seen anything more beautiful, more fresh and green. As we climbed higher we found traces of the devastating fire that only the previous week had swept through the district, destroying everything as it went, and imperilling the safety of both La-La and Warburton themselves. The fresh bright green of the ferns was replaced by charred stumps, some of them still smouldering. As we sat out on the veranda after dinner that night talking to the proprietor of the Mountain Grand, who was a man of Kent and a great photographer, clouds of smoke were still sweeping down the valley. In the twilight we strolled along the banks of the Yarra, where a lyre-bird's nest was pointed out to us, but the bird unfortunately had flown.

Next morning we started out for the ascent of Mount Donna Buang, the "Giver of Water," that rises 4,000 feet high in the great dividing range between Murray and Yarra. We were urged on all sides to make a detour of eleven miles along a new road that was being cut through the forest. Nothing daunted we accepted the advice, and though it made an extra strenuous day we did not regret it. Except where past fires had charred the countryside, tree ferns were growing luxuriantly in every creek, and but for the difference in the vegetation we could have believed we were in Switzerland. The Warburton district is called the "Switzerland of the South," and in winter time deep snow is no uncommon sight on the summit of Mount Donna Buang. The road twisted and turned in its upward course, revealing the most marvellous views across the valley below us. Not until 3.30 in the afternoon did we climb the steps of the rickety wooden structure that serves as a tower on the summit of Mount Donna Buang. The view was sadly limited by the haze from the smoke of the forest fires, but it was our immediate surroundings that attracted our attention. It was like a field of battle. All the trees round the summit had been cut down and lay strewn around us, and beyond them was a circle of dead, barkless, white giants of the forest holding up their arms for pity.

We retraced our steps to the road and then followed Richards' Tram Track down the steep mountain side, a track used for hauling timber, and a most trying and fatiguing descent. As the English trees shed their leaves, so the Australian trees seem to shed their bark, and in some cases it hung down the boles in festoons or flapped about in the breeze,

Melbourne has both benefited and suffered by its modernity. The manufacturing city of to-day is at the best far from inspiring or beautiful. But the haphazard growth of ages is ill suited to modern requirements, and Melbourne has the advantage of having been definitely planned and laid out with fine broad streets. Although the unpleasant side of the great city is in consequence less obvious, it is there none the less. One is not confronted with slums, but one can see them in the making; and, though there is probably less real need, Melbourne is not without the big city's quota of destitute. One of the most remarkable things about Australia was, to our mind, the abnormally large proportion of the total population to be found in the capital towns of the various States, so that while the country was crying out for workers, and there was opportunity for all, the "lure of the town" left vast tracks uncultivated and the cities overcrowded. We were amazed at the Australian city man's lack of knowledge of the back blocks of his own country.

The splendid openings on the new irrigation settlements were being extensively advertised, and many of the younger generation were beginning to realize that there was a better, happier, and more prosperous future awaiting them "on the land" than as a cog in the business machine.

We were alive to the many good features of Melbourne. First and foremost of these were its parks and gardens. We were told, and though we could not verify the statement we could well believe it, that no Melbourne child need walk more than four minutes to find an open space in which to play. Certainly there are gardens on all sides, and even St. Kilda Road, that broad highway that rivals the Unter den Linden of Berlin, is planted with flowers.

The Cable Tramway Service, though doubtless highly profitable to the shareholders, did not seem to us worthy of Melbourne. It was both expensive and inefficient, and we were not impressed by either the Australian postal or railway service, and would have liked to assure the authorities that, though

67 The *Ruby* was a queer-looking craft

68 The woodman led a solitary life in his "humpie"

69 Tree ferns on Mount Donna Buang

70 Sultanas and muscats at Mildura

they had reported to the contrary, they had *much* to learn from other countries! That attitude of having nothing to learn from outside is all too apparent in Australia, and we could not conceive of anything more likely to retard the progress of this vast country—a country teeming with possibilities, a country with an immense future.

During our stay in Melbourne some Japanese training ships put in for a few days. The cadets wandered around everywhere, and it was most interesting to watch the Australian attitude towards them. The feeling against the Japanese is very keen here. They are feared as much as the Germans were at Home in 1913. There is a poll tax of £100 on every Japanese entering the country. But the papers could not help commenting on the clean and orderly appearance of these cadets, and on the whole they were very hospitably treated.

One night we dined with Professor Payne, who had kindly promised to show us something of the University and the Working Men's College. The latter proved exceptionally interesting, and corresponds to some extent to such places as the Battersea Polytechnic. It was the opening night of the session, and there were crowds of young fellows entering their names for instruction in one or other of the numerous practical subjects—carpentry, printing, etc., in which instruction is given for a nominal fee.

I had several more calls to pay, including the editors of the *Argus* and the *Age*, and I also wanted to look up some "Single Taxers." The local secretary proved very kind, and telephoned to several enthusiasts to say I was in town! A group of eight or nine of them had lunch together every day, and it ended in my joining them. We had a most interesting round-table talk, and I learnt much of local affairs. They were all well-informed men, and one, a leading lawyer, was born at Midhurst, and remembered visiting the Cobdens with his mother.

The weather in Melbourne was for the most part hot, but by no means unbearable. But the day before we left it touched 107° *in the shade*. Even so it was not oppressive, though it "hit" us as we left the hotel.

Chapter VII

TASMANIA

THE crossing from Melbourne to Launceston is like the English Channel trip, a regrettable necessity. The S.S. *Loongana*, then a fairly modern and very rapid steamer, covered the distance in about fourteen or fifteen hours. The posters advertised "Tea in Melbourne, Breakfast in Launceston," but luck was agin' us. So long as we were in the shelter of Port Philip Bay "life went by like a song," as the poem has it. We ate a substantial dinner and looked complacently at our fellow passengers. But the moment we passed the heads "everything went dead wrong!" Now we are told "that the man worth while is the man that can smile" in such an emergency, and knowing from experience that I can only pass that test in a recumbent position I hustled into my bunk. It was a very near thing, but the rapidity with which Johnnie followed me turned my smile into a broad grin.

To cut a long story short, we did *not* breakfast at Launceston; in point of fact, we did not breakfast at all! Our steering gear broke down and we described circles and other geometrical figures until the officers became bored. We then hove to. We were, I suppose, about five miles from the Tasmanian coast, and there for several hours we stopped. Gongs were rung violently for lunch, but no enthusiasm was shown, for the movements of a stationary vessel in a rough sea do not stimulate enthusiasm for food. At 4 p.m. we felt the throbbing of the engines once more, and a few minutes later we were steaming up the calm and peaceful waters of the River Tamar. At 6 p.m. we saw Launceston.

Mr. W. J. Westrope had been waiting with one of his daughters for us on the quay since 8.30 that morning! We spotted him at once, and he gave us a most hearty welcome.

The Homestead at St. Leonard's

Owing to its being race week he told us the hotels were all full to overflowing, and he had therefore most kindly arranged to drive us both out with him to his farm at St. Leonard's, about five miles away.

Mr. Westrope proved a genial and cheerful philosopher-host. He was overjoyed to welcome a son of his old friend, Edward Unwin, and a friend of his brother. It was nearly thirty years since he had been in the Old Country, and he had seen no old friend from Home out here since.

Mr. Westrope's two daughters, who ran the house and farm, and their brother all gave us a homely welcome. They had a hard life and seldom got an hour off, for the cows *must* be milked, so that, although our coming meant extra work, it was in reality a little change for them.

Even if this life left no time for intellectual development, it certainly produced a type of womanhood for whom one could but feel the greatest respect. They must not, for instance, be daunted by the necessity of providing and cooking food for an extra twelve to fourteen men, and hungry men at that, for the law provides that, when the threshers or reapers arrive, if you employ them you must feed them. This actually happened whilst we were there. Feeding these men consisted of breakfast, tea at 10 a.m., dinner, tea again at 3.30 p.m., and supper, besides numerous *extra buckets* of tea if the weather were very hot. The men were waited on hand and foot; all they had to do was to eat and drink; half a sheep and a free run of the orchard was nothing to *them*, so one can well understand the extra work such an invasion entailed. Not only that, but if the threshers elected to stop on the place over a week-end, between two periods of employment by the same farmer, they were entitled to demand food on the Sunday at 6d. per meal. So did the workers of the Antipodes protect their interests, and seeing that they were paid 8s. per day it did not seem to us they were badly off, for living in "Tassy" (Tasmania) was not excessively dear at that time. We thought of the agricultural labourer at Home and his few shillings per week.

Our five or six days at this farm near Launceston were a welcome respite after the rush we had at Melbourne. It was altogether delightful to sit outdoors after tea and listen to the opossums chasing one another over the roof above, while a new moon and the Evening Star glistened in the sky.

From the farm we visited Launceston, where we paid business and other calls. We were taken to see the famous Gorge and the beauty spots of the North Esk River at Cora Lynn. It was certainly a very pretty part of the world, and more like England than anything we had seen since leaving Home. The view from our bedroom window at the farm, across the hedgerows and fields of newly cut barley, to the willows lining the stream side, was just as one might obtain from the window of an old English farm, whilst the heavily laden mulberry tree in the garden and the quantities of greengages in the orchard completed this homelike scene. We motored along country lanes lined with hedges of hawthorn, whence flights of brightly coloured parakeets rose with much screeching at our approach. Thus we went through Perth, Longford, Bishopsbourne, and Hadspen to Carrick, over vast corn-bearing lands where harvesting was in full swing, and beyond loomed the distant mountains—Ben Lomond, Arthur, and Barrow, whose flanks were swathed in the curling blue-grey smoke of the bush fires.

Another day our host's son-in-law, a Mr. Smith, himself a farmer in a large way of business, motored us out to the Nile district to meet the owner of a "little block" of some 45,000 acres; his land covered roughly an area ten miles by eight miles! He "sheared," as they say in these parts, 20,000 to 25,000 sheep per annum, and he told us that he "could shoot stags from the bedroom window" if he wanted to. He had recently been returned a senator to the Federal Parliament, and his ideas, which were far from harmonizing with our own, were nevertheless typical of an officer in the army, from which he had recently retired.

We returned to St. Leonard's to find the chickens suffering from an overdose of mulberries. It was really too absurd to watch them sitting about under the tree waiting for the fruit to drop! The supply was plentiful so they did not bother to seek other and more solid food. But undiluted mulberries produce "collywobbles" even in chickens, and they presented quite a forlorn appearance and were growing steadily thinner.

We were sorry to leave this part of the island without seeing something of the "chocolate" lands of the north-west, where tons and tons of potatoes are grown and they harvest 100 tons of hay on a thirty-acre paddock. The tin mining, too, we left unexplored, for our time was limited and the beauties of the south called us. Once more we found ourselves in a train that was following a winding track among the hills to climb and descend again some thousand-odd feet. The joy of Tasmanian scenery lies in its mountainous background, and as we neared Hobart the slopes were covered with orchards and hop gardens. It was the beginning of the apple season, and even now the great mail-boats were coming out of their way to collect this golden cargo at Hobart.

Our first view of the capital was not so dramatic as might well have been the case, for Mount Wellington was completely hidden by clouds, but the next morning these had lifted and a perfect picture greeted us as we sat on the balcony of our very comfortable boarding-house called "Vallis Vale." Below us, on ground that sloped gently to the water's edge, lay the outskirts of the capital of Van Diemen's Land. The River Derwent spread itself out into an enormous estuary, and here, on a grey-blue expanse of water, two sailing-ships were tacking in an almost imperceptible breeze. Beyond, fine ranges of hills ran north to south, indistinct in the heat haze but evidently well wooded, and the light brown of the scorched stubble fields was evident everywhere. Behind towered Mount Wellington, concealing half its massive strength beneath a flimsy veil of bluish mist. An apple orchard was close at hand, whither we had already been to gather the rosy fruit, for we were already tiring of apricots, peaches, and pears, luscious as indeed they were. A trellis of rambling roses—a trellis of cherry pie—completed the foreground of our view of Hobart from the balcony of "Vallis Vale."

Having completely filled one day with calls and sight-seeing, which included the famous "Domain," we set out early next morning, knapsack and camera on shoulder, down Davey Street for the wharf, whence the S.S. *Cartela*, one of the numerous river-boats that steam to places of interest along the beautiful shores of these winding fjords, bore us across the Derwent Estuary and Frederick Henry Bay to Taranna and Eaglehawk Neck.

A freshening breeze had cleared the sky of the ominous-looking clouds that for some days had been hovering overhead in an unseasonable manner. Only a small chaplet of vapour still clung to the peak of Mount Wellington, whilst other clouds, swept together in long ranges across the sky, caught up the early-morning sunlight with a splendour of effect that completed the perfection of the scene.

Thus we steamed round the lighthouse at Cape Direction, perched on the end of a dangerous reef that protects the Derwent Estuary from the fury of Storm Bay, and, passing behind Franklin Island, we entered the broad, calm waters of Frederick Henry Bay.

Bounded to the north by a beautiful curving beach some seven miles in extent, this bay gives birth to two fjords. The smaller, Pitt Water, is gained by a narrow entrance at the end of this northern beach, and bears the important township of Sorell on its farther shore; but the larger fjord, or Norfolk Bay, as it is called, runs in a south-easterly direction, penetrating far into Tasman's Peninsula, with the village of Taranna at its head.

Hell in Paradise

Here again a continuance of these tidal waters goes eastwards to Eaglehawk Neck, where a narrow strip of land, but 150 yards wide, joins Tasman's and Forestier's Peninsulas, which form the great south-eastern portion of Van Diemen's Land.

Hither we were bound, and, as we steamed along gazing at the gum forests that lined the banks of these fascinating fjords, we noticed here and there, where a bush fire was starting, the flames running up the oily eucalyptus boles and the blue odoriferous smoke trailing out across our course.

Having had lunch on board with many horny-handed but none the less worthy companions, we hurried to Lufra House, which for some years had been run as a private hotel by an Indian named Nuroo. Here we procured accommodation for the night, and having left our belongings we set out to explore.

Eaglehawk Neck might be described as a natural drawbridge, composed of broken sand-hills, that just prevents the great Southern Ocean joining hands with the tiny Eaglehawk Bay. From our hotel we looked down upon these two bays and the frail "neck" that divides them, across a green meadow where grew luxuriant blackberries asking to be gathered; and around us towered the gum forests, gaunt and grim, where fires of long ago had sucked the strength from the now ghostly rotting stems. To our left the sea was a brilliant blue, and in the far distance the great rocks at Cape Hany stood out grey and menacing. As we strolled along the white sandy beach of Pirates Bay southwards to the Isle of Fossils, it was hard to imagine that this golden morning sunlight had been the only redeeming feature in the scene some seventy years before, because this beautiful but ill-fated spot presented a spectacle *then* the memory of which fills one with horror *now*.

Then it was impossible to cross this narrow neck of sand without challenge from an armed sentry, or if one *had* essayed to run the gauntlet one would have been pulled to the ground by one of many furious curs which were tethered across the isthmus. Some of these dogs even stood on platforms in the water, so woe betide the absconding prisoner who attempted to swim, and there were sharks to contend with as well.

This, then, was the gateway that led from the outer world of hope, freedom, and so-called justice to the hell upon earth —the old convict settlement at Port Arthur in Tasman's Peninsula.

Gigantic gum trees growing on the edge of the shore now cast their shadows over the pure white sand, and their reflections ripple in the brackish pools where cattle come to slake their midday thirst. But in the days when men and boys were transported to Port Arthur to undergo long terms of imprisonment this peaceful little beach was often the scene of many daring and ghastly attempts at escape, and once the prisoners had contrived to elude their would-be captors and gained the mainland of Tasmania, it meant certain death from starvation in the impenetrable bush, or murder and cannibalism amongst their own ranks if there were several in their party.

But when we come to describe Port Arthur and its picturesque situation, it will be better understood why these unhappy convicts wished to escape from the place, and what led them to descend to such acts of untamed barbarity.

The shore is thickly strewn with minute shells, and close by the Isle of Fossils is a blow-hole of considerable repute in Southern Tasmania; we were somewhat disappointed by it, for the memory of the blow-hole at Boscastle in Cornwall was still fresh in our minds. True it is that we could approach quite close to this one at Eaglehawk Neck by means of some broad ledges of rock, and we could peer right into the rocky maw through which the treacherous swell heaved and gurgled and went spewing forth on the other side.

The cliff track continued through deep bracken and low scrub to Tasman's Arch and the Devil's Kitchen, both awesome precipices of sheer rock into which the ocean appears to have eaten a subterranean way. We were pressing on along the coast to Waterfall Bay when the dry weather that we had been enjoying for nearly eight long months broke again in one of those miserable wetting rains, and it was not long before the tall bracken had drenched us to the skin.

That evening at supper we made the acquaintance of a Mr. and Mrs. T——. The former was an honorary assistant at the Natural History Museum, London, and his speciality was the collection of a certain species of the wasp family. Mr. T. was very shy of manner, and hesitated in his speech as if half afraid to disturb the siesta of his would-be captive; his wife, on the other hand, was bright and talkative, although none the less ardent in the chase. The following morning they set out each with net in hand, and returned to lunch having made twenty-seven captures of various wasps and one or two varieties of bees. Personally we were congratulating ourselves on the absence of wasps in Tasmania, yet here we were sitting opposite to a professional wasp-catcher who had been busily employing himself for some months in the capture of these unpleasant insects in the immediate neighbourhood of Hobart! This was sufficient proof that in *some* matters the Two Young Men's eyes were *not* so fully open as some reporters in the Colonial Press had flattered us by maintaining.

We spent a few hours, while at Eaglehawk Neck, eating blackberries and scrambling over the rocks to Nuroo Island, which forms the northern point of Pirates Bay. On our way we crossed what is known as the Tesselated Pavement, broad stretches of rock that have been scarred or split up into almost regular squares by some unimaginable power.

It was a most perfect walk back to Lufra House, along the white sand of this umbrageous foreshore, with the blue curving waters of the bay stretching away on the one hand and the rising hills thickly clad with bush and gum trees on the other.

After an early lunch we set out on a coach for Port Arthur.

Our road lay for the most part through very thick bush country, where fires were burning freely in spite of the heavy showers of rain through which we kept passing. At about three in the afternoon we came in view of the ruined village of Port Arthur, tucked away in a fold of the hill around a little bay that is an offshoot of another of the many estuaries that eat into Tasman's Peninsula. A more charming position for a village would be hard to conceive, the water was so blue, the grass and foliage so green, and the hills so thickly wooded. "What an ideal place to send those who have sinned against the law! Who could have chosen a more beautiful prison than this?" Thus we innocently soliloquized as we followed the guide who was leading us to those roofless buildings which were once the Model Prison of Port Arthur.*

"Here," explained the guide, in his professional jargon, "is the central row of cells where the prisoners were kept in solitary confinement. The jambs of the doors were burnt by the fire that destroyed the shingle roof. Sparks from a big bush fire swept the settlement some years ago and reduced them to their present ruinous state." He then showed us the silent cell, where a prisoner could rave without being heard. It was a pitch-black chamber, so small that a big man could not fully extend his arms; it was enclosed by solid walls and approached by four unassailable doors.

Then there were the exercise yards, long triangular cages. Each man was let loose in a cage to himself for an hour or so a day, during which time he could neither speak nor make signs to the man in the next cage to him without earning an extra punishment. Here he clanked up and down, up and down, in his heavy irons that tore the skin from his ankles and wrists, more unhappy, poor wretch, than the wildest of wild beasts!

* An interesting description of Port Arthur, and a successful escape therefrom, will be found in *The Escape of the Notorious Sir William Heans*, by William Hay, a remarkable novel of early Tasmanian life; and also in *Pageant*, by G. B. Lancaster (both published by George Allen & Unwin Ltd.).

Within, the silence of his prison was all but absolute; even the warders wore slippers, and no sound was heard except the clanging of keys.

For one man a special cell had to be built, so desperate had he become that his agility and strength were like those of a gorilla, and ordinary iron bars doubled up in his grip. For another a special run and house even had been erected, for he had had all reason tortured out of him in the chain gangs and other horrors of the Penitentiary, and became so dangerous a madman that no one dared go near him.

At a little distance stood the Penitentiary itself, a huge ruined building of two floors. Here the convicts worked at various trades, the chief of which was boot-making; and here also they slept in long dormitories under very overcrowded conditions. The men who worked here were far better off than those who had to haul timber in trucks along wooden rails laid through the bush, or drag great logs through the dense undergrowth to these trucks, struggling and stumbling as their bonds caught them around leg and arm, doubtless goaded on by the rude curse and heavy lash of their gaolers. Under these and worse brutalities it is not surprising that a spirit of revolt was raised in the heart of the lowest criminal, taking the form of insubordination or attempts at escape; whereupon the unhappy convict had the severest punishments inflicted upon him. His irons were made yet heavier, his meagre diet was reduced, his term of silent and solitary incarceration was prolonged, or, worst of all, he would be put on to grind cayenne pepper!

After a time these unfortunate criminals became hardened against all forms of violence, and sometimes, it is recorded, when two prisoners were confined together, they drew lots as to which should strangle the other, when, of course, the survivor of such a ghastly tragedy was hanged. Others, on the contrary, were offered and accepted the post of warder, and these men proved the most brutal warders in the settlement. Considering these things, we can well understand the attempts at escape and the consequent recourse to barbarism of which we have already spoken!

Across the water was another building called Point Puer.* Thither juvenile criminals were deported, and at a spot where a steep rock overhangs the blue lagoon these youngsters used to throw themselves with cool deliberation to a certain and welcome death to escape the inhuman tortures which they were expected to endure. This point is now called "Suicide Cliff."

Half-way between this gruesome promontory and the mainland at Port Arthur lies the Isle of the Dead. Here some hundreds of bodies were interred. Some were those of warders; some those of the high officials of the prison; but for the most part, where nothing but a low mound denotes the final peaceful resting-place, the graves are those of convicts. Perhaps they had been thrashed to death for not disclosing some plot of escape; perhaps hard toil or lack of food had killed them, or suicide or murder had relieved them at last from further hopeless lingering in a world of darkness and grim unending suffering. This was only ninety years ago, and now the grass is green, the water blue, the wooded hills just as impassable as before; but the place of suffering is reduced to ruins, and we look back in wonder at the callous inhumanity of those days! Only the ivy-clad walls remain of a beautiful church which one of the convicts designed, buying his freedom for a piece of work that is superb even in its ruined state.

It was with a lighter heart that we were able at last to leave our guide and set out on a brisk four-mile walk to the "Remarkable Cave," but, in spite of pretty peeps at sandy

* From the Records of the Office of Comptroller-General of Convicts may be learnt the tender age, 12 to 14 years, at which some of these children were transported from England for petty thefts, such as "stealing a watch, value 50s.," "stealing clothes from my brother," "theft by housebreaking," etc. One young convict of 12 years of age was sentenced to 7 years' imprisonment at Point Puer. During 6 years of this he received, for various acts of insubordination, 165 stripes on the breech, 168 days' solitary confinement, and 5 months' labour in chains. Another youth went to Point Puer at the age of 13 for a term of 14 years. During the first 10 years he received 65 stripes on the breech, 124 days' solitary confinement, and 23½ months' hard labour in chains.

shores where lazy wavelets sighed as they fell in a captivating and regular cadence, we were not yet free from the haunting convict element. On our right was a big farm building, and on the disused land that surrounded it convicts used to be harnessed to the plough. We tried to dispel our uneasy thoughts by gazing across the estuary at the noble cliffs that guarded the entrance to Port Arthur, on which the evening sun was casting a rosy hue. A tall flowering heath lined our track on either hand, its pink and white blossoms reminding us of the charming flora of Cape Colony, and as we pressed on along the sandy path we presently began to descend towards the edge of the cliffs at a rapid rate, until suddenly we came to the lip of one of those strange deep chasms in the ground with a sandy bottom, which show that the ocean has in some incredible way managed to creep through. Descending by some wooden steps we gained the bottom and gazed up at the towering walls of cliff which rose to a height of some 500 feet all around us. On one side opened an enormous cavern into which we penetrated for some distance, until we were confronted by a strange double entrance facing the boiling rollers of the Tasman Sea. This was the "Remarkable Cave," remarkable for its double entrance and for the fact that we were nearly cut off by an incoming tide owing to our undue curiosity to observe the rocks on the seaward side!

However, we returned to our little hotel at Port Arthur without mishap, and after a wash and brush up in our garret bedroom we descended to a solitary but strangely over-loaded table, where we discovered, cleverly concealed amidst the Christmas decorations, which, seeing that it was now February, we thought peculiarly out of place, every conceivable luxury in the manner of good things to eat, from luscious peaches and rich cream to preserved ginger and other sweetmeats.

Our waitress spoke with a dignity and refinement which placed her at once, in our minds, as being Home-born, but imagine our surprise when she informed us that she was

German, but Tasmanian born. Her father and mother, Mr. and Mrs. Furk, had been pioneers in this island; she and her sister had never been to Germany and could scarcely speak the language, although their English was perfect!

Later that evening a married couple arrived, and we enjoyed our first big wood fire since leaving Home, for the night was chilly, and it was with much difficulty that we ultimately tore ourselves away from a blaze filled with so many homely reminiscences to slip between chilly sheets and sleep soundly in spite of a terrible din in the garden, where they were hiving a swarm of bees by moonlight.

The next morning we made an attempt to scale Mount Arthur, but in spite of careful directions from the guide we managed to miss the way in the maze of woodmen's tracks that ran in every direction. However, we succeeded in climbing to within a few feet of the summit by dint of forcing our way upwards through a dense wonderland of fern and bush, and for a time we could well imagine ourselves to be escaped convicts battling for freedom. In such a place as this only a few months previously a woodman made a gruesome discovery—a human skeleton with the broken iron fetters still clinging to arm-bone and leg-bone, and beside it, in a straight row, lay the buttons that adorned the convict's clothes in those bygone days of harsh tongue and cruel lash. This man had evidently escaped, had contrived by almost superhuman efforts to break his fetters, and had struggled on until overcome, for even the hand of Nature was turned against him.

Half-way down again we rested on a fallen gum tree to smoke a cigarette and gaze at the blue waters of the port through the hazy smoke of a fire that was burning slowly right across our track. Such fires are slow but destructive in their course; sometimes the tree boles smoulder for many days, come crashing down, and go smouldering on.

Later that day we left by coach for Nubeena, and proceeded to cross Storm Bay in a steamboat which seemed all too small for the size of the waves, which caused us to roll, pitch, and toss in every direction with such alarming rapidity that presently a tragedy ensued which is best untold. It will be enough to say that one of us attempted to be sick over the windward gunwale.

After passing Cape Direction we were in smooth water again, and late that evening we were back at "Vallis Vale," none the worse for our adventures in convict land.

I could never make out why Stan always had rubber heels fixed to his footwear. *He* maintained that they were economical, whereas *I* voted them a waste of valuable time. Everywhere we went we did an enormous amount of walking, and these wretched heels were always being cast by the wayside. One day as we were passing down one of the principal thoroughfares of Hobart, and had arrived opposite an important Government building where a high official of state was laying the foundation stone of a new wing, one of Stan's rubber heels went spinning into the gutter. The street was thronged with fashionably dressed people who were crowding round to watch the important event that was about to take place across the road. Stan always insisted that I should act blacksmith to him immediately and wherever these little accidents occurred. With a groan of disgust he kicked off his shoe and hopped to the wall of a house, where he supported himself on one foot and raised the other, which was clad in a bright purple sock, out of the mud, whilst I salvaged the shoe and heel from among the hurrying feet of passers-by and began the task of screwing them together with my penknife. I really believe the public thought *more* of Stan's purple sock than they did of the ceremony of laying the foundation stone.

Hobart was not without its peculiar characters, nor did we miss the doubtful charm of their acquaintance. We were endeavouring to telephone at the post office one day when we were rudely interrupted by an unpleasant disturbance. On looking out from the box where I was assisting Stan, I saw a shabbily dressed man gesticulating and shouting in front of the counters, and shaking hands with the clerks, and slapping on the back those people who happened to be writing telegrams at the desks. Then, after a lengthy soliloquy in the centre of the office, during which he informed himself about many startling "facts" as to how he had managed to get into his present condition, he raised his battered old bowler to his amused audience and took his departure. But we were destined to meet him again on various occasions, and Stan always crossed to the other side of the road and put on the pace to avoid him. The old fellow seemed attracted by Stan, and I assured the latter that, avoid him as he would, he was *sure* to turn up to a meal at our lodgings one day. I must admit that it was a great surprise to me when, one Sunday afternoon, as I was sitting near our front door at "Vallis Vale" smoking a pipe of peace, who should come trotting down the garden path but old Mr. Dotty! He was dressed all in his Sunday best, a baggy tweed suit and an old straw hat with the brim bent down all round and a yellow daisy in his buttonhole. "He has evidently come to pay his respects to Stan," I thought, and as no one came to answer the ringing bell I kept the old fellow in conversation until our host appeared at last. I dashed indoors to tell Stan that an old friend had called to see him, and as we came rushing back to the front door in wild anticipation as to whom our caller might be, we saw poor old Mr. Dotty being pushed out of the garden gate by our host, who received a volley of oaths for his trouble. Poor old Mr. Dotty was a well-known character in the city, a sorry example of his own admissions—"drink and other things." He was one of the many "remittance" weeds that, after frequent uprootings and replantings, run up into perennial seed and get blown across the oceans from the Homeland to be a blight upon the fair names of these unlucky colonies.

We Explore Still Further this Beautiful Isle

We were off up the beautiful winding road to the Springs Hotel that lies half-way up the slopes of Mount Wellington. The views of Hobart and the harbour were superb, as also

71 Shea oaks, Monge Bay and Cape Hany

72 Where cattle come to slake their midday thirst

73 A charred monarch of the bush

74 The River Liffey at Carrick

was the quiet nook called Fern Tree Bower, which we were allowed to visit whilst our horses rested on their upward climb. We arrived at the Springs Hotel for lunch, after which we climbed to the summit of Mount Wellington by an easy path.

Just over 4,000 feet in height, this mountain rises steeply at the back of the capital, and our pathway lay right across its face, gaining the crowning cairn after traversing the rocky summit for some distance. From the cairn we could look inland over the inferior heights to more distant peaks where snow was still lingering, but at our feet lay a panorama that, for its own peculiar charm, can be scarcely rivalled in the whole world.

The entire district of Hobart was laid out like a map, and never have we seen, from any height, a more interesting geographical study of land-locked lagoons, curiously shaped peninsulas, hills, hamlets, and winding roads and streams. From the verdant valley on our left, where the silvery waters of the Derwent curled like a broad ribbon, our eyes followed it to where it widened into an estuary. Here great ships lay at anchor in the ample natural harbour, or were busy discharging cargo alongside the wharfs that fringed the little city; and there lay the city itself in all simplicity, the houses seeming to stand apart, each like a toy dwelling in its orchard, or clustered around the more imposing buildings of the municipality. Everywhere lines of fruit trees dotted the landscape, and away to our right, where the Derwent estuary opened out still farther into Storm Bay, there began that extraordinary indentation of coast-line formed by the fjords and peninsulas of which we have already told.

The boulders immediately around our cairn were shockingly defaced by painted names, most of which were followed by Australian addresses. We could but deplore the bad taste of a few foolish individuals which had spoiled the beauties which Nature has placed here for human delectation. On our way back we had an exciting encounter with a 2-foot snake, which we succeeded in blotting out, much to the satisfaction of some ladies who passed us on the track at that moment; and lower down we came upon a tablet erected to a man who fell dead at that spot in a "Go as You Please" scramble to the summit that had taken place some years ago.

After a refreshing cup of tea at the Springs Hotel, overlooking almost as glorious a view as we had obtained on the summit, we mounted our charabanc once more and were drawn home by four cream-white ponies with pale blue eyes and pink noses.

Another expedition we made from Hobart was to Huonville, in the centre of the Tasmanian Apple Land. Here again was a beautiful drive lasting some hours, all along the face of Mount Wellington, with superb glimpses of blue-watered harbour and fjord, between stately gum boles, or over the tops of apple orchards where the rosy fruit clustered against the azure sky.

By noon we had covered the twenty-three miles and drove into Huonville, a one-eyed little place that attracted us hardly at all except for a delightful stretch of river, whence the township takes its name, and down which we were soon gliding on the M.S.S. *Excella*.

Thus we had a fleeting glimpse of the jam pulp industries at Franklin and some glorious peeps at Sleeping Beauty and the Hartz Mountains, and so back up the D'Entrecasteaux Channel to Hobart. Owing to an accident that had overtaken our vessel earlier in the day, when she and her mechanism received bodily harm, we did not get back to "Vallis Vale" until late in the evening. But this did not daunt us from catching the 8.30 boat for Bellerive the next morning, whence we took a miniature train for four miles to Red Gate Halt and then tackled the magnificent walk up Mount Rumney (1,236 feet), from which summit we had a still more gloriously coloured map panorama view than that afforded by Mount Wellington, on to which we now gazed as it raised its colossal splendour above Hobart Town.

75 Kangaroo on a Tasmanian farm

76 A beautiful reach on Brown's River

77 The Russell Falls

78 Assisting the hop-pickers

It was on a sunny, windless morning that we found ourselves being borne by the train up the beautiful valley of the Derwent to Macquarie Plains. Poplars, willows, and gums were mirrored in the broad unruffled surface of the river. Orchards in full fruit lined the steep banks and hop-yards covered the cup-like dales with the luxuriance of their dark green verdure.

The train took a long time to reach our destination, but with imposing blue mountains as a background to so beautiful an outlook time slipped by all too quickly.

Sir Phillip Fysh, late Premier of Tasmania, on the arm of his daughter, Mrs. Forest, was on the platform to meet us, and soon we were speeding along in his beautiful car to take morning tea with some wealthy friends of his who own a large sheep station some few miles away.

Bushey Park, Sir Phillip's residence, is an old rambling Tasmanian homestead, hidden from the hills and fertile valleys that surround it by well-grown timber of many varieties. Magnificent specimens of Spanish and horse chestnut, acacia, elm, and oak gave the beautiful garden a homely look which was greatly enhanced by the presence of a huge white magnolia bush in full flower at the time of our visit. A port-wine magnolia was an interesting variety that I do not remember seeing before; it blooms twice in the year—in the spring when the bush is a mass of reddish-purple flowers, and later in the year when these exquisite blossoms appear again amidst the deep green foliage.

As we sat on the long veranda that ran along the front of the low house it was a delight to let one's eyes revel in the feast of colour that decorated the irregular flower-borders. But more often we sat in a little summer-house perched on the high bank of the River Derwent, and as we leant our backs against the trunks of the trees that, shading our bower above, penetrated its roof and floor, we gazed upon the glinting rapids and listened to the whispering harmony of their song.

Returning to the house by a winding path, we would cross a small stream of clear water which could be diverted through the various beds of flowers at will, and into this racing current large green frogs would jump at our approach.

Sir Phillip Fysh was a fine septuagenarian with a long white beard and thick white hair, whose dignity of manner and fine stature led one to respect his rather biased opinions on matters of State.

During our two short days at Bushey Park we managed to put in a good deal of motoring. The first evening to the Salmon Ponds, Tasmania's beautiful trout hatchery, where luxuriant green lawns and stately lines of poplar and willow trees backed by blue hills were mirrored in charming pools. And here fish from a few ounces in weight to many pounds leapt from the water as lumps of sheep's liver were thrown to them by the keeper. We were also shown fish in the embryo state, preserved in spirit, some with double heads and one tail, others with double tails and one head, others again with one eye and crossed jaws, etc., and then we went to the banks of the stream where huge 15-pounders lay lurking in the shady pools!

The following afternoon saw us racing along in the car over hill and dale, through burning bush and peaceful orchard, to the famous Russell Falls. Here again was a fairyland in the form of fern-lined glades and running streams with giant gum boles rising foot above foot from the thick undergrowth into the blue sky. The falls themselves were graceful rather than wonderful; as the water was low, they formed a wide thin veil of water in a frame of tree and fern, falling in three leaps from a considerable height.

We had visited some hop-yards that morning where we chatted to and assisted the pickers, photographing them and the threshers who were also busily at work at a farm close by Bushey Park.

In the evening some played bridge and others read in the soft lamplight of the drawing-room, whilst without the moon shimmered on the Derwent rapids and the wind whispered in the elm boughs as in the elms at Home.

For a long time it had not been our good fortune to enjoy so perfect a "slack" as we had in Sir Phillip's garden one morning, in the deep shade of the summer-house overlooking the river, or on the warm sunlit veranda surrounded by trees and flowers. So when three o'clock came, and we had to say good-bye, it was with a pang of regret that we looked for the last time on this happy corner of so wide a world!

Again we had a glorious train ride back to Hobart, but when we arrived there we found the city reclothed in her mantle of grey overhanging cloud. So it was with somewhat disheartened feelings that we took up lodgings in a rather frowsy hotel until we should be borne away by the T.S.S. *Maunganui* for New Zealand.

Before leaving Hobart, being young and irrepressible sightseers, we climbed to the summit of Mount Nelson (1,113 feet). This was the only peak in the district and the only "sight" that remained undone, and although the sky was grey we were well repaid for our energy. This is the signal station for incoming craft, and on the veranda of "the Captain's" little house we were served a delicious tea by "the Captain's" rosy little wife, while far below us lay the long stretch of the Derwent Estuary and Storm Bay, which we had by now learnt to love in all their varied aspects.

Two Young Men See the World

NEW ZEALAND

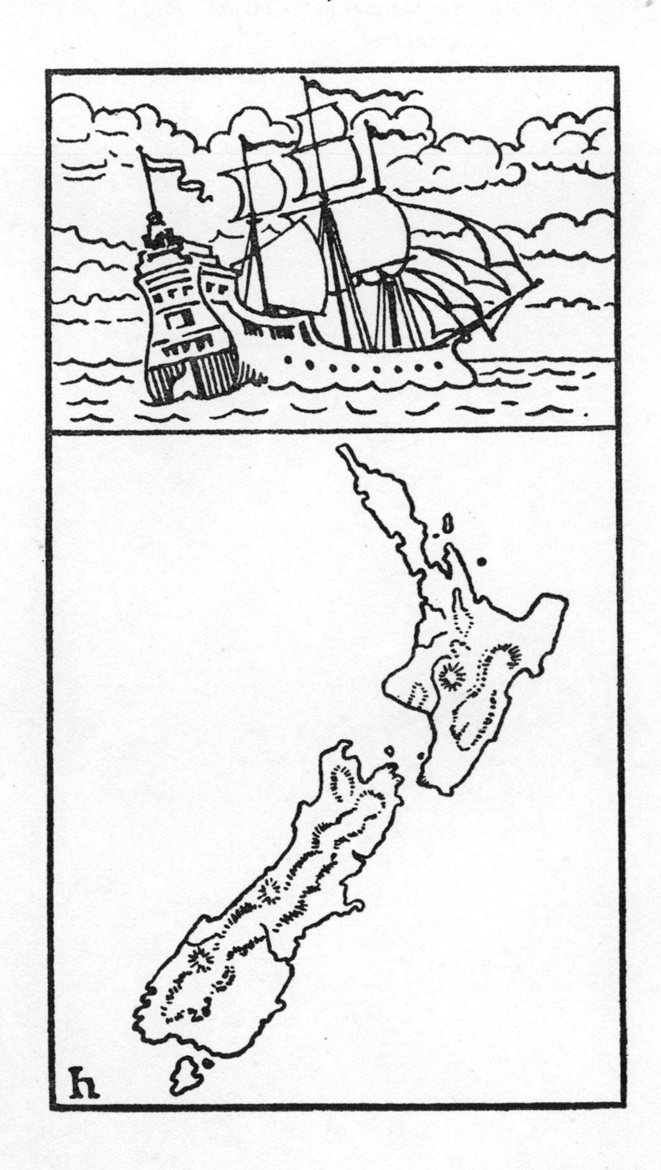

Peaks piercing the silence of heaven,
Snows gleaming in luminous space,
See her waves round a hemisphere driven
Fling their crests to the winds as they race.
God filled from the life of their motion
Her nostrils with breath of the sea,
And gave her afar in the ocean
A citadel free.

William Pember Reeves

Chapter VIII

ACROSS THE TASMAN SEA TO MILFORD SOUND

THE T.S.S. *Maunganui* of the Union Steamship Company of New Zealand left the crowded harbour at Hobart for that grim-sounding port, The Bluff, only a few lengths astern of the great *Ruahine* of the N.Z.S.S. Co. The *Maunganui*, however, was a much faster boat, and at Cape Direction we passed the *Ruahine* as if she was standing still.

It was dull and windy as we steamed down Storm Bay and out into the Tasman Sea. The gradually vanishing coast-line was capped with grey clouds, but was none the less wonderful in its rugged beauty. Cape Raoul with its shattered basaltic pillars, and Tasman's Island with its high perched lighthouse guarding the entrance to Maingon Bay, and Port Arthur were passed by and faded away into the mystery of the ocean wilderness, and the smoke of the *Ruahine* was also lost to view as she steered away on a north-easterly course for Wellington. We were at sea, hopelessly at sea, the ship rolling to a steady swell with the wind chanting in her spars. Thanks to the severe schooling we had had by now on ships of all sizes, we were as fit as the fiddles that decorated the tables during the whole of this voyage, and we were much amused at the first meal when fiddles were not in use to watch the bottles of beer and wine being scattered in all directions, and knives and forks creeping this way and that, while plates slid suddenly away, and gravy kept spilling all over the cloth! We glanced with much glee at the faces of "the chair people" as they lay all wrapped about with rugs, whilst we stepped briskly along the sloping decks, lurching to the swing of the boat.

There were many interesting people, both to talk with and to look at: le Comte and la Comtesse de Z——, the famous French seed-grower and his wife, were undoubtedly the most elegant of our company. There was a dear old gentleman well advanced in his sixties who was on his way to *see* his daughter, aged thirty-two, for the *first time in his life*. It was also during this week-end at sea that we made the acquaintance of Dr. Wellbeck and Mr. Spinney, in whose society we were destined to spend many delightful and some unpleasant days. Thus with a little deck quoits, a little reading and talking, and a few meals, the day was done, and we would lay ourselves down to rest and be rolled unwillingly from side to side in our bunks. As we drew nearer to the coast of New Zealand the great Pacific swell increased, the wind shrieked in the rigging, and a host of giant albatross swept, with motionless outstretched wings, across the unbroken crest of this vast ridged ocean.

Early one February morning we awoke to a sensation of unaccustomed stability that told of our arrival in calm waters at last. On deck the scene was grey and uninviting, the rack from the previous night's gale hung everywhere about the sky in ominous festoons. The Bluff, a dirty green headland, rose in unimposing grandeur on our starboard bow. People call it "The end of the world that God forgot to finish off," and certainly it had a most God-forsaken appearance when we set eyes on it that dreary morning. For miles on either side of it the grey coast-line could be distinguished, fading far away to where sea and sky and land merged into a shapeless smudge of leaden hue. To starboard were the high peaks of Stewart Island towering into the scudding cloud, whilst all around lay the dim ugly shapes of smaller islands, plentiful traps to shipping when the sudden and dangerous squalls so frequent to these coasts sweep up out of the dark Antarctic.

At noon, after lying idly in the roadstead for some hours, we entered the narrow fairway to the wharf, and there, nestling among a few scattered trees and surrounded by brilliant emerald grass, stood the little red houses of the town.

This indeed seemed more like Home, but it was in reality the land of the Maoris, "Ao-Tea-Roa," the Long White

Cloud. After waiting nearly an hour on the windy platform at The Bluff, when a pipeful of John Cotton gave additional charm to the fact that we were on terra firma once again, a tiny train steamed into the station to take us up to Invercargill.

The train was slow—oh! so tediously *slow*, and the country we passed by was of a sandy nature covered with low unimposing bush. Here and there a cabbage tree reared up from the thicket, but it was a dreary entry into a land of such reputed beauties.

Invercargill is the capital of the Southland district of New Zealand, and it is what is known as a "dry" town. Those who wander into the public bars of hotels or inns are faced with a large notice, "Soft Drinks Bar." The shock is a severe one at first to those fond of something stronger than lemonade and soda water. Gore, Oamaru, and some other New Zealand towns have similar restrictions. Invercargill, in spite of the fact that it is "dry," is largely a Scottish community. The buildings are solid and the streets wide, but one has only to see the city on a day when the wind howls and the raindrops leap up into the air to give it the name of the "last town in the world."

The place depressed us beyond words. The only redeeming features were the vivid green of the grass in the paddocks, where even the cattle were browsing in mackintoshes, a few fine pine trees, and the view from the top of the water-tower.

The "Finest Walk in the World"

From Invercargill the train took us through an undulating pastoral country that reminded us very much of the Salisbury district, to Lumsden. Fine sheep, cattle, and crops were in evidence everywhere. The land was divided up into small paddocks lined with hedges of gorse, and the whole scene, from the round white clouds in the sky to the homesteads dotted here and there in the fields, seemed very much like the

Old Country; the cabbage trees alone aroused us brusquely from our dreaming.

Lumsden, where we had perforce to stop for luncheon and take motor thence to Te Anau, is a very "wet" place. Four hotels, selling the most fiery of drinks, supply, no doubt, the grocers' and the bakers' shops, for we could see no other habitations of much account.

We found five other passengers besides ourselves in the motor-bus that left for Lake Te Anau that afternoon. There was Spinney, an English gentleman of uncertain age, a fellow World Traveller, ex-schoolmaster, and ardent fisherman. He was chiefly remarkable for his very skinny legs, his languid voice, and his droll face upon which, as we afterwards found, he had some trouble to grow a sufficiency of what the late Frank Richardson used to call "face-fungus," and on which a smile but rarely manifested itself. Then there was Dr. Wellbeck,* whose huge head and round cheeks quite overbalanced his sturdy frame. In fact, his head, like his tongue, seemed quite uncontrolled, and into every item of his conversations he brought his *métier*—osteopathy. The Misses Beatrice and Florence Timber came from the North Island, and were spinsters fairly well advanced in years to undertake such an expedition as lay before us. Miss Beatrice was thin, Miss Florence was stout; they were "both going to walk through to the Sounds," they told us. We thought to ourselves: "*Are* you! Anyhow, if you *can*, it must be a pretty easy stroll!"

The remaining female member of our party was a rosy-cheeked, auburn-haired Colonial, but she got out at Mossburn, our first place of call. Oh! the hair of these New Zealand girls! This and their pretty colouring were the very first things we noticed on landing, all so infinitely superior to the pasty faces of the Australian towns. We were later *disillusioned* by a Timaru doctor as regards the New Zealand girls' hair!

* We may remind our readers that in this, as in many other cases, the name given is fictitious.

At that time apparently "buns" and "additions" were not unbeknown to those charmers! Should a doctor tell?

The car in which we found ourselves was old and noisy, the road bad and bumpy, and the country—well, the country between Lumsden and Lake Te Anau, a distance of fifty miles, reminded us of Scotland, the West of England, and the high veld of South Africa, whilst others declared it resembled such distant places as Corsica, Egypt, or Palestine. Above all else, the colouring of the landscape was extraordinary: deepest mauves, blues, and reds wrapped the cavern-scarred sides of the volcanic mountains in a most bewitching mystery. Unruffled pools, where a silent cabbage tree stood sentry, mirrored the most exquisite natural pictures, whilst rushing torrents of green and foaming water often barred our passage. On their banks grew tall reeds and pampas grass, and the apparently useless tussock grass covered the treeless hillsides.

We stopped at the Key Hotel for a few minutes, a lovely wayside hostelry in the centre of a good stretch of arable and pasture land, and we shall always remember the lovely Takitimu Mountains, whose corrugated spurs and terraced slopes were tinged with the mauve and blue of a perfect evening light that glanced along the backs of the browsing sheep in the tall dead grass of the pasturage.

The Whitestone River was crossed without difficulty, but, although an innocent enough creek the day we saw it, it can at times hold a car up for hours and be almost impassable by the coach. This vehicle, which had left Lumsden at eleven that morning, we passed at nightfall about two miles from the lake, and as we dropped from the highlands to the water-level we only obtained a glimpse like a silvery line of this beautiful inland sea.

It was a five hours' journey from Te Anau to Glade House,* up the thirty-eight miles of this narrow lake. Our little steamboat was diminutive in the extreme, so that the smallest waves made her leap about in most lively fashion. It had been raining

* Since burnt down and replaced by a new building.

all night, and was still raining now, to add to our discomfort, so that we could see little or nothing of the beauteous landscapes that surrounded us. In fact we were soon on our backs in the stuffy little cabin forward, feeling very uncomfortable indeed. The mirror-like reflections portrayed on picture post-cards had led us to believe that Lake Te Anau could *never* be rough!

We were all glad to land at noon, and a half-mile walk brought us to Glade House, and after lunch we set out, in the pouring rain, on the first ten miles of the "Finest Walk in the World," for the Pompolona Huts up the Clinton Cañon.

Having been ferried across the Clinton River without difficulty we started off at a good three miles an hour along the narrow track that lead through a wonderful forest of moss and lichen-covered timber. Dripping vegetation hemmed us in on every side, and now and again we had glimpses of the narrow Clinton River, which was rising steadily owing to the increasing fall of rain. Here it would tumble along in a series of roaring rapids, and farther on it would be an emerald pool. Unfortunately the clouds hung low over our heads, so that we only obtained surreptitious and awe-inspiring glimpses of the enormous peaks and precipices that towered immediately above us whenever our narrow track traversed a clearing in the forest.

At first we endeavoured to avoid the innumerable puddles that covered the surface of the track, but at the end of the second hour this became a useless precaution, as overflowing streams frequently flooded our path.

Stan and I had been maintaining the lead, but we were soon caught up by Dr. Wellbeck, the big-headed young osteopath, whose company we did not cherish. We soon got into clearer country, and the clouds, drifting again, showed us the precipitous mountain sides down which numberless cascades were falling from a height of over 1,000 feet. This was the result of only a few hours' rain, in dry weather, which is rare in these regions; scarcely any falls are to be seen from this valley.

We had seldom seen anything more remarkable than the sight afforded by these cascades, falling as they do from the very summits of the peaks, where it is hard to imagine any water could collect, and tumbling in supremely beautiful leaps, sometimes disappearing into the tangled woodlands that cover the lower spurs of this narrow cañon.

Thanks to fording ankle-deep through several small but swollen mountain torrents that crossed our way, and the saturated state of the foliage overhead, we were now beginning to experience all those unpleasant sensations of unwatertight kit. The Doctor walked along holding up the corners of his mackintosh before him for the better protection of his knees. He advised *me* to do likewise, but I explained to him that my hands were otherwise engaged, for with one I was carrying my camera legs, and with the other I kept relieving the straps of my well-laden knapsack and well-stocked camera case, which began to pull heavily upon my shoulders. This, together with the fact that we were labouring along in overcoats buttoned up to the neck, will give some small idea of the unpleasant side of our walk! At one point we saw a waterfall shooting over the mountain's lip, but the terrific wind that was howling in those lofty regions caught the falling volume of water and scattered it in a fantastic cloud of spray before it had time to leap from another rocky ledge.

However, we stumbled along the last two miles, the beautiful cascades spouting onto our very track, and we passed deep, silent pools, beneath the brushwood, into which great drops of moisture fell. No bird sang, no beast crossed our path, only the roar of the ever-rising river accompanied the sound of our slipping feet as we struggled on over rocks and through pools, longing for the welcome shelter of the Pompolona Huts.

The miles seemed to drag out towards the end; our burdens became more irksome, and we cursed our folly for bringing so many useless things. Our knees were clammy with moisture, and our bodies a revolting indignity of inward sweat and outward rain! At length we scented a sweet perfume of burning logs, and, on pressing forward, we saw a clearing with a tree bole laid across the track. We crawled under the barrier across our path, and then, round a bend, we suddenly came upon the welcome sight of the Pompolona Huts!

We had covered the ten miles in three hours and twenty minutes, which Mr. Graham, the caretaker, thought was very good time under such conditions. He was preparing a fire with large damp logs in the gentlemen's sleeping hut, and here we changed into other garments which we found had suffered little from our wet tramp. The remainder of our party came up in twos and threes; the ladies had weathered their difficult task well, and by now had almost entirely dispensed with their skirts, even the more elderly Miss Timber arriving with her skirt tucked round her waist and showing, unbashfully, a pair of very serviceable blue serge knickers. But poor Spinney came in in a sorry plight; his stockings had descended around his ankles, leaving bare his remarkably thin legs, and his languid voice had quite lost its charm and almost its power of expression, through a heavy cold which had suddenly come upon him.

Marooned at Pompolona

It was a queer-looking crowd that sat down to tea that evening in the kitchen-dining-room at Pompolona, some of us collarless, in all kinds of scrap garments. It really might have been a fancy dress tea. Mrs. Airey was clad in a blanket, Mr. Airey had bare legs and feet. Johnnie, looking exceedingly dishevelled, with his scanty hair brushed back, sat next to Dr. Wellbeck, whose enormous head was capped with a shock of shaggy locks. Then there was poor Spinney, whose mournful expression and doleful hoarse voice uttering cheerless complaints about the weather could but bring sallies of laughter from us all. Opposite to us sat a Mr. and Mrs. X——, who had been already weather-bound one day. They were a rosy-faced, middle-aged couple; he looked like a cross between a gorilla and a pig, a most extraordinarily ugly little man. At

79 Native Bush, Milford Sound Track
By courtesy of The High Commissioner for New Zealand

80 On the Milford Sound Track

81 The Quinton Huts

Photos by courtesy of The High Commissioner for New Zealand

the other end of the long table sat Mr. Challice, who had come over from Glade House on a tour of inspection, and, incidentally, to mend the telephone, which was to be the only source of excitement during our imprisonment at Pompolona. With him were two guides or tracksmen, and Mr. and Mrs. Graham. This last-named personage was a very bright little woman, an excellent cook and hostess, and our thanks are due to her for keeping our spirits so high.

The kitchen-dining-room at Pompolona had a wide, open fireplace; an array of pots and kettles stood on a high grid, or swung over the fire of damp logs from sooty hooks. Beneath the fire was the oven, where Mrs. Graham manufactured her life-saving dainties, and on either side were piled sodden logs a-drying.

After our meals we would all sit round the fire in a semicircle, discussing our chances of escape, or the cessation of the downpour, or we would write on what available paper we could collect, or read a number of third-class novels that had seen better days.

The gentlemen's sleeping hut was a few yards away from the main hut. It was a fairly airy apartment, with two rows of bunks around three sides and another wide fireplace, a door, and a tin washing-basin and jug on the fourth side. The ten bunks were comfortable and clean enough, and the whole room was adorned with drying garments and paraphernalia of all kinds.

Tobacco was running short, and one cannot overestimate the companionship of tobacco during such an imprisonment as this. Our only moments of real excitement were when the telephone bell rang and we knew that we were in communication with the "Outside World," as Spinney mournfully called it. The "Outside World" was only the accommodation quarters at Glade House, which is about five hours' steamer trip from Te Anau. This steamer only runs twice a week, and is the *only possible* means of communication with Glade House. Te Anau itself is fifty miles from Lumsden, the road between them being liable to heavy floods. Forwards, we were divided by impassable streams from the next huts at Quinton, and a telephone message told us that we could not go back, for the Clinton River at Glade House was nothing but a roaring torrent, having flooded its banks, and the boat that ferried us across was tied to the veranda posts!

Thus we found ourselves at the mercy of this incessant element, rain; entirely cut off, but fortunately with a solid roof above our heads and no lack of food for the moment; but there were thirteen of us all told in this hut—— Ah! thirteen, by Jove! Here's the reason for it all!

We spent a second and a third day at Pompolona. We were told that no wayfarer had ever been forced to shelter there so long before. These huts are owned and run and the track is boomed by the Government, which accounts for a deal of the comfort one can get, though the track itself could not boast of over-attention in those days.

The weka birds afforded us constant amusement. They are flightless birds, with plumage like a hen pheasant, and they have very sturdy legs, red eyes, and substantial beaks. In size they resemble a small fowl, and although usually very timid, here a number of them walked about close to the hut, and sometimes their inquisitiveness made them venture inside. They appeared pitiful creatures in the wet, their shabby tail feathers looking especially droll. They are protected, together with all other animal life in this enormous National Park, which extends for many thousands of acres. But many were the threats of slaughter which we made against them if our food supplies had happened to come to an end! They make a curious harsh, penetrating cry, and appear to be very quarrelsome and great bullies among themselves, but they display undaunted courage in fighting with weasels, stoats, and rats; the first two of these animals were introduced into this country to destroy the rabbits, but now they prefer all kinds of birds and their eggs.

The following afternoon brought a startling change from

our three days' hopeless contemplation of the continuous downpour. The rain was falling less heavily and the sky brightened somewhat. It was proposed that we should don our overcoats and go for a stroll of a few hundred yards to see if the creeks were subsiding. I refused to go out, but sat in a fit of spleen over the fire in our sleeping hut, smoking a pipeful of my rapidly decreasing supply of John Cotton.

About thirty minutes later the Doctor and Spinney rushed in to say that a party of four ladies, whom we knew were in the neighbourhood of the Sound, had just arrived in an exhausted condition, having spent all the previous night on a bridge over the Arthur River, some fourteen or fifteen miles the Sound side of Pompolona. "If *they* can get through," said the Doctor, "I can," and he prepared himself for the track, and dragged poor Spinney after him as the skies resumed their sullen look.

These four ladies had a thrilling tale to tell, and, as we sat at the long table eating our evening meal, they, clad in blankets and other borrowed coverings, held forth in an excited manner.

On the way out, they told us, they had had a wet journey over to Milford Sound in company with a Mr. Stevens. It was imperative that they should catch the Monday's boat back to Te Anau, so they set out at the height of the downpour on Saturday morning, homeward bound from Milford Sound, without Stevens, who was not so pressed for time. Sutherland's accommodation house, whence they started, is about two miles across the water from Sandfly Point, where the actual track ends. This they accomplished in safety in Sutherland's motor-boat, but neither he nor the guide stationed at the point warned them of the possible flooded state of the track owing to the heavy rains.

So they started from Sandfly that Saturday noon, having waited some time for the weather to moderate, which, of course, it did *not*. By 3 p.m. they had done seven of the thirteen miles to Quinton, and arrived, after terrible experiences, which included wading breast-high through water, at the suspension bridge over the Arthur. This river was found to be nothing less than a roaring torrent overflowing its banks and rising some distance up the high flight of steps that led up to the bridge from either bank. The unfortunate women, who had already shown great pluck by wading through such a depth of water in the swollen creeks, now feared to advance or retreat, and decided to remain on the bridge until the river should go down. The rain continued to pour down all through the night, and here on this narrow swaying structure of planks and steel wires, with the cold night wind shaking the moisture from whatsoever trees might possibly afford protection, the women huddled together, now sitting with arms locked and legs dangling from their sodden seat of planks, now rising to stamp their numbed feet. The three horizontal wires that formed the side of the bridge were insufficient protection against their slipping into the foaming torrent that swept over sharp rocks and grinding boulders beneath them, and when squatting arm in arm they would doze and then start into a horrible awakening!

One lady counted "One, two, three" all through the night in order to keep herself awake, and all the while the rain lashed down upon them, and, more terrible still, *they had no food*. Thinking they would get to the Quinton Huts in good time for the evening meal, they had provided themselves with only a few biscuits. These were now sodden beyond recognition, or had been thrown away with other articles to lighten their packs.

So the night passed on, whilst the women cheered each other bravely, longing for the dawn to break or that the rain might cease. At 5 a.m. there was sufficient light and they decided to advance. To their joy they could see that the river had gone down considerably.

They eventually escaped from the suspension bridge, after being imprisoned there for fourteen hours, wet to the skin and without food, and they arrived at the Quinton Huts at about 9 a.m. There they only tarried for some hot tea and something to eat, and were fortunate to find the head guide, who escorted them over the nine miles of track, across McKinnon's Pass, to Pompolona.

This distance is beset with dangerous creeks whose waters rise with alarming rapidity in stormy weather. The most notorious is Roaring Creek, where again they had to wade breast-high through the torrent. Here their foothold was among unseen boulders, but, thanks to the presence of the guide, they managed to complete their journey to Pompolona in safety, arriving at about 4 p.m. in a state of excitable exhaustion.

When we awoke on Monday morning it was to see the rain coming down as steadily as ever. I was the last to traverse the muddy stretch of track between our sleeping quarters and the main hut, and as I passed along I noticed a very milky and scarcely perceptible portion of blue sky along the peaks. I rushed into the hut where the others were breakfasting and shouted out the joyful news.

The four heroines of the suspension bridge* bade us good-bye, as they were off to Glade House, at all hazards, to catch their boat. Among our ranks there was much hesitation before we decided to press on to Quinton. Some of our party had actually abandoned all hope, and had started out after the girls back to Glade House, but returned as others shouted after them persuasively. And so it was that, after spending three days and four nights in the Pompolona Huts, our original party was able to proceed.

The rain ceased as we set out, the mists rose up the steep sides of the Clinton Cañon and broke away from the mountain peaks in the form of beauteous clouds. Our track was wet, but our hearts were light, for the creeks had already shrunk away into almost insignificant trickles, and the sun's rays urged us onwards and upwards through the wonderful tunnel of moss-draped bush and rock, where drops of moisture

* This bridge was carried away by the flooded Arthur River during a similar storm a few weeks later.

hung for an instant like sparkling gems ere falling into some dark green or peaty pool, in the shadowy depths of which lurked weeds and water plants of rare luxuriance. The tiny fantail and the wax-eye flitted from twig to twig, whilst the reeking stems of beech and rata and the sodden moss-covered boulders bore rich clusters of ferns, and the whole bush breathed forth a strange odour into the moist, perspiring air.

Save where our passage was balked by dislodged boulders, our track wound on in an easy gradient to the foot of McKinnon's Pass, which now towered above us, forming an enormous saddle between the protecting pinnacles of Balloon Peak and Mount Hart. After passing the deep and many-coloured waters of Lake Mintaro, we crossed the stream of the Clinton River, that descends from the snowy heights of Mount Hart, by means of a rough timber bridge, and then began in earnest the ascent of the pass in easy zigzags that, at every turn, gave us magnificent views. First we were walking towards the moraine under the shoulder of Mount Hart, and then, as our pathway changed direction, we faced down the peak-crowned valley whence we had come beside the roaring Clinton River. Every now and then these glimpses of snowclad summits were glorified by a framework of curious lichen-covered boughs which reminded one of the prints of the Japanese Masters, for even at these ever-increasing altitudes this endless luxuriance of ferns and other vegetation clung to the precipitous slope of the mountain side.

The extraordinary rainfall of this region is, of course, entirely responsible for such a wealth of verdure. The average is, I believe, somewhere about 150 inches per annum! This accounts for the almost continuous rain storms that sweep the neighbourhood of the Milford Sound track for days without intermission.

We were, indeed, well repaid for our long tarrying at Pompolona when we gained the summit of the pass, which is about 3,500 feet above sea-level. It appeared to be a vast bog of peat, covered with long coarse grass, and, where it was saturated by the voluminous supply of water which poured onto it from the towering rocks on either hand, large pools of clear water formed which mirrored the summits of the higher peaks. Midget-like we gazed up at the barren but colossal splendour of Balloon Peak, or, creeping to the spongy lip of the pass, we were almost terrorized by the awful drop into the widespreading valley where Roaring Creek shrieks a warning to the unwary mountaineer. As from the eyrie of some bird of prey, we could distinguish the open rocky bed of this treacherous torrent and trace it backwards to its source; firstly, to two stained snow arches, and further to where numerous falls dropped over thousands of feet of sheer crag from the bluish cliffs of the Jervoise Glacier. From time to time this mountain monster spat out a tooth of ice that came thundering down in a splendour of shattered fragments, whilst he could be heard groaning as it were in the very bowels of the earth!

Scudding cloud-rack swept over Mount Elliott still farther away, while to the left, standing out sharply in magnificent array, draped in blue and capped in white, were the widespreading sides of the Arthur Valley, with the Quinton Huts like a little hen-house far below us and right in the centre of this stupendous scene.

After resuming our journey we came upon another grand view down the Clinton Cañon. A tiny spot of red marked the roof of Pompolona, with a small white line of washing drying in a gentle breeze.

Stan and I maintained our lead of the party down the zigzag, Mr. Airey and the three ladies bringing up the rear. My big toes began to give me some pain, and my load pulled heavily upon my shoulders; but soon we came upon Roaring Creek, which we crossed without difficulty, though the wide bed of ugly boulders showed us what caution would have to be exercised when the torrent was in full flood. We congratulated ourselves that we had not been with the Doctor and Spinney, who, having preceded us, crossed here the previous evening knee-deep in a failing light. When the four ladies of the suspension bridge crossed, the water was breast-high, and some time ago an artist was swept off his feet and hurled a considerable distance down its tumultuous course before he could scramble out. He was so badly bruised as to be unable to proceed for many days.

I now dropped to the rear of our party, for the path led through the woods again over rough rocks and streams, and this tried my feet, which had become badly chafed owing to the wetness of my boots. Eventually, however, we arrived at our destination at 3.30 p.m. We three men found a glorious pool of icy water in a secluded spot up the creek surrounded by ferns and moss-clad birches. Here we thoroughly enjoyed a soap-down and a bathe, which warm sunlight penetrating the overhanging boughs made all the more enjoyable.

The Sutherland Falls

We decided to walk another one and a half miles after getting something to eat to see the Sutherland Falls, which are, perhaps, the chief sight on this wonderful tramp.

The track was more boggy and rocky than any we had yet struck, but our struggle was amply rewarded; firstly by the imposing grandeur of Balloon Peak, that now towered supreme in the distance at the valley head, bathed in the brilliance of the evening light, and secondly by the sudden revelation of the falls themselves. Splashing through the flooded streams and scrambling over the rocks in our way, we heard presently a sound as of crackling artillery, and on turning round a ferny corner of the track we beheld a spuming volume of water spouting and roaring as it crashed down the face of the mountain side nearly 2,000 feet in height! We had been told that it fell in three leaps, but when we set eyes upon it in its swollen state it appeared like one straight column, towering high above us. We were unable to approach closer than about a quarter of a mile, for the wind caused by its downward rush carried the spray in every direction. Stan and Mr. Airey made a dash towards some rising ground, whence a view can be obtained of the water's headlong crash into a deep basin, but the driving mists obscured their view, and they returned hastily, wet to the skin. A lady we had met at Pompolona suggested that the only costume to wear when visiting this fall was a bathing dress, and, as we returned to Quinton, we could but regret that we had no such serviceable garment with us! I endeavoured to take some photos of this awe-inspiring fall, but found this impossible until we had retreated fully a mile, and even then I had to tilt my camera considerably to obtain a good view of the entire precipitous drop of the water.* This fall, which is in reality an overflow from the little mountain lake named Quill, was discovered by Mr. Sutherland, whose accommodation house we were on our way to patronize at Milford Sound. It is claimed for the Sutherland Falls that they are the highest in the world, being 1,904 feet in height, or four and a half times taller than the Victoria Falls. But in width, of course, the Sutherland Falls are insignificant compared with the wonder of the Zambesi!

The arrangements at Quinton were very similar to those at Pompolona. Tinned food was our staple diet; tea, condensed milk, or water, our drinks. Wet clothes again had to be slung from wires before the fire or along the beams of the hut. Mr. and Mrs. Mulqueen, who were in charge, were as attentive as we could desire, and we all sat down to meals with a sprinkling of guides and tracksmen as before.

When we turned in it was a beautiful starlight night; the enormous peaks rose menacingly above us, but the wekas called uncannily to each other, which, we were told, always means rain. The bunks at Quinton were so hard that none of us slept over-well, and the gusty wind that blew down the gulley rattled our iron roofing and whistled in and out of various cracks in our cabin. When we awoke in the morning we found the floor and everything in the hut covered with

* Unfortunately all the photographs we took on the Milford Track turned out failures for some reason unknown.

wood ashes that had been blown from the open fireplace! At 8.15 we were on the tramp again, with the last thirteen-mile stage to Milford Sound before us.

These last thirteen miles of our walk were even more beautiful than the earlier portion. The track was better than it had been, but the bridges and overflowing streams were very troublesome in places.

First of all our way lay beside the winding Arthur River, till we crossed it by the suspension bridge where our lady friends had spent such an awful night. Here we too stopped to rest and eat something. The river had resumed its normal appearance, but we could see where the grasses on its banks had been beaten down by the terrible flood water. Nearby this bridge and close to the track is a curious boulder called Bell Rock. At first glance there would appear to be nothing peculiar about it, being covered with moss and overhanging bush like thousands of others along the track. But on nearer inspection we discovered a narrow entrance underneath it through which one can just squeeze, and once inside one can stand upright in a bell-shaped hollow. Close by is Mackay's Fall, and it is thought that at one time this rock stood in a reversed position high up in the fall and received the rushing waters that gradually wore it away, and that it finally became dislodged and fell upside down as it now is. Inside, the wall of rock is quite smooth, denoting the constant wear of water.

Farther on again we crossed a deep green pool at the foot of Giant's Gate Fall, an indescribably beautiful point on our walk, and, when we were almost too weary to go farther, Lake Ada was suddenly spread at our feet. As we gazed down upon it, calmly lying there in its mountain framework, we could see the white-headed Paradise duck, teal, shag, and black swan peacefully fishing on the silent, silvery stretch of water.

From here our path took the form of a rocky ledge that had been blasted out from a low precipice that dipped into the deep water of the lake, and then, for the last few miles, it lay through the bush again, improving somewhat in surface and foothold.

We were leading a long way ahead of the others in order to reach Sandfly Point and arrange for a boat to take us across the upper reaches of the Sound to Sutherland's house. Large pigeons of delightfully blue plumage flew off from their feed of fuchsia berries as we approached. In places we managed to travel at a fair pace, in spite of our irksome burdens.

Presently we met the Sandfly guide, an open-faced young fellow of few words, and with him we returned to his hut at the point, where he prepared tea and placed cheese, bread, butter and jam on the table.* Sandfly Point is well named; these minute insects are in full possession. The window-sill of the hut was heaped with their dead or dying carcasses; kerosene had been their sorry end. But even as we sat there, breathing in the heavy smoke from the damp log fire, the sandflies pounced upon us and nipped us unmercifully.

Tired and footsore as I was, I could rest there no longer, and whilst Stan *ran* back, with his usual energy, to meet and relieve the ladies, I paced up and down outside the hut. Here I found the little pests pursued me in multitudes, and only by maintaining a brisk pace could I keep free from them.

Stan soon returned, so we entered the hut and fell to on the good cheer, whilst the guide went outside to explode a cartridge of dynamite as a signal to Sutherland, two miles away, that his boat was wanted; for, although the telephone was installed from Glade House to Sutherland's house, a distance of thirty-four miles, only the first ten miles of line to Pompolona was serviceable at that time. The remainder lay beneath log and bush in a hopeless state of disrepair!

The guide's home-made bread was the best we had tasted on the track, and, when I had a great lump of it half-way down my throat, the cartridge exploded with a roar that shook and

* We understand that this old hut has been replaced by a new accommodation house.

reverberated among the mountains, and nearly caused me to choke to death!

After a delay of half an hour we espied a little white boat, containing a crew of three elderly bearded men, speeding up the fjord, and it soon came alongside a roughly constructed landing-stage.

The famous Mr. Sutherland was at the tiller, his step-son McKenzie controlled the petrol engine, while his friend Black, a jovial old man with grey whiskers and a red nose, sat in the bows with a rope and made fast.

Milford Sound

Soon we were gliding over the mirror-like water of the Sound. The broad-shouldered Sutherland sat like a great owl in the stern, his calm blue eyes gazing steadily ahead, on the look-out for snags, those ugly tree-stumps that stick up in the deep water and are a menace to navigation. Here we were on the bosom of one of the most beautiful fjords in the world, the climax of what is claimed to be the "Finest Walk in the World," and as we turned round the arm at the head of the Sound we came into full view of Mitre Peak and the crouching Lion. Ahead of us boomed the great Bowen Fall, with its magnificent tail arching out from the mountain side, and away to our left, where the waters of the Sound vanished in a mystic haze between converging precipices of rock, were the towering ice-clad peaks of the great Pembroke Glacier.

Before our arrival at Milford Sound we had already heard a good deal about Sutherland. For years he had lived here at the head of the Sound, entirely cut off from the world by practically impassable mountain ranges, and visited only at rare intervals by a steamer that brought sightseers and provisions to this solitary family of backwoodsmen. In his early days he was a fisherman on the North Sea, but eventually he migrated to New Zealand, and here he led the life of a pioneer, prospecting and exploring.

The solitude of such a life had made him morose and unreasonable, and he was looked upon by most visitors as a curiosity, which only made him more misanthropic. When any women came to stay at his accommodation hut, which was not an infrequent occurrence, he always referred to them as "hot waters," and in such small matters as the amenities of comfort he and his wife were completely deficient. Mrs. Sutherland had, I should say, been a fine woman; Sutherland was her third husband, but *still* her eye had an imperious look. Her short hair was grey, and she wore, I was told, a man's costume under her overalls!

Sutherland had never been known to wear an overcoat. A shirt, open at the neck, covered his singlet, and these, with trousers, socks, boots, and a seaman's cap, were the only garments he wore year in, year out. Age alone caused him to stoop from his former six feet of height, and it had also tinged his sandy beard with grey.*

But *Miss* Sutherland was *the* attraction of the place. She was a niece of the household, and had been living there for the last two years. We heard, unofficially, that she had received over a hundred proposals from various swains who had toiled all those miles to win her affections. But she "had kept them in their places," and was still free, still the *only* maiden at Milford Sound. We ourselves escaped the toils of this Antipodean Circe, but Stevens, whom we discovered when we finally arrived at the house, seemed to have lost at least a portion of his fickle heart to her.

Rain spoilt that evening for us at the Sound, and rain was falling heavily next morning, when the Doctor and Stevens set off on a forced march through to Glade House. The weather improved later on in the morning, and we decided to go down the Sound in the motor-boat. Of course, we had not been going long before the downpour came on in renewed

* Some few years after our visit Mr. Sutherland passed on along a still finer track than the one that leads to Milford Sound. His end was a tragic one, I am told, for it was some days before assistance could be obtained to give him a decent burial.

torrents and wetted us to the skin again through our saturated raincoats. Despite this, and the roughness of the Sound, we enjoyed ourselves none the less, and marvelled at the sheer height of the mountain sides above us, rising to an altitude of four to five thousand feet. The water beneath us was quite as deep as the mountains were high, and we could not help shuddering at the thought of some rock detaching itself from above and crashing into our midst, submerging us beneath its weight and bearing us down to the fathomless bottom of this submarine cañon! At one time we surprised a school of porpoises that were gambolling within two feet of the rocks; they darted ahead of us, and seemed almost inclined to jump into our boat. We could see their great ghostly outlines as they dived away into the deep green water to continue their frolics in the underworld. So we went on down the Sound; we drew in close to graceful waterfalls resembling bridal veils, or put about to avoid some ugly peak of rock; we peeped up mysterious gulleys where men seemed never to have trod. One, Sinbad Gully, looked particularly sinister, and formed the main approach to Mitre Peak.

Vegetation grew everywhere in dense profusion. The red flower of the rata was visible on every hand, also the orange-brown rimu or red pine, one of the most beautiful of New Zealand's trees; whilst others in the jungle were the birch in its four varieties, black, silver, red, and white, the fuchsia, lancewood, ribbon wood, and veronica, called by the Maoris Koromiko, and a host of others.

The afternoon proved too wet to go out, and so we rested on our beds, while the sandflies feasted merrily upon us! No attempt was made to keep these infernal insects out of the house, and even as we put on our clothes in the morning they would settle on and bite the uncovered portions of our anatomy. Fortunately they were slow to move, and we had the satisfaction of killing them in hundreds, but it was like shovelling a spadeful of sand from the desert! Having been round the Sound, our interest in remaining longer at

Sutherland's was gone, for these pestilential sandflies gave us no peace.

We decided to start back the very next day, and, of course, it was raining hard! This time we got the Sandfly guide to row us up Lake Ada, which saved us a three-mile tramp along the track, and the rain obligingly ceased, giving us an opportunity of admiring the scenery. Lake Ada was formed years and years ago by a big landslide that occurred in the valley near the head of the Sound. The Arthur River flooded the forest, and the rotting tree-stumps can still be seen in the lake.

Our walk back to Quinton Huts was only remarkable for the rain and the wetness of the track, but the next day was fine for our return over McKinnon's Pass.

I went to the expense of a guide (12s. 6d.) to carry my swag to Pompolona, but thanks to a bad memory and Mr. Challice's forgetfulness, my debt to the Government remains unpaid! The man who carried my knapsack was a graduate at the University, and had come on to the track as woodsman during the vacation.

After lunching on the summit we began to descend to Pompolona. We met several people on the pass going over to the Sound, among them a Mrs. and Miss S——. I had a long conversation with Mrs. S——, a middle-aged lady, who was travelling *very* light indeed. She had taken off her skirt and had an abbreviated arrangement around her knees in the shape of a knitted coat, which she had fixed up as a kind of kilt.

After another night at Pompolona we made a great effort and got back to Glade House. The rain was coming down more heavily than ever, so that it was with a feeling of thanksgiving that Stan and I found ourselves at last, installed in dry raiment, after a luscious hot bath, drinking tea in the comfortable smoking-room before a roaring fire. One by one our fellow travellers arrived, and we received them with cheers, and spent the rest of the day in discussing our past experiences.

Next day Mrs. and Miss S—— returned in the pouring

rain; the river was rising steadily. Both these ladies were in a terrible plight when they arrived, being practically shoeless. They had only got as far as the Quinton Huts.

We managed to get out on Lake Te Anau for an hour or two that morning and gathered kidney ferns that grew in great profusion on the banks, but, coming back, the rain nearly drowned us again. We were just in time to witness an exciting incident. Three drenched travellers had arrived on the farther bank of the Clinton and wanted to be ferried across to Glade House. The river was running swiftly and bank-high, and swept the heavy boat downstream in its ugly swirl. It was with considerable difficulty and at great risk that they were finally brought across in safety.

So that was the end of the "Finest Walk in the World." It had taken us twelve days to complete the sixty-eight miles! It certainly is magnificent, and the variety of scenery, for so short a distance, is extraordinary—mountain and vale, torrent and lake, sea and fjord, bush and barren, bog and rock.

Captain Roberts, or rather Stan, piloted us down Lake Te Anau that afternoon in safety, and next day we left on a coach for Lumsden. The creeks were too high and the road too bad for the motor to run, but at a place called Mossburn, about twelve miles from Lumsden, a car was waiting to take those passengers who wished to catch the Kingston train. These included the Misses Timber, Spinney, and ourselves, and after a regular old-time transference of luggage had taken place we set out at a terrifice rate.

We skidded this way and that, burst a water-tube that delayed us ten minutes, and then, after going on again, we had to stop owing to boiling water in the radiator.

Finally we arrived at Lumsden as the train was on the point of leaving. We just had time to get some letters and photos from Home, and these we eagerly devoured until our train arrived at Kingston, and a little later Spinney, Stan, and I were steaming up Lake Wakatipu on that fine boat, the *Earnslaw*.

Compared with Te Anau, Lake Wakatipu is much more

82 The famous suspension bridge across the Arthur River

83 Arthur Valley and Diamond Gully
By courtesy of The High Commissioner for New Zealand

84 Mount Tutoko, Milford Sound Track

85 Glade House and The Clinton River

Photos by courtesy of The High Commissioner for New Zealand

rugged. Being farther from the coast, its rainfall is much less, and the vegetation is not so luxuriant on the slopes of the mountains that surround it on every hand. I was told an ancient Maori legend about Wakatipu, and only remember the drift of it, which was to the effect that in olden days the Maoris trapped a huge giant, who had been carrying off their most beautiful princesses, and that he fell to the ground, making a huge dent. This, filling with water, became Lake Wakatipu. The lake is just over fifty miles long, and is 1,000 feet above sea-level; but the bottom of the lake is considerably *below* the level of the sea! A range of steep crags, from five to seven thousand feet high, runs from Kingston to Queenstown along the eastern shore. These are called the Remarkable Mountains.

About seven o'clock that evening we arrived at the lakeside township, and were not long in discovering Hamilton House, where we dumped our bags and tackled a substantial meal.

We had come to Queenstown at the commencement of the Easter rush, so had to sleep in a tent in the garden. Otherwise we were comfortably housed and well looked after, and certainly our position, high up on the hillside, overlooking both arms of the lake and the full jagged line of the Remarkables, was ideal, whilst below us lay the pretty township which was built up at the time of a prosperous gold find, and now enjoys the reputation of a quiet and stimulating health resort. Here we decided to rest for a couple of days before spending Easter in Paradise. What better place could be found?

On March 20th we climbed Ben Lomond, 5,747 feet. It is *the* walk hereabouts, and an easy one. The track is good, and the view we obtained from the top, over the snowclad peaks and the glaciers of the Southern Alps, exceedingly beautiful. The strange volcanic ridges of the lower spurs held all those mystic purples and blues and reds that one learns to seek and love in all these gorgeous landscapes. And there, against the clear, pale blue sky, which for once had put aside its cloak of grey cloud, rose the shining white summits of Mount Aspiring and Mount Earnslaw.

Next day at 8 a.m. we sailed for Glenorchy at the head of the lake, and Paradise, which lies beyond.

We Find Ourselves in Paradise

There is a certain hillock that rises higher than the rest of the undulating ground of Paradise, it is covered with close grass, and riddled on every side with rabbit burrows. This hillock swarmed with little hunch-backed bunnies, who were busy eating their supper of sweet grass and washing it down with the sparkling dew of a cool, silent, moonlight evening.

Down yonder, beyond the Gate of Heaven, beyond the darkness of the birch forests, the gleaming waters of Diamond Lake, and the broad treacherous rapids of the Rees River, were rows and rows of fences, horrid things made of delusive tree-stumps with barbed wire stretched between. No rabbit who had courage to venture so far, and many did, for the grass of Temptation is sweet beyond the Gate of Heaven, ever passed these fences without feelings of unutterable horror. For there, in lines many yards in length and many rows in depth, hung the grotesque, smirking corpses of their brethren. Jack Rabbit or Jenny Rabbit, no matter which, all hung on those wires, dancing a jig of death, rotting and stenching, until their white bones dropped one by one from their weather-beaten skins!

But *that* was not Paradise. No! Paradise lay all round about the hillock I have already mentioned, where the grass was really sweet and cooled by the soughing night breeze as it rustled the Manuka boughs. How the rabbits worshipped these Manuka bushes! In their dense labyrinth all pursuers were instantly shaken off.

It was to this grass-covered hillock that I repaired one bright moonlight night. As I crept up the slope I could see the bunnies scattering in all directions. They did not wait to enter their burrows, but, stamping their hind feet on the ground, as if in contempt of my approach, they raced away to the Manuka bushes, whose dark forms startled me for an instant as I came panting up to the top of the rising ground. These bushes lay on the less steep side of the hillock and stretched away, in an undulating jungle, to the not-far-distant Garden of Eden. No sound came to my ears, save that of the gentle breeze, as I turned to face it, and the white nightcaps of the mountain monsters seemed to quiver on the firmament. Earnslaw, Comos, and Somnus appeared to move in turn as I gazed up the dark valleys between their enormous spurs.

Presently I heard a woman laugh, and then, after a long silence, the voice of a man. These sounds came from the direction of the Garden of Eden, and by their increasing volume I could tell that someone was approaching through the bush at a rapid pace. But the forms were not white; they were clothed. It was only Stan and Olive B——, and the magic of my hillock, on the outskirts of the Garden of Eden, was shattered beyond repair! This Eve, whom Stan had picked up during our sojourn in Paradise, was a very "sporting" damsel, the daughter of wealthy New Zealand residents.

That morning, whilst she and Stan were exploring the bush, Spinney and I took three other damsels out on Diamond Lake, which in depth and colour and surroundings is a very small example of all these other mountain lakes. Large trout lurk in these deep waters, and so manage to elude capture for years. Sometimes, however, a monster is netted or hooked, and during our short stay at Aitken's we had delicious, delicately-tinted trout flesh for breakfast every morning, except on those occasions when we overslept and sat down to breakfast to find that the trout and the Devonshire cream had been utterly consumed by the large assembly of Eastertide guests.

From Paradise to Glade House there is a track similar to that going to Milford Sound, cut through dense bush and crossing creeks and mountain passes. This is called the Routeburn Track, and according to some a lady could walk to Glade House by it almost "on her head." It is interesting to note how experiences differ on these western mountain pathways of the South Island.

When we left Glade House by the little steamboat, the *Tawera*, three men from Invercargill set out with a guide to make Paradise by the Routeburn Track in four days. All were sturdily built and in good training, for they had just returned from Milford Sound.

Four days later we were steaming up Lake Wakatipu on our way to Paradise. At the tiny landing in Elfin Bay, which was a long cry from our destination, we were surprised to see our three friends from Glade House walk on board. They had had a terrible experience, wading through water waist deep, and encountering the most frightful weather, thunder and snow and hail-storms. Conditions were so bad that they had to abandon the last stage of their trip to Paradise and strike aside to Elfin Bay. The tinned food of the mountain huts disagreed with one of their party, who only escaped being dangerously ill owing to their timely arrival in the blackberry country. This fruit formed their staple diet for two days, and when we met them their lips were scabby and sore, and they had to admit that they had had enough! Our friend, Mr. Airey, was thinking of taking his wife over this very track with them, and had been recommended to do so by the Government tourist agents. However, such an experience did not daunt the ardour of a young lady whom we met at Aitken's; she intended, she said, to walk to Milford Sound from Paradise at the earliest opportunity.

Rowing up Diamond Lake one day, we obtained a good near view of a large flock of Paradise ducks resting on the sandy shore. It is from these curious birds that Paradise really takes its name, originally it was called "Paradise Duck Flats." When we were there it was a long close season for these and many other birds, so that they were comparatively tame. The hen has a white and the drake a black head and neck, their bodies being a brownish red, and as they fly overhead or stand gazing at one on the shore they make a most curious noise, the ducks calling shrill replies to the gruff questionings of the drakes.

In these countries where rabbits are such a scourge and where pheasant preserves are unknown, hawks abound in great numbers, and are indeed encouraged to flourish. They become so tame as to hold men in contempt, and as I lay on my back on a grassy knoll one came and perched on a stump hard by. I got up and walked to within 2 feet of it, took my camera out of my pocket, and was just about to photograph it when it flew slowly away. I saw a similar bird in Queenstown, which had flown close to a man on horseback. He had put out his hand and caught it as it flew past.

So we spent our Easter holiday. The days were warm and sunny in the lap of the snowclad mountain ranges, and we shall never forget the crisp, sweet air of the evenings, the sparkle of the summits and lakes in the cold beauty of the moonlight, and the glory of the sharp mornings, when the white frost forsook the grass only as the golden sunlight crept across the vale—and we sat down to hot coffee and pink-fleshed trout!

We left Paradise on Easter Monday. We came very rapidly to Purgatory, or Glenorchy, as it is now called, nearly dying of boredom there, while the cars which had brought us down rushed an excursion party back to Paradise for a few hours.

We derived a little amusement from watching these trippers from Queenstown disembark from the *Earnslaw*. An enterprising cinematograph man, who had rigged up his apparatus, took us several times over as we purposefully went to and fro, mingling in the crowd of disembarking trippers.

The same evening we slept at Hamilton House again, and learnt something of the regatta which had brought great holiday crowds and crews with their outriggers from far and wide. Next day we left at 8 a.m., and arrived in Dunedin at seven that evening, after a tedious journey of many changes and many crowds.

Otago and the Canterbury Plains

The country alters completely as one crosses from the west to the east coast. Snow-capped mountains, forests, dense bush, and deep river ravines give place to undulating pastures, preceded by very hilly country and followed by large flat plains which have been turned to agricultural purposes, or where the tussock grass waves among flocks of browsing sheep. All the flat country around Gore, where we had to change trains, had lately been inundated with flood-water from the rivers, which, rising with an alarming rapidity, swept into the very town itself, carrying off cattle and sheep, and doing damage which had involved the inhabitants of the district in heavy losses.

When in Dunedin, capital of Otago, we put up at Wain's Hotel, where we paid 12s. 6d. per day, and one afternoon we were shown over Messrs. Sargood, Son & Ewen's warehouse by our friend Mr. Airey, the manager, and he took us out to afternoon tea with his wife and baby girl. How many business men in England can or care to free themselves in the middle of the afternoon, and with such natural pleasure as do these good Colonials? Previous to this Mr. Airey had "put us up at the Club," but unfortunately we had no time to patronize the comfortable chairs and fire.

On the top of all this hospitality, a Mr. Smith, cousin of the late Rev. J. S. Moffat of Cape Town, invited us into a two-horse landau, and we drove along the Town Belt, a delightful bush-lined road winding along the hillside above the city. As we drove along, our host pointed out places of interest. Here his father in earlier days had disturbed a wild sow and her litter of young, now the spot indicated was built over and roads and houses surrounded it for some distance. There above us was Flagstaff Hill, and there Mount Cargill, named after a Dunedin pioneer whose energetic works and aims had been recognized farther south and were embodied in the city of Invercargill. Mr. Smith also pointed out to us land that had been reclaimed in the harbour, and beyond rose the productive slopes of a peninsula which, running alongside the mainland for some miles, forms the narrow waterway that terminates in Port Chalmers.

That evening Stan reported that his business was nearly cleared up, so we decided to start for Oamaru next morning. At breakfast a fat man of the Jewish persuasion, who sat beside me, confided in me that he had what is known as an athlete's heart. It was his birthday the day before, and he had had a night out with his chums. Eleven sherries with one man and three whiskies with another terminated his evening and almost his life! From this it will be understood that Dunedin was a "wet" town!

We left the capital of Otago at 11.15, bidding farewell to Spinney. We were all sorry to part after our three weeks' companionship. Soon we were steaming along at no great speed towards Oamaru. Skirting the coast, the line runs up and down steep gradients, with pretty peeps of ocean and shore, pastoral and arable land on every side, and flourishing townships every few miles. Near Oamaru we saw numberless limestone quarries, so we were not surprised to find, when we got there at about 3 p.m. in the pouring rain, many substantial buildings of this stone.

We put up at the Queen's Hotel, where we were told by Mr. Jones, the energetic proprietor, that our bedroom "was one of the best." He also escorted us down the corridor and showed us "the first bathroom and the second bathroom; this one I have just had re-enamelled, gentlemen; and my tariff, gentlemen, is 5s. a day if you take your meals in the ordinary dining-room, or 6s. a day in the Commercial-room."

We elected to take our meals in the "ordinary" dining-room, and did so later in the day, together with labourers and the crews of various yachts. The food was good, however, and all very well cooked. If we had chosen, we could have eaten our chops with our fingers, as some young men *did*.

Whilst I wrote that afternoon, Stan polished off his calls,

and after an excellent night's rest we set out to visit a Mr. Rose, whom we found in his office at the National Mortgage and Agency Co. We talked for half an hour of our doings and his family, then he put on his hat and showed us round the delightful little Gardens. They are, indeed, of unusual appearance—trees, flowers, pools, streams, and green lawns combining to produce an effect altogether unlike the ordinary municipal gardens. He also took us over the Municipal Opera House, a charming and useful building, which, together with the business and municipal offices attached thereto, make a paying concern. Streets in this "dry" town of Oamaru are named after English rivers.

Around Oamaru is one of the finest agricultural districts in New Zealand, but, in spite of this, the town was not expanding; a steady commerce, however, kept everyone contented, and certainly, as far as an outsider could judge, the inhabitants of Oamaru should have nothing to grumble at.

At noon we entered one of those long side-seated second class corridor cars which can boast of everything but comfort, and at 1.30 we arrived at last at Timaru.

Chapter IX

LIFE WITH THE UNWIN BROTHERS

DR. UNWIN was on the platform to meet us, and soon we were speeding along in his little Rover car. We drew up at a pretty bungalow house with a profusion of brass plates on the gate-post. The family was speedily introduced, and we were instantly at our ease in this delightful and typically English home. Two days later we went out to Winchester. Here Stan's two brothers, Sid and Cyril, had a farm, where, later on, we were destined to spend some few weeks. It was Show Day at Winchester, and a good many people were travelling thither.

Sid and his neighbour Fothergill were both at the station to meet us, and in a moment we had hoisted onto their cart the trunkful of secondhand clothing and odds and ends which we had brought for these farmer brothers to wear out with hard toil. Fothergill cracked his whip and was off in his large milkcart. He stood up in it with the assurance of Boadicea in her chariot, and he had just a touch of the Early Briton about him. We followed at a more sober pace drawn by old Topsy. It was obvious that we were "out for the day," for Sid looked quite immaculate in his new Norfolk. His pretty dog Spot followed alongside as we drove through the charming little village of Winchester, a homely little place and very English in appearance with its large public-house and groups of small cottages, and surrounded by green fields, streams, larch and pine trees, backed by distant blue and snow-flecked mountains.

"Stonycroft" is about two miles from the station, and most of the way lies along the main north road to Christchurch. As we drove along Sid pointed out a long and very narrow strip between the railway and the road, amounting to three or four acres in all, which they lease for grazing purposes at £1 per annum. We were thus already at the outskirts of their holding. We turned down a small lane, drove through two or three streams that have an unhappy knack of flooding, and pulled up at a four-roomed wooden homestead. We had arrived at "Stonycroft." It looked very bare, and one sighed for a creeper or two, but a casual glance at the various out-houses showed that "utility" was and must necessarily be the watchword of settlers with limited means. In the early struggle "necessity" is the deciding factor.

We made our way in and found Cyril had an excellent dinner in readiness for us. It was a feast for the gods, and worthy of so great an occasion! An excellent Irish stew, cooked, I need hardly say, in a boilerette, was followed by a most tasty macaroni cheese. "A very excellent finish to an excellent meal," said I, but Cyril only smiled and, mindful of old boating tours and family tradition, produced a large Camananda or Summer pudding and custard!

We spent our afternoon walking round the Show, and, for all the world, this too might have been some village show at Home. There was the large meadow surrounded with trees under which the cattle exhibits and horses were tethered. Innumerable buggies and motors and vans were drawn up on every side. Large marquees contained grotesque side-shows, into which thin-faced men with harsh voices endeavoured to allure us. In others were to be found vegetable exhibits, homely looking mangel-wurzels, turnips, potatoes, and onions; whilst cakes, jams, honeys, and other delicacies were also in evidence. On a high platform a skinny man and two women with ugly figures pranced about in coloured tights, firing revolvers, blowing trumpets, and shouting; and outside another booth a fat man declared, in feigned foreign accents, that McDougal was about to fight Sovizco. All this around a large enclosure where the judging of horseflesh in all its aspects was being carried out by attentive judges; and here proceedings concluded by a "fine military display" of four territorial troopers, two ditto officers, and a riderless horse!

During the afternoon a military band discoursed in dulcet tones the clap-trap class of brass-trumpet music customary at a village fête.

The wealthy farmers had mostly made their money out of sheep and crops. Frozen meat had revolutionized New Zealand farming, and here sheep were bred more for the carcasses than for their wool.

But not merely the wealthy were present at this Show; all classes were there, for we are all one class in New Zealand. The uneducated "squatter" is not so securely seated in his thousand-pound car as the man of culture in a milkcart. The squatter is overawed by his own wealth and knows not what is expected of him. The man of culture goes blithely on his way with the natural dignity of his kind, secure in the knowledge that nothing else is expected of him.

Coming back to Timaru that evening, our train was 2½ hours late in leaving Winchester. The recent floods had damaged the Rangitata bridge a few miles to the north, and for some days had considerably inconvenienced traffic.

Frozen Mutton

The Smithfield Freezing Works of the Christchurch Meat Company are situated about two miles from Timaru, on a cliff not far from Dashing Rocks, where the swell of the great Southern Ocean ends in the boom of breakers and the scattering of clouds of spray. Thither we went one day by car, for there is a fair prospect inland from the works, overlooking the fertile Canterbury Plains and the distant snow-flecked peaks of the Southern Alps. A siding runs from the main line of railway, which passes close by, right up to the main buildings of the works, and on our arrival this was busy with shunting trucks bearing their double row of sheep and lambs to the slaughter.

We were introduced to the chief engineer, who escorted us round the works. The engine-rooms were filled with the usual whirring machinery, and this kept the stores, where hung the carcasses in neat shrouds and duly classified, at a freezing temperature. Here we watched the stiff packages sliding down wooden chutes, white with hoar frost, whence they were borne away by men whose feet were wrapped in sacking. We could not linger, owing to the cold, so we mounted to a floor above where the headless, hideless forms hung from racks to cool before being passed into the refrigerating rooms next day. The smell here was as of a very musty butcher's shop, unpleasant in the extreme. Through a doorway came a procession of these corpses swinging from travelling hooks; they were marshalled into the way they should go with lightning rapidity by a handful of men.

We passed through this doorway, following our guide and dodging the bloody carcasses as they swung by. Here were the shambles. As Stan said afterwards, "I would sooner sweep a London crossing than earn a pound a day at killing sheep!" First of all we saw the dead sheep swinging from a long row of hooks. A deft sweep of a knife and a few long pulls at the woolly hide, and off it came, like turning a glove inside out. Another man removed the insides of the beast as easily and as nonchalantly as if he were lifting a baby from its pram, thrusting his arms into the belly and bringing forth the steaming guts. This done, the less-revolting carcass is passed down the travelling hooks and trimmed; quickly jostled on and weighed; ticketed with a number and initials that in a simple cipher tells its whole history: whose it was when it was alive, its quality, weight, and, I believe, destination as a carcass.

We took a few more steps, which brought us to the killing stands. Seventy-two slaughterers were at work; 5,000 lambs had to be killed that day! At a signal the pen doors were opened, and in each pen stood about a dozen large-sized lambs. The butcher looked upon his victims for a moment as if selecting the best-formed beast, then, seizing it by a hind leg, he lugged it forward, held it between his legs, and with an effortless movement of his arm he nearly severed its neck with the long knife he held in his hand.

Six beasts were thus despatched in as many minutes, and all lay there in a long agonizing row, heaving and quivering in every nerve, their eyes still appealing to us for the breath that it was beyond our power to restore. As we watched this revolting spectacle, standing in pools of blood, we had now and again to step aside as a handtruck was pushed rudely past us, containing a slush of entrails and gore that splashed over the sides on to the floor, where we were constantly slipping on pieces of cold fat or bloody hide. The fetid atmosphere, the sight of the spurting blood, and the necessarily callous movements of the slaughterers were quite enough for us; we felt ready to be sick, and above all we could not help marvelling at men choosing such a profession as this! In various tubs other men were sorting out the kidneys, which are frozen separately, and were handling the various items of the sheep's insides like so many fishmongers.

Glad indeed were we to return to the Doctor's house for lunch and find that Mrs. Unwin had *not* provided mutton!

We never want to go to a shambles again, but it is just as well that people should go, for it gives one plenty to think about.

For many days during our stay in Timaru the weather was gloriously fine with cloudless pale blue skies and crisp, invigorating air. Winter was at hand, and such weather as this is enjoyed for many weeks on end at this season on the Canterbury Plains. The twilight is very short; the deepening yellow light changes to orange, the orange to a dark rich red, and this red light becomes at length the green and deep blue, star-spangled sky of a frost-bound night. And it was in such weather that we started out for our long-planned visit to Mount Cook.

Among the Glaciers of the Southern Alps

We had an exciting drive from Timaru to the Hermitage in the Doctor's Rover car by way of Burke's Pass. After leaving Lake Tekapo, where we passed the night, our road lay over the Mackenzie Plains; open undulating country, covered with tussock grass, absolutely treeless, and swept by the cold winds from the distant snow ranges. This is a great sheep country, and from time to time we passed pretty homesteads sheltered by some hollow or small valley and surrounded by tall poplar trees, whose leaves bore the russet hue of autumn. The mountain peaks were lost in an angry rack of dark cloud, but ahead of us the sky was clear and blue, while here and there banks of mist were trying to force their way over the high tableland which we were traversing.

Now and then, as we passed the boundary fence of the various "runs," as large areas of land are called out here, we noticed that a couple of dogs were invariably chained to stumps on either side of the road. These had a most ferocious and lonely appearance, and barked furiously at our approach. The Doctor told us that no gates were allowed to these "runs," so that dogs had to be posted there to prevent the sheep from passing. It seemed very rough on the poor dogs!

At eleven that morning we stopped at the top of Dover Pass, which overlooks Lake Pukaki, a huge stretch of chalky-coloured glacier water, collected from the giant icefields of the Mount Cook district; but alas! Mount Cook itself was not visible among the heavy clouds that hung about. We had morning tea at the little Pukaki Hotel. From there the road, which now ran along the left bank of the lake, became rapidly worse. At the head of the lake the Tasman River enters, and in floodtime its waters cover the huge swamp and stony reaches that spread some miles backwards towards the great Tasman Glacier. As we came along this road the clouds lifted for a few moments and we had a glimpse of Mount Cook (12,349 feet), the great "Ao-rangi," the "White Cloud in the Heavens," pointing upwards, high above a myriad other peaks.

This was a signal for our troubles to begin. Already we were crossing the beds of what had been furious torrents, which, in the recent flood, had destroyed the bridges for light traffic or left them standing in the middle of a wide stony watercourse with all the earth washed away from the end approaches. Presently we came to one of these bridges, but could not see if there were a safe way over or not, so I walked forward to ascertain. I found two men at work *under* the bridge and asked them if it were safe to bring the car over. They seemed rather amazed at my question, and, on looking down, I saw there was *no water* at all in the creek so that the car could go straight ahead!

It was shortly after this that we made a dash at a stream, or rather a point where the lake overflowed on to the road, and here we stuck fair and square in the middle. There was nothing for it but to undress and start salvage operations. The Doctor and Stan took off boots and stockings, but being shorter I took the further precaution of removing my breeches and pants and hitched the tail of my shirt around my waist. It was bitterly cold, and we must have made a most humorous picture wading thigh-high, tugging, pulling, pushing, and hauling at that beastly little car! We got her out after sweating and shivering for three-quarters of an hour, but not until we had found that the Doctor had left her *in gear with the brakes on!*

Soon after this the road became impossible for our low-powered car, and after innumerable difficulties we gave up, just as the larger Mount Cook car came upon the scene.

We stabled the Rover outside a tin shanty, where we found a convenient tarpaulin to throw over it, and then, removing our luggage to the bigger vehicle, we continued our journey on the top of mailbags and luggage. The road had been absolutely washed out. We were toiling up a river-bed, and finally we stuck once more in a narrow mountain stream, the bottom of which had been so scoured out that we dropped into it at an ugly angle. There was nothing for it but to jump out—clear of the water if possible—and by dint of pulling and setting the engines at full power we managed to get her out.

Finally, after picking our way up another stony but waterless river-bed, for the road proper had long since disappeared, we arrived in safety at the Hermitage. And now we found that our retreat to civilization was once more fairly effectually cut off, thanks to the fact that it had been raining for a number of hours at an average of *over* an inch of rain per hour! The caretaker said that he never remembered such rain, certainly we did not! The water was up to the front door, having overflowed the stony watercourse which yesterday was as dry as a bone.

Many of our fellow visitors at the Hermitage,* who vividly remembered the disastrous overflow of this torrent only four weeks previously, when it carried away an eleven-room annexe, a garage, and an outhouse or two, were anxiously watching the rising stream. At Christmas time there was another heavy deluge of rain in this mountain region, where the excessive flood that ensued caused a modification of the customary watercourses. One of these carved a new way for itself across a strip of land to the very door of this accommodation house, but rain and flood both subsided before any damage was done. About the middle of March, however, there was another torrential rainfall in the district. The water swept down this newly formed course of rounded stones and silt and, rising above its banks, began washing out the foundations of the annexe during the night.

"With a horrible groaning and snapping sound, we watched the eleven-room building reel over and break up in the fury of the torrent," one eyewitness told me, and then she went on to describe how one lady, who was asleep at the time, had to leave her bed hurriedly just as the water entered her room!

We set out one afternoon for the Ball Hut, on the edge

* The old Hermitage in the valley.

86 An exciting time fording the Hooker River

87 The water was up to the front door

88 Mount Cook from the Hooker River

89 Ice Cave on the Tasman Glacier
Photos by courtesy of The High Commissioner for New Zealand

of the great Tasman Glacier, with the late Charlie Milne as our guide. Two horses were also of our party: they carried our swags and sundries, and were ridden by Milne and myself most of the way. The day was gloriously fine, but the heavy rain had done much damage to the track. Fortunately the flood quickly subsided from the Hermitage, and we suffered no inconvenience from it except that Stan's and the Doctor's rooms were rendered almost uninhabitable, owing to the rain coming through the roof!

We had an exciting time fording the Hooker River. A bridge had been swept away by a previous flood, so that we had to cross the dirty frothing torrent on horseback. Milne and I went over first; the water came up to within an inch or two of the saddle. Every now and then we heard the rattle of blocks of ice that, coming down in the stream, bumped against the boulders as they passed. Milne had to return twice to the opposite bank with my horse to bring off the Doctor and Stan.

Our track then wound along the spurs of the Mount Cook Range, close to the wide, stony waste of the bed of the Tasman River. At times we had to dismount and lead our horses over gullies of mountain torrents or around steep grassy slopes at the bottom of which the track had been eaten away by the river, and now and again the beasts would jib altogether and flatly refuse to step over an impossible-looking piece of rock.

After fording one or two more streams the track became better, running through low scrub and beside the terminal moraine of the Tasman Glacier. The moraine of this great glacier, beside which we still continued our way, is the most extraordinary I ever remember seeing. The ice itself is covered with debris and large boulders for some miles of its length, giving it a most unpleasant appearance. Mountains rise on either side of the valley, and are scarred with numerous rock slides. The discharge from these slides gathers about the sides of the moraine and over this loose shale we had to pick our way for a couple of hours. Looking down the valley, the view is extremely desolate, especially as in the far distance the wide bed of the Tasman River gives no relief from the dull monotony, until the eye observes the faintly white-capped Grampian Range on the horizon, where the sky is of the lightest blue.

But ahead the imposing peaks of the Minarets, coloured by that enticing golden light of late afternoon, urged us and tempted us onwards, and, although the path was stony and grey to-day, to-morrow there was promise of nearly ten miles over clear glacial ice, after which we should be in the centre of the snow- and icefields of the Southern Alps.

The Ball Hut is a tiny tin shanty on the rocky skirt of the moraine, protected by a steep low-bushed slope, where the kea, that evil, hook-beaked, sheep-killing parrot, calls eerily to his mate. The interior of this hut is very similar in arrangement to the Milford Track huts; there are comfortable bunks and decent food. We went fuel gathering before supper. Supper itself was cooked on a kerosene stove, and soon the dry twigs were making a merry blaze before which we warmed our toes before slipping between the blankets.

It was a glorious starlit and moonlight night; the dark moraine and the gay white peaks had a dream-like appearance which baffles description. On the morrow at 7 a.m. we were to start for the Malte Brun Hut on foot, across the Tasman Glacier.

There was a gorgeous but ill-omened sunrise, and as we set out we could see the dreaded nor'-wester piling dark woolly clouds around the Minarets. None of us had slept too well, in spite of six thicknesses of blankets, socks, and vests, but we awoke quite fresh, and Milne's excellent breakfast filled us with a fiery ambition for the track. All carried swags, and I had, in addition, my camera and its tripod.

The first few miles of track lay along the moraine of the Hochstetter Glacier, and was pretty rough going over loose rocks; then we crossed on to the great Tasman Glacier, and obtained glorious views of innumerable peaks and ice-falls.

To our left rose the triple summit of Mount Cook, defying

the cloud-rack that was gradually creeping along the range. Mounts Tasman, Dampier, and Haast were still sharply silhouetted against the sky, and from these peaks the Hochstetter ice-fall descended in jagged splendour and shed a continuous series of avalanches over a steep piece of rock, known as Hot Place.

We pulled up for a spell while Milne pointed out the various routes which climbers took when scaling these snowy heights.

Before our serious work began, Milne halted us again under the lee of a protecting rock that sheltered us from the increasing force of the nor'-wester. He then brought to light, from the recesses of his ample ruck-sack, a loaf of bread and a tin of quince jam, which consoled me somewhat for the loss of my camera tripod, which had slipped down a crack at the bottom of a small crevasse we were negotiating earlier that morning. Milne said I need not worry, it would work its way out of the ice in a few months' time, and he would post it to me. Sure enough it turned up in England some months later!

Now began the most tiring part of our morning's work—the crossing of the Tasman ice-fall, caused by a steeper gradient in the glacier. The ice, instead of being flat or rounded off in easy undulations as heretofore, now broke up into pinnacles and crevasses whose sharp points and steep sides it seemed at first sight impossible to traverse. Milne, however, with that extraordinary instinct of his profession, knew exactly where to go and how to act, which appears all the more wonderful when one realizes how rapidly the appearance of these glaciers change and how quickly the ice is really moving down the valley.

We were nearly two hours getting over these ice-falls, crawling round the pinnacles as Milne cut out steps for our feet. But quite the most terrifying part of the whole business was walking over the crevasses on knife-edge ice bridges and endeavouring to balance ourselves against the stiff breeze that was blowing. It was not dangerous enough to call for the rope, yet we could have broken a leg or twisted an ankle with the utmost ease had we been careless.

I was last in line as we carefully followed Milne, and, being a little behind, I did not pay sufficient attention to my footing as I went over one of these narrow ridges, with the result that I slipped and fell! For a moment I lay sprawling on the edge of ice, an arm and a leg vainly endeavouring to get a hold on each side, and finally, after hanging on *by my chin*, I slipped over into a shallow crevasse. It gave me a bit of a turn, and I was unable to scramble out again until Milne had cut some steps with his ice-axe for me. The incident rather unnerved me for the rest of the day!

Soon after this we had done with the ice-falls and proceeded over a smoother surface for another mile or so, and then we left the glacier altogether, and had a steep scramble up the mountain side to the Malte Brun Hut.

The mountain of the same name, and a long range of peaks also called Malte Brun, towered above us; below us the wide valley was filled with the mass of ice which we had been traversing, while across the glacier, as far as the eye could see, rose a magnificent panorama of majestic snow-capped summits, backed and topped with a fiery bank of cloud. Huge ice-falls scarred the mountain sides, and my glasses showed them to be riddled with crevasses, wide, deep, and horrible.

No sooner had we consumed a hearty meal of tongue and tomatoes, bread, butter, jam, and tea, than Stan was eager to be off on skis to test the slopes with which the head of the glacier abounded. We pulled some sorry specimens of skis from the rafters of our hut, and, having spent some time in adjusting them to the borrowed mountaineering boots, Stan and the Doctor set out. I decided that I had done enough for one day, so remained in charge of the hut, but Milne followed them after he had washed up and tidied the place. I watched them scramble down over the mountain side and from the moraine on to the ice-field, and I followed them with my glasses as they grew into tiny dots in the distance. They looked for all the world like three black fleas on an enormous white counterpane. By and by it was most amusing to watch their antics as they started to dart down the icy slopes in various grotesque postures.

They returned in time for tea, rather exhausted and disgusted with their exertions, but another wonderful repast from Milne's mysterious knapsack soon put everyone in an excellent frame of mind. What more does one want than sheep's tongue and tinned peaches, with tinned tomatoes as vegetable and tomato sauce as appetizer, helped down by excellent bread, butter, various jams, and plenty of hot tea?

The Doctor thought that he was far enough away from civilization to devote some of his time that evening to family correspondence, which he had neglected for two years, but he was much more inclined to help me do jig-saw puzzles. The night threatened to be bitterly cold, and we could not but offer a thought of thanks to all those brave strong men who had carried every morsel of wood and every sheet of iron, of which our hut was built, on their backs, over the ten miles of ice from the Ball Hut! *They* might well have grumbled as they staggered along under their burden of 75 lb. or so!

Before turning in we went outside. The moon was at the full, and this snowy world dazzled and sparkled in her brilliant light. It was a scene to which we were well accustomed; yet here in this far-off land, cut off as we were so completely from civilization, it had a different meaning: the air was pregnant with the uncertainty of true adventure.

The Malte Brun Hut is exposed to the fury of every storm; it is held to the ground by stout wires, and even the little window of our sleeping quarters had been broken by some gale. I must have been roused from the warmth of my blankets at an early hour, for rain was then falling on the iron roof, and not long after I heard Milne's alarm-clock go off: it was 4 a.m., dark and still.

Overnight we had discussed the possibility of climbing the Hochstetter Dome if the next day was fine. I heard Milne moving about in the next room, and not long after a sizzling and a pleasant smell told me that breakfast was being prepared. At five o'clock he came in to waken us, lighted candle in hand, and reported that we must return to the Hermitage with all speed as it was snowing hard!

Breakfast was another surprise: we sat down to porridge and fried mutton and bacon, among other delicacies, and then, after packing up and washing up and attending to other duties, we turned our backs upon the Malte Brun Hut, plunged down the mountain side, and were soon facing all the dangers of the treacherous glacier which in the denseness of the blizzard were completely hidden. We followed in line behind the faithful and patient Milne, heading towards the falls, but unable to see more than a few yards on either hand. With eyes glued to the footsteps of the man in front, with no sound save the crunching of our feet in the snow, invested on every side by the dense mist of falling flakes, our conversation naturally drifted to the terrible experiences of Captain Scott, or, when no one spoke, the whiteness of the snowfield, the silence, the steady tramp, tramp onward, acted as a kind of narcotic, and with half-closed eyes we really seemed to be walking in our sleep, until a sudden slip or a warning exclamation brought us instantly back to the seriousness of our situation.*

Charlie Milne soon had us in the midst of the ice-falls. The freshly fallen snow made the way over ridges and crevasses difficult to find, and brought him down very frequently. We fared a little better, for we could see where he slipped and follow in safety and with confidence wherever he led. Sometimes we straddled a sharp ridge of ice, with a young crevasse on either side, working our way along with hands, toes, and knees. Then there were other awesome places where we had to let ourselves slide down a face of ice and land in the bottom of a crevasse within an ace of an ugly ice-hole that probably

* Some few years later a sad accident befell a party of young tourists who were caught on this glacier in a similar blizzard. They were without a guide and all lost their lives. A new hut, dedicated to their memory, has been built not far from the scene of the tragedy.

penetrated the glacier like a grim blue funnel for hundreds of feet.

Coming last, the Doctor and I had rather a rough time, for the other two had worn away the snow as they slid, and we had the bare bumpy ice to fall upon. However, we all came in for our share of knocks and bruises and skinned fingers, and added to those were the unpleasant plunges into water-holes. Milne came in for most of these as he was leading, and once we really thought he was going to disappear altogether. He skidded down a small face of ice and crashed through the thin surface that covered a hole at the bottom, and, losing his balance, fell across the hole with his feet on one side and his shoulders on the other. Arching his back and using his ice-axe to good effect, he righted himself in a marvellous way, whilst we all followed down the face with due caution. By degrees Milne got us out of it, though at times he had to confess that he "did not like it." What we should have done without him I cannot imagine, for we all thought *we* knew the direction better than he did, and at one moment when I considered our position hopeless I mildly suggested to him that I had a compass! I have repented saying that ever since, for, of course, he knew "the Glarcier," as he called it, inside out.

Eventually we got on to the moraine again, much to our relief, and to our joy we saw the snow-covered roof of the Ball Hut, looking like a large boulder, among the mass of rocks below us.

Soon we were eating tinned salmon and drying our saturated coats before a twig fire, and, wrapping blankets about our shoulders in true Maori fashion, we waited until Milne had discovered the two pack-horses and brought them back to be loaded and prepared for the route home.

There were the difficult places where we had to dismount and lead our horses, and there was the dangerous crossing of the Hooker River, but at length we all got back in safety and were wallowing in stinging hot baths and revelling in the adventures we had just come through.

We were surprised to be greeted on our return to the Hermitage by Miss Du Faur and her guide, Peter Graham. They had left for the west coast by the Copland Pass the same day we had gone up to the Ball Hut. But they experienced even worse weather than we did, and so were forced to give up their climb. Miss Du Faur has climbed and made the traverse of Mount Cook and several other important peaks in the district. A citizeness of Sydney, Miss Du Faur had spent many seasons at the Hermitage, where her ambition to become a mountain climber had gradually matured. Peter Graham was head guide at the Hermitage, and, together with his brother, had a wonderful repute among New Zealanders. He was certainly a fine specimen of manhood, and a more kindly soul it would be hard to find. He told us many yarns of the mountains, the most thrilling of which was one of the accident that befell Lowe, a mountaineer who was crossing to the Hermitage from the West Coast. Although an experienced mountain climber, he was accompanied by a guide part of the way, and shortly after the latter had turned back the accident took place. Lowe slipped on an innocent-looking piece of rock and fractured a small bone in his ankle, which made walking impossible. He crawled on hands and knees over rock, ice, and snow for two miles to a large boulder, where he knew he could get shelter, dragging behind him as he went a heavy swag, the contents of which were to save his life. He was not found until *ten* days later, and he had kept himself alive all that time on a small tin of cocoa and a little tobacco. When they discovered him, his knees were worn through to the bone by his crawling efforts, and this was giving him much more pain than his ankle. The Doctor remembers him being brought to the hospital at Timaru; soon after he was hail and hearty, and climbing again!

On the morrow Miss du Faur very kindly offered to escort us up Mount Sebastopol. Johnnie took a day off for photography, but my Doctor brother and I accepted with alacrity. It is one of the easiest climbs round the Hermitage, but quite enough after our strenuous doings of the day before.

We took lunch with us and a "billy" and made tea at the Red Lake half-way up. Although the day was fine, the clouds were very low. When we finally reached the summit, the recent snow made the climb along the top ridge needlessly terrifying; there was a level blanket of cloud below us stretching for miles around. Every now and then the warm sun would dispel the upper mist that hid the higher peaks, and we caught glimpses of Mount Sefton, Mount Cook, or the Nun's Veil. It was truly remarkable that the by no means athletic-looking damsel standing beside us had surmounted every obstacle and had climbed those gigantic peaks. Whilst still on the top of Sebastopol we noticed a wonderful "fog bow" behind us, not encompassing the heavens like a rainbow, but small like a horseshoe. When we stood up, behold our forms were in the circle. This was surely a premature halo!

The way down Mount Sebastopol was speedy enough, for there is a shingle slide a large part of the way. You put your feet down and the shingle does the rest.

Next morning, with a pack-horse to carry our belongings, we set out for Birch Hill, where the Doctor had left his car. We said farewell to the climbers, and expressed the hope that we should hear of their overcoming Mount Everest. Before we had gone far, we saw yet further evidences of the recent storm: telephone poles split into shreds by the lightning, and as we came round a bend in the track we found a workman awaiting our arrival. He had heard, he said, that the Doctor was on his way home from the Hermitage, and asked if he could have a very painful tooth taken out on the spot. There and then we laid our patient down on the grass, and the Doctor very soon had it located and extracted, much to the relief of the sufferer!

The car proved none the worse for its week under canvas, and we soon started off on our way. What is more, we got through the creeks and over the rough places without misadventure. As we were homeward bound, of course the day was brilliantly fine, even Lake Pukaki was blue in the sunshine.

It was 4 p.m. when we arrived at the little hotel on the edge of the lake, and here we had to stop to carry out a few minor repairs to the car. Meanwhile the Doctor paid a professional visit on the landlady, who in return for his good advice gave him a pint of oil for the Rover.

The sun was setting as we passed by the end of the lake and climbed back over Dover Pass, and worked our way into the heart of the wide McKenzie Plains. Long will that last glorious glimpse of Mount Cook, rearing her grandiose triple peak above those of her snowy sisters, and the blurred reflections of those sun-tinted white mountain ranges on the chalky-coloured surface of the lake, wind-ruffled by an errant evening air, remain graven in our memories. And then the McKenzie Plains, that endless, apparent waste of yellow tussock grass, bounded at last by hills all crimson and purple in the evening sunlight, whilst Rona sat by her tree in the circle of the yellow moon; they hung there, a warning sign, in the deepening blue of heaven. Rona was a beautiful Maori maiden who one evening went to the river to get water. She stumbled against a rock and hurt her foot, whereat she uttered an impolite epithet intended for the moon. But the moon, incensed, reached down from the heavens and caught up the maiden, together with the unfortunate *ngaio* tree to which she clung for protection. Both are now to be seen in the circle of the moon, where they will ever remain as an example to those on earth.*

Darkness crept gradually over the sky; the moon, planets, and stars increased in brilliance and enabled us to obtain occasional visions of our road, a great dark endless serpent that we never seemed to overtake.

It was to this bleak but useful upland plain that the daring

* See *The Long White Cloud, Ao-Tea-Roa,* by W. Pember Reeves. George Allen & Unwin Ltd., 1924, p. 68.

McKenzie drove the flock of one thousand sheep that he had "lifted" from the run of a Mr. Rhodes near Timaru. That was so long ago as 1855, and the tussocks still rustle their silvery manes and tails to the north-west wind. Fine flocks of fat sheep have been reared here since, and thousands have perished in the deep snowdrifts which invest the surrounding mountain slopes in winter time. So here it was that the adventurous McKenzie was captured after a fierce struggle and taken to Christchurch on horseback, manacled and covered by the firearms of his captors. He had shown that apparently useless tussock grass was in reality grand sheep-rearing country, but his reward, apart from giving his name to the district, was a sentence of five years' imprisonment, three dashes for freedom, a severe wound, and finally a permit to leave the country.

Soon we dropped from the plateau of the plains to the shores of Lake Tekapo, whose waters were gleaming in the moonlight. We decided to stop here for the night, and tea and bed were most welcome; but as our host sat over a cosy fire in the bar parlour, we had to shiver beside the visitors' book in the drawing-room. Such cold comfort made us decide to press on to Burke's Pass for breakfast next morning. It was the break of one of those gloriously sunny New Zealand winter days with golden light and crisp clear air; as we sped along we criticized the various sloping hillsides which one day may make this part of the country a fashionable ski-ing centre.

We arrived in due course at the pretty little village of Burke's Pass, embowered in willows, pines, and poplars, all so homely-looking in their orange, green, and yellow tints. Calves gambolled on the greensward, and innumerable sheep-dogs lazed in the sunny shelter of the verandas, or rose stiffly to enquire into the health of some passing doggy neighbour. Up above us were the hills, the tussock, and the sheep, and here we were watching a big black lowing bull leading a herd of fine dairy cows out to the pastures; we were reminded of a certain Alpine village, but we did not hear the clamour of the many cattle bells.

The Doctor, whose reputation was well established in this thinly populated district, was asked to cure the irritation in a farmer's eye, and this done we set off on the final stage of our return journey to Timaru.

When we got back to Timaru the Doctor's small son wanted to know whether Daddy had brought home some "Females." When asked what he thought "females" were, he replied: "I seen one." What sort of animal or vegetable he thought a female was I know not! During our absence a paragraph had appeared in the Timaru paper under the heading: "Of interest to *Ladies*. Mr. Unwin and Mr. *Store* [*sic*] have gone to Mount Cook. . .!"

One night we accompanied Dr. Burns to the Opihi River to try our hand at fishing for trout by night. We came to the conclusion that we preferred our beds. We got back at 1.40 in the morning, to find that Dr. Unwin had just been called out; he returned home at 5 a.m. Who would be a doctor?

*We Become a Couple of "Rouseabouts"**

A few days later we found ourselves at "Stonycroft" again, this time for a spell of hard work. But for the gorse hedges and the weird appearance of some of the smaller shanties, dumped down without any pretence at a garden or a path leading to them, we almost thought that we were in a country lane at home. The golden hue of the poplars, of which there are many hereabouts, showed that autumn was well advanced, and in a day or two the deciduous trees would be bare.

"Stonycroft" could boast no garden, and the fact that the soil is 80 per cent. stones damped our enthusiasm to make one; and how much garden would the fowls leave if one had been made? Of outhouses there were a goodly number, all of them built by the indefatigable Sid and Cyril Unwin. Perhaps

* Handymen on small-holding or sheep "run."

the most substantial piece of work in this line was the cowshed, or rather the building of which the cowshed formed a part. It included a coach-house, harness-room, and workshop.

On going round the stony meadows which form a large part of the estate, we were at once struck, now that we knew a little more about farming, by the excellence of the fencing and the gates—all made and put up by the brothers. When one considers the amount of time absorbed by the daily routine of housework, cooking, washing up, milking the cows, feeding the pigs and poultry, separating the cream, making the butter, collecting the eggs, attending to the bees, and finally marketing their own produce, the amount of work the two of them had done seemed colossal. And not merely construction work, but the "clearing" of their land as well, for a large part of it was covered with gorse 10 feet high! Our only regret was that lack of capital had prevented them from expending their labour on more profitable soil. The land itself, or most of it, is too poor to justify much in the way of improvements. If they were to stop on, it would be essential to buy some better land near by which they could use for orcharding or cropping, but this would involve another £400–£500 capital. Even if they applied for a Government grant under the Closer Settlement Act, they would require at least that amount of additional capital. There is no risk, for, with a competent man and hard worker such as Sid at the helm, farming is a dead certainty over here, and a paying game at that.* But one must have some decent land—thirty-three acres does not go very far here—and a reasonable amount of capital.

The way they had avoided spending a single penny on anything that was not absolutely productive was marvellous. Sid possesses infinite resource and ingenuity. Everything was put to use, and especially petrol tins. Sid had a model chest of drawers made out of petrol tins and their wooden cases! Our most efficient coal-scuttles were but petrol tins with a

* Alas! no longer true.

corner cut off and a handle added. Most people threw away their tins; Sid used every one. Remove the top, fix a handle across, and you have the most excellent bucket or slop-pail. If it is too big, one has merely to cut the petrol tin in halves and fix two handles, and one has two small pails. For storing rice, sugar, etc., petrol tins are better than biscuit tins, for they hold more. The Romance of a Petrol Tin would make an excellent article, had one but an hour or two in which to write it. Undoubtedly the most important of the four rooms was the kitchen-sitting-room. This was no luxurious kitchen-sitting-room as exhibited at the Ideal Homes Exhibition. The room measured but 10 feet by 15 feet. It contained an excellent range, with hot water on one side and an oven on the other, a substantial table covered with American cloth—they had no time for linen tablecloths—and four wooden chairs. Two or three good cupboards and as many shelves completed the outfit, save for innumerable pegs and hooks.

In this household, even though a bachelor establishment, tidiness and method held sway, and everything had a place. Odd bits of wire had been converted into convenient racks for newspapers and correspondence, and even the drawers of the table were carefully partitioned off for spoons, forks, and knives, so that anything that was wanted could be found in the dark.

In the front room great changes had been made. When we first saw it, a honey extractor filled one corner; beekeeping utensils of all sorts were there in profusion, and bees buzzed round anyone who dared to enter. But a great transformation had taken place. The entire window was taken out to enable the extractor to be removed, and a couple of folding bedsteads replaced the beekeeping paraphernalia. The stains of the honey on the wall still remained, and, as Sid said, it looked very much like the spot where Luther threw the inkpot at the devil in the Wartburg. The front door of the house was blocked by one of the beds, but in any case it was seldom used, for a back door is as good as a front door in a four-room shack.

Cyril had expended £1 in having his room decorated with green wallpaper, so that it looked comparatively respectable, despite the dilapidated state of the furniture and water-jug. However, he found his bed comfortable, and his basin held water, so what did it matter if his jug (like the Yonghy-Bonghy-Bò's) had no handle? No, the small settler has to content himself with necessities, and if he has good food, a roof to shelter him, and sufficient raiment, the amenities of civilization must wait.

And for our own part there are few of the other amenities we cannot be happy without. In the words of Haykar, the sage, which were displayed on the wall of our living-room, "The transport of stones with a man of wisdom is better than the drinking of wine with one blamed for folly."

I may say that I at once installed myself as "maid of all work," and made a point, therefore, of being up first to light the fire. We rose about 6.45 (very late for farmers). The first morning I was quite enthusiastic over washing, but later on became convinced that it was an entirely futile proceeding before fire lighting, house cleaning, and filling lamps!

The routine of the housework was as follows:

Rake out stove; remove ash to box in shed opposite; break coal and fill scuttles; clean grate and (under my régime) polish it; light fire; fill both kettles and boiler with water, also large saucepan if it is butter-making day; put on porridge and milk (both in double saucepans); sweep out kitchen then or after breakfast; empty slops; fill water-jugs; fill lamps; make beds; sweep out a bedroom or clean out a cupboard; lay the breakfast table. By this time it was probably about 9 a.m. Sid and Cyril would have fetched the cows in, milked them, fed the calves, the pigs, and the poultry, and also separated the milk. Meanwhile Johnnie helped me, or, more probably, had cut some mealie stalks (maize) for the cows' feed.

After breakfast, of which porridge, coffee, bread, butter, jam, honey, stewed fruit formed the staple fare, there was the inevitable washing up. During breakfast the next day's porridge was made, for in a household of this sort it is essential to get all the cooking done at one time and when the fire is going strong. The sooner you can get lunch prepared, therefore, the better. For most things, such as a stew, or an old chicken, the boilerette came into use. There was nothing like it for both ease in cooking and excellent results. One could go away and leave it, or, if the contents were cooked, place the whole bag of tricks into a Swedish oven—the Swedish oven being a large wooden box carefully lined with cushions containing bran or hay. Immediately the saucepan or boilerette was placed inside, another cushion was placed on top and the lid closed. Needless to say it was a "home-made" article, like most things at "Stonycroft." It acted like a Thermos flask, the bran being a substitute for the vacuum.

Household duties over for the time being, one was free to join the others who were already at work at one of the thousand-and-one jobs that urgently required attention, such as getting more feed for the cows, or getting an old sow into a cart—no light job! and digging potatoes, or grubbing up gorse. The last was a hard job and we put in many a long day at it.

A few minutes before 1 p.m. the man on household duty hurried in to lay the table, and a moment or two later his welcome shout of "dinner" reached the ears of the hungry toilers in the paddocks. There was no cooking to be done, and the boilerette was put straight on to the table, so that everything was piping hot. I found cutting up raw beef both tedious and distasteful, so, at Sid's suggestion, I put it through the largest cutters of the mincing machine, a plan that worked excellently.

On Mondays and Fridays butter was made, a strenuous morning's work, and on Tuesdays and Saturdays one of the brothers went into Timaru with their produce, so that Wednesdays and Thursdays were the only two whole days in the week when they were both free to work on the place.

It was Cyril's Sunday off. Topsy was harnessed to Cyril's old cart immediately our breakfast was over, and we set forth to the base of what are known as the "Four Peaks." "Stony-

90 We found ourselves at "Stonycroft"

91 The bachelor establishment

92 Here and there were clumps of Toé-toé grass

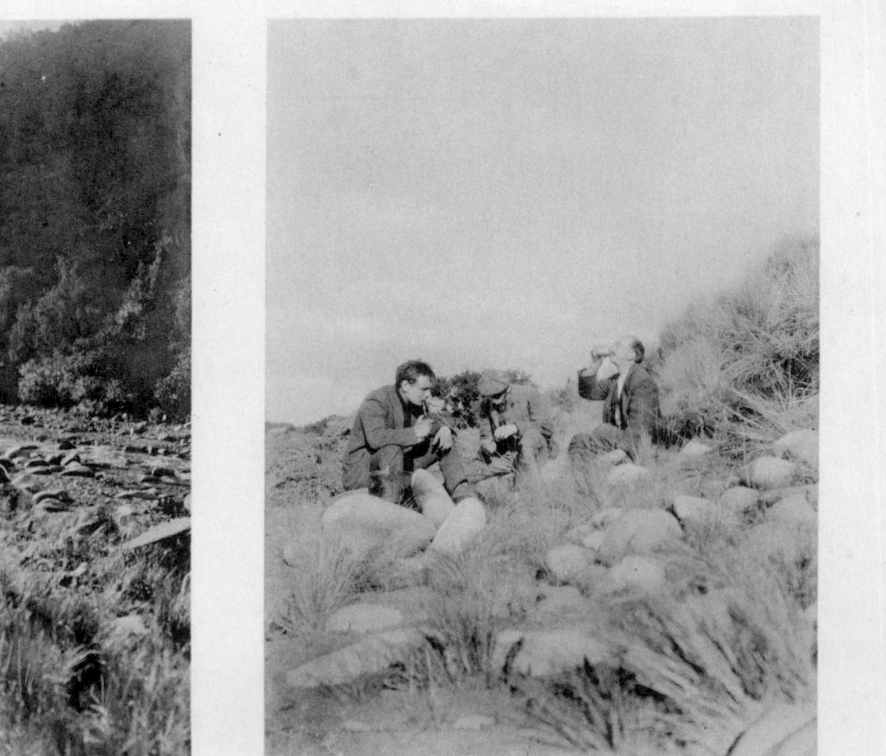

93 It is like smoking a pipe of peace together

croft" is certainly blessed in regard to its surroundings. It would be difficult to picture more beautiful country lanes than those which we at once found ourselves passing. The gorse hedges, the grassy verges of the road, and, above all, the tall poplars clothed in gorgeous yellow, made a picturesque scene, despite the thick mist that still covered the land. Geraldine, the only township through which we passed, seemed a prosperous little place, and, possibly to its chagrin, was, owing to an alteration in the electoral area, in a "dry" district. At that time, however, it was on the borders of a "wet" area, so that the liquor lovers had merely to walk into Winchester for their weekly "drunk." But that is only one of the disadvantages of gradual transition from one order of things to another.

From Geraldine onwards our road slowly ascended, and gradually we left the mist behind. What surprised us most was the number of really first-class homesteads that dotted the valleys in this neighbourhood. Every one of them evidence of material prosperity, and built up, not as in Australia on vast areas in single hands, but on smaller holdings, farms of, say, 300 acres. As we neared the mountains the farms increased in size, for here the land was only suitable for sheep-runs, and much of it would be covered with deep snow in winter. A "run" might include the sides of a mountain, and the task of mustering the sheep would be a colossal labour, for, as in South Africa, the sheep seem to find the top the warmest spot of an evening. Our road led us through such a "run" into the Waihi Gorge, until it came to an abrupt end at the bank of the Waihi River. From here there was but a bridle-path under the trees beside the rippling waters of the stream.

It was nearly 1 p.m. What more charming place to "boil our billy" than in the shade of a sylvan glade? We had forgotten the bread, but what did that matter? We had everything else, and the sun was shining. One side of the gorge was completely covered with Native trees down to the very water's edge, including Totara, the New Zealand *hard* wood.

Here and there were clumps of Toé-toé grass, a small bush which we grew with such care outside the morning-room window at Home.

There is something very fascinating about dipping your cup in the "billy" as you sit round a camp-fire. It is like smoking a pipe of peace together, and in surroundings such as these we were not surprised that a feeling of perfect contentment crept over us—a feeling of absolute satisfaction after a week's strenuous manual labour. I often feel that the worker on the land gets the most real joy out of life. I knew that when I settled down to London life again I should often sigh for the days when I wielded a gorse-grubber and acted as Rouse-about on a New Zealand farm, or ploughed with a team of fourteen donkeys under a hot South African sun.

As we sat down in dirty shirts, without collars or coats, to a meal we had prepared ourselves, we thought with pity of those we had left behind us condemned to do the same thing in the same way, day after day and year after year, in that most hideous of all places, a dirty London office. We would stop for a brief moment, whilst washing up the dinner things, and picture them hurrying back from their Lyons or A.B.C. And at the close of day, what had a cinema show to offer compared with the joy of sitting in front of a blazing gorse fire, our limbs all a-tingling and the satisfaction of knowing that what was once barren was now fertile; that what was once useless was now productive; that what once grew gorse will now grow grain.

It was getting late, but Cyril and I thought we might as well have a scramble while Johnnie took photographs. The bridle-track leads right over the pass to Fairlie, a distance of twelve to fourteen miles. After following it about three miles—a very delightful walk—we caught sight of two of the four peaks. The temptation was too great; we decided to see how far up the lower mountain we could get. It was a veritable Marathon race, but we climbed to the top, and we were well rewarded by the view. Above the mist, in which Timaru lay shrouded, we could see Banks Peninsula away to the north, jutting out into the sea that now appeared to be lying at our feet. Inland there were groups of mountains, and in their midst Mount Peel. The sun had just set, and suddenly we thought of Johnnie sitting patiently over the camp-fire with the "billy" boiling in readiness for tea, so we hurried down. The twilight lasted till we reached the main road once more, and after that it was plain sailing. At 8 p.m. three cold and hungry men arrived at "Stonycroft" to the welcome meal that Sid had laid ready for them.

A Piggy Interlude

One morning Sid and I had to drive one of our sows home from a place about a mile away, where she had been on a visit. We had armed ourselves with a whip, a rope, a cycle, and the good dog Spot, in case of eventualities.

All went well for the first half-mile. At cross-roads and turnings Sid cycled ahead to prevent the sow from breaking away, but becoming deep in conversation we omitted to safeguard a neighbouring schoolmaster's carriage entrance. The beast rushed in, with Sid, Spot, and myself in hot pursuit, and we had an anxious fifteen minutes as the wretch charged about over kitchen garden and flower-beds. Eventually we got her out, but soon we came to the first of the three creeks that cross the road on the way to "Stonycroft." The sow made for the foot plank, slipped, and dropped into the deep stream. She swam against the current, and passing under a wire fence she emerged in a field of rape where a flock of sheep was browsing. Spot, encouraged by the shouts and oaths that we were uttering, chased off after the sheep, whilst we began clambering over the thick gorse hedge into the field where the sow was having a quiet feed of rape. After a good deal of bother we got her on the road again, and in doing so we came across a sheep suffering from stomach staggers, and this we had to kick on to its feet. Once more we drove our old sow towards the creek, and this time she found a gap in the *opposite* hedge and went careering across another paddock! At this stage in the proceedings I cycled off to the homestead to fetch Stan and Cyril to our assistance, and on our return we found that Sid had the sow in the road once more, and was addressing her in uncomplimentary language. Twice more we essayed to drive her across the creek, a man on either side guarding the hedges, and two men and a dog forcing her forward. Twice she evaded us, and after an exhausting chase Sid and I caught her by the hind leg and fastened our rope securely to it. *Then* the fun began! We had to pull her backwards under a low wire fence. The screeching, the swearing, the yapping, and the biting were awful, but at last it was done.

But still that cursed creek had to be crossed, and, what was worse, there were the two others after that. There was nothing for it but to pull her backwards through the ford, so whilst Stan and I stood on the footplank hauling for all we were worth on the rope, the others whipped and pushed, and Spot barked and bit. At one moment her head went under water, and she sat quite a long time in the shallows breathless and waterlogged, and then with a yell of triumph we pulled her at last to dry land! When we came to the other creeks reason seemed to enter the stupid beast's head, and we had little trouble in getting her to cross.

No sooner had we housed her safely in her sty than it was decided to slaughter her companion, and Sid came up with his humane killer for that purpose. I hastily absented myself, suddenly remembering that the cows' evening meal had to be prepared, and just as I was mixing the treacle and chaff I heard the gun go off. The customary silence followed, but a second report and a third made me wonder what was amiss. Apparently it is not always easy for an amateur butcher to stun his pig with the first shot, and this pig was a wriggler.

Fothergill now came galloping up on his bare-backed steed, and, clad only in a short-sleeved vest tucked into his breeches, he quickly set to work with Cyril's help to steep the animal in boiling water and shave off her bristles with our *bread*-knife and another one which went by the name of "visitors' cutlery" in our pantry cupboard. All this happened as darkness was coming rapidly upon us, whilst Spot danced round the stretcher upon which the pig's prostrate form was lying, yapping with delight and licking his whiskers in anticipation of a supper of tripe and "innards."

The butchers completed the operation of gutting by the light of the moon, assisted by that of our bedroom lamp, a large white-globed luminant whose opalescent glow harmonized to perfection with that of the mother planet and contrasted with the bright embers in the furnace of the portable copper. Meanwhile the other members of the "Stonycroft" staff were busily employed collecting the eggs, milking the cows, and frying sausages for tea, a most appropriate dish wherewith to close such a porcine day. When our bedroom, where the frying took place, was well filled with the blue and appetizing vapour, we sat down to an enjoyable meal. During our repast we kept spotting curious shining particles on each other's coats, shirts, and trousers, which on closer examination proved to be what Sid picturesquely termed "Schwein's blawd." Next day Fothergill took the carcasses of two of his pigs and ours in to the curing works at Temuka, and brought back the heads, ribs, tails, and other fatty oddments that were of no use for turning into bacon. We had a review of these gory fragments, pulling them out of the sacks and placing them on our tea-table. It was a most gratifying display, for here was plenty of fat to boil down for cooking purposes, and we could almost count the number of eggs that the fowls would lay after consuming all those odd pieces of flesh, not to mention the tit-bits we thought of reserving for ourselves, the cats, and Spot. It was well said that "there was no waste at 'Stonycroft.' "

On this and similar festive occasions our room was known as "the front room," and, except when Fothergill came to tea, everything therein was spotlessly clean, thanks to the constant besoming of head Rouseabout Stan; but with the advent of our neighbour a good deal of mire and offal was trodden into our carpet, and we would get very merry sampling draughts of Cyril's excellent mead. Sid's bedroom was everything that a true Cockatoo's* room should look like. It was a strange medley of baskets of apples, scientific books, worn-out clothing, dirt, and "sundries too numerous to mention," as the auction announcements put it in these parts. In one corner was a heap of old pyjamas, where Spot delighted to sleep and harbour fleas in summer time, and Sid's pillow-case was an old imprinted flour-bag, and the pillow consisted of a canvas sack stuffed with chaff. When the Rouseabout went to tidy up Cyril's room he constantly found dead bees in his hair-brushes and chicken food in his blankets.

One day I had my first experience of ploughing with horses; one was an old carthorse that was stone deaf, and the other an old carriage-horse that answered to a whisper. It was a hair-raising job over the rough land of the Cemetery Reserve that Stan had just succeeded in clearing from its fine crop of gorse. Fortunately no corpses had ever been buried here, otherwise I am sure they would have been disturbed in their graves, either by the plunging nose of the plough or by the exotic language we used as we addressed our horses Dandy the deaf and Topsy the trotter. A gale of wind was blowing at the time, and it was necessary to raise our voices to their utmost capacity to make old Dandy respond to our wishes; if we did not yell at him he would go steadily on, and Topsy would stop; and when we said "Gee up-er!" Topsy would move forward and Dandy remain rooted to the ground. Never did a retired schoolmaster and a retired auctioneer use their voices to better advantage outside a classroom or the rostrum! It proved a much more formidable undertaking than any of us anticipated; we were prepared to find little but stones and gorse stumps, we were not ready for willow roots as big as our wrists and extending for yards. The plough bumped

* Headman or boss.

and jumped over the stones and stumps until one was worn out holding on to it, but, in addition, continually to be brought up with a jerk by a hidden root was wearying to both man and beast.

Catering was greatly assisted by the fact that an almost unlimited supply of fruit had been bottled, and pounds and pounds of jam made. Housekeeping expenses were thus reduced to a minimum, for milk, butter, poultry, honey, and occasionally half a pig all came off the farm. Actually it worked out to about 1s. each per day, or 7s. per week—the amount they used to spend on one meal when they drove down to the pub for lunch.

On my way down to fetch the cows one morning, Fothergill and Johnnie were crossing the far paddock, and I was not surprised when they announced the arrival of a fine heifer calf, but I *was* surprised when Fothergill said: "You will have to carry it up." The cow, of course, had to be milked and given a good feed, and without the calf the cow would not budge. I walked on to inspect, and found the mother proud and excited, and by her side was the weirdest little bundle of legs with a body still more or less the colour of a newborn chick. The calf was too weak to do much more than stand, and, at Fothergill's suggestion, I went back for a wheelbarrow. Cyril, however, pooh-poohed the idea. "What you want to do," he explained, "is to get the weight evenly balanced on your shoulders. The best plan is to put your head under its body and have two legs over each shoulder to hold on to!" Precisely! But by the time we arrived the calf had got tired of standing, and lay like a lump of yellow custard pudding on the ground. It was born, of course, in the farthest corner of the farthest paddock.

Cyril and I staggered along alternately carrying this slimy mass on our shoulders, and the old mother cow barging us all the time. Never have I got my hair, neck, and shirt in such a filthy mess! But for Fothergill's authority, both Johnnie and I would have announced the arrival of a *bull* calf; the difference is very vital to the owner, because a bull calf is not of much account, unless it has a pedigree.

Life at "Stonycroft" was all-absorbing, and left little time for the affairs of an outside world. Work was never done. The cows had to be fed and milked Sundays as well as weekdays, and the pigs and the poultry were equally inexorable in their demand for attention.

Our "three weeks' " visit extended into more than a month's strenuous work at "Stonycroft." Others may see one of these days the trees we planted, over seventy in number, which will, we hope, live after us. Many of them were placed in front of the house, and in time would make the place look a trifle less desolate than when we first set eyes on it. But the greatest transformation was wrought in the exterior appearance of the house, for during our stay it was repainted from top to bottom. A warm red roof and creamy white sides gave the shanty a bright and homely appearance it did not possess before. The painting of the chimneys was not included in the estimate, but the contractor strongly recommended it, and offered to provide the paint and brush if we cared to do the job ourselves. Were the "Two Young Men" daunted? No!

They mounted the roof and the deed was done, and a good deal more painting besides. Many other jobs would have been finished before our departure but for the endless and unavoidable interruptions and other work that intervened. A neighbour's cow broke through, and a morning that ought to have been devoted to ploughing was spent in mending a fence. Barbed wire or paint had to be fetched from Winchester, and the Home mail had to be taken in and posted there. By the time the horse was found, harnessed, driven there and back, unharnessed and fed, another morning was gone. My London friends would have smiled if they had met me driving Topsy with Cyril's old cart stacked up with barbed wire, paint-pots, and on top of all a pair of steps! But perhaps they would have smiled more if they had met me leading the old Jersey cow in to the Geraldine sale—a job that wasted an entire day for two of us, for we got no bids. Still, it was an interesting experience, and fortunately one of those glorious New Zealand winter days we had heard so much about. We had to be up before the sun and start at daybreak, for the pace of the cow, like the pace of the ox, "is steady and slow." Most mornings Johnnie found there was little time to think about washing or brushing his hair, and, after all, what was the use, when as soon as one was dressed one had to assist in such jobs as catching the bull calf that was destined for the same sale with its mother? This generally resulted in a fierce encounter, during which one was invariably rolled in the mud and filth of the cowyard before the youngster was safely under the seat of the cart. It is no light thing to lift, as Cyril and I discovered when we had to tackle the job at Geraldine by ourselves! We wended our way along pleasant by-roads; the crisp air, the blue sky, the warm sun, the tall pines (*Pinus insignis*), and the snow on the mountains ahead contributed to an almost Alpine picture.

Evenings Out

I must also tell of the Zests' musical evening. Mr. Zest is now a prosperous farmer who can afford to take his trips Home with his family periodically, on which occasions they "do themselves proud." Of course, Scotland, Ireland, Paris, and perhaps Naples, are included in such a trip, and as we all sat round in a circle in uncomfortable positions on the flash furniture we talked of our hard times and their hard times that were. Mrs. Zest got so confused with the three Mr. Unwins present that she "took the liberty" to call them all by their Christian names, so they became *Mr*. Sidney, *Mr*. Cyril, and *Mr*. Stanley.

Other guests arrived, and one caught visions of Colonial loveliness unveiling itself before a mirror in a bedroom across the corridor. Presently tea was announced as ready, and we all walked into a large dining-room where a noble spread met our eyes, and a bright wood fire glowed in the hearth.* Several introductions were now made as we stood awkwardly around the table or professed to admire the water-colours that hung upon the walls. Mr. Zest, upon whose left I had the honour of sitting, told me in an undertone: "All the paintings in this room, except one, are the work of my daughter, Vera." Of course my professional eye instantly spotted the *one* drawing which was not the work of Vera; it was an oleograph!

Mr. Zest was portly and grey-whiskered, his hands were thick and brown; he evidently knew what hard work meant; but his morning coat and the white slip in his vest surely were purchased in the Old Country, for they were in the style of the Junior Carlton Club, whilst his conversation was *unmistakably* Colonial. He kept my plate liberally supplied with ham and mutton, but there was an awkward hitch at the commencement of proceedings—"Vera" had forgotten the forks!

Eighteen of us sat down to that meal, and it was strange to think that no servant ever entered the room during the whole time, nor did we speak of them. At the end of the repast, Mrs. and Miss Zest and one or two of the more intimate guests absented themselves, returning by and by when the colossal "wash up" was completed. Then, after the gentlemen had been decorated with buttonholes from the conservatory at the suggestion of our active-minded hostess and by the hands of the fair young ladies of the party, we began a musical programme that was to last nigh up till midnight. Mrs. Zest called forth the artists, once she had got the running of who could perform, with the regular monotony of a drill sergeant, and would follow up the concluding bars of song or instrumental solo with the same appreciative interjection:

"*Now*, Mr. Stanley, will you play us something, please?"

Stan would oblige with his *Arietta*.

"*Thank* you, Mr. Stanley. *What* a charming *old* tune! *Now*, Mr. Sidney, won't you recite us something?"

* On nearly all Colonial farms the evening meal takes the form of "high tea."

Sid spouted forth some bloodthirsty Kipling or similar verses interspersed with plenty of damns and other curses. Most of the audience hardly knew how to take it, whether to be shocked or amused by it, but Mrs. Zest *always* knew what to say. As Sid sat down:

"Oh, *thank* you, Mr. Sidney," said she. "What a quaint rhyme it is, isn't it, Mr. Poacher? But there now, I think you must give us a song, Mr. Poacher, won't you?"

Contrary to my most cherished expectations, Mr. Poacher *could* sing; he had a sweet tenor voice.

Cyril next played Handel's *Largo* on his 'cello, whilst Sid accompanied him. After it was over and the thundering applause had died away, Mrs. Zest could be heard saying: "Oh, *thank* you, Mr. Cyril. *What* a charming old tune! I never remember hearing it before."

One or two other village maidens sang, whilst their mamma or sister did the necessary on the piano. Needless to say they all seemed to be following the regulation for motor-cycle traffic in London, i.e. their silencers were *on* and what sound *did* come through was not unlike speaking through tissue paper covering a comb!

Nevertheless all these good folks were most charming and friendly. "Vera" came and chatted to me during the evening about Paris, Versailles, and other places. She wore a quite charming frock—it was such a *rare* sight then to see a well-dressed woman in these parts.

Our evening ended with the consumption of tea, coffee, or chocolate, and innumerable rich cakes that "Vera" had made. Jove, most Colonial girls can make good cakes, too! Then we sorted ourselves out, and we mounted our spring dray, 'cello and all, and drove off home.

Spot greeted us on our return to "Stonycroft." He was a dear and affectionate dog, with pink eye rims and a pink root to his nose; he had a great affection for the two cats. He used to play with them all day long, and his favourite game was to grip them in the centre of their backs with his teeth; they seemed to like it, and only occasionally rebuked him with spit or claw.

The late John Stewart Fothergill (an old Bedalian) owned the adjacent holding to "Stonycroft." In all he had about twenty-four acres, with a similar little four-roomed shanty.

He asked us over to tea one evening. We were invited for 6.30, and it was already dark by the time we had finished milking and the separator had sung its song. Suddenly we heard a gunshot in the direction of Fothergill's abode. That was a signal to us that the feast was ready, so we trooped forth lantern in hand. Our host had felled an enormous blue gum tree across his main entrance, and had been busy for some days previously splitting its great limbs with charges of dynamite. Such a tangle was no easy one to penetrate on a dark night, but finally we worked our way through and arrived at the back door. We announced ourselves with some shouting, but were requested by the gruff voice of our host to remain outside for a few moments. Meanwhile a great banging, puffing, and hammering was going on within. Finally we were allowed to enter.

Aladdin's Cave could not have presented a more wondrous spectacle to hungry eyes. The open fireplace was radiant with roaring logs that leapt into renewed fiery energy as we entered, for the burly figure of our host was silhouetted against the tongues of flame, kerosene tin in hand. Harness, hams, and farm implements hung around the walls, and on these we placed our hats and coats. Candle stumps burnt in bottle-necks or cracked cups, and, I believe, there was a lamp of sorts. Among the flames hissed boiling "billies" and a frying-pan sizzled and filled the room with an appetizing reek.

An extra table had been erected to accommodate his guests; it consisted of Fothergill's bedroom door, which he had taken off its hinges for the occasion, supported on kerosene cases, with the same useful articles of furniture placed round about to sit upon. We had brought over our own cutlery, *silver*, and cups. We took our seats and a steaming pan was passed round and, dipping our forks into it, we drew forth curious-looking chops. Stewart apologized for the absence of breadcrumbs, "but," said he, "perhaps the *wood ashes* will do as well." Certainly the chops tasted excellent and went down with relish. Next came a "billy" full of prunes and these we helped ourselves to with the same forks, using the same plates on which the mutton fat had by now congealed. It is true that Fothergill did condescend to cleanse one or two platters for the more fastidious amongst us by holding them in the flames for an instant and then wiping them with newspaper.

The atmosphere became very thick after a time, and he evidently felt the heat, for he peeled off his jersey and sat down again in his short-sleeved vest which exposed his massive anatomy to advantage.

After we had fed, we were shown round the establishment. Our host's bedroom was an example of tidiness. His bedding seemed to consist of old sacks; the floor was littered up with old odd socks, boots, tools, and anything one would least expect to find there; whereas his spare room and sitting-room were both *full* of chaff, almost to the ceiling!

After this inspection, we sat round the fire yarning. I reposed on a sackful of paper, with a scythe as a back to my couch; others sat on cases, and one or two on *chairs*. We spoke of the merits of a bunch of onions hanging from the ceiling to keep away disease, and the remedy of pouring kerosene on the floors in summer time to keep down the fleas. Also there were the evergreen topics of cows and fencing, and the flooding of paddocks by the oft-overflowing streams that abound in this picturesque neighbourhood.

So we went on; lighting our pipes and throwing fresh sticks of gorse or willow onto the dying fire that blazed up merrily on being coaxed by the addition of more oil.

There, with unshaven cheeks, in dungarees and toil-stained clothes, we sat and yarned and smoked and dreamt of the days that were, and the prosperity that was to come out of cows and butter, eggs and swine, until Sid said:

"If we're going to get up at six to-morrow, boys, it's time we went to bed."

And so back we went to "Stonycroft" and slipped into our blankets and slept. In such a brotherly community as we had at "Stonycroft" it was a very joy to live. The dog fondled the cats, and they, in their turn, arched their backs around the snowy feathers of the cocks and hens.

Ah! I was forgetting the evening we spent with old McGill before a huge log fire in *his* little parlour. His son and daughter were there too, and a poor imbecile boy of his, whose one delight in life was music. We sang songs and smoked pipes, and listened to the old man's memories of Hereford. At last he sprang to his feet, and, with his back to the fire, he sang us an old country song about a man with carroty hair. Simple souls were these, and unpretentious. Our concert ended with the singing of *Forty Years On*, the martial strains of which seemed to please them very much.

To-day, no doubt each shack and homestead has its wireless set, and aeroplanes drone over the entire length of "Ao-tea-Roa." Old McGill's grown-up imbecile son can hear music all day long, and old McGill, were he alive to-day, could rock himself to and fro in his armchair as the loudspeaker emits the refrain of "A man with carroty hair." Fothergill lies in Flanders' Fields, Cyril has (alas!) died whilst this book was in the press, whilst Sid still toils on, and we would fain be back with them all, working and singing in our own sweet way.

Long shall we remember the beautiful neighbourhood of "Stonycroft," where streams abound and poplars line the highways and byways as they do in France. Watercress and mint choke the rivulets, and are considered as weeds, whilst the snow-covered mountains are close enough to frame this great pastoral plain with dignity; and they gave the eye something to rest upon and the mind something to yearn for when we raised our aching backs for an instant's pause during the labour of the day. The sea, too, sometimes coloured the horizon between the willow boughs, as we drove to market or took train to "Town," and here and there, by stream side or in open paddock, the swaying heads of the Toé-toé grasses and the shining leaves of the lily palm trees called one back to New Zealand from dreams of the Homeland, Switzerland, or France. We still often think of Spot, and how he used to take an evening off to visit the local slaughter-house, whence he would drag home putrid sheep heads, on which he delighted to roll—*dear* dog—and then took forty winks on the most comfortable bed in the shack! And the rising at dawn, just as the full yellow moon hung in the heavens for an instant and then sank behind the snow peaks as the sun rose clear from the murky clouds. Civilization with its washing and its shaving, with its pleasant talk and cleanly raiment, seemed strange at first, and somewhat distasteful. One learns to appreciate the amenities of the over-civilized world more for a temporary retirement from it, and our stay at "Stonycroft" had not been time wasted, for we saw and learnt *much* that was unbeknown to us before.

Life in Timaru and Christchurch

It was May 24th when we returned to Timaru to find a serious strike was just over. We were sorry for some things, for it would have added yet further to the variety of our experiences had we earned our 22s. per day (including overtime) loading frozen mutton. And we should have done so without a moment's hesitation, because we found ourselves devoid of any sympathy with the strikers. The workers were simply in clover in regard to both conditions of work and wages; so much so that they could afford to strike for the amusement of it. The whole trouble arose out of a personal quarrel. Three Union men started jeering at one of the old employees of the freezing works. It was not the first time, and the man, much exasperated, turned on his persecutors and threatened that if they continued to molest him he would do for them. This occurred somewhere in the outskirts of

Timaru. The Union men retired and insisted on this man's dismissal on the ground that he had threatened them with a revolver. The story goes that it was either a pipe or a penknife. The manager replied, very rightly, that he was not concerned with their personal quarrels, that the man was a good and faithful workman, and that if he had threatened or assaulted them there were courts to deal with such matters and judges to decide them. Whereat the workers at the freezing works went out on strike and the wharf labourers with them. Feeling was so strong that wealthy farmers, tradespeople, employers of all sorts, volunteered to fill the gap and get the boats loaded.

And they broke the strike; and the last state of the strikers was worse than the first, for the "free labourers" formed themselves into a competing union, and to the workers of this new union preference was naturally given.

The week that followed will long be memorable to the Timaruvians, for it was the week in which "*Their*" Dreadnought lay off the harbour. Never was excitement greater, and although they had only just had a public holiday and another one was due in a week or so, all work had to be closed down for such an event. The people came in their motor-cars and their traps, on their horses and on their bicycles, to gaze at that unproductive mass of steel and iron on which they had spent the generous sum of two millions. They were like children with a new toy, and could have cried with disappointment when Captain Halsey* decided it was too rough to attempt to come ashore.

Our numerous visits to the banks and shops in Timaru caused us much merriment. Seldom had we struck greater incompetence and self-satisfied assurance combined. Never have we laughed internally so much as we did at the bank clerk who, after keeping us waiting a "month of Sundays" while he leisurely entered a few items, made every mistake it was possible to make over a simple transaction, and ended by paying

* Now Admiral Sir Lionel Halsey, G.C.M.G., etc., Comptroller and Treasurer to H.R.H. The Prince of Wales.

94 Aladdin's Cave could not have presented a more wondrous spectacle

95 Our host's bedroom was an example of tidiness

96 Maori Canoes on the Wanganui River

97 Wanganui from Flagstaff Hill

us out £20 for each of the £10 Circular Notes we had presented! This, despite endless calculations on two slips of paper kept for the purpose. And when we pointed it out, with an appreciative remark as to his generosity, he was not at all perturbed, but contented himself with making another mistake. He quite overlooked that the "exchange" payable on £10 would be less than that on £20.

On our last Sunday at Timaru the youngest child of our host was christened. A Mr. Hunt came to Church Street for that purpose. He had had an interesting career in the South Sea Islands. He accompanied R. L. S. and his wife when they went to settle in Samoa, and curiously enough their only other fellow passengers on the boat were Chalmers of New Guinea and his wife and another famous missionary. They seem to have had a most interesting and happy time, and Stevenson refers to it in his *Letters*. Mr. Hunt kindly gave us two or three introductions in Samoa.

When Tuesday came I should have found it even more difficult to tear myself away had not this "Wander Year" consisted so largely of meeting and parting. Indeed, it was a succession of partings: first our hostess and the children at the house; then the Doctor at the station; and lastly the brothers at Winchester—Cyril quite satisfied and contented with New Zealand life; Sid infinitely too absorbed in the work on hand to give much thought to aught else. When should we four meet again?

As our train drew out of Winchester and passed their railway paddock I could just see the now red roof of "Stonycroft" in the distance. I thought of the difference the advent of a woman would make to that household—and I wondered what the future had in store.*

We were soon passing over the Rangitata River bed, at one time a vast stretch of boulders and pebbles, at another a roaring torrent carrying all before it and sweeping bridges aside as if they were but a pack of cards. New Zealand rivers

* Both brothers married soon after and had children.

are indeed a problem. They are so extravagant in their use of land, and withal so difficult to control.

The bareness of the famous Canterbury Plains has been much relieved by extensive tree plantations, largely put there as a protection against the strong north-west winds. Even the wood and galvanized-iron shanties would give the country a picturesque appearance had the inhabitants but the slightest idea of colour. The staple paint that was used was a vile shade of magenta, and why people should choose it I do not know, for a jobbing painter assured me that it is by no means one of the cheapest.

But the sun had set and the colours were no longer discernible by the time we reached Christchurch. Tom Steele was on the platform to meet us. We had soon left our trunks in the cloakroom and were driving through the streets of Christchurch, or, as it is invariably spelt out here, "Ch-Ch." By the shop lights it really looked as if we were passing through some suburb of London, for one did not observe the verandas that constitute the chief difference.

No. —, Papanui Road is a fine two-story house, but, like most Colonial houses, made of wood and with a galvanized-iron roof. It is of a type that is now, I imagine, likely to become difficult to sell. It is so impossible to obtain servants that people are building bungalows and doing without them.

Our week in Christchurch was not only an extremely happy but also an extremely busy one. Mr. G. H. Whitcombe, head of the firm of Whitcombe & Tombs, was extremely kind to us, and made us members of the Canterbury Club at Christchurch and the Wellington Club, as well as showing us around.

As we looked at Christchurch from the Cathedral tower, we came to the conclusion that the Port Hills should be climbed. The very next day we received a telephone message from Mr. Ell, then Member for South Christchurch, that he was going over the ground with a surveyor and would we come too?

It was a glorious walk up the Kashmir Hills past Victoria

Park and across Hoonhay Park to Kennedy's Bush. Christchurch and the Canterbury Plains lay stretched before us on the one side, and Governor's Bay, Lyttelton Harbour, and Banks Peninsula on the other. Mr. Ell proved to be an enthusiast, and one of whom any country might be proud.

As we climbed the Kashmir Hills, we learned that where we then saw fashionable dwellings, only a few years before sheep were grazing. We were told that the land purchased not so many years before by a retired Indian official for a few pounds an acre would be worth nearly three-quarters of a million sterling by the time a certain youth who was being educated in England became of age. Of destitution we saw no evidence in Timaru, and it therefore came as a shock to read of the existence of a coal and blanket society in Christchurch. On all sides, however, we were assured that there was no destitution that could not be directly traced to drink or desertion. So long as there is land still waiting development and work needing doing, this may well be the case. But how long will that be? And what then?

The magnificent forests of New Zealand are rapidly being cleared because they often occupy the best soil. We therefore rejoiced to find Mr. Ell quite indefatigable in his endeavour to preserve some of this Native bush for posterity. It is well that someone calls out, for the danger of its extinction is very great, because a forest of Kauri gums, for instance, cannot be replaced in one or even two generations.

Our visit to the Kaiapoi Woollen Mills was most interesting. It is probably one of the very few cases of a "protected" industry producing the finest article. But this remark applied to rugs only, for the blankets did not appear to us to be up to Witney standard. And although they claimed to have the latest and best machinery, they did not seem to make an attempt to utilize by-products, such as the oil extracted from the fleece. The racket in the weaving-room was unbearable, but otherwise the conditions of work were pleasant enough.

We spent one afternoon in the company of many interesting

people walking over the hills from Heathcote to Sumner. We learnt much of the work of the Peace Society, the Anti-Militarist movement, and the many prosecutions of boys for refusing to serve.

Amongst our party was Mr. Saunders, the editor of the *Lyttelton Times*, at whose charming little bungalow at Sumner we partook of tea. Sumner is beautifully situated, and the syndicate that bought the slopes of the hills at £10 per acre had no difficulty in selling quarter-acre sections for £75, and these were often again subdivided! But what they had done to "earn" these fabulous profits we did not learn.

Chapter X

THE NORTH ISLAND

OUR last day was yet another wild rush for us, and that evening we were on our way to Lyttelton, whence the S.S. *Maori* bore us across the "Windpipe of the Pacific." A strong south-westerly gale rocked us to sleep and woke us again with needless violence, but by morning the *Maori* was in the calm waters of Wellington Harbour. Thus we came from the hospitable shores of "Te Wai Pounamu" ("The Place of the Greenstone") to the land of that great monster "Te Ika a Maui" ("The Fish of Maui"), as the Maoris call the North Island. Maui, a demi-god of Maori mythology, when fishing one day hooked this great catch and drew it to the surface of the ocean. It is also told how he lassooed the sun with a cord made from the hair of his sister Ina, and was so able to make the days longer by checking the progress of the great fiery orb.

But there was no sun to greet us on our arrival at Wellington; a cold wind, a drizzling rain, and the hills surrounding this fine harbour shrouded in clouds were all the welcome Maui had prepared for *us*, but not inappropriate we thought as we turned out from our cosy cabin and faced this fish-like atmosphere—cold, wet, and clammy. True it was the month of June, the depth of winter, and doubtless the cord made from the hair of Ina was slackened to its extreme limit—the sun was enjoying his holiday in almost unbridled liberty!

During our stay in Wellington we were guests in one of the many delightful houses that are built on the steep slopes of the hills surrounding this city. "The Firs" was exceptionally well situated, for it overlooked the whole harbour, and every boat that entered and left Wellington passed beneath the dining-room window and could be seen over the top of the tall pines that surrounded us. We took many delightful rambles among these grassy summits where blow the cold winds for which this capital city is noted, and where are to be found the suburbs either perched on some exposed cone-shaped hilltop or nestling in the irregular folds of its down-like spur. As in many another Colonial household, our hosts had got over the servant problem by dispensing with them altogether. It certainly makes life infinitely more simple and less formal, and it is a more natural existence; and with it all they seemed to be able to have a good time.

One day we went to York Bay, adjoining Day's Bay. It was a sort of "Royal Command," for the invitation came from some friends of the Cobden family, to whom we had been given an introduction. It is a perfect spot right across the harbour, and was still covered with Native bush. Ratas and beeches grew there in the wildest profusion.

We took our lunch out into the woods, and the "Englishman" was put on to light the fire, which he did, to their surprise, with great success, despite the dampness of the wood, for this Englishman had handled gorse! It was a glorious day, so we climbed to the summit of the hills behind, and lo! there in the distance lay the South Island which we thought we had left for ever. Just across Cook's Strait were the white towering forms of the "Kaikouras" standing out against the clear blue sky, the very peaks that we had seen from the Port Hills at Christchurch. Returning to Day's Bay we walked along the beach, picking up "pawa" shells, iridescent with blues and rich greens, and lounged on the rocks listening to the pounding waves.

One of my many calls led me into the Houses of Parliament, and during an hour spent there with the Librarian I ran across two interesting people: the Hon. J. Rigg, M.L.C., and the Hon. R. Heaton Rhodes, the then Postmaster-General and *Minister for Tourist and Health Resorts* respectively. This was a stroke of luck that enabled me to ventilate my views as to the condition of the Milford Track!

There is a decided charm about Wellington that is apt to

grow even on a passing traveller who has already seen so many other beautiful scenes. There is a busy coming and going of men and ships; large, prosperous-looking business establishments and wide thoroughfares whose names tell how, in former days, they served as quays. These now form the principal streets in the centre of this busy city; whilst parts of the former bay have been replaced by new wharves, new buildings, and new roadways.

Earthquakes are not uncommon in Wellington. A severe shock of some minutes' duration startled the inhabitants of the city some few years ago, when a tidal wave swept across a narrow isthmus that protects a portion of the waters of the harbour. When the wave receded it was found that the land on the isthmus was about 6 feet higher than it had been before. Undaunted by this unpleasant occurrence a large number of people built houses on this land, and an important colony of suburban residences can now be seen dotting the isthmus, as one gazes down upon it from Mount Alfred.

But the inhabitants think nothing of these earth tremors. A dear old lady, who had spent the greater part of her life in New Zealand, said to me: "First there comes a roaring noise, and then the pictures begin to swing out from the walls and the ornaments totter to the edge of the mantelpiece. Sometimes they fall, but more often they remain on the shelf after balancing at a dangerous angle for a second or two. But the worst of all the sensations of an earthquake is one's own inward discomfiture, which is worse than being on a rough sea." She seemed to treat it all as a big joke.

This old lady was charming in every way, but she had an unfortunate knack of misplacing her aitches. We had been telling her of our proposed visit to the South Sea Islands when suddenly she said, "*My* sons have been to the Highlands." I at once asked her how they had enjoyed the beauties of Edinburgh, when another member of the family interposed hurriedly: "She means the Islands, the South Sea

Islands," he muttered. In some confusion I changed the subject as hastily and diplomatically as I could!

Up the Wanganui River

The country north of Wellington is very different from that surrounding Christchurch. As the train went on its leisurely way we passed through many tunnels that pierced the high, closely grouped hills, from which it would emerge to creep along the steep ridges of deep ravines. On every side burnt and decaying timber showed how the dense bush that once covered these hills had been "whacked out." Then came a beautiful run along the coast with views over French Pass to the South Island. Great clusters of ferns grew in the topmost forks of gaunt trees, like mistletoe, and from sand-dunes we passed beside vast flax swamps where the hemp hung drying on wire fences around the mill.

At Palmerston North we left our train, intending to put in a night there, but we had struck "Winter Show Week" and the place was filled to overflowing. There was nothing for it but to hustle through my calls and catch the next train on.

Palmerston North is one of the many prosperous inland towns which, as a writer in the *New Zealand Herald* rightly states, afford such an excellent index of the healthy progress the country is making.

We had noticed a large number of Maori schoolboys about, and we learnt that the great football match of the year had just been played, viz. Te Aute (the Maori College) versus Wanganui College. The Maoris are fine players, for they are well built and thoroughly adapted for the game. A South African would find this intimacy with a coloured race unbearable, even though he would admit that they were of a higher type than his coloured people, and he would find it intolerable that they should be treated as his equals at the refreshment bar of a station or a parcels office. Force of habit makes one forget the fact that here the coloured folk are a small minority, not an overwhelming majority.

When one realizes that some eighty years ago they were in the Stone Age and were cannibals, it is amazing to note the progress that they have made. One of the chief obstacles in their way is the easy position in which many of them find themselves. They are a landed aristocracy "who toil not, neither do they spin." They just live on the rents of the "Pakeha" (white man), and enjoy the luxuries of civilization without working for them—a demoralizing thing for white men, doubly so for a coloured race.

Our train meandered along from Palmerston North to Wanganui. New Zealand trains are painfully slow at the best, but we found this one bore the name of "Weary Willie," and it must have been very weary that night, for it stopped at innumerable "flag" stations, and it was nearly 10 p.m. before we arrived.

Next morning we were greeted by a clear blue sky and the invigorating air of a perfect winter day, so we panted up the steep flights of steps that led from the river bank up Flagstaff Hill. From the top we had an ever-memorable view overlooking the town of Wanganui, the winding river, and a vast expanse of the Tasman Sea. Over the broken ridges of the horizon landward we beheld the wonderfully symmetrical sugar loaf summit of Mount Egmont, the pride of Taranaki, and eastwards the broad shining shoulders of Mount Ruapehu gleamed enticingly in the brilliant atmosphere.

We learnt from the Old Salt who was in charge of the flagstaff that his duties were to signal the approach of inward-bound vessels and their safe negotiation of the harbour bar. He told us that he had sailed on every sea in ships of every kind, in the good old times when it took months instead of weeks, and weeks instead of days to sail from one port to another.

When our little steamer left Wanganui early next morning for its journey up the river the mist precluded any view. It was "out of season," so that our companions were nearly all Maoris instead of tourists. Our journey was thus full of interest, for the human element more than compensated for any lack of beauty for which the river is famous. The costume of the Maoris is now almost entirely European, but they are fond of gaily coloured rugs, in which they wrap themselves most dexterously as if they were shawls. The way they manage to balance a baby on their back while they envelope themselves, baby and all, is a marvel to behold. The women, particularly the old ones, are great smokers. One old dame, with a tatooed chin and an ill-fitting but costly coat, plumped herself down opposite us and immediately brought out her pipe. There she sat placidly puffing away till her son or some friend came up to greet her . . . and they "rubbed noses." No! They did not *rub* noses. They took each other's hand and with foreheads touching they just lightly pressed their noses together in a most affectionate, natural, and charming way. It seemed almost a sacrilege to look on while they were doing it. The girls, particularly the half-castes, are quite good-looking at a certain stage, but they seem rapidly to become very fat and coarse, but their smile remains bewitching. They lay around on the deck in graceful positions which look so comfortable, but which I know from experience would be torture to a European. Therefore we felt we could excuse a grey-haired courtier who, on bended knee, wooed an enormous maiden wrapped in a loud check blanket, who was reposing in a deck-chair at our feet.

The way the Maoris manage their children is a treat to behold, or is it that the children are different? It would be hard to conceive a boat-load of white mothers with their children and babies being a comparatively *peaceful* party, especially so far as the children and babies were concerned! But it must be admitted that these Maori parents made up for any lack of noise on the part of their offspring. Our fellow passengers were exceedingly talkative, and their speech was very musical to listen to; the way they raise their voices at the end of every phrase reminded us very much of the French language.

As the day wore on the mist lifted and the sun shone upon the tree ferns and willows that lined the banks of the stream. We stopped at many villages to drop passengers and cargo, and passed a party of wealthy Maoris in their motor-canoe, whilst many of the more primitive Native craft, carved out of the trunk of a tree, were moored to the river side and greatly added to the beauty of the scenery, wherein reflections played an all-important part. Here and there eel-traps dangled from overhanging boughs, and in places rapids flowed so swiftly that it seemed impossible for our boat to pass, but once only did our stern wheeler bump over some projection in the stream, much to the amusement of a Maori passenger who happened to be steering at the time.

The many evidences of Native life along the river banks were an odd but pleasant contrast to our previous journey up the Murray River in Australia, where nothing but memories of past associations with the nearly extinct aboriginal race remain. The absence of bird and animal life along the shores of the Wanganui is regrettable, but due perhaps to the fairly large number of human inhabitants in this region, though fallow deer are not infrequently seen grazing on the river banks.

The last reach of the river just before we arrived at Pipiriki, when darkness gradually closed around us, was the most beautiful of all. We passed through a deep cañon, a bush-clad ravine, which made us wish we had been able to explore the still narrower and more wonderful course of the Wanganui above this little village.

We found Pipiriki House greatly to our liking, from the Winter Garden embowered in tree ferns to the excellence of the hot baths. It was owned by the firm that ran the boat service and more or less owned the Wanganui River. Although built solely for the tourist traffic, we noticed it was used to no slight extent by the settlers of the district in their journeys to and from their sections. The Government had opened up a considerable quantity of land in this district for closer settlement, and although a very lonely life, it could hardly be called an isolated one with a steamer passing every day. Land of this sort involves exceptionally arduous work during the first three or four years, but at that time it offered one of the quickest roads to prosperity. And when once the ground was cleared there were then few things to touch sheep farming for bringing in the shekels with a minimum of effort.

From Cinders to Grass

For some miles after we left Pipiriki we passed through the most gorgeous "bush" country. In New Zealand the term "bush" is applied to forests of Native trees, and at one time nearly the whole of this southern portion of the North Island was thus covered and there was an almost unbroken stretch of trees from coast to coast. But the advent of the Pakeha brought speedy demolition in its wake, and with the exception of the Government Reserves this devastation of the bush continues to-day, though here and there the process is just a trifle less wasteful.

After passing the boundary of the Government Reserve at Pipiriki we plunged from the beautiful to the utilitarian, and the cleared bush was a very ugly sight. The dense undergrowth, the beautiful Native shrubs and trees, many of which will not survive if planted alone, were all swept away. Here the process had been completed some ten or fifteen years and grass replaced the bush, but the gaunt figures of the charred and limbless tree-trunks still stood there as a reminder of the glories that had been. And out of the ashes has sprung Raetihi, a thriving little township that prospers with the busy settlers round it.

Here we and our four companions of the drive, contractors' men paid to fence at so much a yard or to clear bush at so much an acre, were glad to break our journey for a warm by the fire and a cup of tea.

It was a bitterly cold night when we journeyed onwards into the darkness. Our old wagonette was replaced by a coach and five horses, the box-seat of which we had taken the precaution to book. Our only companions on this part of the ride were two Salvation Army lassies who were "unwise virgins" in that they had foolishly packed their rugs. But a S.A. lassie will take greater hardships than that with a smile!

Out of the darkness came the sound of much shouting. At a turn in the road we saw a blaze of light. Here were great goings-on, people moving backwards and forwards between a blazing pile of logs and a quaintly carved Maori building. A Maori had died, and all the friends and relatives had come to feast so long as the chief mourner would provide the means; and it would not do for the supply to be skimped. A *tangi*, as it is called, may last a month and cost hundreds of pounds, and the preparations are often commenced before the person is dead. But they take the precaution to assure the person that he or she *is* going to die, and, with a Native, that practically settles it! Between the feasting the young folk dance, and those who are too old or fat sleep.

The occasion of a *tangi* gives the Maori an opportunity to indulge his oratorical skill, which often attains a very high standard. Below we quote the oration of Rakaherea Pomare at the funeral of his elder brother Naera, both sons of the late Sir Maui Pomare, who for many years was a member of the New Zealand Cabinet. "Thinking in Maori," says a correspondent in *The Times*, from which our quotation is taken, "and speaking in English, Rakaherea Pomare pronounced the following oration":

We are gathered together on this courtyard to praise God and honour the dead. In all things be honest, more so to the dead than to the living, because the living can always have the sympathy of others. To-day is the anniversary of the passing of our father and the day of the burial of his son—my brother. Many are the canoes tethered by cords of love in this courtyard of our illustrious forebears. A noble brother and son has gone, and those who had been associated with him, both Pakeha [white men] and Maori, will revere his memory and mourn with us his loss. His ashes, borne on a canoe of flowers made by the loving hands of Pakeha friends who appreciated his Maori thoughts and ideas, have floated up to be alongside the ashes of his father as long as they might remain here—a great emblem of the cementing and unity which should and does exist between the two peoples. Come, therefore, and see the fallen leaf whose bloom hath fled. Come upon the wings of love. Bring our common grief and let us weep together.

Man holds the string of life but for a moment: then the bird returns to the great forest of Love. My brother has taken his stand at the stern of Fate's canoe, and has set its prow for mystic Hawaiki, on whose shores he will greet his father and rest in peace. Meanwhile the waves whisper sadness as they break on the shores of his homeland, the West Coast of this Island. He has gone to join his youthful companions along the path o'er which man never returns.

What matter if the roof, the side walls, and the reeds of a house be strong when the centre pole is levelled to the ground? The house will collapse, and we are bereft of our shelter. A mighty totara of the forest has fallen and the sapling which was growing up to take its place has now been torn away. It was my father's wish that he should be cremated, and following in his footsteps my brother's wish was that he too should be cremated. Time alone will tell whether they are right or wrong.

It is true that our precious jewels have been lost to us, but God, the Great Creator, has found them. Yet how often in my longing for them shall I wonder why Man was made so imperfect that he needs must die. However, their deeds will live, and will in the future be for me a guiding star.—*The Times*, August 13, 1932.

At Ohakune Mr. W. Seth Smith was at the post office to meet us, and the following morning our hostess showed us something of the country around them. Apart from a Government Reserve round what are known as the Twin Lakes, the district might well be termed an abomination of desolation. The process of clearing had only recently been undertaken. It was as if some Brobdingnagian reaper had swept the country with his scythe. The ground was just littered with trees. It had the appearance of a field of battle, and the dead and the wounded were lying on all sides. It was cheaper to set fire to what would burn and to leave the rest to rot than to make any effort to remove or use the timber. But in settled districts trees over a certain diameter were specially treated. There were hundreds of saw mills at work, and many of them moved from place to place. One of them was at work at Ohakune, and we followed their trolley line into the virgin bush. Before the hand of the spoiler set to work the saw mills marked out the best timber, ran trolley lines in to secure it, and then moved on. All the rest was felled and at the close of the summer burnt where it lay. The better the "burn," the better the ground is cleared for the grass seed, sheep, and cattle that follow in their turn. Ten or fifteen years after, the charred logs having rotted, the ground would be unencumbered and fruitful; but the Native bush and its beauties has disappeared for ever. We can bow to the necessity, but we do it with regret. We can acquiesce in such a process but we cannot bless it.

The bush that we entered, with its infinite tints of green, its gorgeous ferns and birch-like beech trees, took us back to the Milford Track, the one place where it will always be seen at its best.

One of the redeeming features of Ohakune is its unique view of the snowclad peak of Ruapehu (nearly 10,000 feet above sea-level), but although the sky had been cloudless for a fortnight prior to our visit, we were only treated to intermittent glimpses.

Railway travel in New Zealand was a sad falling off after the luxury of South Africa. The second class compartment in which we jogged along from Ohakune to Taumaranui was of the side-seated variety, like the inside of an old bus. They were even more difficult to ventilate than a bus. If one opened the large windows the back of one's head became frozen and one's neck stiffened. We tried it and paid the penalty! The alternative was to sit in a hermetically sealed compartment containing perhaps thirty people with the atmosphere growing steadily more fetid than a German railway carriage.

The Waitomo Caves

At Taumaranui we were not far from the centre of the North Island. It is what is known as the King Country, and the land is largely held by the Maoris. For the most part they are content to lease it to the Pakehas and live in luxury on the rents received, but occasionally a Maori can be found working his own ground. That this is not more frequently the case is possibly due to the fact that much of their land is owned communally, so that, unless they adopt some co-operative system of working it, as they are being taught to do in some parts, it is hard for the individual to make any move. I am afraid, however, that the Maoris share many of the characteristics of the Corsican: I refer not only to the love of fighting and the love of ease, but the love of disputing over the ownership of land!

The King Country is for the most part covered with bracken fern and ti tree (Manuka), and although not amongst the best it is by no means unfertile. In the main it is excellent for grazing, and settlers whom we met spoke well of it and of the freedom of the life.

The Waitomo Caves are about six miles' drive from Hangatiki through country that in the distance gave a suggestion of the Surrey hills. The Government runs a most excellent hostelry on the hillside near the caves, and as the other guests were all departing we were given our choice of rooms.

Once again we had one of those beautiful New Zealand winter days that are at the same time both invigorating and trying. Crisp frosty mornings and evenings when the thickest underclothing leaves one cold, and an hour or two in the middle of the day like an English summer. There are three caves to visit: the Ruakuri, the Aranui, and the Waitomo. The first two, which are a few miles farther on, we drove to see in the afternoon. The Ruakuri, or "Dog's Hole," has the most characteristic entrance, a sort of gash in the side of the hill down into which it is necessary to climb. At certain

98 Near the Hamurana Spring, Rotorua

99 We in our turn came to Wairoa

100 The whole mountain side seemed to be ablaze

101 The bare, relentless slopes of Tarawera

periods of the year, when the rivers are in flood, it is impossible to visit it, for the river that we could hear surging along below us, apparently under our very feet, swells and blocks the way. It was quite uncanny to hear the thud of the waters below and the sound of a waterfall in the distance as we followed our guide through long and winding passages. On every side there was a wealth of stalactites and stalagmites, many of the purest white, others tinged with iron; some thin and smooth like hollow tapers, and some enormous like gigantic cones.

The wealth of detail in the so-called Bridal Chamber must be unrivalled, and the coral-like sides make the place into a veritable fairyland as it sparkles in the bright light of magnesium flares. Here and there the stalagmites have formed themselves into weird and fantastic shapes, and in the ever-changing light the cave seemed peopled with strange beings.

But we had yet greater wonders to see. The Aranui, or "Great Surprise," had been discovered by a Maori chasing after a pig which suddenly disappeared. In some ways it is even finer than the Ruakuri, though they are both very beautiful, for it has a more wonderful climax. At the end of some entrancing passages the cave opens out. It is as if one were in the nave of a crystal cathedral. We stood spellbound by the railing at the entrance of the chancel while our guide walked slowly forward. A peal of church bells resounded through the chamber as he tapped a row of stalactites that hung down like organ pipes to the right of the chancel. Presently there was a blaze of light, and we could see yet more clearly the glories of this buried temple. The decorations appeared like marble and coral of the purest white, and Nature's carving was more beautiful than hand could fashion or heart desire. As the light slowly died away a tenor voice rang out. And then all was darkness and silence—a darkness blacker than the night and a silence deeper than the grave.

In the cool of the evening, lantern in hand, we made our way through the bush to the Waitomo, or "Water Cave." The doorway is in the solid rock with thick undergrowth all around. It reminded me irresistibly of Holman Hunt's picture. Outside it was a cold and frosty night, inside the air seemed warm. We were glad to discard our coats before penetrating farther. Once more we found ourselves in a labyrinth of underground passages. Stalactites hung down in the greatest profusion, and many of the stalagmites assumed the weirdest forms. Whether pure white like wax or tinged with iron yellow, they shone out transparent in the brilliant light. Once again we found the passage opening out, this time into the dome of a vast cathedral, into the recesses of which the light scarcely penetrated.

After crawling along endless passages, stumbling over stalagmites, and imagining multitudinous forms of sublime and horrid character, our guide brought us at last to a place of mystery where our lights had to be left behind. Striking a vesta and holding by a rail we followed him down a slippery track, and soon, in the uncertain flickering light cast by our matches, we espied the dim outline of a boat and the gleam of a pool.

Observing our guide's strict instructions to keep silence, we took our seats in this craft while he blew out his light after slipping the painter and seizing a wire that ran along the side of the tunnel. By holding on to the wire he thrust the boat out into the darkness of these unknown waters.

Whither were we bound? A cold shudder ran down my back. Had we then found our way to the Lower World of "Po" or Darkness? Was our boatman in reality the ferry woman Rohé in disguise, and were we even now bound for that "farther shore" where she would tempt us with rare foods? And what if we ate thereof? Had not our fathers told us the mythological Maori tale that if we ate of the food proffered by the ferry woman Rohé we should be condemned to remain in the bitter darkness of this underworld? "But if you refuse to eat," they added, "if you have strength to *refuse*, you shall awake upon the Earth as from a trance." So we prayed to have strength to abstain from Rohé's offerings, and our boat glided silently on, nor could our eyes fathom the dense obscurity until, with almost alarming suddenness, the entire roof of the tunnel we were traversing became illuminated with fairy lights—a myriad blue jewels they seemed, studding a cloth of velvet blackness just above our heads, and by their light we could just discern the dim form of our boatman stooping in the prow.

For a long time we passed spellbound beneath this subterranean constellation, till presently our boat bumped against the side of the tunnel: "Look," said the boatman in a more audible voice, "you see, we have come to the mouth of the cave!" Looking up we beheld the stars of heaven twinkling between the branches of the trees; we believed that these were the tempting offerings of Rohé, so we resolutely turned our eyes away and asked to be taken back to Earth across the river of fairy lights.

It was night when we returned to the world of men. The gateway of "Po" clanged behind us, and lantern in hand we stepped through the hoar-frosted Manuka, and as we gazed up at the stars we knew that we had refrained from temptation and recovered from the trance into which we had fallen in the famous glow-worm cavern of Waitomo, the "Water Cave."

Afterwards, as we sat around the open fire at our hostelry, pipe in mouth, we still shuddered at the thought of our underground wanderings. Long will the recollection of that appalling silence, broken only by the hollow "drip-drop" from the overhanging stalactites, remain with us—a remembrance of the silent terrors of "Po," the World of Darkness.

There were great festivities in the neighbourhood that night. The manager of the local store was taking his departure, and in a "no licence" area that is sufficient excuse for a case of whisky to be ordered along by rail and an invitation to the settlers to take an evening off and make merry. In the King Country, as one settler was careful to explain to me, there are no class distinctions, and a display of "side" is unknown. "Back-block settlers ploughing their lonely furrow" day after day and week after week naturally pine for any opportunity that brings them in contact with their fellow men and women. The longing to see a little life is natural enough, and with many it includes a desire to drown their loneliness in whisky, and it is not for the town dweller to cast the first stone.

It seems a strange task to spend your lifetime walking up and down moving railway trains selling newspapers, magazines, and books. But it appears strange merely because of its novelty. Here in New Zealand it is a recognized occupation, and though very hard work there is apparently a living to be made at it. The monotony of the journey from Hangatiki to Frankton Junction was broken by an account of his work that was given me by Mr. J. J. Busby, who had what is known as the Taumaranui Run (i.e. the railway line from Taumaranui to Frankton), and he turned out to be one of those with whom I had discussed Prohibition in the hotel smoking-room at Taumaranui. But for him many a settler would have had but scanty news of the outside world, for besides selling papers in the train he dropped many along the line at regular places.

The Beautiful Face of a Boiling Underworld

It was dark by the time we reached Rotorua, for we were nearing the shortest day and the anniversary of our departure from Home. The Two Young Men, ever on economy bent, left the Grand Hotel (12s. 6d. per day) to the officers of H.M.S. *New Zealand*, and patronized the Empire Boarding House (6s. per day), where about twenty of the crew were being entertained.

We learnt that the Maoris were giving a special entertainment for the benefit of the sailors, and as this was a thing not to be missed we promptly booked seats and took our places in the hall, which was packed from floor to ceiling. It was a most interesting performance. The part-singing reminded us of the Welsh choirs, which is high praise. The dancing and games were unique, and the Rev. F. A. Bennett (himself a Maori) was doing good work in keeping alive, and in many cases reviving, the best Maori customs and traditions.

The *Poi* games were performed by six *wahine* (women), and are generally part of the ceremony on religious and state occasions. The player holds a round hard ball made of flax, and about the size of a tennis ball, by means of a cord. She has a ball in each hand, and whilst the chorus chants a melody in strains that would be impossible to reproduce on any European instrument, these maidens swing their *Poi* by a wrist movement with such ease, grace, and dexterity that one can but marvel at their accomplishment.

This was followed by a very ancient Maori game or ceremonial, known as the *Potaka*. After an impressive incantation from the crowded chorus, two men set spinning a couple of tops that were suspended from the ceiling. If the tops climb up the cord, as one of them did on this occasion, up to the roof of the building, then the omen is good, but woe betide the particular Maori tribe taking part in the ceremonial if the top refuses to rise.

The Hat Dance was a most amusing game! A crowd of *wahine*, wearing red and white blouses untucked at the waist and great wide-brimmed straw hats, were drawn up in lines across the stage. All sorts and sizes were these women, from slender, beautiful girls to enormous, gross-looking matrons with tattooed chins. All stamped their feet rhythmically to the song, swinging their hips and arms and clapping their hands in spasmodic accompaniment. Eyes and tongues and smiles and scowls played an important part in all these Maori games and dances. But the peculiarity of this one was the simultaneous taking off of the straw hats with a united and tremendous shriek, and then laying them on the floor with a most hilarious gesture. The whole dance went with a terrific and ever-increasing speed, and the performers worked themselves up into such a frenzy of excitement, especially two of the fattest women, who displayed most extraordinary energy in the front row of dancers, that the audience was prostrated with merriment and persisted in an encore.

We were treated in the second part of the programme to the charming tale of the love of a celebrated Maori chief's daughter, the beautiful Hinemoa, for Tutanekai, the commoner, who dwelt on the island of Mokoia in the middle of Lake Rotorua. The story, which was presented to us in the form of a series of tableaux, was exquisite in every detail of Native dress and setting.

We were glad that this very interesting entertainment came to a close with an exposition by the entire company of that most stirring of all Native dances, the *Haka*. The body action in this dance is very violent, and the vocal accompaniment of blood-curdling yells and shrieks from those taking part even more so, whilst the incessant vibrating of the hands of the dancers produces an astounding effect analogous to that of the tremolo in European music. The *Haka* is an almost daily pastime with the Maoris, and in tourist districts children, alone or in groups, will perform the dance by the wayside in exchange for a penny; they call them locally "The Penny *Haka*"!

We felt we could not have had a better introduction to this part of New Zealand, the thermal region, where the continuous restlessness and mystery of underground phenomena blend so harmoniously with the Native life and legend that is closely associated with the many beautiful lakes and scarred mountain sides of this intriguing district. The sailors, like ourselves, thoroughly enjoyed the entertainment, and at the railway station next morning, where there was a large crowd of Maoris to see them off, they gave an excellent imitation of the *Haka*, greatly to the amusement of the Maoris present, for they have a keen sense of humour.

Amongst the letters at the post office was one from a lady friend of Johnnie's (a pretty little nurse!), Miss May B——, whom we had met at Wellington, to say that she was now installed at Rotorua, and on our first inspection of the place whom should we meet but the lady in question! She at once took us through the Sanatorium grounds, where simple fountains are replaced by jets of evil-smelling vapour and hot water that come belching up from the bowels of the earth.

"While you are here you ought to have a bath," she said, "and you had better have a Priest."

We suggested we were not Catholics, but she merely laughed and added, "You will find a Public Priest all right. Meet me at two, and I will take you to Whaka" (Whakarewarewa).

So we entered the portals of the large Government Sanatorium and remarked with some hesitation that we wanted a Public Priest. We were given a ticket and a towel, ushered along a corridor, told to turn to the left and take such-and-such a door on the right. Which we did, despite much temptation to enter a door marked "Rachel, Gentlemen only." A strange sight met our eyes: bald-headed old gentlemen with hairy chests as fat as the Lord Mayor's coachman, together with bearded bags of bones, were seated in a large square bath up to their necks in steaming water of a suspicious colour and unpleasant smell. Two minutes later the Two Young Men, any absurd little ideas of modesty thrown to the winds, were themselves seated with the rest and were eagerly discussing the temperature of the water and the merits of the various baths: the old Priest, the Mud Baths, and the Postmaster, with its three baths of increasing temperature.

It was quite pleasant to be out in the sunshine again and the crisp air. It is impossible to say fresh sweet air, for so long as one is in the thermal region one must accustom oneself to the fumes of H_2S.

On our way out we met our friend May again, and as there was still time before lunch she escorted us through the Government Reserve. There were many notices warning visitors to keep to the path, but when once they had seen some of the many pools of boiling water and mud that lay hidden in the Manuka scrub there was little fear of anyone desiring to wander. It was an uncanny walk, but very mild compared to what the afternoon had in store for us.

On our way back we passed through Ohinemutu on the shores of Lake Rotorua, which was the site of the original town. It is now a Maori village, and here we saw, for the first time, the boiling holes being used for cooking purposes. How useful one of those steaming holes would have been to us at "Stonycroft"! Fancy being able to take your kettle to your backyard to be boiled without the necessity of lighting any fires!

Whakarewarewa, to give it its full name, is nearly two miles out of Rotorua, and here are to be seen some of the most wonderful geysers, but, unlike many others, they do not play at regular intervals. It is a weird place, and scarcely a site one would choose for a village, but the Maoris live there within a stone's throw of all this volcanic action. It is just a crust of dried lava exuding steam from every pore. In places the very sulphur of which it is partly composed is still burning hot. From a dozen or more holes in the rock great quantities of steam and boiling water are continually belching forth. In other places there are porridge pots, pools of boiling mud through which the steam is continuously escaping. Here there are gurgling holes that may at any time burst forth; there pools that petrify all that is placed within. The whole air is laden with sulphurous fumes, the odour of bad eggs, and one marvels at the hardihood of the Manuka that seems to thrive almost on the very edges of these boiling cauldrons.

As we were surveying the scene and waiting for the big "Pohutu" geyser to play, we wondered at man's temerity. Were we not skating on rather thin ice? A few hundred yards from where we stood is a large pond of mud known as the "Devil's Reception." That very morning the whole thing had shot up into the air to a height of 40 or 50 feet, but when we saw it it appeared dotted with small blow-holes all busily engaged in spitting mud pellets into the steamy atmosphere, to an accompaniment of flopping, puffing, and sucking sounds that were far from agreeable to listen to.

In one of the most sinister-looking corners of this unpleasant neighbourhood there once dwelt a notorious Maori cannibal and his servant. Whenever this recluse felt hungry he would venture forth from his cleverly concealed lair and slay some well-fed member of an adjacent tribe. At times, if ever an errant Maori passed by the boiling pool beside his hiding place, this dark-skinned ogre would trip up the traveller and throw him headlong into it, when the necessary cooking did not take long in this natural model kitchen. At length, however, the vicious cannibal was entrapped and slain in his turn by his neighbours, and the brains of this Tohunga or wise man, as his captors thought him to be, were cooked in a curious hot sulphur basin near by and divided equally among the victorious tribesmen. "For," said they, "if we eat of this wise man's brains we, in our turn, shall gain something of his wisdom." Our inspection of the "Brain Pan," as it is called, terminated our visit to Whakarewarewa.

At ten o'clock next morning the three of us were seated in a little motor launch making our way across Lake Rotorua past Mokoia Island; here dwelt the commoner Tutanekai. We were bound for the Hamurana Spring, where it is estimated that about twelve million gallons of beautiful cold water well up daily. So strong is the upward flow that pennies will not sink. Be that as it may, we recommend the use of somebody else's pennies, for they soon get washed out of sight. The clear stream, like so many others in New Zealand, was alive with trout, and they seemed to know it was a close season.

Joining the launch again, we made for the Ohau Channel that leads into Lake Roto-Iti. (In Maori names, every syllable is pronounced; therefore it is Ro-to-ee-tee.) We landed at the Okere Falls, which are spoilt by an electric power station, and, after a picnic lunch on the bracken-covered hills, climbed down Hinemoa's Steps to a cave at the side of the falls that was once a Maori's habitation.

Tikitere and Tarawera

Our drive back was by way of Tikitere,* one of the most extraordinarily unpleasant places we ever want to see. The atmosphere of Rotorua was flavourless compared with what now assaulted our nostrils. All around us were boiling lakes; dense clouds of steam arose on every side, and the very ground seemed to be seething and sizzling. It was as if hell's gates were opened. In one place there was water 20 degrees hotter than boiling point, and not half a dozen yards away, but at quite a different level, water that was little more than warm. At other points boiling mud was being spewed up, mud that, if dried, would form the most delicate Fuller's Earth. Here hot and cold streams were running almost side by side, and everywhere were signs of violent disturbances below. Sulphur and alum were present everywhere, and minerals of every variety and in every form. In one pool, quantities of sulphuric acid were present; in another, oil. Nature's chemical laboratory seemed to have been turned out for our benefit. A boiling pool of mud at one place would be a foot or more higher than another not a yard away. The levels and the temperature varied at each spot. And against this white background of dried lava and crater was the green Manuka scrub, unconcerned with the *Sturm und Drang* around, ever anxious to cover the earth.

Early on the morrow we set out for Wairakei, near the head of Lake Taupo. There was much to see on the way as we intended crossing Lakes Tarawera and Roto-mahana. The road took us by the Government larch plantations and the beautiful blue and green lakes to the buried village of Wairoa, destroyed in the great Tarawera eruption of 1886.

We feel justified in giving here a short quotation from Mr.

* Tikitere was owned by seventy-eight Maoris who shared the proceeds after paying a Pakeha 6d. out of the 2s. per head received for acting as guide.

W. Pember Reeves' book, *The Long White Cloud*,* in which he writes: "In the heart of this uneasy region of startling sights and satanic smells the traveller is shown the cloven volcano, Tarawera, the long chasms of which are a memorial to the most terrible natural convulsion witnessed by white men in New Zealand. On June 10, 1886, in fine, cool, winter weather, the heavy-looking mountain mass, until then regarded as extinct, and which certainly had been quiet for so long that thick-stemmed trees had grown in its crater, exploded with a roar that made windows rattle in the city of Auckland, 140 miles away. The eruption was preceded by earthquake shocks in rapid series, which those who felt them likened to the blows of titanic hammers striking upward beneath the earth. Then a huge column of fire was spurted aloft, from which red-hot stones shot through the air, bombing the country round for miles. With fire came first mud and then dust, for, after a while, a vast black cloud, mushroom-shaped, shadowed the land eastward of the burning mount for many leagues. The dust was thrown up 8,000 feet into the air.† For hours the sound of the eruption deafened beholders, and a tempest of wind, icy cold, though varied with hot gusts, blew wildly enough to prostrate tall trees. As the red fury of the explosion abated, darkness settled down on the overshadowed territory, and grey volcanic dust continued to fall, soft and dense, like an infernal snowstorm. All herbage was destroyed . . . wild birds and rabbits were starved. When daylight at last struggled through the black canopy it was found that Lake Roto-mahana, with the islets therein, its fern-clad shores, and neighbouring lakelets, had been blown to the skies, and that where these had been was an expanse of boiling, steaming mud. The pink and white terraces . . . perhaps the most singular features of these islands, were utterly destroyed. After a time Lake Roto-mahana re-formed, and is now to be seen a larger sheet than before, but the loss of the terraces was irreparable. Only

* London: George Allen & Unwin Ltd.

† Some of this dust fell on the decks of vessels 500 miles away at sea.

four whites, two of them children, lost their lives in the eruption, but more than one hundred Maori perished, smitten by falling stones or smothered by the mud that overwhelmed their huts."

It was such a day in June as Mr. Reeves describes when we in our turn came to Wairoa "in fine, cool, winter weather." Of the little village there is but sparse evidence to-day. But there are the remnants of a little wooden *whare* (shanty), and to anyone who knows its story those remnants are very sacred; for, thanks to the pluck of a couple of Maoris, that *whare* saved over thirty lives. Wairoa is seven miles from Tarawera, but boiling mud to a depth of 5 feet was flung upon it. Most of the buildings collapsed, but this little *whare* held out, and many crowded into it. As the eruption continued it became obvious that, despite additional supports from inside, it could not hold up much longer. It was at this point that two Maoris went outside and shovelled away the mud to relieve the weight. A little farther on, the top of an iron bedstead is visible projecting from the ground.

There was an hotel here once. A young Englishman was writing on the veranda when the roof gave way and crushed him. It was a letter to his mother he was writing, and they found it near the body. Yes, that is the top of a buggy that has been buried in the ground these forty-seven years. It was near here that a lady saw her child killed in front of her very eyes, and was at the same time herself pinned down by a fallen beam from which she was not extricated until the legs of the chair on which she was sitting were sawn off. It is Wairoa, and the many buried Maori settlements of which we hear less, that make one gaze at Tarawera in wonder at those bare, relentless, mud-covered slopes of the gaunt inanimate volcano, towering from the waters of the lake like some modern ship of war with her weapons of offence concealed. But who shall say what is brewing below?

Saucily our petrol launch raced across to the sleeping monster that looked placid enough, its lower spurs clothed in a patchy mantle of ubiquitous Manuka that hardly hid the scars of bygone days. But our boat pulled up within a few yards of where the huge mountainous bulk sank into the quiet water, and then our little craft dodged away again, like a mischievous puppy from under the nose of a drowsy hound, and slipped by the dead village of Moura, which was covered, like all the hills around, by the alternating layers of mud and ash which rained upon them from lake and mountain in the great upheaval of 1886.

We landed on a shore strewn with cinders and with pumice, and followed a track to the shoulder of the hill whence we viewed the great Tarawera Chasm and the waters of Lake Roto-mahana (Hot Lake). Undaunted by the assurances of our guide that a second eruption might take place at any moment we boarded another motor-launch, and were soon speeding alongside the famous burning cliffs of Roto-mahana. As we approached, the whole mountain side seemed to be ablaze: steam rose in dense columns from the water's edge, and with the sun's rays penetrating from behind, a picture of unparalleled magnificence was formed. At one moment our craft was enveloped in steam and the water all around was hot, whilst a moment later, having sped round a projecting point of land, the water beneath us was cold! The rain has washed great gullies in the mud and ash of which the hillsides are composed, and these resemble the ribs of some vast prehistoric skeleton.

From the shores of Lake Roto-mahana we walked to the great Waimangu Geyser, great no longer for, since some time, its activity has ceased. Our track followed the course of a stream of boiling water from whose banks steam jetted out, and even from under the very path we trod. But we followed our guide quite unconcerned, so readily does man take things for granted. He took great pains to point out to us the exact spots where four bodies were found in the stream after an eruption of the geyser.

The Waimangu Crater is about one acre in extent, and in

the days of its activity it would shoot this terrific volume of boiling mud and ashes into the air to a height of several hundred feet about every thirty hours, whilst the immense white cloud of steam that followed each explosion would be hurled many thousands of feet upwards. The four unfortunate people referred to above had come to witness this awesome spectacle; they ventured too near, alas! and were caught in the scalding downpour and swept away in the torrent of boiling water and black scorching mud!

Presently we were looking down on the Waimangu Crater. Near to it is a lake of boiling water, the rise and fall of which used to be a certain indication of the height the geyser would play. On the other side, in the middle of a stream, a small geyser was still at work, and we could see the steam and spray of boiling water that was continually ejected. Here we were detached observers looking on from above, but five minutes later we were *in medias res*, for we had descended to what is known as the Frying-pan Flats. The name describes the place exactly. The ground in every direction was sizzling. A thin hard crust had formed, and over this we followed the Government guide. We felt that the proverbial ice was getting very thin indeed! Our feet tingled with the heat below while we stood in the frying-pan and watched the frying! Here was everything at work in miniature: boiling pools, mud volcanoes, and a blow-hole that emitted large quantities of steam every four or five minutes. In the little streams of hot water that flowed on all sides of us we noticed those wonderful little algae reputed to be the first to grow on the earth from the fact that they are the only plants which can live in water that is almost, but not quite, boiling. They seem to have the power of absorbing the minerals in solution in the water. They were a beautiful shade of peacock green which added yet another to the many colours in the frying-pan, and as a contrast to this continuous effervescing and excitement, sheep and cattle were grazing not fifty yards away, untroubled and unconcerned.

At the summit of a hill near by, the Government have built a hostelry, and to this we were glad to retire for a cup of tea and a bird's-eye view of the weird places we had been visiting. Somehow we felt happier at a distance!

But, although we were soon driving away from Waimangu, we had not left geysers behind. We were travelling southwards to Wairakei, "the wonderland of the thermal district." Ahead of us in the far distance we could see once more the snow-clad peak of Ruapehu and the black and white streaked sides of smoking Ngauruhoe.

A large mud volcano, busily coughing up the same mud again and again, which we inspected *en route*, gave us another unpleasant reminder of the thinness of the crust that separated us from the unknown.

We spent that night at Waiotapu, and when we awoke the next morning we found the wattle trees which surrounded our hotel draped in hoar frost and a thick mist hung over the countryside. No sooner had the sun dispersed the fog, and thawed the hoar frost on the boughs to sparkling gems of moisture, than we ventured forth once more under the guidance of a Maori maiden to inspect the fine collection of coloured lakes and pools, fumaroles and solfataras that surrounded our hotel. From our window we had gazed out at the great expanse of rising steam, and now we were in the middle of it, picking our way over crumbling tracks that sounded hollow beneath our feet. Perhaps the finest sight at Waiotapu is the Champagne Cauldron, a large boiling pool of blue water which effervesces as freely as the best of Heidsieck, when a spadeful of earth from a neighbouring alum bank is cast into it. Terraces made of a substance like the "fur" that collects at the bottom of a kettle covered a large area over which the hot water gently rippled.

But it is almost impossible to convey in words surroundings so unique. Like Tikitere the place is owned by a group of Maoris, who live in ease on the visitors' toll of 2s. a head.

Our journey on to Wairakei was by car, but the coach and

car services had been amalgamated for the day and we had the parcels to deliver. The whole back of the car was stacked up with brown paper parcels, mostly containing bread, and mail-bags. These were delivered by the way mostly into Tate sugar boxes stuck up on their ends on a couple of poles by the side of the road. One would not perhaps think it from their appearance, but they were the letter-boxes and parcels' receptacles for homesteads miles away.

At one point, after we had disposed of a lot of the parcels, a Maori dame with tattooed chin expressed her desire to join the car, and room had to be made for her next to me. The chauffeur was a trifle apologetic, but I was much amused. With the desire of making myself affable, I asked the good lady if she liked motoring. "Yes," she replied, "if it is a good car. I am going to have my own next month!" Her husband was apparently a large landowner, so that they had plenty of money. I was, in fact, talking to a Maori aristocrat without knowing it!

A little farther along the road—I think it was at a place called Whakamarumaru—we stopped to have "a liquor up," and here we took on board a roadmender, who found a seat on the step of our overloaded car, and his collie dog curled himself up on my lap. So we sped on over the sandy road with views overlooking the dreary Kaingaroa country that stretched away in long blue distances, dotted here and there with white puffs of steam, to where Ruapehu and Ngauruhoe rose into a pale blue sky; and thus at eveningtide we came to Wairakei, the greatest Wonderland of Te Ika a Maui.

Wairakei

On our arrival at the Wairakei Hotel the proprietor invited us to take a swim, but forgetting that perhaps in these parts it would be hot water we shivered at the thought and voted for tea and a quiet stroll. We found ourselves in luck's way, as it was out of season and we had the place to ourselves. There

102 A bird's-eye view of the weird places we had been visiting

103 The Frog Pond and Manuka bushes, Waiora Valley

104 We crept into the Dragon's mouth at Wairakei between the explosions

105 A fall of boiling water, Waiora Valley

was a comfortable sitting-room with a sensible table and a blazing log fire.

After our long accounts of geysers, fumaroles, and solfataras, what is there left for us to say of the Wairakei Geyser Valley? This: that it is perhaps the most wonderful of all. Along that little narrow steaming valley, clothed with Manuka and an occasional *Pinus insignis*, all the wonders of this thermal region seem to be present.

Staff in hand, we followed our guide through the Native scrub. Below us was the little stream that, starting cold, gets heated in its onward course, for its path is beset with geysers and hot springs on either side. Attracted by vast clouds of steam, we descended from the main track and found ourselves by the Champagne Cauldron. Here pure soda water, hotter than boiling point, is continually gushing up in uncertain rushes, hissing and bubbling at its release from the pressure and heat below. The earth beneath our feet throbbed with the subterranean concussions; great unseen forces were at work feverishly creating these sudden gushes of water, which overflowed the cauldron on to the terraces of kettle "fur," green with the algae that cover them. It was difficult to tear ourselves away from that boiling cauldron; the mighty power behind it, the uncertainty of what it would do next fascinated us.

But we moved on to the Pack-horse Mud Geyser, where a pack-horse with a load of sugar, butter, and flour fell in one day, and German sausages and batter pudding were spewed up, according to local legend, and so on to the Great Wairakei Geyser which every ten minutes, with the regularity of clock-work, throws up vast quantities of boiling liquid. A few steps farther we were crossing a cold stream with a boiling hole not a foot from it, and at another place the ground was covered with salt.

Of the Great Wairakei Boiling Pool with its magical colours, the gold and the greens, and of the Fairy Baths, what shall we say, for no words can describe them? They were a feast to the eye, and we long to return to them.

The Dragon's Mouth Geyser is an unpleasant-looking fissure in the red rock down which it is just possible to scramble between its regular eruptions. Its waters flow in a boiling cascade to the Lightning Pool, where a continuous discharge of electric current seems to be at work.

Looking down into the valley from the other side, we could see red, yellow, and black geysers all within a yard or so of the cold stream. We turned to go back and were confronted with another variety of geyser, one that throws up a sort of mud jelly which contains various oils and has wonderful curative properties: the Maoris used to apply it to their wounds. A little farther there were mud geysers whence the most perfect Fuller's Earth could be obtained. On all sides the ground was full of mineral pigments, with which our guide painted pretty patterns on a little card.

One rivulet, with creamy bed and mossy sides, we shall never forget, for it formed such a perfect picture amidst the fern and bush. Everywhere we went we heard strange sounds, which were interrupted for a moment by the shrill blast of a whistle. We turned and saw our guide had poked the neck of a bottle towards a jet of steam that was emanating from the earth about a yard away. A little farther on he stooped and picked up a handful of pink earth from a small hole. It was the most perfect plate powder, and would bring a fortune to anyone who exploited it.

Our walk through the valley was nearly completed, but there were three more geysers still to see, all close together, two of them in fact in the same pool with apparently nothing dividing them, one—the Paddle Wheel Geyser—going off every quarter of an hour, and the Twins (Na Mahanga) every four and a half minutes. Deep down in the pool was a huge rock, and a few seconds before the geysers played we could see it moving up and down like a ball! Behind was yet a larger geyser that gives a display every half an hour. It is the only one over which the guide had any control.

Lest we should depart with too much confidence in earth's

narrow crust, the most uncanny event came last. We were standing by a large calm pool. Suddenly there was a report and a sound like the cracking of huge ice-floes. We instinctively stepped back. Was the earth crust cracking? The guide smiled.

"We call that the Great Steam Hammer," he said. "It is always at work somewhere below here, and has been known to hurl people off their feet at times."

The Two Young Men hastened away. That ice was becoming unbearably thin, and the whole valley one haunting nightmare!

After such an experience we felt in comparative safety when, later in the day, we balanced ourselves on huge boulders by the side of the Waikato River and gazed down upon the Aratiatia Rapids. It certainly was a grand sight to watch the water roaring and raging in its haste to get through the narrow rocky channel in which it suddenly found itself confined. The current was so swift that one felt nothing could make headway against it, but the large trout with which the river abounds seemed to find it no effort, and we watched them jumping almost incredible heights to pass the many waterfalls that blocked their upward course. Moss covered the rocky sides of the torrent, but the country around is desolate enough save for the picturesque path by which we approached the place.

It was higher up the stream, where the Waikato thunders over the celebrated Huka or "Snow Water" Cataract, that the Maoris of the Lake Taupo district took revenge, many years ago, on a party of visiting Natives from the Wanganui River, who boasted that these falls would prove no obstacle to *their* canoe. In their attempt to shoot these rapids, in which they were aided by a Taupo guide, the visitors were drowned to a man, with the exception of the guide, who sprang to the bank and laughed mockingly as the canoe and its crew turned turtle in the frothing swirl of this wonderful mass of seething water.

We had heard so much of the baths at Wairakei that, although it was twilight by the time we returned from Aratiatia, we felt we must try one.

"A very excellent time," said the manager. "There's not the slightest risk of catching cold; we often go last thing at night, when it is freezing 10 to 12 degrees, but I recommend the small bath, as it is the hotter of the two."

Accordingly we proceeded down the long avenue of pine trees which led to this natural open air hot bath. At the far end of the pool, which was well surrounded by trees and undergrowth, there was a large waterfall, and here one could allow the hot steaming waters to massage one's limbs. We never felt so much refreshed as by that hot bathe.

Early next morning the hotel manager informed us that a Maori had just arrived on his way to the Magistrates' Court at Taupo, that his horse was spent, and that he (the manager) was going to take him on by car. Would we care to come?

Now, although we knew this "invitation" would be duly charged on the bill, we felt it a pity not to avail ourselves of the opportunity. We wanted to see the Court at work. The weather was not very cheerful, so that we did not see the celebrated Huka Falls in the Waikato River to their best advantage. Most of Lake Taupo and the mountains beyond were buried in mist, nor was there much to be seen at "The Terraces" to which we afterwards drove on, but the wattle trees in blossom and the many fantails flying about were both pretty sights.

The Court was much the same as a County Court at Home, and the cases were nearly all concerned with the non-payment of debts. Mr. Aramiahaungatia would be called, would smilingly admit he owed the money, though he may have denied it *outside* the Court, and would have judgment given against him with costs. In many cases judgment went by default. The magistrate was a genial old chap, and both kindly and considerate in his treatment of the Maoris, unless they played the fool. The only amusing incident transpired in

Maori which we did not understand, and the only case of interest was between two white men regarding the non-payment for a horse. The defendant said that since he had had it no less than three other people had claimed it as theirs!

Next day we had the honour of lunching with the magistrate and his suite at the Waiotapu Hotel, where we all broke our journey on our way back to Rotorua. Stan took upon himself the magisterial right of asking questions, and cross-examined the distinguished Justice of the Peace on political matters at Home and abroad. When their conversation came round to the subject of women's suffrage, the portly old Clerk of the Court became very excited. His hands shook as he tackled his chop, and his face turned a purply red as he declared that *no* woman ought to have the vote who spent more money on pretty clothes than men spent on drink!

But to return for a moment to Taupo. On our way back to Wairakei we visited the Waiora Valley, the like of which is not, we sincerely believe, to be seen elsewhere on the earth. It contains no sensational geysers and is not visited by the "many," but it is none the less unique.

Imagine, therefore, a fairly wide valley covered with dense undergrowth and an occasional tree. Along it flows a little stream, and we are tracing it to its source. The water as it passes through this moss-bound creek is hotter than the hand can bear. The warmth affects the vegetation around, and ferns abound that are not to be seen elsewhere. Our little path winds in and out among the bushes; here and there the way is partly blocked by fallen branches. There is a sound of gurgling water; we are in the presence of three springs or miniature geysers. They are different in appearance, and the water coming from them is by no means the same. The mouth of the largest is encrusted with some yellow substance, and the water is strongly flavoured with iron. Were this spring in Europe the water would be bottled and its fame spread through the world. Here it just flows on undisturbed. The other springs are not so pleasing to the taste, and one of them is acid. The water is so hot that it is difficult to taste it. These three geysers only form a tributary to the stream we are following. A few hundred yards farther up we are faced with a novel sight: a waterfall of boiling water! Through the steam we could see the gaily coloured rocks of red and green that give it the name of "Rainbow" Waterfall. It is a magic spot, and we came upon it suddenly amidst the undergrowth and rich green moss.

The boiling water, carrying as it does endless minerals in solution, seems to colour everything it touches.

The farther we went the more wonderful it became. Here was a spring of boiling water containing much hyposulphite of soda; there a mineral creek with a green water bed; here again a pool that looked as if the laundry had been washed out in it, and not far away the "Spectacle" Pools, one hot, the other cold, though they are not a foot apart. Farther on were pools of varied colour, yellow, green, and blue, and yet another just like claret. The last smelt strongly of iodoform. Traces were still to be seen of some old Maori sulphur *Vapour* Baths, which unfortunately it was dangerous to approach too closely. An acid water bath and a "Frog Pond" (so called from the way the boiling mud hops up) were a few more of the "sights" of this extraordinary valley.

But to us the climax was to scramble over the still smoking crater of an extinct volcano. We were walking over ashes and smoking sulphur, and the chemical action at work is still so great that even pieces of metal left there literally rot away.

We returned in time to have another sylvan bath by starlight. The following morning we were on our way back to Rotorua. The journey was uninteresting, save for two things: the "Rainbow Mountain," so called from the variety of coloured sands exposed to view, and the extensive Government tree plantations. Many of the latter are the work of convicts, good-conduct men being drafted off for the purpose. It impressed one as an intelligent and beneficial way of using their labour from the points of view of both State and convicts.

For miles along this rather dreary stretch the mountain tops are now covered with young trees. Many varieties are planted, but larch predominates. Prior to the clearing the ground was largely covered by coarse bracken and Manuka.

Our return on Friday night gave us Saturday and Sunday to have a little quiet before the inevitable "hustle" at Auckland. Johnnie's charming friend, Miss May B——, the little nurse (and a little nurse, like a little widow, is a dangerous thing), was there to welcome us and to take us to Whaka and Ohinemutu once more. We even went to the Pictures at her invitation, but then I was the *fourth*! Tell it not in Gath: it was the first purely picture show I had been to! I was not vastly impressed. But one item was splendid: "London Street Scenes." The sight of Ludgate Circus and St. Paul's, and later a No. 13 bus off to Hampstead, moved us deeply.

I left Johnnie to his own devices in Rotorua for twenty-four hours whilst I went on to Hamilton.

Hamilton, on the Waikato River, is the outcome of the breaking up of some big estates and the founding of the dairying industry. Its prosperity was based on those regular monthly cheques from the cheese and butter factories the amount of which depended in each case largely upon the capacity of the individual farmer. It is another of those prosperous inland towns that gave evidence of the general well-being of the country.

Business over, I made use of a spare hour or two to visit the "Ruakura" Government Experimental Farm a couple of miles away. It is one of some half-dozen similar institutions that do invaluable work which no private individual could undertake.

My tramp along the muddy roads was amply rewarded, for, thanks to the kindness of one of the staff, I had a personally conducted tour round the place. When the Government took over the farm (rather under a thousand acres) it was largely swamp land. It was carefully drained and improved, and when I was there the land they purchased for £8 per acre would fetch £45 per acre and more.

But dairying is only one of their very varied activities. I passed large paddocks cut up into half-acre sections where experiments with various manures were being carried on. Each section was carefully labelled with the particulars of the manure used and its cost, so that farmers could come and see for themselves.

The same crop is planted throughout the paddock, and as an ocular demonstration one section is left without manure. At another place the use of "green manures" was being shown, i.e. crops that are grown and ploughed in. And here also could be seen specimens of every conceivable grass and innumerable varieties of lucerne. Many of these are tested in all parts of New Zealand to see under what conditions they do best. After a glance at the fruit trees, the poultry, and the bees, and a sip of their "mead" in memory of Cyril, I had to take my departure to join the Auckland "Express."

We were soon in country that was amongst the first to be settled. At one or two sidings we noticed trainloads of sheep and cattle, evidently making their last journey, and as we neared Auckland we observed the unusual sight of walls around the paddocks instead of fences, but walls made from the lumps of brown lava which was poured from the craters of the many volcanoes hereabouts long ages ago, and now fortunately extinct.

Good-bye to Pakeha and Maori

Our week in Auckland, where we made the Northern Club our temporary home, was certainly a very busy one. Beside various bookseller friends, not to mention editors and librarians, we had many people to look up. Wherever we called we were given the warmest of welcomes and treated with the utmost kindness and hospitality.

It seemed quite strange after the cold and frosty nights at Ohakune, and even Rotorua, to be able to stroll back to the Northern Club at 10.30 p.m. without feeling the need of an overcoat. Our journey northwards towards the Equator was beginning to tell at last. But, although it was never very cold, it was a climate we did not much appreciate. There was never a day without half a dozen showers of rain, though some blue sky was always to be seen and there were periodic bouts of sunshine that made a mackintosh or coat extremely irksome. As compensation for the overdose of moisture, the grass in the parks and elsewhere was a most luscious green.

Our tour of the town under Mr. Bush's guidance proved most interesting, but it was not until we were on the top of Mount Eden, and later when we climbed to the summit of One Tree Hill, that we were able to obtain an adequate idea of Auckland's growth. Here we could see the many suburbs with which this city is surrounded, and which stretch in an almost unbroken line across the narrow isthmus that divides the great Hauraki Gulf from the port of Onehunga. North of that isthmus the noble Kauri gum tree raises its stately form. But the days of the Kauri bush are numbered. Its timber is highly prized, and what has taken a thousand years to grow to perfection is remorselessly cut down in a day. The gum itself, that wonderful amber-like substance we have all seen in exhibits of New Zealand produce, is dug from the sites of the forests of long ago.

Throughout the main thoroughfares there are notices: "Keep your city clean," and in the public parks and gardens, "Protect your own property," together with many other instructions that are less well observed.

One evening we accompanied Mr. Bush to the Savage Club concert, a most entertaining function. The level of both the music and recitations was extraordinarily high, and we thoroughly enjoyed ourselves. One of the recitations, written by a New Zealander and beginning "Give me the man," still rings in our ears. And how we laughed over that Irish recitation *Drink, the Curse*!

They were temporarily vaccination mad in Auckland, and we were debarred from leaving by rail or steamer unless we submitted and obtained our certificates. Protests were of no avail. A whole day was wasted, but I found a doctor who did not believe in it, who said, "I have got to do it, but don't blame me if it doesn't take!" And it didn't! But we got our certificates.

Many and long were the conversations we had during our short stay in Auckland with the leading men and women of the day on political, religious, and educational matters, and we learnt much of interest concerning the difficulties and ambitions of this alert little country.

The burning topics of the day at the time of our visit—topics that not only affected Auckland but the entire country—were Prohibition, the closer settlement of the land, and better roads and bridges and communications generally. In many parts of the North Island transport was impossible for long periods every year. Lack of material with which to metal the roads was the chief difficulty. Where material had been readily available, as in the neighbourhood of Christchurch, in the South Island, the roads were really very good.

The railways, which were being steadily pushed forward in many directions, though slow, prided themselves on being sure, and there was no question that they were run first and last for the benefit of the people. Any extra profits that they were able to make were used for a reduction on fares and freights, or to such purpose as was considered best to benefit the country as a whole. Lime, for instance, was carried free, so that any farmer who wished to improve the soil of his holding could do so for the cost of procuring and carting the lime from his nearest station.

When travelling through the North Island one heard a great deal about undeveloped land that is in the hands of the Maoris. There were bitter complaints, for example, that the

Natives did not put it to the use that a Pakeha would, and a great deal more that is reminiscent of Naboth's Vineyard. The abuse of land is a sad thing the world over, but the Pakeha in New Zealand has by no means a clean record. The total amount of land held by the Maoris that is undeveloped is but a fraction of the total of undeveloped land in the hands of the white man. When all the rest of New Zealand is developed to its highest extent it will be time enough to talk about the land that was reserved for the *future* of the Maoris. Reference has already been made to the conditions under which the Maoris hold their land, and much good work has been done and no doubt *will* be done both in simplifying those conditions and educating the Maoris in the advantages to be gained by a proper use of their land.

Auckland possesses two most excellent schools for Maori children: the Queen Victoria School for Girls and the St. Stephen's School for Boys. At both the pupils receive a thorough training. They have to carry on the entire work of each establishment themselves, and the organization is such that each pupil has to take his or her turn at every part of the domestic work, at first as an assistant, but later in charge of others. Thus a boy or a girl who commenced as junior assistant in the kitchen would end by becoming chief cook during the week on duty. If anything was amiss with the food the scholars would know whom to blame. Even medical work is carried out by the pupils themselves, so that they may know how to act in many emergencies. In this class of work some of the boys become particularly skilful, and in the holidays when they are back in isolated districts among their own people the knowledge thus gained is of immeasurable utility. The work throughout is eminently practical, and a St. Stephen's boy can turn his hand to anything, from the making of furniture to building a house! Thanks to their fine physique the lads excel both at gymnastics and football, into which pastimes they enter with the greatest enthusiasm, and the girls play basket-ball with vigour.

In a Maori family the difference between "mine" and "thine" is almost unknown. The one great difficulty is in the after-school life of these children, and the criticism is often made that on their return to their families they sink back to the level whence they came. But it must be borne in mind that only ninety years ago the Maoris were cannibals; it is therefore not to be expected that they can make, in that period, the progress that has taken Europe more than twenty times as long.

Again, the value of such education cannot be fairly judged by its effect on a generation or two. The Maoris have made exceptionally rapid progress, and there is no sign of this rate of progression diminishing, whilst the lot of the Native who is educated far in advance of his fellows is not an altogether enviable one. Take the case of a young Maori doctor—and there have been some particularly clever ones. If he goes among his own people he will be compelled to live as they do and bestow his services for nothing, for they will never pay one of their own people for medical attentions. And although he might have exceptional talent and qualifications, what chance will he stand amongst a white population?

In most places public opinion is not sufficiently far advanced for him to prove successful, but there have been some exceptions, and there is no doubt that progress in this matter is being made. Although Maori and Pakeha are on more friendly terms than in most countries where mixed coloured races are living together, yet the inseparable barrier is not altogether invisible. No! the lot of the highly educated Native is *not* an enviable one.

"We thought they were goblins with eyes in the backs of their heads, otherwise how could these sailors row their boats with their backs turned to the shore?" So said Horeta-Taniwha (Red-Smeared Dragon), an old Maori, in 1853. He was but a boy when Captain Cook's "goblins" landed in New Zealand, yet he remembered the "Great White Birds," as they called the exploring ships that came from beyond the horizon of the sea, whence also came the ancestors of all the Maoris from their mythical home in Hawaiki.

These were the forefathers of a magnificent race of brave and intelligent warriors, men who fought between themselves "for fun," and also more seriously against the invading English forces. War was an honourable profession with the Maoris. It was after they had suffered a defeat in the Waikato War that the leading chief was asked why he had neglected an opportunity to attack the ammunition and provision convoys of our troops. "Why, you fool," he answered indignantly, "if we had stolen your powder and food, how could you have made fight against us?"

As well as being great warriors the Maoris have keen eyes and a charm of poetic spirit. Nature is symbolized in their thoughts and expressions, and the drudgery of labour, whether on land or water, is relieved by the singing of what appear to be monotonous choruses. War songs are sung with audacious ferocity and brimful of uncomplimentary epithets; love songs, on the contrary, are lengthy serenades of seductive tenderness of expression. Songs of loneliness or despair are always sung in a minor key, and are combined of notes that cannot be reproduced on European instruments. These laments are heart-rending in the extreme, beautifully expressive of the deepest pathos.

As in music, so in art, the Maoris are grotesque yet capable masters of their profession. Tattooing alone is carried to a fine art. The process is such a painful one that only a portion of the design can be carried out at a time, whilst the craftsman sings songs of encouragement to his long-suffering client.

The Maoris were very superstitious, but how far modern education has eradicated this in recent years is difficult to estimate. Their lives were practically in the hands of the Tohungas, or wise men of the villages. In olden times these men were responsible for handing down the traditions with regard to the origin of gods and heroes. They taught in the Whare-kura or Red House, the old Native sacred schools.

Here it was that the Maori boy of high rank learnt his ancient legends and racial incantations, the rules of *tapu*, the treatment of disease, agriculture, and other useful arts. A mistake in teaching was punishable by very evil consequences, and this made the Tohungas exceedingly careful teachers. The Maori pupil learnt everything appertaining to his tribe by heart, and his extraordinary memory was not surpassed by that of any white man; and even to-day the Maori is a great orator—he speaks musically and with intense feeling.

He was a believer in ghosts or Kehua and Atua, demon spirits, and he believed that the spirits of the dead returned to earth, entering the bodies of other men, as well as birds, spiders, and lizards.

There were no tortures for those who were condemned to the land of "Po" or Darkness. Punishment was meted out to an evil-doer whilst he was still alive, and was suitably administered by Wiro, the Lucifer of Maori mythology, and Taniwhi, a holy and gigantic lizard. The souls of chiefs and priests resided in Rangi, the temple of the sky; the souls of common men went to Reinga, a mythical heaven in the midst of the sea.

Tapu, or forbidden things, lent an intricate complication to Maori life, and of this we shall have more to say when we come to the "Islands of the Blest," whither we must now pass on; but before we depart let us say it was among a race nourishing such ideals and so unfailing in their retribution of wrongdoing that the pioneers had to live in the early days of this great Dominion. After lengthy and painful wars, through vast areas of dense bush and deep fern, the gallant Maoris were overcome. Civilization spread rapidly among them, and as rapidly spread its attendant evils, immorality, drink, and disease. The Great Old Men of the race are gradually passing away, but although men of high ideals are still to be found the old spirit of the race is on the wane. Let us hope the Maori, even if bred and educated in a new spirit, will long remain to inhabit his rightful land of "Ao-Tea-Roa."

And so we said farewell to this interesting and beautiful

land of "The Long White Cloud" and its charming and hospitable people. The time had come for us to board the great trade canoe of the Pakeha and sail the northward seas that lead to the traditional home of the Maori Pilgrim Fathers, the fair land of Hawaiki. On our way we would pass close by "the extreme north end of New Zealand, a spot called Muri Whenua—Land's End. Here was the Spirit's Leap. To that the soul travelled, halting once and again on the hilltops to strip off the green leaves in which the mourners had clad it. Here and there by the wayside some lingering ghost would tie a knot in the ribbon-like leaves of the flax plant—such knots as dull-witted Pakeha attribute to the whipping of the wind. As the souls gathered at their goal, Nature's sounds were hushed. The roar of the waterfall, the sea's dashing, the sigh of the wind in the trees—all were silenced. At the Spirit's Leap on the verge of a tall cliff grew a lonely tree with brown spreading branches, dark leaves, and red flowers. The name of the tree was Spray-Sprinkled.* One of its roots hung down over the cliff's face to the mouth of a cavern fringed with much seaweed, floating or dripping on the heaving sea. Pausing for a moment, the reluctant shades chanted a farewell to their fellow men and danced a last war dance. Amid the wild yells of the invisible dancers could be heard the barking of their dogs. Then, sliding down the root, the spirits disappeared in the cave. Within its recesses was a river flowing between sandy shores. All were impelled to cross it,"† in the boat of the ferry-woman called Rohé, of whom we have already told.

* Pohutu-kawa.

† *The Long White Cloud*, by W. Pember Reeves. George Allen & Unwin Ltd.

Two Young Men See the World

SOUTH SEA ISLANDS

Soon, too soon, the time came for us to leave the South Sea Capua. I was so happy there, that I verily believe I should have been content to dream away my life, without care or ambition. . . . Perhaps after a time a man's feelings and thoughts would become degraded and numbed by such a life; he would lose that power of enjoyment that made it at first so charming and pleasant to him. Peace, and quiet, and perfect freedom, are useful medicines, but not a wholesome diet. Their charm lies in contrast; there is no spark without the concussion of the flint and steel; there is no fine thought, even no perfect happiness, that is not born of toil, sorrow, and vexation of spirit.

South Sea Bubbles, by THE EARL AND THE DOCTOR

Chapter XI

THE FRIENDLY ISLANDS

WE were due to leave Auckland at 10 a.m., but we did not get under way until 2 p.m., owing to the refusal of a passenger and a fireman to submit to vaccination, but they had to capitulate, and after this tedious delay of many hours, Captain Crawford, of the T.S.S. *Tofua*, rang up his engine-room; bells sounded all over the ship, and the great siren hooted impatiently. The doctor had just gone ashore with his nurse and calf's lymph; the smoking-room was still filled with howling babies and men and women with bleeding arms. Many of us had stoutly resisted vaccination up to the eleventh hour, but the Antipodes was white-scared at this outbreak of supposed smallpox, and authorities and shipping companies alike had run amok with lymph tubes.

The gangway was down, and hawsers slipped, and our friends, tired with hours of standing and neck-craning in anticipation of our departure, were at last relieved to watch the *Tofua* back cautiously into the broad waters of the Waitemata River from the Queen Street Wharf. Slowly we steamed down the beautiful harbour, leaving behind us the City of Green Hills, here basking in sunlight, there veiled in a cloud of moisture shot with rainbow hues.

We passed close to the island of Rangitoto, which is an extinct volcano, conspicuous all around Auckland for its trinity of peaks. In Maori it is said that Rangitoto means "A Blood-stained Sky," and when in eruption it must have been an impressive spectacle indeed, for the rim of the crater is nine hundred odd feet above the sea. Rangitoto is joined to the little "forbidden island" of Motu Tapu, immediately to the east, by a strip of sand at low water, but their geological formation is entirely different. Other beautiful islands we passed near were Tiri Tiri Matangi, where is the guiding light to the harbour; and then came Kawau, on the port bow, once owned by Sir George Grey, who made a paradise of the place. Then we saw the Little Barrier Island, preserved as a sanctuary for birds; and lastly, at sundown, we steamed under the rugged cliffs of Great Barrier Island, at the entrance to the Hauraki Gulf. If it had been light enough we should have seen giant kauri trees standing on the steep slopes of the island, that are bush-clad right up to the summit of Mount Hobson, 2,330 feet, but darkness closed quickly around us; the shores of Te Ika a Maui were shaded from our eyes for ever by the pall of night, whilst our palace of fairy lights sped over the tossing sea bound for the "Islands of the Blest."

At last we were at peace, save for enthusiastic deck billiards players, who found this one-handed game the "very thing" after vaccination. There was not a soul on board—and there were between two and three hundred of us—who had not been vaccinated, or whose medico had not "endeavoured" to vaccinate him or her. No official doctor was carried on this ship; many people had awful arms, though ours did *not* "take," and as our medical man asked us not to "blame him," we thought of him with nothing but the highest praise, and we hoped that his half-crown certificate would see us through the "scare."

The Kingdom of "One Hundred Isles"

It was early morning when we first sighted the outlying southern atolls of Tongatabu crouching in a rolling sea, grey, like so many battleships in fighting array. We came up to them and turned our glasses upon them, and behold, as the murk of early day cleared away from the sky these islands revealed themselves, densely green with swaying palms and circumscribed by narrow belts of sandy shore, at which great spuming breakers lashed unceasingly. Presently our curiosity was aroused by the sight of many buildings on a distant isle. "Look," said Miss Bennett, excitedly, "there stands our church on the only hill in Nukualofa! And there, below it, that white building is the Royal Palace, and the wharf is farther to the left."

Miss Bennett, whom we had met in Auckland, was returning to her duties at the Native Girls' College at Nukualofa.

We turned our glasses on them all in turn, the church, the Palace, and the wharf, and then someone drew us aside and pointed out the hull of the wrecked *Knight of St. George*, stuck on the coral reef among the pounding rollers of the Pacific swell. But we had no mind for such things, for nearer at hand, in fact under our very bow, the sea was tinted with an entrancing medley of brilliant hues, orange and old gold predominating. Pink and mauve were there too, and all gradations of the ocean blue marked our channel between these wondrous reefs that lured us towards the sandy shores of Nukualofa. This island, like the many outposts we had passed, was as flat as one's hand, nothing appearing above the row of coco-nut palms along the foreshore save the slight eminence on which the pretty Wesleyan Church was perched. Under the "Yellow Jack" we crept up towards the wharf, but we did not go immediately alongside, for we had come from an "infected port," and many wondered if we should be allowed to land.

Our fears were soon dispelled, however; the *Tofua* swung to her helm, and engine bells were ringing, whilst a launchful of great brown half-naked Tongans raced around us, towing cables and hawsers to buoys and wharf. Several of the crew of this smart little motor-boat dived into the sea and, in half a dozen strokes, gained the coral reef, scarce up to their middles in water. Here they made fast a hawser and then plunged off in pursuit of their craft again.

So it was that we came to be made fast alongside the wharf at Nukualofa, the capital of the kingdom of Tonga—the kingdom of "One Hundred Isles." Before disembarking we took a closer view of what we could see of the town between the palm groves. The roadways seemed to consist of beautiful grassy tracks, and through the branches of curious trees we caught glimpses of Native huts, corrugated-iron buildings, and the white towers of the Royal Palace and chapel.

Only a few official figures clad in white—Europeans for the most part—were on the quay, but as soon as the mails were landed a host of Natives in gaily coloured raiment flocked along the jetty. Everyone seemed very lightly clad to face the strong Trade wind that was blowing, but as soon as we got ashore and had left the straggling wharf behind us we were "stewing" in a tropical climate with a vengeance!

We wandered off to explore on our own, and in a few seconds we found ourselves in the midst of a most enchanting scene. The soft grassy track we were following, green and luxuriant, led among clusters of Native huts, quaint of shape and built of woven and dried palm leaves. The Tongans came and went about their daily business, their naked feet fell noiselessly on the verdant roadway. Fine, broad, almost handsome men were they, and buxom maidens, smiling and long-haired. All greeted us enthusiastically, shouting to us from their *abis*, or whispering as they passed, "Malolelei! Malolelei!" whilst we would answer with this same musical expression of good will in which we had been coached beforehand. Some women waved to us from the dim recesses of their huts; others we surprised stripped to the waist attending to their clothes washing, and they, observing our approach, modestly drew some garment about their shoulders. Superb palm fronds, glinting with sunlight, rustled in the tropical Trade; breadfruit trees and mummy apples, scarlet poinsettias, and other curious plants and trees flourished in abundance, whilst the red hibiscus and other flowering shrubs impregnated the atmosphere with seductive odours, and brilliant butterflies fluttered lethargically from bloom to bloom.

The Tongan is not so dark-skinned as the Kaffir, nor so light, perhaps, as the Maori; he is a handsome brown colour, with kindly eyes, delightful smile, and distinctly intellectual appearance. His only clothing is, as a rule, a "lava-lava" or loin cloth, and this shows off to advantage his massive chest, back, and limbs. The women are more modest in displaying their equally excellent figures, at least so it appeared from what we saw of them in Nukualofa. They generally wear a loose blouse and a slightly more elaborate lava-lava.

On our wanderings we fell in with a group of pretty Tongan children, or rather we coaxed them to us, a task needing some niceness in execution, for although we could have been but a mile from the wharf these kiddies were unaccustomed to seeing strangers along the side road. On holding up our camera, pointing to it, smiling and beckoning, they at last crept from the foliage and under the incongruous barbed wire that surrounded their *abi*, and approached us timidly like a flock of half-tamed birds. Of course we were unfortunate in not being able to talk their language, but presently we made them interested in the movements of our camera, and they were much amused at peeping at each other through the view finder. At the critical moment, however, just as we were about to operate the shutter, the sun disappeared behind one of those magnificent "clouds of the Trade wind that are alone for sublimity," as Stevenson puts it, and so a good many of the snaps we took of our pretty little dark friends were not very successful after all.

That same afternoon we penetrated into the interior of the island along a somewhat tedious road, lined on either side by various Tongan holdings, with here a grove of coco-nut palms, there some paw-paw trees, a pineapple patch, or plot of taro. The road was busy with the coming and going of Natives on foot, in carts, or on horseback. The animals were exceedingly poor-looking creatures for the most part, and although there is plenty of grass for the beasts to eat, we all know that you cannot work a horse on grass alone, and corn is almost untasted among the horses of Tongatabu. Everywhere we were accorded the heartiest of greetings, and on our way back we were overtaken by a handsome mounted man of Tonga. He was returning from his work, for he carried a sack of yams at his saddle bow and a couple of implements in his hand. He wished to know whence we came and whither we would go, and expressed much interest in Stan's gesticulations on the subject of London.

"Houses, houses, houses!" said Stan, pointing to the numberless palm trees at the roadside, "and so *many* people!"

"Prince Tugi he been London, yes?" said our escort.

"Yes, he been London," replied Stan, and added: "We go see him Vavau; Prince Tugi *fine* man."

And indeed he spoke the truth, for we had two introductions to the Prince, at that time Governor of the Vavau group of islands. It would not be out of place to mention here that the line of succession to the Tongan throne has until quite recently been through the mother and not through the father. Thus there was no hereditary succession of the eldest son as we know it in Europe.

The late King George Tabou II was unfortunately away on a yachting cruise during our visit to his capital. According to report, he was of a shy and retiring disposition, but well educated and Europeanized in manner. He stood 6 feet 4 inches high, and must have been a most imposing personage.

But to return to our narrative. Our guide brought us ultimately to where Miss Bennett lived at the Ladies' College (Tongan ladies, be it understood). She welcomed us to afternoon tea, that was carried round on trays by two handsome Tongan maidens, who showed evident signs of bashfulness at the sight of so many strangers. Here we were introduced to Miss Frazer, who, like her colleague, was an Australian lady. Miss Frazer's duties were to instruct the white and half-caste children, whilst Miss Bennett dealt entirely with the Native girls.

After tea these ladies escorted us round the College precincts, which are described elsewhere, and they also told us of the horrors of earthquakes and hurricanes. Tongatabu, as well as many other islands in the South Pacific, had been recently visited by both these devastating phenomena, to the utter temporary ruination of all crops. One has only to read Stevenson's *Vailima Letters* to understand to what extent a hurricane is dreaded. It is heralded by a gathering of dark suspicious clouds and a rapid falling of the barometer. Then comes wind and rain; the palms are bent to the ground, and many are those whose tops are ruthlessly torn off by the tempest. Buildings are often destroyed, and in many places we beheld very sinister-looking ruins. We were told of many heroic acts in the last hurricane; how people crawled on their hands and knees to lend assistance in the houses of others, and how some of them were even then picked up by the wind and hurled to the ground in its fury! It is surprising how anything will stand in the face of such an overwhelming force, screeching across a boundless ocean and sweeping over these flat and defenceless Friendly Islands. We noticed that many of the buildings at Nukualofa were built with rounded ends, not unlike the bonnet of a racing car, whilst the pavilion in the College grounds and the Wesleyan Church on the hill, both roomy buildings, were supported internally by a series of huge ironwood boles, lashed and counter-lashed, in an almost indestructible manner. The effect thus produced was quaint, but not unpleasing to the eye, and the acoustic properties in the church seemed in no way destroyed. Other houses in these islands are secured to the ground by steel hawsers, but what would these avail against an earthquake!

A friend on board the *Tofua*, Mr. Attwater, who had been spending a month's holiday at Nukualofa, came in for one of the most severe earthquake shocks they have had there of recent years. He was reading on the back veranda of a friend's house, some guests were playing tennis, and others were in a room on the first floor. Suddenly, without any previous warning, the earth began to shake. Mr. Attwater ran out on to the court, where Ata, a Tongan guest, was standing with his legs spread apart and looking very grave. By this time the ground was heaving up and down with an undulating movement. Mr. Attwater said that the sensation was as if they were standing on boards that someone was pulling from under their feet in every direction. The house now began to tremble and sway to and fro in a dangerous manner, accompanied by the sound of cracking timber. The Native girls ran out from their quarters in alarm, whilst upstairs the ladies were beseeching their host to allow them to descend, but he very wisely forbade them. The shock lasted fully two minutes, but severe as it was little damage was done beyond the stopping of all the clocks and the smashing of medicine bottles. Curious as it may seem no cracks appeared upon the earth's surface, yet for some time after the vibrations had died away people were feeling sick and ill at ease. It was an old custom among the Tongans to turn out on such occasions and beat the heaving earth with sticks, "To drive the devil out," but, we believe, such a practice is very uncommon nowadays. As we wandered among the Native huts we were much amused to see so many of their inhabitants with whitened and carefully combed hair, looking like that of some West End flunkey. This, we were told, was coral lime, with which they were cleansing their heads for the Sabbath. It had the extraordinary effect of bleaching the coal-black locks to a ginger colour, and in some cases to an almost golden tint!

Everyone seemed pleased to see Miss Bennett (or "Bennett" as the Tongans were given to calling her behind her back) among them again, and many were the tender and strangely effusive greetings that they interchanged with her.

We were taken to see the tomb of King George Tabou I. It is a graceful white monument erected on a spacious platform of concrete, and approached by a broad flight of steps. At the top of these, and on the right-hand side, is a white figure of a lion; its mate, for which one looked instinctively, was missing, and littered about the enclosure was an incongruous collection of cases and kerosene tins. Other tombs are here, too; some in the Tongan fashion, heaps of small dark or coloured stones, often with a *sisi* or Native garment of honour suspended over them from a bamboo pole. One of the tombs in this royal enclosure is that of the King's father, Prince George Fatafelu, or to give his name its full honour, H.R.S. Prince Jiaoji Fatafelu Tu'i Belehake, who passed away at the age of seventy on November 20, 1912. According to our informants, the lying-in-state in the Palace summer-house was a most impressive affair. Tongan guards with arms reversed stood about the coffin, which was draped in the royal colours of red and white. The grounds were ablaze with lights suspended from ropes and trees, and groups of candles stood burning in the earth. Outside the Palace walls parties of Natives clad in finely woven but dishevelled mats, for such is the sign of mourning in the Friendly Islands, squatted about large fires of palm fronds, and each group represented the family of some chief. So, to the dirge-like music of the royal band, the vigil was kept all through the night.

It was eventide as we strolled back to the College, along the soft turf tracks; the air was sweet with the scent of flowers, and from the distance a curious hollow drumming sound was wafted across to us on a cooling breeze. It was the beating of the *Lali* that we heard, and presently we came to where a young Tongan stood between two hollowed tree boles, and with small clubs of wood was sounding this resonant curfew that calls all students within the confines of their College grounds.

Later that evening, after our early meal on the boat, we returned to Miss Bennett's house, and under her guidance we were taken next door and introduced to Mr. Page, head of the Wesleyan Church in Nukualofa, with whom we enjoyed a long talk on Tongan affairs. Just previously to this we had been listening to the "call over" of the maidens in Miss Bennett's charge. A man stood outside the house and called their names, and each replied with a short gruff exclamation, intimating that she was within. Personally we could not distinguish between the many answering voices, but we were assured that the keen-eared "caller," far away as he seemed to be, could distinctly detect a falsified answer for an absentee. Miss Bennett told us that these girls were excellent workers, and all seemed most interested and devoted pupils. One or two, of course, proved incorrigible from time to time, but expulsion from the College was a rare occurrence, and any severe reprimand was taken deeply to heart by these easily affected girls, who always came to their teacher with tears in their eyes and presents in their arms, as tokens of their repentance. The generosity of the Tongans knows no bounds. We were told many instances of people coming to take up work in Nukualofa, or even to make a lengthy stay there, who were visited by a number of Natives laden with gifts of *tappa* cloth, *sisis*, fans, vegetables, live fowls, and even pigs. In the same breath as the speech of welcome, the headman would add how poor they were that year on account of the devastating cyclones; but, even under these circumstances, it would never do to refuse the gifts.

We had deeply regretted not availing ourselves of Mr. Page's buggy and "boy" that he had so kindly placed at our disposal all the afternoon, but which, through a stupid blunder, we had missed the chance of utilizing. So it was with additional gratification that we accepted his and Miss Bennett's proposal that the College girls should dance a *fiva* in our honour, and even now we were entering the long room in which this performance was to take place. Some seven or eight of us, the ladies clad in cool white dresses, sat in a row on a long bench running the length of the wall. Opposite to us, squatting on mats on the floor, was a line of some twenty Tongan maidens, clad in skirts and blouses of mingling and harmonious colours, their hair turned up in the European fashion, a special permit having to be obtained before they can wear it down the back. The room was lighted by oil lamps that flared in the draught from the increasing Trade wind, and the atmosphere smelt evilly of coco-nut oil and the curious beans and flowers employed in the decoration of the *sisi* or native tippet, mainly manufactured from palm fibre and arrowroot.

The singing and dancing now began, the first being started alone by the *première danseuse*, who sat in the centre of the line, in a high-pitched minor key that was almost instantly modulated by the breaking in of the chorus in a surprisingly rich bass obbligato with a tenor and falsetto accompaniment. Considering that the choir was entirely composed of young girls, one could but marvel at the extraordinary compass of their voices. But, above all, we were captivated by the grace of their swinging and interlacing arms, the expressive movements of their tapering fingers, and the rhythmic clapping hands and stamping feet of these lissom maidens who leapt from the squatting line and danced with rapt fervour to the increasing rapidity of the theme. Now and again one dancer would decorate another by placing a huge red hibiscus blossom or a variegated leaf in her jet-black hair, or by taking off her *sisi* and placing it around the shoulders of her comrade. Such an act was considered a high honour, and was applauded by smiles and shouts, emphasized by an extra energetic attack upon the song. Then another song and dance began, very similar to the first, and this would be suddenly dissolved by the appearance from a back apartment of a wild figure in a gruesome red mask, and the song ended in shrieks of hilarious laughter and a general stampede of the two or three damsels who were crouching and toeing it before the squatting chorus.

Such a performance was a much more passive affair than the fierce Maori *Haka*, yet it was just such a prelude as this that one longed to have as an introduction to this peaceful Native community of the Southern Seas. The evening's entertainment ended with the singing of the sweet ditty of farewell common to these enchanted isles, "Tofa ma Feleni" ("Good-bye, my Friend"), and with this haunting melody ringing in our ears we returned to our vessel for the night; and as we went the moonbeams were mingling with the fragrant air and lit up the waters of the reef in dazzling magnificence, whilst the palm fronds rustled in the breeze or hung listlessly silhouetted against the spangled firmament.

The Tongan Land System

Perhaps the most interesting and instructive thing about Tonga is its land system. No land can be bought, nor can land be sold. Not a single acre in any of the principal islands is alienated. Europeans or outsiders requiring land for any purpose can lease it, but that is all. A lease, in most cases, is for fifty years, but in the neighbourhood of any town or village it is for twenty-one years only. The land is the people's and they have a very effective way of dealing with it. Nominally it is divided out amongst the King or Queen and the big chiefs, but every youth on becoming a taxpayer (i.e. on payment of the £2 poll-tax, to which every male over sixteen years of age is liable) is entitled to a plot of land from his chief, sufficient to support himself and his family. The amount to which he is actually entitled is about 8¼ acres, but owing to a lack of proper surveys it has often exceeded this quantity. It has been found that 8¼ acres is sufficient to keep a Tongan family in comfort, and if the holder cares to prepare copra (dried coco-nut) he can make a very pleasant cash income besides. Over and beyond this 8¼ acres, every taxpayer is entitled to a small plot of land in his village on which to build his *abi* or Native hut. Only the surplus lands, above what is required for the foregoing purposes, may be leased by the chiefs, or even the Queen, to outsiders; but there is a slight tendency already creeping in for chiefs to consider their rent roll more than the needs of their vassals. Any abuses of this sort are dealt with by the Minister of Lands, whose duty it is to see that all taxpayers receive the plot of land which is due to them on arriving at the age of sixteen. The chiefs were entitled at the time of our visit to a nominal yearly payment of about 4s. from each of those to whom they allot land, but this is seldom inflicted; its equivalent is, however, often paid in a different way. If, for instance, a chief is going through a district he sends word beforehand and preparations are made for his entertainment.

For some years past Tonga has been under Constitutional Government, and the Sovereign is assisted by various Ministers, most of whom, including the Premier, are Natives. But the Chief Justice and the Auditor-General are white men nominated by Great Britain through the High Commissioner of the Pacific. There is also a Privy Council, but we did not learn how this works, except that apparently the Sovereign makes use of it whenever he wishes to avoid a decision on any particular subject. Parliament meets every three years, and consists (1) of the hereditary chiefs, (2) of elected commoners.

As yet, however, the Tongans have not shown the freedom in civil life that they exercise in dealing with Church affairs; they tend to elect the man whom the chief approves, who is generally his principal aide-de-camp. It will be seen from this that the chiefs still maintain a very effective control over their people, a control far in excess of their actual legal status.

The use of alcohol is forbidden amongst the Tongans, unless they obtain a special permit. Most of the chiefs and some of the wealthy men have permits; beyond this there is very little abuse, though here and there one hears cases of illicit grog selling. More money is, however, to be made at less risk in other directions, so that there is little temptation for traders to break the law. At Nukualofa there is a resident British Consul acting under the High Commissioner for the Pacific. His function it is, while avoiding as far as possible any interference, to see that the Constitution of Tonga is adhered to. From the foregoing it will be gathered that Tonga, while being an independent kingdom, is a Protectorate of Great Britain. No step outside the scope of the Constitution may be taken without the British Consul's approval.

Tonga is by no means a poor country, and the State, as well as the individual, is in a prosperous condition. The revenue almost invariably exceeds the expenditure, and there is a nice little amount standing to the credit of the country at one or more of the Sydney or Auckland banks. Apart from the poll-tax already mentioned, there is a customs tariff which, with a few exceptions, was on a 10 per cent. *ad valorem* basis. The Sovereign is allowed a salary of two or three thousand a year, but, as against this, we believe that the revenue from some of the land around Nukualofa goes into the coffers of the State.

At the time of our visit Tonga was not in such a prosperous position as it had been, and no doubt *will* be again, for they had had two very bad years. The hurricanes had done much damage to coco-nut trees and curtailed the supply of copra, on which the cash income of the average Tongan depends. In this group, as in nearly all the South Sea Islands, copra is the staple product, and at the high prices then ruling it was undoubtedly a very profitable one. Oranges, which grow in large quantities, particularly in Vavau, were useless for export purposes owing to the presence of a fly pest which, it was feared, might spread.

Although a British Protectorate, the trade of these islands was then largely in German hands, though curiously enough the German firms were given to employing English assistants. The timber, for instance, of which the Tongan Government, the Tongan Free Church, and the Wesleyan Church were the principal buyers, had all to be imported through the Germans. Practically speaking there was no local timber for building purposes; it was all brought in schooners from 'Frisco.*

The mention of the Tongan Free Church recalls the fact that Tonga is a Christian country, and has been so for some time. As in Samoa the London Missionary Society has been to the front, so in Tonga the Wesleyans have had an almost undisputed field to themselves. Some years ago, however, there was a split on the subject of outside control, and the Tongan Free Church was founded. Though Wesleyan in origin, it is quite independent of that body and has absolute

* Since this was written the position has probably changed.

106 A handsome mounted man of Tonga

107 The *Tofua* at Nukualofa

108 A glorious avenue of coconut palms at Haapai

109 Native passengers from Nukualofa to Haapai

control of its own funds. There was a great deal of bitterness at the time and the adherents to the Wesleyan cause were much persecuted. One very eloquent Tongan preacher, whom we had the pleasure of hearing, was even left for dead by those who resented his faithfulness to the Wesleyan Society. To-day the breach has been healed, and it has been generally recognized that much of the best work throughout these islands has been and is being done by the Wesleyans. The Natives are tremendously anxious to learn and extraordinarily generous in supporting their own schools and churches. During our all-too-brief stay in Nukualofa we were able to see something of the work of the Wesleyans. They were indeed fortunate to have at the head of their affairs such a man as the Rev. R. C. G. Page. No one could work with greater enthusiasm or take more pains to enter into and understand the life of the Tongan than Mr. Page, and like all who come in contact with Polynesian races he has learnt to love and respect the Tongan people as they have learnt to love and respect him. It is to him that we are indebted for much of our information regarding their customs and system of land tenure.

A Tongan Church

We were fortunate in being in Nukualofa on a Sunday, and the service at the Wesleyan church, which we attended, was one which neither of us is likely to forget. We were a trifle late in climbing the one small hill on the island on which the church has been built. Long before we arrived at the doors we could hear the joyous singing of the Natives—singing without an organ or any other accompaniment. It reminded us once again of an enthusiastic Welsh choir. The church is a large one, and not the only one in Nukualofa, and it was nearly full. The service was in Tongan, and a Native minister occupied the pulpit. We, like the other Europeans present, occupied a seat on a dais surrounding the pulpit, and from here a quaint sight met our very astonished gaze. It is not the custom for the Natives of Tonga to wear hats, but for church-going the women are taught to consider a hat indispensable, and never was seen such an array, or such an incongruous selection. We just shook with suppressed laughter. In the front row there was one very aged Tongan woman with a dilapidated old straw hat tied on to her head with a bit of string and hopelessly askew. Her costume was an odd medley of garments, finishing up with bare legs and feet. If anyone ever looked hopelessly drunk that woman did, but in reality she was all attention and a very devout worshipper. In fact, if there was one thing that impressed us more than this fantastic display of woven hats, from which it was literally impossible for the eye to escape, it was the rapt attention of the congregation. Their eyes were glued to the minister, one or two of the very young or aged always excepted, and they seemed to be drinking in every word. All the doors and windows were open, so that a gentle breeze passed through the building, and, with the breeze, other things entered by these open doors. Dogs, for instance, wandered hither and thither in a way that would have distracted nine-tenths of a European congregation. One we noticed solemnly walking round the pulpit, but nobody heeded. When two curs started misbehaving themselves not a couple of yards from us it was too much for an aged Native near by, and with considerable effort he separated them with an umbrella.

The back part of the centre of the church was occupied by the students, male and female, looking very charming in their white costumes and blue sashes. Those who had passed matriculation are entitled to a mortar-board hat, of which they are vastly proud.

We have never heard a more eloquent prayer, not that we understood a word of it, than that which closed the proceedings. As we rose to go the most important Natives present came and shook hands with us in a most friendly and natural way. Everyone is independent in Tonga, and there is a dignity about the bearing of the people which independence brings.

On leaving the church our eyes were greeted by a very pleasing sight. The students had left by another door and were now marching down the steep grassy track back to their College quarters. The sun shone brilliantly on their spotless white uniforms and blue sashes, and in double file they marched past the quaint Native huts overshadowed by coco palms. Presently they arrived in the spacious green enclosure of the College grounds, that reminded one somewhat of a county cricket-ground at Home; here they were marshalled into closer ranks, brought to a halt, rightabout-faced, and dismissed. It was an orderly and imposing conclusion to the morning service, and none but the Tongans could have made this little piece of militarism seem so purely unmilitary and pleasing to the eye. The pleasant green sward was instantly alight with the dispersing figures of the white-clad students. We followed a number of them across the grass to where their houses stood in a neat double row. Before each was a sunken patch of pineapple plants, and from the central paths branched other verdant footways leading off to the corrugated iron or Native-built hut on either hand. Into these we were cordially invited and were shown various curiosities. We noticed coloured portraits of the English King and Queen on many of the walls, and the huts seemed well kept and, of course, airy.

Throughout these islands the yam and the purple-coloured taro form the staple foods. The yam grows to a goodly sized root, or at least *will* do if the Tongan is not too slothful in making the preliminary hole in the ground. The bigger the hole, the larger the yam will grow, and they say you can always judge of the diligence of a Tongan accordingly. In a land where every tree is richly laden with nourishing fruits and a fertile and well-watered soil can bear such a wealth of vegetation, it is not necessary to starve. But a single hurricane will reduce a prosperous community to poverty by the wholesale destruction of these fruits on which a livelihood depends.

Round About Nukualofa

The Royal Chapel, into which we crept by stealth, for His Majesty forbids the tripper within his Palace grounds, was in a state of lamentable disrepair, and was mainly used in those days for choir practices. The first thing that met our gaze was a huge blackboard erected in front of the pews. This was covered, back and front, by what appeared to be a carefully worked out mathematical problem: a mass of numerals so densely packed together that you could scarce place a pin between them. We discovered afterwards that this was the manner in which the Tongans are taught to sing; it is a numerical Tonic sol-fa, and judging by results an excellent method. Here, also, we saw the Throne, and near by was the actual Palace. Not a soul was about, and we knew His Majesty to be away in his yacht. We crept on to the veranda and peeped through a french window right into the Royal Bath! At that instant an excited handmaiden appeared.

"May we come in?" we asked politely. "We understand the King is not at home."

But without replying the damsel fled in dismay.

We were about to retire when the pattering of naked feet on the veranda deterred us. Round the corner came half a dozen more maidens in morning *déshabillé*. We raised our hats and asked if we could glance inside, whereat the ringleader replied "Yes"; but as we approached the bathroom door they put out their hands and exclaimed "*No*."

Finding ourselves completely unable to understand each other, we thought it advisable to withdraw before the Royal white-uniformed policeman with the red pugaree around his helmet was called from his duties on the wharf to eject us.

Many of the Tongan girls we spoke to evinced much coyness. Miss Bennett introduced us to one of her pupils, the only girl to pass her matric. examination—a most charming and intelligent-looking creature.

It is said that the Tongans make excellent husbands, and

prefer to relieve their wives of any heavy or burdensome work, so that the beauty of their maidenhood may remain with them the longer. For this reason the fair young women of Samoa have no hesitation in accepting the many handsome suitors who flock to their shores from the "Kingdom of a Hundred Isles" and return with them to Nukualofa, "The Place of Kindness," or, as some people more poetically name it, "The Sands of Love."

The last few hours of our stay in the capital of Tongatabu I spent with my camera, and in the company of a little Tongan boy who, with proud and friendly eagerness, volunteered to act as my carrier and figure-subject until the deep-sounding church bell called him off to Sunday School.

For once photography was a dream to me; everything went as it should do, and my little carrier bossed up the inquisitive children into charming groups around seductive Native dwellings.* When the time came for him to leave me he waved his hand long and affectionately; nor did I reward him in any way, except by kindly words. Generally a Tongan is embarrassed by gifts of money which the average tourist will so foolishly persist in making as recompense for the slightest service, which most Natives are only too honoured to perform for the stranger.

There are many interesting excursions to be made into the interior of Tongatabu, but which we were unfortunately not able to undertake in the short time at our disposal. The first of these is to the graves of the Tui Tongans at Mua, where the bodies of the earthly and heavenly Kings lie buried. The earthly King was, we learnt, merely a governing figure-head, whereas the heavenly King was hereditary and held in the esteem of a god. These burial-grounds appear to be colossal pieces of coral limestone rock, split into blocks of such size that it would seem almost impossible for anyone to have brought them hither without some form of mechanical assis-

* I did not realize then that the tropical heat had warped the back of my camera, resulting in the ruination of many excellent exposures!

tance, which modern history proves that the Tongans of recent years never dreamt of. The whole is overgrown with roots of great antiquity, pointing to the remote period at which the monuments must have been erected.

At Haamunga, about sixteen miles from Nukualofa, is a still more remarkable link with the days of long ago. This consists of three gigantic rocks, one lying across and fitting into the other two in the form of an arch about 20 or 30 feet in height. From all accounts it is reminiscent of Stonehenge, and the mystery of its construction is veiled behind an uncertainty almost as dark as that which envelops the ruins of Zimbabwe.

Another twelve-mile drive from Nukualofa brings one to an enormous avava tree. Here, it is said, Captain Cook made friends with the Natives upon his arrival in the island, and not far away is an avenue of other large trees that are always densely covered with flying foxes. These unpleasant-looking brutes are about the size of a domestic cat, and hang, head downwards, from the branches all day long. At sunset they rise in an enormous flock and spend the hours of darkness in plundering the fruit plantations. At daybreak they return to these particular trees again and digest their feast in a topsy-turvy position! The flying fox is tabu in Tonga: that is, he rejoices in the privileges of being a sanctified beast, and no one may destroy him save the King or chiefs.

Someone likens Tonga to "a country of Comic Opera," but during our brief stay we could see nothing to give foundation to this impression, except that they seem to use their verandas as coach-houses and their fowls appear to wear curious feathery pyjamas. Rather would we name it "The Place of Great Kindness," for as the *Tofua* backed away from the wharf that Sunday afternoon, stirring the deep sea beside the tinted reef into frothing and effervescing pools, nearly all of us felt that a large portion of our hearts remained on shore, amongst that gaily clad throng of Tongans and Europeans, who had welcomed us so sweetly to these "Islands of the Blest." And as we drew away still farther into the reef-bound sea, our Native passengers, densely packed amongst baskets of yams, groups of lean horses, and grunting pigs, that covered the well-decks fore and aft, kept waving incessantly and as enthusiastically chanting their haunting farewell, "Tofa ma Feleni," in which the words, "Oh, I *never* shall forget you," rose in a sudden and unexpected harmony from the incongruous jargon of the song.

Haapai

Early the following morning we awoke to find that we were lying about a mile off-shore from another of these flat atolls. The white bungalows and Native huts that we could discern peeping out between the grey and red boles of the palm trees composed the township of Haapai, and Haapai is the chief village of the central group of the Friendly Islands, situated on a little atoll about seven miles long by three miles wide.

By this time our cargo of live-stock and copra (sun-dried and sliced coco-nut), of which we had shipped a goodly supply at Nukualofa, was beginning to raise a most disagreeable stench! Some five or six horses, crowded out from beneath hatches, were tethered to the bulwarks of the after well-deck, and in the filth about their feet several long-snouted, hunch-backed Native swine, secured by the trotter, grunted and squeaked discontentedly. Every other available space not occupied by the Tongan deck passengers was devoted to and piled up with their parcels of yam and taro; parcels, not of brown paper, but of roughly woven palm leaves. The Native passengers themselves sprawled or squatted about the hatches wrapped in their gaily decorated *tappa* cloths that are beaten, at the expense of much labour, out of the bark of a mulberry tree. They had whiled away most of the night in song; in fact, the Tongan is always singing, and well he may, for, as far as we could see, his lot is a particularly happy one.

The expanse of deep blue water between us and the yellow line of the shore was busy with the coming and going of boats; alas! not Native ones, but ordinary whale-boats or jolly-boats, many skimming along under the brightest of white sails. In these some of the Natives were leaving for the shore; in others new arrivals came. All the while there was a great deal of shouting and gesticulating as the brown boats' crews clung to the towering sides of our ship. Other folks passed precious baskets of yams up and down the precariously hanging gangway, whilst the donkey engines plunged a collection of startled ponies, screeching swine, or terrified sheep into a deep-bellied lighter alongside.

Upon this scene we looked down with unabated interest until the breakfast gong called us to our places in the saloon. As we hurried through the meal in our eagerness to get ashore, we noticed many dusky faces peering in at us in rapt wonderment through the open ports. Among these I was startled, almost to choking, by one individual in particular. He had a mop of ginger-coloured hair as dense as a door mat, and about 4 or 5 inches in thickness. His cast of countenance was sinister in the extreme, his features being much more negroid than those of any Tongan I had seen. I gathered afterwards that this man was a Fijian, and one among many other "boys" that we had taken on at Nukualofa to work the cargo up to distant Lautoka. We went ashore in the ship's motor-launch—a heavy cargo of us—and we men, who were sitting in front, got well soused, in spite of protective blankets and umbrellas, by the flying spray. In-shore it was very close, but we were not long in finding the Rev. Collocott's house, prettily situated in a banana plantation. Mrs. Collocott laid the table with morning tea, cakes, and fruit, and for this refreshment we were already very thankful. There could be little doubt that we were drawing near to the Equator. Capricorn was a few degrees south, and we were sleeping, every night, under a sheet with an electric fan running full tilt, ports and cabin door wide open. Even then we sweated; but by day it was a joy to revel in cotton shirt and trousers, collar, socks, and shoes again as one's only covering.

We were soon driving along one of the principal roads with Mr. Collocott and Mr. Attwater. On this island the recent hurricane had been particularly violent. We saw all that remained of two handsome churches and several dwellings, and it was also evident that the coco-nut trees had suffered severely. The road was deep with sand that had been washed up on it at the time of the storm.

Ugly-looking swine were fattening in the captivity of deep, hollowed-out tree-trunks used as styes, which struck us as a novel manner of preparing breakfast bacon! We passed the hospital buildings and isolation tents where, Mr. Collocott said, a startling number of patients were dealt with annually. Both Natives and whites alike suffer from that most dreaded of all diseases, Elephantiasis, conveyed by the bite of a mosquito, which is very prevalent in most of these islands of the South Pacific. A peculiar skin disease is also common among the young Native children, covering them with odious sores, and lasting many months and not infrequently running into years. Tongan parents regard this malady as we do measles; they think it is almost inevitable, and that it is just as well that the youngster should get it over early in life. To gain this end they will actually associate their children with those suffering from the complaint, but the missionaries and doctors were doing their best to combat this evil habit.

We drove along the island road almost as far as a curious mound mentioned by Captain Cook, and then we came back and across the island through a glorious avenue of coco-nut palms that suddenly revealed to us a panorama of exceeding beauty. A strong wind drove the unbroken Pacific swell onto an endless reef about half a mile from the shore. It stretched as far as the eye could see, a frothing, spuming line of rare magnificence. The white beach, overhung with palms and other fantastic trees, spread in company with the reef far into the distant haze, but each was divided from the other by an inviting calm expanse of water, shot with a myriad colours from a garden of brilliant corals over which it rippled.

Here was the spot to pass the livelong day, basking on the hot white sand, or dallying with a thousand shells of rare exotic hues. But for us there was no time for the enjoyment of such pleasures, scarcely sufficient to wonder at the fringe of finely broken pumice that edged the shore; it had not been there some days before, and must have been cast from the fathomless ocean by some recent submarine upheaval.

So we retraced our steps to the shaky four-wheeler, in which we passed through the rustic streets where we saw sliced coco-nut drying for the copra market, and women assiduously painting great sheets of *tappa* cloth. A young Tongan of two or three summers was seeking shelter from the midday heat in a bucket of water placed on the threshold of his home, and a solitary plant of the prickly pear could but remind us of our happy wanderings in the land where it abounds.

At the landing-stage we took our farewell of Mr. Collocott, and whilst waiting for the launch we watched some half-dozen Tongan youths diving for pennies in the clear green water, their foreshortened legs resembling, in their active evolutions, the limbs of gigantic frogs. In the sunny hour or so between luncheon and our time of sailing, Stan endeavoured to dictate to me a portion of these notes. We had placed our chairs in a secluded corner of the deck where we were the least likely to be disturbed. Whilst he paused to think between his sentences I had time to feast my eyes on the familiar scene before us. The ultramarine swell toning to the palest green as it swept over the coral bed and broke, in a billow of lace-like foam, upon the narrow strip of beach. Beyond, the host of criss-cross palm trees swaying in the Trade; the Native huts and European bungalows peeping from beneath them, the grass that was so wonderfully green and, on the water, boats with sails that were so wonderfully white! Such a scene was sufficient to distract both of us, but when a row-boatful of gaily clad and singing Tongan damsels came cruising around our starboard quarter we were *completely* demoralized. At one moment we seemed to have overcome the fascinations of these alluring sirens, but an irresistibly enchanting harmony was wafted up to us from below:

> Tofa, tofa ma Feleni,
> Oh! I *never* shall forget you!

Our eyes wandered to the boat again; they were waving us farewell with their gaily coloured scarves, and we, casting aside our writing materials, pulled out our handkerchiefs and waved and waved whilst the great boat turned to her helm and bore us away to another island of this enchanted sea.

Prince Tugi Entertains Us at Vavau

We steamed for some hours; towards the end of the second dog-watch our straining eyes were rewarded by the appearance of some great hunch-backed forms looming out from the uncertain light of cloud-rack crossing a waning moon. The engines slowed down to half speed, and in a glory of fleeting shadow and elusive tracts of silvered waterway our ship glided along between steeply sloped islands. Presently some coloured guiding lights broke into view with dramatic suddenness and led us up a magnificent harbour, at the head of which the white dwellings of Vavau peered like ghostly forms from beneath a tangle of palms and orange trees.

An almost preternatural silence hung over the wharf as we crept to our moorings. A few black-faced figures, clad in loose white garments, stood spectre-like and inanimate on the quay; then sprang to left and right as the curling black hawsers went circling among them. The gangway was lowered on creaking blocks, and whilst moon and clouds cast a flickering network of light and shadow upon the restful water we slept and sweated the tropical night away.

Most people were early astir the next morning, for *the* thing to do is to climb a high hill on the island called Talau, and from the top watch the rising sun. But there was no sunrise at Vavau that morning, so we did not hurry to leave our bunks. However, we were not going to be outdone by the few adventurous spirits who *did* attempt the expedition, and so we strolled along later at our leisure. The sky was overcast, and the heat, even at 6.30 in the morning, almost unbearable.

Our way lay along a grassy track lined on either side by coco-nut palms and, at frequent intervals, a grove of orange trees densely hung with fruit formed a tunnel across our path that was strewn with rotting windfalls. Gay and sweetly scented flowers sprang from the rich grass on either hand; jasmine mingling with the dangerous foot-catching tentacles of the lianas, whilst the imported and pestilential sensitive plant was very conspicuous by its tiny ball of bloom. A quantity of enormous spiders hung motionless overhead in their webs. Of other wild life there was no sign, except the soft cooing of some pigeons that remained hidden from view in the bush. From time to time we passed a plot of bananas or pineapples, as yet deserted by its Tongan cultivator, and as we went we sucked at oranges plucked from the tree or gathered from the thousands of ignored windfalls at our feet.

In about half an hour we came to the foot of Talau Hill, up which we climbed easily, though the track was slippery with clay, but good foothold could be found on curious protruding rocks resembling lava or coral in their form. From the top, although the morning was dull and hazy, the view over lagoon and hill, harbour and open sea, was very impressive. Numberless coral reefs tinted the becalmed landlocked water with colours innumerable, and from a Native village across the deep lagoon came a sweet sound of singing from the mellow voices of Tongans at early-morning prayer.

Later that day, with our friends Attwater and Thompson, we called on the Governor of Vavau, Prince Tugi* (pronounced Toong-ee, *g* as in *tongue*. Also with Tonga = Tong-ah). We found him in his office, together with a strange

* Now the Prince Consort and Prime Minister.

individual whom we afterwards discovered to be the son of a Samoan chief.

Prince Tugi seemed to be a trifle embarrassed by our pile of introductory letters. There was much bowing on our part and smiling from him. He was very European in manner, having been educated in Sydney, and represented his country at the coronation of King George V in London. In dress the Prince was also completely Europeanized, and had a most dignified bearing. He contrasted oddly with the Samoan, who, although his collar, coat, and vest were of the latest cut, yet wore, as his nether garment, the native lava-lava, and was bedecked about his shoulders with an elaborate and extra evil-smelling *sisi*. He shook hands with us, bowing low from the waist in true German style.

At Prince Tugi's invitation we all adjourned to his house near by, and sat round in a circle on elbowed bentwood chairs. Whether it was our embarrassment at being in the combined presence of a personage of blood Royal and of a chief of even higher rank than the reigning king or what, I do not know, but conversation lagged uncomfortably to start with; all we could do was to sit at attention, make an inane remark or two, and smile very coyly. In the long intervening silence the son of the Samoan chief kept muttering to himself or leaning over to whisper in Tugi's ear, much to the Prince's apparent discomfiture. At first we could not make out what was wrong with the Samoan, and not until hc completely overbalanced on top of Tugi when trying to deposit his cigarette ash in the tray did we realize that he had had "a drop too much."

It was during a rather painful silence immediately following this lamentable episode that the chief's son rose to his feet, removed the *sisi* from his shoulders, and striding across to Thompson placed it with a flourish and a low bow about his ample form. Such an act is considered a very great distinction among the Island folks, and Thompson, who was taken aback as much as any of us, bowed and stuttered out some appropriate word of thanks. So there we all sat, we three nearly bursting with laughter at the strange figure of Thompson sitting bolt upright with the *sisi* adorning his blue serge suit.

Soon after this the Samoan took his departure, much to the relief of all, and immediately our conversation livened up and we talked to Tugi about London and the places he had visited on his travels. He had been greatly impressed by the Coronation procession he told us, and above all by the marvellous control of the police over the traffic in our streets. On a table standing in the centre of our circle was an album containing miscellaneous photographs and post-card views of his travels, and beside this stood a tray on which four tumblers were placed. Each tumbler contained, egg-cup fashion, an enormous coco-nut, freshly plucked from the palm. The fibre husk had been deftly stripped off by means of a pointed stake driven into the ground, and this left the large brown kernels now resting in the glasses, and the tops of the fruit had been severed with a knife. Around the walls of the room hung enlarged photographs of the famous Finau family. It was the celebrated chief of this name who adopted William Mariner, the only survivor of the ill-fated *Port-au-Prince*, a British privateer captured by the Tongans off Haapai in 1806. Mariner spent some few years in Tonga, and his book, *Mariner's Tonga*, is *the* classic on the history of these beautiful islands.

The Prince now gave orders to an aged female retainer to prepare Kava for us, and whilst our curiosity was heightened to burning point on learning that we were at last to taste the national beverage of the Pacific Islands, we were at the same time disappointed that a Tongan beauty had not been chosen to masticate the Bacchanalian root! The Kava root is usually chewed into a pulp by the most beautiful maidens of the household, and then placed in a round bowl of varying size, but usually supported on a dozen legs or so. The whole vessel is carved from a solid block of wood, generally of a rich brown colour, and the interior of a bowl that has seen much usage is often stained with a rich bluish bloom which, in the eyes of its owner, greatly adds to its value.

The chewed root then has water poured gently upon it and it is thoroughly well stirred with the hands and wrung out in a cloth of coco fibre. This goes on until the operator's hands are well cleansed and until the liquid assumes an unpleasant muddy hue. Unfortunately the advance of civilization has persuaded the educated Native that the *chewed* Kava habit is an evil one, and with the abandonment of this custom others have gone with it.

Prince Tugi ordered the Kava makers to sit on the veranda before us, and as we watched the process from the deep shade of the room we sucked at oranges that had been prepared in a most fascinating manner. The skin had been skilfully removed by a sharp knife, but the white pithy covering remained. The fruit had been sliced across the top; all one was supposed to do was to suck out the sweet juice and cast aside the useless remainder. But to return to the Kava making. Our disappointment increased when we noticed that a man—a mere man of far from prepossessing appearance—beat the root into fibrous strips, as he sat cross-legged on the veranda. Then he placed the chopped root into a goodly sized bowl and the aged retainer referred to above poured water over it from a coco-nut shell. The man then proceeded to wash his hands in it, and gathered the pieces of root up in the fibre cloth and wrung it out. This went on for some time, the coming and going of servants for orders interrupting the rather tedious monotony of this unromantic Kava making. In fact there was no romance about the whole performance until a not unbecoming damsel, in a transparent blouse, stepped into the room bearing a trayful of small coco-nut shells filled with the precious liquid. We all forgot to clap our hands sharply together before taking the cup, except Attwater, whose month's apprenticeship to island life had not left him lacking in Tongan etiquette. However, the Prince excused us with many smiles, as the curious beverage slipped down our throats. Too much Kava, they say, paralyses the legs, so that one cannot rise from the floor, although the brain remains free from this intoxicating effect. We found the taste of Kava not unpleasant, though to many it is extremely obnoxious at first; it seemed not unlike some preparation of arrowroot or one of the more palatable of allopathic medicines. The after-effects of a small draught in the mouth is cooling and pleasant, and to a stomach that had not tasted alcohol for some months it produced an agreeable tingling sensation. There can be little doubt that Kava contains a certain amount of alcohol, though exactly *how* much it would be hard to judge by its effect upon individuals. This delicacy was followed by a Tongan cigarette, an irregular roll of leaf tobacco that refused to draw and when it *did* tasted uncommonly strong.

Before leaving we refreshed ourselves again with coco-nut milk, poured with some dexterity from the kernels into tumblers by Attwater. This sweet and sparkling drink is as unlike as can be the acid and coagulated liquid that schoolboys swallow with such avidity at fairs in the Homeland. *This* was the real thing, fresh from the tree, and no hard shell has to be broken first—only a stiff, green, fibrous husk that is hacked off on a wooden stake, as we have already explained.

Tugi, as the Prince was often called by his friends, now placed a trap and horse at our disposal, and a mounted guard to show us the way across the island to a view famed for its romantic beauty. Unfortunately there was only room for three of us in the buggy, so Stan very nobly said that he would stay behind. So we set off over the rutty road, Attwater driving, whilst I belaboured the bony, fly-bitten nag with my camera strap and Thompson sat on the other side of me still decked out in his elaborate *sisi*. On our flank, over the green turf, cantered our Tongan escort, bare toe in stirrup, on a more restive beast, and we created a great impression among fellow passengers from the boat and Natives along our route!

110 Coastal scene near Apia, Samoa

111 Thompson, wearing his *sisi*, at Vavau

112 Could there be a greater victory than Stevenson's?

113 We were on the threshold of Vailima

A gentle rain fell from time to time, yet it was too hot to wear more than a cotton shirt and trousers and a jacket. Looking back, we saw Stan close behind us lolling in a buggy which the Prince, so we afterwards learnt, had, with that generosity so peculiar to his race, invited him to take at the last moment.

Of course the usual palms lined our way, and from one to another fluttered a bird, not unlike a kingfisher of exceedingly brilliant plumage—a Japanese-blue back and wings and pure white breast. Kindly Natives greeted us as we passed, calling "Malolelei! Malolelei!" And so along this umbrageous road, past taro and yam patches, up a long steep rise, to a Native village built about a grassy clearing in the bush, in the centre of which an imposing new church was in course of construction.

Stan appeared to be having a lengthy conversation with his driver who stopped to show him over the church. The fact that Stan was a Free Churchman, as nearly all the Tongans are, and a friend of Tugi's was duly impressed upon all those inquisitive Natives who pressed around, and he was invited to a neighbouring *abi* to partake of Kava or coco-nut milk. Kava not being in his line, he accepted the offer of the milk. Whilst he was being greeted in the most friendly way by his unknown hosts his driver ascended the nearest palm tree and quickly kicked down a couple of nuts. To remove the green husk was but the work of a minute, though to an inexperienced hand it is no easy task. Though work is looked down upon with contempt, the Tongans are never too proud to do cooking. While the foregoing operation was proceeding, Stan's host continued to stir a huge cauldron containing a suspicious-looking brown liquid. Unfortunately the Natives' knowledge of English and Stan's knowledge of Tongan were insufficient to discover what the cauldron contained.

As our mounted escort led us along the track to the coastal scene of rock and cliff and waving palms, he carried on a long conversation with us.

"Is it a fact," he asked, "that there are people in England

who have no food nor clothes? How can this be? Is not England a great and wealthy country?"

To the Tongan mind such a state of affairs is incredible, and such questions are not easy to answer except to point out that in olden times the land of England was held much as the land of Tonga is to-day, but that the kings and chiefs at Home had abused their power and kept the land for themselves instead of holding it in trust for the people to use. It made us feel what a lot we have to learn from Tonga.

We had to force the pace of our stumbling nags on the return trip. We could not help wishing that they would introduce a few good stallions into these islands. True it is that most of the horses one sees *are* stallions, but they are so broken down with labour and so ill that they are useless for the improvement of the breed.

The Swallows' Cave

Immediately after lunch an expedition was setting out from the *Tofua* for the famous Swallows' Cave, and after a hasty meal we found ourselves taking our seats in the motor-launch and the two ship's lifeboats, and away we went, a merry throng, across the beautiful natural harbour of Vavau.

Captain Crawford took the helm of the towing launch, but "Dummy" was the real commodore of our little fleet that afternoon. The poor fellow was, as his name implied, unable to speak except by extraordinarily expressive signs and uncouth sounds; he kept up a running conversation with the Captain all the afternoon, much to the amusement of those who could see him hanging out of the engine-room and gesticulating with arms and legs and intelligent face. In the cave itself "Dummy" was at his best, bossing up the boats for the tricky entry into the lofty chamber. Beneath us were fathoms of light green water showing the corals growing below, and in front a long gallery penetrating for hundreds of yards, raised above our heads like the stage of a theatre from the stalls.

Into this gallery two or three Tongans crawled and presently the nave of a glorious cathedral was revealed to us in a ruddy glow of light which faded and then blazed up again a brilliant green.

On leaving the cave which, so far as we could see, had no connection with swallows, our motor engine refused to start, and in the meanwhile we were being smothered by the escaping smoke from the coloured lights. However, our discomfiture was only temporary, and we were soon steering towards an exquisitely picturesque sandy shore on an adjoining island, but we could not approach nearer than about 20 yards owing to the reef shallowing. This meant being carried to the shore by the boats' crews and any male passenger who volunteered to help—no easy task over the sharp coral for those with tender feet. Stan got me ashore early in the proceedings, and I had the good fortune to see nearly everyone else carried or heaved or dragged to land. One of our party, a Mrs. Telle, had waited in the boat till the last. She was very stout, and naturally timid of being carried ashore like a baby in the iron grip of "Dummy" and his mates. There was a good deal of excitement about getting her over the gunwale of the jolly-boat. The first position, seated on the edge, was all right. She placed an arm around the necks of her stalwart carriers, and then, with a twist, they brought her clear of the boat. What we saw then was nothing to what followed. Shrieking for mercy, Mrs. Telle implored the staggering Natives to set her down, and this they did on a dry portion of the reef. Before anyone else could assist her Mrs. Telle made a sporting bolt for the beach, plunging recklessly over rocks and through puddles. At every stride she raised her skirts higher, shrieking with excitement at her adventure, whilst everyone on shore roared an accompaniment of good-natured laughter!

Some good-looking Native damsels now assembled on the shore would have us bargain for shells of quaint shape. Everything was "seexpence" or "sheeling." When we offered them a shabby piece of white coral we had picked up at the same price they saw the joke and laughed most bewitchingly. Having sauntered some distance to the Native village, we returned to a typical grove of palms and other tropic bush, where a picnic tea was served.

Later on we had to embark again, and once more Mrs. Telle made a wonderful exhibition of herself getting from shore to boat. She stood for some minutes ankle-deep in water, laughing hysterically, nor would she allow anyone to assist her, and I do not think any ladies in our party, from the continent of Europe to the Antipodes, had ever seen a finer display of lingerie at any White Sale!

It rained pretty heavily on the way back to Vavau, and as soon as the sun went down a flock of flying foxes covered the sky; gruesome-looking vampires were these tabu creatures of the Friendly Isles.

I had been worried by a tropical headache all the day and so was glad to get to bed early. Through a light, restless slumber I heard the songs of the joyful Tongans as they laboured with heavy sacks of copra, whilst a solid rain beat the devil's tattoo, and those merciless donkey engines banged and rattled an accompanying chorus. Most people were on the shelter-deck watching it all, and marvelling, moreover, at the good nature and untiring strength of these dusky "landed gentry" who were labouring under the copra sacks in a deluge of rain.

Some time that night we slipped from our moorings, and, thanks to the moon, passed in safety from this magic harbour, for when we awoke the fresh wind of the open sea was blowing through our porthole and around us the great Pacific heaved in a restless, endless swell. So for the whole of that day and the whole of the night that followed we steamed northwards, and came, with the break of dawn, in sight of the hills of Upolu, at the foot of which, nestling in palms, was Apia, the capital of Samoa.

Chapter XII

SAMOA

AT Apia there is no still and peaceful anchorage as at Vavau. The ship lay off about a mile from the shore, and the rollers swept past only slightly moderated by the reef. An ugly place to rest in during a hurricane, as the rusted, fern-covered ribs and broken back of the ill-fated *Adler* showed us. She was once a German cruiser, and has been a grim warning to other masters of ships for four and forty years.

The sun, which sulked behind oppressive clouds during our visit to Vavau, now gleamed on the myriad swaying palm fronds that covered the steep slopes of the hills, and on one of those umbrageous summits stood the tomb of R. L. Stevenson. Years ago he had come here in search of health, and like so many other wanderers to this isle he stayed, built himself a home, and now lies there on Mount Vaea "under the wide and starry sky."

All about our ship swarmed a dense throng of long jolly-boats, and around the decks came Jack, William, and Sam anxiously canvassing for passengers to take ashore. We had previously learnt that the German authorities would not allow our motor-launch to land passengers, so we had to submit to a somewhat ridiculous tariff of 1s. each way, whilst the official charges for inland drives were equally out of reason. Of catamarans we saw only a few, curious outrigged craft bearing a Native paddler and his cargo of green bananas from the shore. As our powerful "William" and his lusty mates pulled us with rapid strokes landward, we gazed at the busy main street of Apia, shadowed by trees and lined with a straggling row of houses and stores. At the boat landing we were enveloped by a covey of Samoan maidens and matrons anxious to sell us pretty necklaces, fans, and baskets, and by youths soliciting the honour of driving us inland behind horses of deplorable meagreness.

But for the present we were bound on more important business, and under the guidance of our Marconi officer we soon found ourselves in the presence of Mr. H. J. Moors, an American trader with whom Stevenson had lived and been friends. We learnt from Mr. Moors that he (Mr. Moors) was *the* agitation in Apia, and that he was "ag'in the Government every time!"

As we sat in his office, talking of Stevenson and the days gone by, we were affording a new and succulent dish to multitudes of mosquitoes! Somebody in Auckland, on hearing we were off to the Islands, said: "Going to the South Seas? Jove! You must look out for the mosquitoes; they're so thick there that you can *push* them back!" But we were fortunate in getting them no worse than we did in Mr. Moors' office. Stan declared that he could see them sucking the blood from the trader's neck, yet Moors winced not, being too accustomed to them and having plenty to spare for them, perhaps!

It was certainly a hot day, and most people were glad to avail themselves of Samoan carriages, but with Mr. Moors' warning ringing in our ears to be careful that they did not make us *buy* the conveyance we decided to walk the mile or so, down the one street of Apia, to the Court House where His Excellency the Governor was supposed to be.* Four miles an hour is an unaccustomed pace for the tropics, and the local inhabitants gazed with wonder upon anyone so indifferent to the heat. The road skirts along the seashore past an enormous wooden building that bore the then familiar initials of D.H. & P.G. The Deutsche Handels und Plantagen Gesellschaft was a wealthy German concern doing an extensive business in all the Islands and owning many large plantations at that time. The resident general manager, Mr. Karl Hanssen, was on the *Tofua* with us, and from him we were able to learn much of trade and general conditions on the Islands. Farther

* Samoa was a German possession then, and is now held under a mandate by New Zealand.

down the road we came to the memorial to the English and American sailors killed in one of the Native risings; they fought together and now lie buried side by side, whilst not far away is an old Native war boat consisting of two gigantic canoes fixed together with a superstructure capable, it is said, of carrying six hundred men. It is an amazing piece of work, for there is neither nail nor bolt in the entire construction: it is bound together by thongs!

Hot and perspiring we at length reached the Court House, a light and airy building of the bungalow type. We entered what appeared to be the offices, but no one present seemed able to understand either English or German, and we were waved across to a building opposite. This consisted of a gigantic thatched roof supported by poles, barely more than 5 feet 6 inches high. Under the shelter of this roof three German officials were seated at a table administering justice; about 15 yards away from them, squatting on the floor some distance apart, were the plaintiff and defendant. None of the officials turned out to be the Governor whom we were seeking, for apparently he had not yet arrived in his car from Vailima, and so there was nothing for it but to turn back along the hot and dusty road. At last we ran him down in the Justice House, and explaining who we were secured from him a pass to see over Stevenson's home.

Vailima

Vailima was then used as His Excellency's residence, and soon, after a great deal of hide and seek, Attwater and Thompson accompanied us in a rickety buggy on our pilgrimage to the home and grave of "Tusitala," as the Samoans called "The Writer of Tales." Whilst waiting for the various members of our party to assemble, we had been speaking with our driver boy and asked him incidentally to which Church he belonged. "I belong Church of England," he said, "but," he added, "all Church same; all same *God*," with an enthusiastic emphasis on the last word and we could not help admiring his broad-mindedness.

To those who have read the *Vailima Letters*, the drive up to Stevenson's house is full of fascinating associations. On our right we passed a school of which we shall have more to say later on, where Stevenson used to pay regular visits to receive instruction in Samoan from Mr. Newell. In those days the road was very different from what it is to-day, and we think Stevenson would be more than surprised to see His Excellency the Governor *motoring* to Vailima along the track he loved so well.*

There are many Native houses on either side of the way, and bananas, taros, coco trees and tall palms line the route. Bright orange-coloured flowers, looking much like a species of wild coreopsis, grow in great profusion, and one has not to look far for the sensitive plant of which Stevenson has written so much. The handsome Natives, with their genial smile and pleasant greeting of "Talofa" ("My love to you"), seemed quite in place, and one could picture them going up on their many errands to Vailima, as often as not to consult Tusitala on some matter of the slightest importance. Mataafa, the great chief, for whom Stevenson had such a deep respect, was dead, but we met with many others who still remembered and revered his name. The road leads slowly upwards through the tropical vegetation to a most gorgeous spot about 600 feet up the side of Mount Vaea. Here, then, we were on the threshold of Vailima: alas! no longer the same, for much of the house has been rebuilt and many rooms have been added. Before entering we turned to see for ourselves the fascinations of the view. It is certainly a unique situation, and one cannot wonder at its

* "Chiefs! Our road is not built to last a thousand years, yet in a sense it is. When a road is once built, it is a strange thing how it collects traffic . . . so that perhaps even this road of ours may, from reparation to reparation, continue to exist and be useful hundreds and hundreds of years after we are mingled in the dust. And it is my hope that our far-away descendants may remember and bless those who laboured for them to-day."—Stevenson's Address to the Chiefs on the Opening of the Road of Gratitude, October 1894.

appeal to Stevenson. Four miles below us lay the harbour. We could see our steamer at her moorings, and alongside her the missionary ship, the *John Williams*, for which in the enthusiasm of his youth Stan had collected £10 or £15. Behind us rose the thickly wooded hills which Stevenson explored with such boyish enthusiasm in his desire to trace the rivulets to their source.

On the large veranda at the front of the house we were met by a Samoan in uniform. After taking our letter from the Governor he returned to say that he had instructions to take us where we wished. It seemed almost like trespassing on sacred ground to walk through the old sitting-room at Vailima and to gaze at the brick fireplace and chimney without which, even in this tropical climate, Stevenson felt his house would not have been complete. The rooms have scarcely any connection with Stevenson to-day, but the *veranda* is where so much of his life was spent, and upon it we stood and gazed, first at the garden and then out to the harbour and the open sea. Our minds wandered back to the vivid plans in the *Vailima Letters*, and almost instinctively we found ourselves looking for the banana patch and the waterfall. There they both were, just as we had hoped to find them, and after another look round the light and airy rooms we strolled down through the garden to the stream. Just below the fall there is a delightful bathing pool, but this, we think, has been altered since Stevenson's time.

Fortunately we did not have to emulate Stevenson and cut our way up the side of Mount Vaea, for the track through the bush, which the Samoans made, is kept open. We found it a steep climb up, and we often paused to wonder at the loving gratitude that inspired the chiefs not only to cut the track but to carry the last remains of their beloved Tusitala to the summit. A glance at the thick growth on either side of us recalled the laborious expeditions that Stevenson used to make, cutlass and compass in hand, and as we stumbled over the trailing lianas we pictured with renewed freshness his inimitable description that we had read and re-read with such infinite pleasure.

From the summit we could see once more the wide expanse of the Pacific. Here, surrounded by hibiscus bushes, with their bright red flowers, was the simple grave we had expected. On one side his own epitaph, and on the other the speech of Ruth to Naomi in Samoan (Ruth i. 16, 17), which the inflections of the Native language render so beautifully. One could not help feeling how much more appropriate were the full-blooded hibiscus flowers than the white blossoms which adorn most other graves.

As we listened to the cooing of the doves and the songs of other birds that now harbour unmolested on these mountain heights, our thoughts involuntarily turned to that other hilltop grave we had but recently visited. Could there be a greater contrast? Here, amidst the richest of tropical vegetation; there, among the barren boulders and kopjes of the Matopos. Could there be a greater victory than Stevenson's? We quote from his letter to George Meredith written in 1893:

"For fourteen years I have not had a day's real health; I have wakened sick and gone to bed weary, and I have done my work unflinchingly. I have written in bed and written out of it; written in haemorrhages, written in sickness, written torn by coughing, written when my head swam for weakness; and for so long, it seems to me, I have won my wager and recovered my glove. I am better now; have been, rightly speaking, since first I came to the Pacific. And still, few are the days when I am not in some physical distress. And the battle goes on; ill or well is a trifle, so as it goes. I was made for a contest, and the Powers have so willed that my battlefield should be this dingy, inglorious one of the bed and the physic bottle."

As we wended our way downwards and joined the Ala Loto Alofa, the "Road of the Loving Hearts" that the imprisoned chiefs built to his house as a mark of gratitude after their release, we thought of Stevenson's conquest of men. Was it not the conquest of love?

We Visit a Samoan Chief

We left our buggy and its two panting, groggy-kneed ponies at the Tivoli Hotel and then we set off with Thompson westwards in search of further adventure. The road led over a bridge and through a portion of the town that seemed to be more devoted to the occupation of Asiatics, and then leaving these behind we came suddenly upon an open view of the reef, a wide stretch of grass, and a Samoan house or two. And so on, past the American Consulate to where the road ends suddenly, dwindles to a track, and in a few yards leads on to the broad white sands.

We had not gone far before a rivulet barred our passage, nor was there any means of crossing it except by fording. We longed for the simple raiment of two Samoans who preceded us; they just tucked up their lava-lavas and walked through the stream in a very matter-of-fact way. Whilst we were struggling with bootlaces and garters, and before I was half through with these elaborations of an over-civilized dress, one of the Natives had returned to my assistance, and taking me upon his shoulders he soon deposited me in safety on the other side. He would have gone back for Stan and Thompson but they were already wading through, and we continued in company with the Samoans along the dazzling palm-fringed shore. Now we left the beach and followed a track penetrating a grassy glade with tropic foliage overhead, yet keeping between the palm boles exquisite glimpses of sea and surf and the distant sweep of a curving bay. As we went we endeavoured to converse with our Native friends, waved to young women squatting in their houses, and finally waylaid some half-dozen of them on their way to evensong. Their delight knew no bounds as they peeped into the view-finder of my camera, and the light being good we managed to secure several snaps of this pretty group.

The Samoans had been vaccinated wholesale just before our arrival in Apia, and we noticed that several of the youngsters' arms were disfigured by ugly lumps and holes, painful evidence of ruthless ill treatment on the part of doctor and patient alike. Around these unpleasant wounds the ubiquitous fly congregated in his hundreds, and for this reason we did not altogether appreciate the eagerness of one young boy to gather innumerable shells and stones which he persisted in our pocketing.

As we arrived in the heart of a large village a good-looking Native came running across the grass to meet us.

"You come steamer?" he asked.

"Yes, we come steamer."

"Then come see my father's house; my father he big Chief."

Two minutes later we were sitting round in a semicircle on mats laid over the white pebble floor of the hut.

These Samoan huts or houses are nothing more than large oval thatched roofs supported on poles. Except in the event of rain or strong wind, in which case crazy-looking Venetian blinds are let down from the eaves to the ground, the sides of the huts remain open so that the air circulates freely.

It was not long before the great Chief himself turned up, his massive body clad only in a lava-lava. This handsome giant squatted beside us on the floor, and although unable to speak English he smiled acknowledgments to our infantile remarks, showing his perfect white teeth and bearing himself with a rather awe-inspiring dignity. We discovered that he was the Chief Asi of whom Stevenson speaks so slightingly in his *Vailima Letters*, and it would appear that great Chiefs are often hard up in Samoa, or at any rate this Asi family was, for later on I had an experience with one of them that disgusted me as much as the Chief's call did Tusitala.

After drinking Kava and taking a few photos of his family and house we took our leave. We essayed a new road back, but had not gone far before we fell in with a ginger-mopped Samoan, cutlass in hand, who expressed the wish that we should go and see *his* house. This deviation brought us back to our old track, and so we followed it homewards, and on the way we came upon a Samoan family drying copra on the seashore. When we came to the rivulet across the sands we observed two Native men and a woman bathing, as is the wont of these cleanly Samoans at sunrise and eventide. The men seemed to lack any form of costume, but the woman was washing herself beneath an elaborate white bathing gown. When we squatted down on the shore and commenced removing shoes and socks she fled affrighted into a clump of adjacent bamboos, modestly fearing, no doubt, that we were about to expose our persons with a ruthless disregard of her presence. Meanwhile the two men grasped the situation and leapt from the water, wrapping white lava-lavas about them, and suddenly we felt ourselves being pressed against hairy but paternal chests and held in a grip of iron. So once again we took our kindly Native friends by the hand and crying "Tofa!" we continued on our way with rejoicing hearts. Presently a bridge spanned another stream, and coming down to it from higher ground we caught a glimpse of more broad, naked backs in the water; but the women were quick to hear our approach, and covered themselves with dexterous rapidity.

A Samoan Girls' School

I had been bemoaning the fact that the shortness of our stay did not permit of a visit to the neighbouring island of Savai'i, where Rev. W. Sibree was stationed. I mentioned the matter to Mr. Moors, and he replied: "I saw his boat this morning. I think he must be over on a visit." Five minutes later, while we were selecting some picture postcards at Mr. Tattersall's, I heard a familiar voice behind me, and turning round I had the pleasure of giving Mr. Sibree quite a surprise! He was over in connection with the visit of the *John Williams*, but, like me, had arrived on the eve of her departure. He at once offered to show me what was possible in the short time still remaining, and I spent the afternoon and evening with him.

The mission-house, where he was staying, is close to the quay, and here I received a very warm welcome from Mr. and Mrs. Kinnersley and from Mr. Morley, who was over from the other side of the island. After tea, however, Sibree and I drove up to the school for Samoan girls, conducted by Miss Schultze. On our way we looked in at the little Congregational Church, but the congregation consisted largely of half-castes, for the majority of the limited white population were Germans. Farther on we passed the Niue settlement. Natives from a little island near by come here to work.

As a nephew of Sir Albert Spicer I received the most cordial of welcomes from Miss Schultze, and we were at once taken into the main classroom where some seventy Samoan girls were busy at needlework. They certainly seemed as happy as could be, and eagerly responded to Miss Schultze's question that they should sing for my benefit. Like the Tongans they are blessed with wonderful voices and a keen sense of harmony, but their method of singing is very different from that to which we are accustomed in Europe. The one or two taking the air are quite in the minority, and to adapt English music to their method necessitates the giving of the air to the bass parts. The most interesting of all are the songs which they improvise for themselves, like the ballads of the old minstrels. If any friend were going on a visit to other parts, they would deal very thoroughly with the dangers of the journey, the joy of return, and their infinite love for the wanderer, with which no affection shown by strangers can compare.

The singing over, they gave us a display of drilling on the green lawn in front of the veranda, and the clubs which they swung so gracefully showed to advantage the suppleness of their wrists and figures. At the close of the performance they filed past and bowed most charmingly to us.

Sibree and I took advantage of a pause in the proceedings to escape to a delicious bathing pool in the bush near by, which was indeed a joy after the heat of the day.

At that time the English language had been replaced by

German in this as in all other schools; it was, therefore, fortunate that German happened to be Miss Schultze's mother-tongue.

On our return to the house we inspected the dormitories, and I had my first taste of bread-fruit as cooked by the Natives. It is certainly very good but extraordinarily filling; just a trifle like boiled chestnuts, in fact. Fried, as we had it at our evening meal, it forms an excellent vegetable. Miss Schultze's sister and a Miss Macey, who was assistant teacher at the school, joined us, and we had a lively discussion regarding things Samoan. As in Tonga, the difference between "mine" and "thine" is very slight. The great thing seems to be to increase your relatives in districts where you are not well connected, and also to obtain good mats. Unless these two considerations have received attention, the consent of the family to a marriage is often withheld.

Will Sibree conducted the evening prayers, and after they were over he talked to the girls in Samoan and apparently told them a great deal about me: that my brother had been at college with him and was now a doctor in New Zealand; that my parents had always been kind to missionaries and to his family in particular, and that, but for my uncle, their beloved Miss Schultze would probably not be in charge of their school. Meanwhile I was all unconscious of this reflected glory that was being thus lavishly poured upon me, but I noticed, with some little trepidation, the eagle gaze of seventy pairs of approving eyes fixed upon me.

Later on there was a rustle among the girls at the back; with no little hesitation one very charming damsel came forward and presented me with a beautiful Samoan inlaid walking stick. Imagine my embarrassment! There was an expectant hush during which Will Sibree whispered across to me, "You will have to say something." Precisely! But what was I to say and in what language? Their knowledge of English was about equal to my knowledge of Samoan, so there was nothing for it but to address them in German, express my appreciation as best I could, and tell them with what joy I should treasure the stick they had so kindly given me. After the applause had died away several girls addressed Miss Schultze in Samoan. Would I give them a song? It really was too much. If they had only known it, I would have done anything for them at that moment, but sing, alas! I cannot.

The Son of a Chief

While Stan was away I boarded the *Tofua* for luncheon, and there, on the stairway of the vestibule, stood the son of the Chief Asi, whose acquaintance we had made the previous afternoon. He said to me:

"I love you *so* much that I come to say good-bye to you. But you go eat now; I wait here till you finish."

I was rather bucked at this little incident, but after the meal I could find no sign of my Samoan, so I retired to the boat-deck to write for an hour or so. Later on I came down to the vestibule again to ascertain how I could best get my mail ashore, and lo! there was the Chief's son waiting with the patient vigilance of a terrier before a rabbit burrow. I took him off to our cabin, where he showed me the beautiful Kava bowl lusciously bloomed with long usage that we had drunk out of the day before. He offered it to me at a ridiculously cheap price, or would take in exchange, he said, any old clothing! I was near falling to the bargain, but remembered in time that my box was in the hold, that my only available wardrobe hung upon a miserable hook in the cabin, that I could part with none of it, and that the weight of our luggage did not permit of my adding an eleven-legged Kava bowl to it.

The Samoan was much disappointed at my decision, and, said he:

"If it was *my* bowl and not the Chief Asi's, my love for you would make me *give* it to you."

This speech was too much for me and I fell an easy victim to such pleasant flattery. After some further conversation I

114 The dazzling palm fringed shore

115 Old Samoan war canoe at Apia

116 Distant view of Mount Vaea and Apia

117 This handsome giant squatted beside us on the floor

wanted to be rid of the man, as I had promised myself a quiet afternoon on the steamer.

"What time boat sail?" asked the Samoan.

"At midnight," I answered in a weak moment.

"Then I stay beside you. I no leave you till steamer sail. I love you so; it is my duty."

He smiled and beamed, and seemed, to my horror, to *mean* what he said. I thought that if I got him ashore I might be able to shake him off, but in another weak moment took my camera in the boat on the pretext that I wanted to take some views. No sooner were we landed that he insisted on slinging the camera case over his broad shoulders and also carried my tripod, and depositing his bowl in a wayside store off we went to explore the back streets of Apia. I never felt so dignified in my life. All the Natives accosted this Chief's son, and I was certain he kept referring to me as his "chum" or "beloved friend." My conversation was but limited with my stalwart carrier, whose name, he showed me with some pride, was tattooed on his arm. I think it was "Faataaooma" or some such title, and I delighted to see that one of the *a*'s was subverted, and that such a detail had not escaped Stevenson's notice in his letters to Sidney Colvin. "Faataa-ooma" also showed me the names of his dead sister and that of his father likewise tattooed.

On our return to the jetty some hour or so later, he appeared to be downcast at the idea of leaving me, and kept on repeating how much he loved me until I became quite embarrassed and, fearing a scene if I bade the good fellow farewell in such a public place, I decided to accompany him half-way to his village. Just before arriving at the American Consulate I declared that I must bid him good-bye, but he, with an obstinacy that made me want to kick myself, declined to leave my side until we had tramped the mile and a half back to the jetty again!

"And now," he said, "my friend, I must say good-bye, and I want to give my wife and family a good dinner to-night in your honour; will you give me two bob?"

I might have guessed as much! Why had he not put in an honest day's work and earned three times the amount? But then he was a Chief's son, and it would have been *infra dig.* for him to descend so low. Fortunately the Tivoli was at hand, and I fled thither ignominously, and because they did not trouble about making afternoon tea I ordered a "Dr. Funk." Poor Dr. Funk! It was he who invented this most delicious of all drinks, which is only obtainable in Samoa. It was he, too, who laboured so valiantly with Dr. Anderson to restore our beloved Tusitala to life on that tragic afternoon up at Vailima. Whenever I read Lloyd Osbourne's words, as quoted in Graham Balfour's Life of our "Writer of Tales," a lump always rises in my throat.

A Native Dance

On stepping aboard the *Tofua* again I found Thompson just returned from a picnic at Papase'ea, where he and others had been disporting themselves with sundry Samoan damsels, shooting the sliding rock of some beautiful waterfalls there. The game, being carried out in bathing costumes of course, had apparently afforded the solicitor endless amusement. He introduced me to a comely Native wench who had been of his party and who was now canvassing for passengers for her brother to take ashore in his boat to witness a dance that she was organizing at the Imperial Hotel. The "Fairy," as Thompson introduced her, was by no means good-looking, and possessed that stolid figure which one cannot help but admire in the Samoan lassies advanced in maidenhood. She spoke in soft deep whispers, and the touch of her tapering fingers was electrical. I enlisted at once for her brother's boat on the understanding that she accompanied me. A few minutes later our boat's crew fought its way through the crush of craft about the gangway, and in another moment we were out of the glare of the *Tofua's* lights. The stars twinkled overhead, and the Fairy's brothers bent to their oars. The

Fairy herself sat so close to me in the stern sheets that the warmth of her great body almost scorched me, and all the while she nursed my knees and crooned into my ear the haunting melody of "Tofa ma Feleni," whilst her four brothers thundered out the refrain with a maniacal fury, and we sped with the billows over the shallowing reef. So to the jetty, all too soon, that led one in a few strides to the veranda of the hotel.

All was in darkness when I arrived, but I sat down on one of a long row of chairs. Presently these began to fill rapidly with half-caste maidens and fellow passengers from the *Tofua*. One of the Fairy's brothers now came and set a line of mats on the open ground in front of the building, and he also arranged two chairs, on which he placed lamps, on either side of the veranda steps. Fantastic figures, clad in white, now began to flock from the darkness towards these illuminations and grouped themselves in a squatting crowd behind the mats. Then there was a sudden burst of merry laughter—the twenty dancing maidens had arrived. They were all dressed alike, in a scanty but effective costume, white rosettes in their jet-black hair, heavy bean necklaces, chests and arms bare, with their breasts mercilessly entrapped in a broad black ribbon tied in the back by a butterfly bow; waists bare, legs almost entirely bare save for a short black lava-lava held in place by a white sash. My Fairy was there looking *enormous* in this simple but barbaric attire. She bossed the girls into a squatting cross-legged line and took the central position herself. I swear I have never seen such backs and thighs in my life before, but one expects scanty raiment at a South Pacific "hop." The Fairy now struck up in the strident notes of her authoritative position, and the white-robed figures, in the darkening shadows of the distance, swelled out a chorus of sonorous melody that revealed all the passion and romance of these Southern Seas. Meanwhile she and her assistants rippled their arms in graceful serpent-like movements, poised their fingers on each other's knees, and their thighs kept up such a trembling accompaniment that one almost blushed for the shortness of their lava-lavas. Between each song and dance we applauded of course, and after the Fairy had come round with the hat for a silver collection the programme was continued on rather more elaborate lines.

As at Nukualofa this consisted in dancers coming to the front and going through all kinds of stamping, squatting contortions, and shrieking, and on this occasion we had men partners who livened up things considerably, especially a hunchback who proved himself to be a most melodramatic performer. The dances became fiercer at every renewal of the song, and the artists' bodies shone with sweat and coco-nut oil, whilst some of the more juvenile damsels could stand their broad ribbon corselets no longer and thus released danced with additional fervour, nor did the picture suffer from this pretty step back into more intimate Native life.

Towards the end, as I was smoking my last cigarette, the Fairy received a burst of applause for the most extraordinary *tour d'estomac* that I have ever seen; it was something horribly but genuinely barbaric. The proceedings ended, not with *Deutschland, Deutschland über Alles*, but with a divine and fully choral rendering of that sad but sweet lament of farewell:

Tofa ma Feleni
Samoa e le galo atu!

Then the meeting broke up, and the perspiring, breathless Fairy led me back to my boat through the deep shadows of that starlit Samoan night. Her arm was about my waist, but alas! there was no hope of passing my arm about hers. On the little jetty our leave-taking was too tender to relate. "Here is my brother," she said, "he see you back to steamer," and taking the cords of the tiller in my hands I steered straight for the big red buoy that marks the reef, whilst the four brothers of my Fairy pulled the craft through the swell to where the dark hull of the *Tofua* loomed, all outlined with dots of orange light.

Until midnight we watched the long white boats coming and going through the darkness; we watched the moon rise in a murk of cloud, and listened to the dulcet tones of the Samoan crews. Away in the night rose the uncertain outline of Mount Vaea, and before turning into bunk we took one last peering gaze over the water in that direction, and then in the restlessness of a tropic sleep we were borne away from the fair shores of Apia.

A Coco-nut Plantation

The following morning our boat hove to off Mulifanua, where, thanks to the courtesy of Captain Crawford, we were allowed to go ashore in the ship's motor-launch, and so we were able to interview the genial Swiss manager (Mr. Helg) of the D.H. & P.G.'s plantation. This consisted of about 4,000 acres, and produced nearly 12,000 tons of copra per annum, which went a long way towards paying the 35 per cent. dividend which this company used regularly to declare. As far as labour was concerned, they were in an exceptional position, for they were the only firm that had the right to import Kanakas (Native labourers) from German New Guinea and the Solomon Islands. These were satisfied with a payment amounting to about £3 10s. per annum, but what these Natives rate more highly than the cash payment is their food, and in this respect they were well provided for, for the simple reason that it paid the company to feed them well, and the twenty or thirty that we saw certainly showed no signs of starvation. There were about four hundred of these Kanakas at work on this plantation, with about ten white overseers, and apart from the coco-nut plantations the D.H. & P.G. kept a considerable number of cattle, for which there was always a ready market in Apia.

As in other parts, the rhinoceros beetle was giving the company very serious trouble, but at the price copra was then making their business was nevertheless exceedingly remunerative. Their plantation was very conveniently placed close to the sea—a position much to the liking of the coco-nut palm, where often the finest crops are grown. The bush country farther inland made about £5 an acre, but the difficulty of obtaining labour prevented development, except by concerns such as the D.H. & P.G., whose cocoa and rubber plantations were elsewhere. The difficulty about rubber was the expense of Chinese labour, which they had to employ. We were told that the Chinese Government had obtained for its people in Samoa an equal status with whites, so that the plantation owners had to exercise considerable care in handling their Chinese labourers.

In a stay of an hour or so it was impossible to see the condition of the workers on this plantation, but a superficial impression was certainly favourable. The Swiss manager was probably right when he said that the Kanakas would repay kind treatment.

Although the Germans were by no means popular with the Samoans, the latter had no real cause for complaint, for the whites took a paternal interest in their welfare, and on the whole the treatment extended to the Natives was good. The sale of land, for instance, was restricted, and no purchases could be made without the sanction of the Government. There were certain regulations which were very strictly enforced, and though they were unpopular there was not the slightest doubt about their being in the interests of the Natives.

As before mentioned, this group of islands, and Upolu in particular, were suffering from the rhinoceros beetle pest, and it was extremely difficult to eradicate it from the coco-nut plantations. Like so many other pests, it was accidentally introduced, and it had no natural enemies to keep it in check. Two prominent scientists were at work studying the problem, but in the meantime it was necessary to do everything possible to keep the pestilence down. The Natives were accordingly compelled to keep their plantations clean, to dig large pits for the rubbish, and periodically to clear them out and burn the contents, for in such pits the beetle delights to deposit its eggs.*

A special stallion was provided for the use of the Samoans with the idea of improving the breed of their horses. No visitor could fail to be impressed by the necessity of this undertaking. By another regulation Natives were compelled to plant a certain number of new coco-nut trees each year, a course which they might otherwise neglect.

Of the exports from Samoa, copra formed by far the greatest part, but cocoa was being grown in considerable quantities.

Of the total Samoan Native population of about 40,000, over 25,000 were adherents of the London Missionary Society, and yet another 6,000 belonged to the Wesleyans. So that it will be seen that the Catholics had not obtained a very great hold, in spite of considerable effort on their part. About twelve miles along the coast from Apia, at Malua, the L.M.S. had a training institution for Samoan pastors and teachers, and quite an extensive printing and book-binding establishment.

* Similar methods of dealing with this pest still obtain to-day.

Chapter XIII

FROM NIUAFUO TO NEW GUINEA

THE day we sailed from Mulifanua was noteworthy for its intense heat. Heavy clouds shed showers from time to time which the sun caught in their fleeting and transformed into veiling of glorious iridescence as they drifted over the sea. The wind was abaft, and it was one of those days when one seemed too prostrated to eat. The coolest place was one's bunk, where one could get a breeze from the electric fan.

Just before breakfast next morning we came in sight of the island of Niuafuo, an outlying possession of the Kingdom of Tonga and a spot of unique interest. Niuafuo is nothing but the rim of a still active volcano that raises its ugly mouth but a few tens of feet above the ocean. From the direction in which we came the place looked innocent enough, for the narrow volcanic rim is clothed in palm trees that provide the finest copra obtainable in these islands. But this "rim" is no more than a mile to a little over two miles broad at any part of its circumference; then one comes to an enormous crater filled with water, and some years ago another crater formed in the centre of this lake, and it, in turn, became filled with water too. So that one might say that Niuafuo is but a magic circle of earth surrounded by water both inside and outside its circumference. The ocean that beats upon its lava cliffs is nearly always too boisterous to launch a small boat in; not so very long ago the one thousand Tongans and few white inhabitants of the place did not know what it was to have even a small row-boat to call their own. They were landed there literally between the devil of the volcano and the deep sea; yet this was a place where money could be made, and so men were willing to take all risks. Owing to the constant swell of the ocean about these shores, the small trading steamers that patrol the islands have considerable difficulty in landing their stores on Niuafuo and taking off the precious copra. For this last purpose they have a chute from the top of the low cliffs, down which the copra sacks are sent. Some people call the place "Tin-can Island," from the method in which the mails are carried ashore. The mail leaves and arrives on the same day once a month, whenever the *Tofua* and *Atua* pass on their way to Suva, and great was the excitement on board when the *Tofua* stopped about half a mile off the coast, and we could see through our glasses the black head of the postman advancing just above the waves!

Niuafuo is the only place in the world where the mail man has to swim for it in the face of adverse currents and a plentiful supply of sharks! It was not long before he came alongside, and we could see that he half supported himself on a bamboo pole in the side of which were stuck two or three shark spears. He carried the outward letters in a cleft stick above his head, and this he now tied to a cord and the letters were safely hauled on board whilst a hermetically sealed kerosene tin containing the inward mail was thrown overboard to the swimmer. And so shouting a cheerful "Malolelei!" off went the half-drowned Tongan, striking out for the shore, and he was thus tossing on the billows as our vessel drew out of sight. These courageous postmen are selected from a number of volunteers of whom there is always an ample supply on mail days eager for the honour that awaits them.

The other side of the island revealed a more gruesome state of affairs, for here a new crater had been formed only six weeks before our arrival, and streams of lava were falling into the sea and devastating a large area of the coast line.

Captain Crawford showed us in his cabin a curiosity that is only to be found on this island, and that was an egg of the bird known as Pritchard's Megapode or the Malau. This bird is indigenous to Niuafuo, and is practically wingless like the kiwi and weka of New Zealand; it is about the size of a pigeon, but the egg it lays is out of all proportion to the bird, being about as large as a good-sized hen's egg and of a red earthy colour. Nor is that all: the egg or eggs is deposited beneath the hot sand and left to take pot-luck, and when the young Megapode arrives he has to fend for himself, and can usually fly better at this early stage than at any other.

Onward to Fiji

Next day we had come to the Fiji group, and all the morning we were threading our way among these mountainous-looking islands, with great reefs running for miles in every direction, and Native-manned schooners skimming along hither and thither.

At noon we came to Levuka on the island of Ovalau, and until 1882 the capital of these English possessions. The township, with its red roofs, nestles at the feet of steep fantastic hills whose summits are lost in clouds and whose slopes are densely wooded in rich and contrasting verdure. Around us, as we dropped anchor to await medical inspection, was the reef all golden and blue, the entrance being the narrowest we had ever seen.

It was a great disappointment to be kept in quarantine for twenty-four hours on board. The authorities decided not to let us land until our fourteen days from Auckland were up. When we did get ashore the following day it was only for a few hours, but in this time we had a glorious peep into some Native villages along the coast. The coiffure of these Fijians is truly charming, and reminded us of *Struwwelpeter*; their whole cast of countenance is much more negroid and their bearing more warlike than either the Tongans or Samoans, a fact that reminds one that the Fijians are of Papuan blood and had little, if any, connection with the Polynesians whom we had left behind us. During our walk we spotted a Native woman fishing in the pools on the tide-forsaken shore with a beautiful double-handled net. The road next led us through villages and round curving shores of exquisite beauty. The steep spurs of the mountains, all lava rock, richly covered in vegetation, towered above us, and the Natives, though unprepossessing to look at, displayed some friendliness along the way.

We sailed at about eleven that morning. On the quay some Fijians had brought baskets of marvellous white coral to sell, and we could have bought for sixpence as many huge lemons as we could possibly desire! Late that afternoon we came in sight of the magnificent range of mountains and hills, all jagged and broken and capped in clouds, that face Suva. The town itself lies right away from the hills on undulating ground, and looks most interesting from the sea. Suva is the capital of the two hundred islands that compose the Fiji group; only eight of these islands are inhabited by a population of about 125,000 souls; of these three-quarters are on the island of Viti Levu, the largest but probably the least fertile of the group. It is on this island that Suva is situated. Here, too, are to be found many of the extensive sugar plantations which, with copra and bananas, form the backbone of the industry of Fiji. The work connected with the plantations is carried out, for the most part, by coolies (Indians), of whom many thousands are to be seen. Compared with the stalwart Fijians they present a lean and half-starved appearance; they are almost living skeletons. To them life is a very serious thing; to the Fijians it is one long joke. It is amusing to notice the contempt they have for one another. If he can be induced to work, the superior physique of the Fijian enables him easily to outstrip the Hindu. But the coolie works steadily on, and without him the sugar planters would be in evil plight, indifferent as his labour often is.

If one is going to employ a Fijian the first question he will ask will be concerning his tucker (food); the second concerning the condition of labour (hours, etc.). Wages, which amount to about 2s. per day, are almost the last consideration.

Most of the land is still in the hands of the Natives, and there is the usual difficulty as to ownership, more than one tribe often claiming the same piece. When we were in Suva a Land Commission was investigating the matter, and when they have decided the ownership once and for all the whole situation will be much simplified. Land belonging to extinct tribes reverts by law to the State, but though to common knowledge many tribes have died out no land has been found without *many* claimants. No land may be sold except to the Government, and all leases are subiect to its approval.

No liquor can be obtained by any Native without a permit. Such permits are for one year only, and are not granted save to a few chiefs. As elsewhere, there is some illicit grog selling by low whites, but it is not carried on to any great extent.

The Fijians are great swimmers. An official with whom we were walking was out fishing one day near the edge of the coral reef. He hooked what seemed to be a large fish, but having difficulty in landing it he suggested to the Native that he should dive in and secure it. He was under water an exceptionally long time, and must have swum down very deep, for although the sea was clear he was entirely out of sight. Presently he returned looking very scared. "Big hole down there with devil in it. Me no like!" he explained. Thinking that there was probably nothing in it, our friend urged him to go down again, which, after some persuasion he did, though with evident reluctance. This time he made little effort, and soon returned, quite unconscious that a shark had now spotted him and was following on his heels. My friend, much relieved that the Fijian had not gone deeper, pointed out the shark to him. "There's your devil," said he.

"He no devil," replied the Native. "My father friend of sharks; no shark touch me," and from that belief nothing would shake him.

There are some quite gay shops in Suva, and a number of branches of the principal Australian and New Zealand banks. But banks are typical of English civilization; we saw none in any of the Pacific towns under German control.

The Chinatown of Suva is notorious for the mixture of races one sees there, and the confusion of tongues that prattle on every side as Chinese and Indian, Tongan and Fijian come and go about their business.

A general and involuntary boycott had been proclaimed on Suva by nearly all the shipping lines serving that port, owing to the absurd regulations which the authorities had made in connection with the Sydney smallpox scare. But when the said authorities found that they had cut off their own supplies they had to amend their hastily drawn up regulations!

Up the Rewa River

The next morning we were off, a large party of us, some by steamboat and others overland by drag, to visit the Rewa River district. We sailed at 9 a.m. in the *Adi Rarogo*, or Lady Mermaid, with a miscellaneous collection of passengers. There was an Indian woman decked out in silver bangles to the value of £28, her husband told us; but the ship's cookboy's wife had a string of forty sovereigns round *her* neck! Then there were more friendly Fijian damsels, who made eyes at Thompson—a married man, too!

Below decks there was a gigantic turtle lying on its back, its eyes glazed and its carcase probed by all who came that way. It had probably been thus helpless for days, and the way the poor brute was seized by its flappers and flung into a waiting row-boat alongside was a sight warranted to give a soft heart pain, but such occurrences are apt to be common in these parts where there is no R.S.P.C.A.

We had to await the pleasure of the tide for an hour or so before winding up the mangrove-covered banks of the Rewa River. Later on we came to the first signs of sugar plantations, into which mongoose had been introduced to destroy the rats which had developed a sweet tooth for the cane. But rat and mongoose soon began to fraternize, we were told, and it is the birds that have disappeared at the coming and thriving of the Indian pest-killer. One bird we saw in great profusion though, and that was a kind of magpie-pigeon, brown in colour, yellow of leg and eye cere, and of a rare inquisitiveness in the neighbourhood of habitations.

The sugar-cane all about looked fresh and green, and at Rewa, where we arrived in a half-famished condition, we rowed across to a big mill after an indifferent luncheon. Here we saw lighters full of the yellow and black cane being off-loaded at the river side by an enormous "grab," a kind of merciless giant's paw that clenched the cracking sticks in its grasp and, carrying them across, laid them on a lifting platform that bore them to the works. Here was a veritable inferno of clanking and whirling machinery, of roaring furnaces, and vacuum boilers, in which the sugar can be brought to boiling point at a comparatively low temperature, and vats of steaming molasses and gradually refining sugar into which the Indian coolie sweated as he worked!

Outside in the sun the heat was scarcely bearable, but in here it was overpowering, and one could not help marvelling how the English overseers and managers could work in such a place, and moreover how they could walk round with a crowd of ignorant visitors, explaining everything to them in a shout which was, as often as not, lost in the din.

Long shall we remember that evening drive back to Suva, a distance of about twenty miles, over an excellent road undulating up hill and down dale, now through rice swamps, and now scaling a height overlooking a forest of trees and an expanse of ocean. On every side were Indian dwellings, filthy-looking hovels that compared unfavourably with the Fijians' huts, and half-scared children and dogs hurried from the roadside as our coach went thundering by.

We passed through an interesting Government experimental farm, where every kind of palm and other tropic trees and plants are reared, including ginger, cloves, cinnamon, and other spices. A number of streams and rivulets flowing between densely foliaged banks crossed our road; some of these a barge could navigate, whilst others formed pretty cascades falling into a series of naturally hollowed rocky cups.

And so, with the setting of the sun, to the heights above the magnificent harbour at Suva, framed in mountains of fantastic outline; and these and the sea alike tinted with soft colouring of blue and pink, and wisps of cloud ablaze with gold.

The scenery of Fiji is glorious, and our great regret was that we had no time to penetrate into its romantic mountain ranges that call one into their fastnesses, and where the *real* Fiji is to be found.

At 8 p.m. we were to sail, and just before this time the whole of Suva, Native and European, seemed to be assembled on the wharf to wave us farewell. A ghostly-looking crowd it was, grouped there in its white array under the brilliant flares of the wharf, and behind it darkness, spangled with the silver stars and the yellow lights of the town. At the last moment came a swift pattering of naked feet, an ambulance, and a crowd of inquisitive Natives surrounding the prostrated form of a white woman, clad in her night attire. Some hopeless case of tropical disease. The poor woman was going home to England to see her people before she died.

Next morning we dropped anchor in Momi Bay farther along the coast. The "Ship's Alarmists," who always thought it was funny to make a noise as early as possible in the morning, had us all up to see a sunrise. This time we were glad, for it was indeed a gorgeous colour effect, and in the distance the awaiting banana cutters just drowsily setting sail from the protection of the reef, with their freight of green fruit for our ever-rapacious hold.

We did not trouble to go ashore at Momi Bay, but spent the day reading and writing, and at eventide the *Tofua* weighed anchor, and, sailing within the reef before a grand panorama of mountains, clouds, and atolls, came at nightfall to Lautoka. Here is another busy sugar centre that can boast of one of the largest mills in the world, but we only tarried for a few hours to land passengers and take on some bags of the *sici* shell (pronounce *si* in Fijian as *thi*). This goes to distant Japan, and is turned into pearl buttons there and probably shipped back to Sydney. This kind of cargo, then worth about £9 per ton, was considered worthless some years before.

That night we set out on our six days' run to Sydney, leaving behind us—for how long who shall say?—these delightful islands of the South Pacific. We watched the phosphorescence on the waves at night and danced one evening away.

As the sun set one day we passed close to Walpole Island; it lies to the south-east of New Caledonia, and its high cliffs shone in the evening glow. A bush-like vegetation clung to and crowned these cliffs, but there was no sign of life except a few very curious-looking birds that hovered for a while around the stern of our ship, and a fine display of whales plunging and lashing in the sea. Someone thought there was a killer after them.

We Arrive at Sydney

It was on August 6th when the Australian coast hove into sight, a broken-looking line of headlands or islands. At 3 p.m. we came to the Sydney Heads. For some time the decks had been crowded with passengers straining their eyes for familiar landmarks. The Cardinal's Palace and Manly Beach, the famous bathing place, were pointed out to us, but the Heads themselves were ordinary rocky promontories of no particular note. Captain Cook passed them by on his way northward in 1770, naming the inlet that he left unexplored Port Jackson. This fine shipping harbour extends for miles in a multitude of locks and estuaries. Of course, a dozen people asked us in one breath, "What do you think of *our* harbour?" or "What do you think of *our* Heads?"

We answered that we had heard so much about Sydney Harbour and its famous Heads during the fourteen months we had been travelling that we would rather reserve our judgment until we had made closer acquaintance with them. There is a good joke told about a clever fellow who wore

118 Fishing in the pools on the tide-forsaken shore

119 Fishing huts near Levuka, Fiji

120 Our long-sought goal "Chilworth"

121 The Three Sisters, Echo Point, Blue Mountains

about his neck, when he came to Sydney, a placard bearing the words: "Yes, I think *your* harbour *very* fine." That satisfies the Sydneyite; he will not trouble you farther, except to be generous and kind to you!

Well, after the doctor had examined our arms and many people had voluntarily undergone the operation of vaccination once again, we steamed up the harbour in the gloaming. In the distance the projecting buildings of the city were shrouded in a pall of smoke, and on the squat hills all around were dense masses of not too beautiful suburban houses and bungalows. As we threaded our way through the hurrying ferryboats all agleam with lights, and came into the very heart of the city in our great ship, we had to admit to the fascination of the scene.

We soon spotted Mr. Byles on the wharf awaiting us, and another strange gentleman who waved and called to Stan we found afterwards was Mr. John S. Dence. About an hour later we four were hustling out of Sydney, the train bearing us towards Epping, where Mr. Dence lived, and two stations beyond is Beecroft, seventeen miles from town. When Mr. Dence left us he said how anxious he was to motor us out to the Blue Mountains, and this pleasant excursion was arranged for the week-end. Of course it was dark when we arrived at our long-sought goal "Chilworth," and it was with no small feeling of joy that we entered its homely portals and received at the hands of Mrs. Byles such a warm "family" greeting.

The Blue Mountains

A few days later we were speeding away through orchard and pastoral country in Mr. Dence's car with his daughter and her cousin.

The day was ideal, a clear blue sky and pleasant breeze, and before us rose the enticing blue heights of the mountains, a long level ridge stretching for miles with an entire absence of imposing peaks. So through Parramatta with its old-world-looking houses and hotels, and Penrith on the Nepean River, where is a busy railway centre, whence road and rail begin the stiff climb together up the mountain slopes, parting to meet again in this continuous forest of the ubiquitous eucalyptus.

We boiled our "billy" farther up the road; these dried eucalyptus twigs make ready and fragant fuelling, and soon we were enjoying a merry luncheon among the gums. From the high lands still farther on we obtained views over a vast expanse of country—a rare panorama of peculiar charm.

At about three o'clock we came to Katoomba, and having found decent lodgings we set off on a short spin to Govett's Leap, passing on our way Medlow Bath and Blackheath, noteworthy for their extraordinary-looking Casino hotels. All these places are in what are known as the Blue Mountains, and hither the jaded Sydney folk flock for rest and recreation in the summer months or for week-ends. Leaving our car among some picnic shelters with which these popular resorts are amply furnished, we followed a track that led with dramatic suddenness to the brink of a long deep cliff. We were suspended, it seemed, on an aerial platform of rock, behind us and on either hand a dripping and unscalable cliff of ferruginous sandstone, from the lip of which spouted a volume of water, like the tail of an Arab steed, that fell away and away for 500 or 600 feet. From our perch among the rocks we looked down upon a sea of treetops that stretched from beneath our feet, and swept away into a mystic distance of blue mists, and the whole of this wild, untrodden-looking country was enclosed by beetling cliffs and wrapped in a silence that held one transfixed in wonderment. On listening more intently we could hear a murmur arising from these depths below—a murmur of gum trees swaying in the breeze, and the singing of the stream as it leapt from rock to rock, far out of sight beneath this wilderness of boughs. Into this mysterious lower world leapt the bushranger Govett, horse and all, when he was hot pressed by the police in years gone by, and after him the place is named—a wonderfully inspiring place that holds a rank among the sights of the world!

We were not sorry to be up early next morning to walk to Echo Point before breakfast, for the night had been very cold. The ground was hard with frost, and Miss Dence was delighted at the sight of some thin, fragile-looking ice. The view from Echo Point is similar to that from Govett's Leap, except that three jagged rocks tower from the shadow of the plain and form a romantic foreground to the scene; they are called the Three Sisters.

After breakfast we descended these cliffs by a myriad steps by way of the Leura Falls into a veritable fairyland of dwarf and giant ferns, of veil-like streams falling over copper-hued rocks, and with these endless giant gums towering above our heads and spreading their boughs in a graceful filigree against the rich blue sky. The birds sang in deep-toned notes, and our bush track wound round about the precipitous rocks, now up steps and now down, now leading to silent pools lined with deep green moss, and then a peep at the distant blue ranges between the framing forest trees. The fierce sunlight penetrated the bush, casting a damask of gold about our way, and this track, known as the Federal Pass, was one of the most beautiful pathways we have seen.

We struggled to the summit of the ridge by way of the Katoomba Falls, up steps innumerable and in view of scenery of surpassing beauty. At the top Mr. Dence was awaiting us with the car. We flung ourselves in, hot and exhausted, and so began the glorious drive home; the first part of it, the 30 miles to Penrith, being nothing less than a swooping flight downhill, with glorious peeps of blue distance as we went. Our total run was close on 150 miles.

Sydney and its Harbour

The two following days we spent most of our time in the city, visited a doctor who vaccinated us again as a "regrettable necessity," and we were once more turned away from the City Town Hall to wait another *seven* days before we could get a permit to leave Sydney! But our diaries show that these seven days were well filled with business calls and the enjoyment of Sydney hospitality.

We spent some evenings visiting friends who lived in the prettily situated suburbs, and long shall we remember the run back from Mosman to Circular Quay at 10 p.m. which was certainly most entrancing: our boat was one of hundreds of such craft, all lit up, hurrying hither and thither on little flaming waves of reflected light like a swarm of gigantic fireflies. We can quite understand that to those living in Sydney, and more especially in these waterside suburbs, the harbour is very attractive. It certainly lends itself to their essentially pleasure-seeking life, with its sandy coves for boating and bathing, the fine area of water for yachting, and the more distant and less spoiled locks of the middle harbour for picnic parties to lose themselves in.

Thanks to the courtesy of Mr. Charles Carey Lance, formerly Agent-General for New South Wales in London, and President of the Commissioners of the Sydney Harbour Trust, we were able to make a tour of inspection under his personal guidance of the wharves, jetties, and building yards of this great harbour, and also the immediately adjoining bays and rivers.

Our launch started from Circular Quay, which in 1788 was the Sydney Cove where Captain Phillip landed his first party. The place was then densely wooded, and a silence-enchanted spot, which from that day to this has been the scene of ever-increasing tumult. *Now* it would be hard to picture a busier place. Much of the old cove has been reclaimed; day and night an endless stream of ferry steamers chase each other in and out on their way from city to suburbs, and as if the rushing to and fro of this mosquito fleet was not enough, the giant mail-boats of the P. & O. and Orient Companies were at the eastern side all the week, and vessels of the Burns Philp Co., Ltd., whilst on the western side the Norddeutscher Lloyd and Eastern and Australian Companies took up a deal of wharfage. To cap this, trams go clanging around the cove and fine business premises tower above it all and mark the way down Pitt and George Streets, the two principal thoroughfares of the city.

With the daily expansion of the suburbs across the water north of Sydney, this ferry traffic was coming more and more into requisition, and it was the aim at that time of the Harbour Trust authorities to tempt the big shipping companies away to wharves of equal if not better merit as regards convenience and position. This would leave Circular Quay free to the ferry services alone, and would help to deal with the serious question of ever-increasing traffic. This traffic problem had become so serious that there had been much talk of an enormous bridge, but many people thought the harbour would be spoilt if this idea were carried out, its then bridgeless condition being a particular attraction in its favour.*

Our launch now rounded Mrs. Macquarie's Point and came right up Woolloomooloo Bay. Here, down the centre of the bay, a big new wharf was in course of construction. In length it was 1,140 feet, and 208 feet in width. It was furnished with double-decked sheds and covered roadway sunk below the floor-levels so as to expedite loading. The cost of this wharf alone would amount to something like £200,000. Up till 1901 nearly all the wharves in Sydney Harbour were privately owned, and a tangle of streets led up to them. The previous year there had been an epidemic of bubonic plague in the city, and not before it was time Government, citizens, and municipality alike made efforts to rid themselves of all unsanitary conditions. A war was waged upon rats—the new theory of these vermin *not* being plague carriers had not come under consideration then—and at a vast outlay the Government resumed all the then existing wharves, stores, and warehouses connected with them and placed them all under the administration of a special trust. This was how the Sydney Harbour

* This bridge is now an accomplished fact and represents one of the foremost engineering feats of modern times and is the largest of its kind in the world.

Trust came into being, and under able management enormous strides have been made. More water frontage is resumed from private owners every year, and in this way the capacity and completeness of the port is increased annually, and not without due necessity. Crazy wharfage has been replaced by good, and every new jetty or quay is made rat-proof. All the old streets and dwellings have been swept away; fine broad approaches have been made of easy gradient; and near Miller's Point in particular, where it was hoped the mail-boats would eventually go alongside, are to be found elaborate double-decked sheds with specially constructed roadways, one running along a viaduct to the upper floor. Electric cranes lift the goods from the ship's hold to the top floor just as easily as to the wharf-level, and a boat can, in this way, be discharged in half the time. At the end of this wharf is a balcony with waiting-rooms attached where folk can assemble to see the last of their departing friends.

Our launch then took us round Double Bay, an aristocratic residential quarter, and then we came back by way of Garden Island, the naval depôt, to Miller's Point, Darling Harbour, and so on to Johnston's, Rozelle, and Blackwattle Bays. We then crossed to Goat Island, where the Harbour Trust has a depôt, and the Harbour Master is accommodated in a pretty house, delightfully situated. Here we got hot water and our engineer made us tea, and whilst we thus refreshed ourselves we sped away again to Cockatoo Island, where we saw a second class cruiser and three destroyers in the building.

Spectacle Island, close by, is an ammunition depôt, and soon after passing this we had left the business part of the harbour behind and cruised up the beautiful Lane Cove River as far as Fairyland. Here are many country residences all along the bank, with lawns and boat-houses at the water's edge.

The evening was drawing in when we returned down this beautiful stream, and then went homewards in the glory of a setting sun, up the more expansive waterway of the Parramatta River, to the railway bridge at Ryde.

The following interesting facts concerning what was then the Fifth Harbour in the world I quote from a booklet which Mr. Lance very kindly presented to me, entitled *Port of Sydney, New South Wales*, 1913.

During the first twelve years of the existence of Sydney Cove as a port, 118 vessels came in, 37 of them transports; in 1900 the number of entering vessels was 1,819, with an aggregate tonnage of 2,716,651. In 1907 these figures were 10,374 and 7,170,139 respectively. In 1912 the number of incoming vessels decreased to 9,524, but the aggregate tonnage increased to 8,191,083! The largest boats running to Sydney that year were the Blue Funnel Company's *Nestor*, of 14,000 tons, and the White Star Company's *Ceramic*, of 18,000 tons. About that time the Commissioners had built a row of seventy or eighty flats for their waterside workers at Miller's Point, and although space did not permit of the allotment of gardens or yards, there is a central common playground for the children, with an experienced directress in charge.

The total cost of improvements to the harbour and resumption of foreshore properties amounted in 1912 to the large sum of £7,000,000, so it can be seen at a glance that much had been done by the Harbour Trust in the early years of its existence. Few people would realize, coming up Port Jackson in their huge liner, that under this harbour is a rich seam of coal. At Long Nose Point the Sydney Harbour Colliery, after many vicissitudes, was obtaining 400 tons a day, and this output was being steadily increased. The company reckoned that it had 100,000,000 tons of coal in its leases, and overseas steamers could be loaded direct from its own wharf.

Many large wool stores are vested in the Harbour Trust and leased to wool firms in the same manner as the wharves are leased to the shipping companies. These wool stores are fitted up with every modern appliance, and 15,000 bales could be shipped into one boat in twenty-four hours. 993,038 bales have been shipped in one season from Sydney Harbour!

Besides the many suburban gardens and the "reserved"

strip that runs around almost the whole perimeter of the outer port one sees, in the very midst of this mass of shipping and seething smoke, the green lawns and noble Moreton Bay fig trees of the Botanical and Government House Gardens. A sight that it is to be hoped will always remain unspoiled to Sydney, and one that goes far to relieve the generally flat appearance of the place.

The population of Sydney and its suburbs at the close of 1928 was 1,127,470. The streets of the city in 1913 were narrow compared with other Australian cities, and its sidewalks covered with the familiar roofings supported on veranda-like posts. These posts afford the crowd of unpleasant-looking, loitering men, who are particularly noticeable in Melbourne and here, something to lean against and to spit at. We felt that the police would be better employed in keeping the sidewalks free from these loungers instead of paying so much attention to the meetings and decent conversations of those who chanced to run up against one another on the pavements. The main streets of Sydney are among the noisiest we encountered, but to the inhabitant and backwoodsman the place is as cherished as London is to us.

Another day, Stan went off on a jaunt to the Hawkesbury Agricultural College, and I set out for Botany and La Pérouse, to see my friend Mr. J. Wassell. His neat little home on the sandy dunes of this part of the world is the outcome of his own patient industry. Mr. Wassell possessed seven acres of sand that were covered with chickens and ducks, if one can put it that way. Every day two or three thousand eggs went into a wholesaler in Sydney, and twice a week offal and grain were carted to this poultry farm in large quantities for feeding purposes. I saw hundreds of young ducks a day old, and thousands of only a slightly maturer age that, as they stood, were worth 1s. each for somebody else to fatten for the Christmas market, but Mr. Wassell had a mind to do all that himself!

It was August 19th when, after taking our tickets for

Yokohama, a most strenuous proceeding, we went to the Town Hall, where we were herded like cattle into long queues, and after waiting and rubbing up against all and sundry for fully an hour, this was for the third time, too, we at last got our passes to leave Sydney, though not before they had tried (without success) to coerce Stan into being vaccinated for a fourth time!

Via Brisbane to Rabaul

Punctually at eleven o'clock next morning we cast away from the wharfside, steamed slowly down Sydney harbour to the Heads in a glory of sunlight and blue sky, and looked our last on the hurrying ferry boats and the innumerable inlets surrounded by low hills bedecked with clustering villas and bungalows.

Our ship, the S.S. *Coblenz*, of 3,300 tons, behaved admirably in the heavy swell we encountered along the coast all day. We rolled terrifically, and fiddles had to be placed on the table. Our second class accommodation was excellent. We had a four-berth cabin to ourselves, and the promise of one each ere long. Four Germans, three of them missionaries, were our messmates, whilst at another table sat four Samoan Native missionaries with their wives and children. These were on their way to German New Guinea,* where they had already attained repute for teaching Christianity to Papuan races. Our stewards were Chinese; was there ever a greater confusion of tongues?

. . . . .

We made Pinkenba, the outer harbour of Brisbane, some hours late, and but for the kindness of Herr Lehner, a German Lutheran missionary, who motored us nine miles to the city, we should have missed seeing anything of Brisbane at all, for our boat was only in port for three hours, and the trains were hopelessly inconvenient. As it was, we saw little enough

* Now under Australian mandate.

of the Queensland capital. On our way thither in the car, Herr Lehner told us something about his work in New Guinea, whither he was returning after a brief leave to visit his wife in Sydney, who had been seriously ill. In his enthusiastic devotion to New Guinea, Herr Lehner impressed us as the type of man one does not come across every day, and he was certainly a worthy successor to the exceptionally fine men who have given their lives to that least known of all countries. He had not been home for fourteen years, and when asked if he did not wish to make the journey, he replied quite simply: "Yes, I should like to some day, and my brothers have often offered to pay my expenses, but there is too much to do in New Guinea. One day I shall not have the health and strength to go on: then will be time enough. I should not have left now had not my wife been so seriously ill."

Brisbane appeared to us rather like the other Australian capital cities, save that it is situated on undulating ground on the banks of the pretty river of that name. The entrance to the Brisbane River is through a beautiful land-locked waterway, abounding with dangerous reefs, and known as Moreton Bay. It is from here that the curious fig trees we saw in the Sydney gardens come.

We had no time to keep our many business appointments, but, as an atonement for our disappointment, we took possession of a four-berth cabin each on our return to the ship. We turned one of the top bunks in Stan's cabin into a library, which we divided into three sections. First came reference books on New Zealand, secondly works on the Far East, and thirdly miscellaneous works and lighter literature, all to be read before we reached Hong Kong! In my cabin were more obvious signs of penmanship, for, owing to the continuation of Stan's writer's cramp, it was still impossible for him even to scribble a short note, though he worked very hard at dictation.

It had not been a calm voyage from Sydney to Brisbane, and now the easternmost currents of the Coral Sea made our ship roll still more violently, so much so, indeed, that hard as it was to write under such conditions, it was even more difficult to *think*. It always seemed a marvel to us the amount of creative work Stevenson got through on board ship, and his vessels were cockle-shells compared to those we had sailed in. We had a good deal of sympathy with the big white Australian cockatoo with a yellow crest, which swung in its cage aft. He so resented his first day at sea that he demolished his stout bamboo perch, thinking to himself no doubt: "The whole blessed ship is nothing but a bough in a high wind, why insult me by giving me this twig to perch on?" That bird thought a lot whilst we were at sea, but he never uttered a word until early one morning at the smell of landfall he condescended to clear his throat and cursed at us all in the full-flavoured language of the vast high seas! That same evening the ocean swell subsided and a torrid sticky heat invaded the ship. Stan sat at the piano in the saloon rippling off some of his old melodies—fortunately his cramp did not incapacitate him from playing—whilst I sat near by beneath a whirling electric fan, and pushed my pen as hard as I could. What a night that was as our ship clove her way through the mirror-like waters of the Bismarck Archipelago! Not a breath of air seemed to penetrate into our cabins, where we lay naked and perspiring in our bunks, fans whirring and wind scoops in the port-holes.

A glorious land view was revealed to us when we awoke soon after dawn. It was a grand sight after days on an accursed heaving sea! We dressed hurriedly and clambered on deck, where a German planter explained the coast to us. It was Neu Pommern, or New Britain, the largest island of the Bismarck group.* We steamed along quite close to the shore, which, to the very water's edge, is richly timbered, and fine ranges of mountains towered inland, in some places capped in cloud, where lived wild men in fastnesses as yet unknown to the European. So we drifted into a beautifully peaceful

* Now under Australian mandate.

waterway, with the high peaks of New Ireland peering over the clouds to starboard, and so on past some gracefully sloped volcanoes and Herbertshöhe, the earlier seat of Government, to Simpson-Hafen, then known officially as Rabaul.

Here we were at the Government headquarters, not only for the Bismarck Islands but for German New Guinea as well.

While we were waiting for the doctor to come aboard we had an opportunity to examine the place. It was not large, for it was not then ten years old, but we noticed the red galvanized-iron roofs of many comfortable-looking bungalows. We picked out a house near the wharf. "To whom does that belong?" we asked a German friend near by. "To an official," he replied. "And the next six or eight more?" "Yes, all officials," he said. It seemed to us that, if nothing else had grown, the number of officials had!

When the doctor came aboard he cheerfully admitted that he had had a night out, and that everything appeared "green" —a most desirable result if it accounted for the rapidity with which we were allowed ashore!

Chapter XIV

FROM RABAUL TO TSINGTAU

THERE was an amazing assortment of Natives on the wharf. Pitch-black Solomon Islanders and chocolate-coloured Kanakas from all the islands round. None of them could compare with the physique of our Tongan friends, though the Solomon Islanders—what incredibly black chaps they are!—looked fairly well built. Their coloured necklaces and armlets and bright red lava-lavas gave them a very picturesque appearance. But a closer inspection of the local Kanakas left a less pleasing impression, for so many seemed to be suffering from some skin disease. A few had their ears or parts of their faces painted a brilliant red, nearly all seemed addicted to betel-nut chewing, which had stained their teeth the colour of the gums, and still further disfigured them. Most of them had large holes pierced through the lobes of their ears, and a few through their noses. A wooden comb, Native made and in the shape of a lady's back comb, was quite *de rigueur* tucked at random into their woolly mops, and made use of for any purpose, from scratching their heads to cooking potatoes! A pipe tucked through their armlets completed their attire. For the most part they looked a sorry lot, and vastly inferior to the South African Kaffir.

Rabaul was as nicely laid out as one would expect with a German settlement. The houses were all built on stone piles, and consisted of two or three large airy rooms, with a broad veranda all round. There were plenty of trees about, and a few minutes' walk in almost any direction brought one into dense bush. Where the ground had been cut, as in the road up to the Governor's house, a layer of ash, 8 to 10 feet deep, was revealed, showing once more the volcanic nature of these islands.

Despite the oppressive heat, of an intolerable dampness, we

were so glad to be on mother-earth again that we set out along the dusty road behind the settlement that led to the hillside residences of the favoured. Broad drains, carefully bridged over with wood, crossed the road every hundred yards—evidence of the tropical torrents with which they have to cope; torrents that often wash away the best of the soil of the mountain side once the forests have been cleared. The air resounded with the singing of birds; gay butterflies, both large and small, fluttered across our track, and led us from one bright flower to the next. Scarlet and green were the colours that stood out most in that rainbow of delight, and was there ever a brighter scarlet than the flowers of the coral tree, or a more satisfying green than the leaves of a massive bread-fruit tree? One red flower we saw in great profusion, with long stamens and petals orange tipped, but its name we know not. It had a pod like a bean.

A party of Kanakas with bright red lava-lavas passed us as we went, but at the sight of Johnnie's camera the womenfolk wanted to scuttle away; they were not very prepossessing in appearance. At the summit of the ridge the sea lay stretched out before us on both sides; one of those divine glimpses that cameras, alas! frequently fail to reproduce.

If Rabaul ever becomes an important centre, it is difficult to see in what direction it is to expand. Behind it lies a steep hill, and on one side the Botanical Gardens; on the other, a valuable coco-nut plantation. No doubt the plantation owner will be expropriated in due course at an exorbitant price; but why allow a plantation to be put in 200 yards from headquarters when there are square miles of unused land at hand? But the difficulty may never arise, for it seemed evident to us that the Government headquarters would have once more to be transferred, sooner or later, and then to New Guinea itself. For German New Guinea, when its turn came to be opened up, would be a vastly bigger proposition than the Bismarck Isles.

On our return to the steamer we found the decks crowded:

the entire population of Rabaul seemed to have turned up for the occasion; and the occasion, you ask? Why, the greatest of all in a German's eyes: the opportunity to drink beer! Think of this poor, thirsty German community, with an unlimited supply of bottled beer always on hand, having to wait a fortnight for the joy of drinking "Bier vom Fass—Eiskalt" (draught beer on ice). So while the Germans put it away, the Kanakas, the Chinamen, and a Parsee bo'sun got to work on the cargo. What a row and what a babel of tongues! No, only one language was spoken, if language it can be called—pidgin-English: the weirdest and most absurd jumble of words that ever assisted human intercourse; but the medium in which the European addresses the Natives of the Southern Seas! Never was more noise made over less work than in the off-loading of this cargo of timber, potatoes, galvanized iron, and all manner of stores. They kept it up all that night! It is bad enough to have the atmosphere so hot and stifling that you perspire with nothing on, without mentioning the advantages derived by your nervous system from having a couple of donkey engines regularly pounding away directly overhead. But the racket these Kanakas made drowned everything else. If there is one thing at which they excel, it is in shouting and screaming, and if they can succeed in dropping a dozen sheets of galvanized iron, a load of timber, or a stack of bricks from a fair height, why, it was to them just the greatest fun in life! The only silent person was the Chinese tally clerk, who solemnly checked off each load of goods as it passed.

Next morning we strolled through the Botanical Gardens, and were surprised at both their extent and excellence. The authorities must have bestowed a very large share of their time and money upon them. Apparently there is a special official to look after them, whose duty it is also to conduct an experimental plantation.

One little difference we could not help noticing at Rabaul. In Tonga, Samoa, or even Portuguese East Africa (Inhambane), no one would begrudge you a coco-nut. Here it would be thieving if you helped yourself to one!

On our westward course to New Guinea we passed many islands, the so-called French Islands amongst the number. Nearly all appeared fertile, and many were inhabited by Natives. Perhaps the one with the most romantic history of those we saw was Peterhafen, so named after the man to whom it belonged. Apparently he acquired it from the Government, who little realized the wealth they were bestowing. Having a monopoly of the trade, he was able to secure copra from the Natives on his own terms. In a very little while he was a wealthy man, and had his own private yacht in which he could trade in the smaller neighbouring islands, which were also his property. On a visit to Sydney he was interviewed by the reporters, and christened King Peter from the style in which he lived. Champagne flowed more freely than water, so that despite his enormous income he was soon living in excess of it. He became indebted very largely to the New Guinea Company, and in the end they bought his islands from him, and he was employed by one of the firms in Rabaul. Had he lived within his income, he might have been a millionaire, and possibly the New Guinea Company would have ceased to exist, because the monopoly of the trade in these islands is one of their greatest sources of profit.

German New Guinea

The following morning we passed Long Inseln, an English-named German island. An hour or two later we were entering the beautifully secluded harbour known as Friedrich-Wilhelms-Hafen. What more magic place could be found than this small hidden harbour, with its innumerable little bays and inlets, its hundred wooded isles, and its palm-clad foreshore, and, as if the measure were not already overflowing, range after range of timber-covered mountains as a distant background? Truly is it *hübsch gelegen*. The whole place is nicely arranged, and

122 Distant blue ranges between framing forest trees

123 Scene near Rabaul, Bismarck Islands

124 Nuts indigenous and otherwise
at Friedrich-Wilhelms-Hafen

125 An official residence at Friedrich-Wilhelms-Hafen

the pleasant-looking airy bungalows, built up on stone piles of course, made one feel that, despite the damp and oppressive heat, life could be very pleasant even here right on the Equator. The Natives looked healthier than those at Rabaul, and they were nearly all clad in the same bright red lava-lavas. Here it was quite the mode for the Natives to have a spoon tucked through their armlet. Perhaps that is merely a passing fashion, but an older one to which they still adhere is to have a ring through their nose like a bull. Nowadays it is often just a ring of small coloured beads. Necklaces made partly of dogs' teeth are greatly prized, and certainly look effective against their dark skins. The teeth for such a necklace are difficult to obtain so the Germans supply the Natives with artificial dogs' teeth!

One of the strangest things about New Guinea is the fact that you will find Natives living but a few miles apart talking a different language, and unable to communicate with one another.

Less is still known of the interior of New Guinea than of almost any place in the world. Only a few miles into the interior from Friedrich-Wilhelms-Hafen, the biggest centre, one is in cannibal land. Here one may or may not receive a pleasant reception. If one does not meet with approval, one will probably be cooked like a pig, and any compunction the cannibals will feel will be due to the fact that apparently the flesh of a European is more salt and less to their taste than that of a black.

Very little has been done so far to open up the interior of this vast country, a country for the most part so fertile that the chief difficulty is to stop things growing where they are not wanted to grow. When the Romans took Britain the first thing they did was to build roads. So far as we are aware they did not ask themselves: Will the traffic on the road in the first year make it pay? Their aim was to open up the country. The road of to-day is a railway, and without it no country of any size can be developed. In this matter we found ourselves in accord with one of the German Catholic missionaries on board. He knew the country well, and was an electrical engineer. He pointed out that there was at hand water power more than sufficient to provide electric current for any number of railways; that were electricity the motive power, the difficulty with gradients would be largely obviated. The trouble is, as he said, that, if one talks of a railway, people are apt to picture a properly ballasted London & North-Western Railway track with corridor trains and elaborate stations. No such thing is either contemplated or wanted, but just the simplest of light railway lines. At first probably two trains a week would be sufficient, and a rolling stock of a dozen trucks and possibly one passenger coach would be ample. The land would cost next to nothing, and fifty miles of line constructed on such a basis would involve a mere bagatelle; in fact, little more than might be saved from the salaries of unnecessary officials and other economies.

But in this matter the German authorities were short-sighted. "What is the good of a railway?" they said. "There is no copra to fetch. There are no plantations." And the planter said, "What is the good of my putting in trees more than a few miles from the coast, when there is neither railway nor road by which I can obtain building material and stores, or transport my products when I have grown them?"

If it were the policy of the Government to retard the development of New Guinea, and it is quite conceivable that such a policy might be wise, well and good! But in that case there should be no complaint about lack of progress. A few years before our visit it was discovered at the eleventh hour that the Natives had plotted to kill all the whites in Friedrich-Wilhelms-Hafen, or rather all the white *men*. As a result all the Kanakas living on the islands or mainland in the vicinity of Friedrich-Wilhelms-Hafen had been exiled to New Pommern. But the danger will always be there until the country is opened up, and nothing does that more rapidly and peaceably than a railway. Up till then the Bismarck Islands had been very isolated, but the Government was contemplating replacing the wireless plant on the island of Yap, and re-erecting it at Rabaul.

The Germans evidently believed in training their Native police in the use of arms. Quite a number of them crossed with us as deck passengers from Rabaul. They were very proud of the khaki hats and rifles which, with a ruck-sack, completed their outfit. To an outsider this training of Natives to the use of arms seemed of doubtful expediency. It was quite humorous to observe a Native sentry and gaudy sentry-box outside some of the official dwellings in a place of this size. But then the dignity and the importance of the "official" must be maintained; that is the first consideration. There is little doubt that officialism and militarism were at the root of German failure in colonization.

While wandering along the palm-fringed shore, we noticed some Natives gardening. One and all were comfortably seated on their haunches, thus obviating the necessity of stooping. It is a profound pity that desuetude prevents our adopting this excellent plan of resting without a chair.

After securing some photographs, we set off along the road that leads a few miles into the interior. Tall coco-nut palms lined our way, through the rows of which we caught glimpses of fairy-like lagoons still glittering in the evening light. Strange Javanese cattle with humpy backs were browsing here and there amongst the long rank grass, existing where Australian cattle die, literally existing, for many of those we noticed were covered with sores. By and by we had left the palm trees behind, and our road was now but a grass track between two rubber plantations. They were quite different in appearance, save for the marks of the "tapping" on the trunks. Those on one side were weird trees, sending out roots from upper branches in the most amazing way, and through their dense shade no light penetrated.

We would fain have gone farther, but the night was drawing in and we felt it wiser to return. Kanakas were still busy off-loading timber when we got back. The Native idea of doing it was to throw the wood (chiefly matchboarding) overboard onto the quay with the maximum number of breakages and the maximum amount of noise. Plank after plank was shattered, but nobody seemed particularly to mind. Meanwhile the *modus operandi* of those on the quay was amusing in the extreme. Approaching the ship with the utmost caution, as if it were an attacking enemy, they would bide their time, then suddenly seize the end of a plank and run like the devil, casting all the while the most terrified glances behind them! They were a queer-looking crowd, and, as Johnnie remarked, if the upper part of his anatomy was like some of the menfolk we saw he really would not know what sex he was!

There was not much cargo to take aboard beyond shells, which the Japanese convert into pearl buttons. Oh, yes, there were some Paradise birds, on which there is a special export tax of £1 per bird, and for whose corpses European ladies gladly paid £4 and more.

There was one rather ghastly souvenir we did wish to take with us, and a few years before it would have been within our means. It would not have proved a pleasing sight, for it would have been a human head! Not, I must add, decapitated for our benefit, but taken from the collection of one of the head-hunting tribes of New Guinea. Their plan was to boil out the brains, then refill the skull with clay and remodel the face in the likeness of the man they had eaten—whether as a perpetual reminder of an excellent repast or with what end in view I know not. In most cases the dead man's hair still remained. Three such heads we saw and examined for ourselves, and probably in the interior of New Guinea this head-hunting is still busily going on to-day.

Imagine our consternation, therefore, on observing apparent traces of blood wherever we went! But we were soon comforted, for we recalled the red teeth of some of the Kanakas, their continuous chewing of betel nut, and their frequent and successful expectoration of a bright red fluid!

We were tempted to follow the suggestion of our good friend the Padre Prefect (the head of the Catholic Missions here) and wait a month for the next steamer. He would, we felt sure, have gone out of his way to show us the work they were carrying on both at their headquarters at Alexishafen, about ten miles away, and elsewhere. They had extensive rice plantations, and made a point of giving the Natives "technical instruction" of all sorts. We learnt that there were no less than fifty Sisters at Alexishafen. The plantations were run as a limited company, the Fathers working without pay.

Then the German Protestant Church had a beautiful station across the water at Friedrichshaven itself, to which our four Samoans and their wives were bound. They were much more pleasant travelling companions than most Natives would be, who were quite unused to sitting at a table. Both the German chief steward and his Chinese assistants treated them with the utmost consideration, and it must have been a new experience for the Samoans to be waited on hand and foot.

One other companion of the voyage to whom we had to say good-bye was an interesting young German who had spent a good many years in New Guinea, and knocked out an income of £1,200 a year recruiting Natives at £5 per head, and trading on his own account, chicfly in Paradise birds. Recruiting Natives from the interior is no easy task from all accounts, and at the best of times risky. Despite his success, our friend had no use for New Guinea, its climate, or its inhabitants. He was all for Australia, and had bought a half share in a sheep station, whither he intended returning at the earliest possible moment.

There is no doubt money to be made in New Guinea, but to start a coco-nut plantation you require considerable capital—say, not less than £3,000. The trouble is that there is *no* return for the first six years, but after about the tenth or twelfth year, you might be making an easy £3,000 per annum. One such planter was aboard with us on his way to Hong Kong to meet his mother. He had been particularly *unfortunate*. His plantation was about forty miles along the coast from Friedrich-Wilhelms-Hafen. His own boat was being repaired, so he chartered the one belonging to the Catholics. With him in the boat were two priests and three Chinamen. The latter had worked well and were going with his permission by the same steamer for a trip home. All went well until they encountered bad weather and their motor engine broke down. They were in perilous plight, and might at any moment be dashed onto the reef if their anchor did not hold. Their only chance was to swim for it, and their only landing-place steep rocks against which they would inevitably be hurled by the waves. The planter led the way, and succeeded after some difficulty in clinging to the rocks and clambering to safety. The priests managed better, for they wisely seized planks of wood to assist them. One of the Chinamen who could not swim was brought ashore by two Natives, who could swim like fishes. All were saved, but none escaped some injury on the rocks, and the planter and the Chinamen lost all their belongings. The boat was soon a wreck, and in this sorry plight they had to find their way through the bush to Alexishafen. A return to the scene of the disaster did not result in much salvage beyond three well-salted birds of Paradise out of seventeen extra good specimens (worth £4–£5 each), which the planter had with him. Amongst his effects were his brother's gold watch, his own gold watch, and another watch which he was taking along to be repaired. The Chinamen, having lost everything, had no alternative but to return to the plantation. Our friend had to come on with his three birds of Paradise and such kit as he could scrape together.

The Hermit Islands

At length our short stay at Friedrich-Wilhelms-Hafen came to a close, but the memory of its beauties will always haunt us. Even now we can see the glitter of the evening light on those fascinating lagoons and the reflection of the tall palms, and hear the throbbing of the insect life interrupted only by the squawk of some unknown bird. How we long to be back amid those palm trees! Who knows, we may yet end our days as coco-nut planters on some distant sunny isle. And if we do, may it be as beautiful as Maron, one of the Hermit Isles, which, alas! like many a beautiful dream, also vanished from our sight with the morning light.

New Guinea has a thousand-and-one islands clustering round its coast, and we passed many such on our journey to Maron; a great number are inhabited by Natives. A few have palm-fringed shores, but, for the most part, they are covered with dense undergrowth. One stands out in our memory, for, owing to its height, it dominated our horizon all one day. Like Egmont in New Zealand or Fuji Yama, the sacred mountain of Japan, its shape was a perfect cone with the summit hidden in a cloud. It is volcanic, as are most of the islands here, and is still active. The Native inhabitants of this island are difficult to see at close quarters, for on arrival of the smallest craft they flee to the fastnesses of the mountain like rabbits to their holes.

The Natives of New Guinea villages seem to live in perpetual fear of their neighbours, and it is no uncommon thing for a stranger to find a village deserted by the time he arrives. Unless you are very well known, you would see nothing of the wives or children, even if you waited a week.

After a particularly hot and restless night, I awoke to find the skeleton of a ship framed in the rim of my port-hole. It appeared to be perched on dry land, but had evidently been wrecked on one of the coral reefs. It, too, was bound for the Hermit Isles, whose palm-clad shores were now in sight, and an hour or two later we were safely anchored off Maron, the centre of a group of ninety isles. Many are the stories that are told of the way in which a clerk in a New Guinea firm obtained these islands for himself and, in a few years, became a German millionaire. One story goes that he inspected the islands on behalf of his firm, reported them as not much good, and the moment his contract was up borrowed the money and secured the islands for himself—such acumen is supposed to be quite up to South Seas' standard. That was thirty-four years ago. When we came to Maron the red roof of the millionaire's pleasant house nestled amidst the palm trees on the highest point of the little island.

On the little quay there were a couple more dwellings, some offices and sheds. A staff of four or five whites and forty or fifty Natives were always at work, besides further Natives on the plantations.

Every alternate ship called here on its way to and from Sydney and Hong Kong to deliver stores and to collect the produce of the islands, which consisted first and foremost of copra from the extensive coco-nut plantations; next in importance was trepang (bêche-de-mer), dried sea-slug that made £100 per ton and is a great delicacy with the Chinese; lastly, innumerable sacks of shells, for the Japanese to make into pearl buttons. All these were very profitable industries costing little more than the labour involved; and that was not much, for the Natives, who were imported and well fed, received 10s. per month, most of which was taken out in trade goods which carried a profit of two to three hundred per cent.

One of the largest islands in the group is as far away from Maron as Maron is from New Guinea, and we should be sorry to travel in the little steam-launch that ran to and fro, but many of them lie close together, and nearly all are planted with coco-nut trees. There is one exception, and that is covered with dense bush. It is reserved for the few remaining original Natives of the group and as a hunting ground for wild pig.

No doubt one could walk round the island of Maron itself in less than twenty minutes, but it has been joined artificially to its nearest neighbour by a narrow embankment.

We wandered amongst the outhouses and watched the Natives of both sexes, clad only in red lava-lavas, handling the trays of copra or cutting up the coco-nut prior to drying it. We peeped into a shanty that served as the Native sleeping quarters, and then looked in at their "hospital," where, on a sloping wooden table, the ship's doctor was shortly to perform an operation. Neither place looked exactly inviting, but both were probably better than their own quarters would have been.

We passed on to some bamboo cowsheds with their thatched roofs, which, though possibly less hygienic, looked infinitely more charming. Here, too, under the shade of the palms, dozens of ducks quacked contentedly.

The foreshore along which we wandered with the Purser was bright with convolvulus blossoms and alive with myriads of the weirdest crabs: crabs that had shells like a snail. Suddenly the sun that had been pouring down so much heat and light disappeared. The blue sea in which we were paddling and searching for trepang lost its brightness, and a moment later we were experiencing a tropical storm. The heavy rain descended upon us regardless of the tree where we had taken shelter. A hurricane rushed upon us from nowhere, and even the smaller animals hurriedly took cover. An unpleasant-looking tree crab of enormous dimensions thought the inside of Johnnie's coat an excellent place to retire to, and started clawing onto his back, whilst a perky little lizard sought safety in the Purser's pith helmet, having run up his back and found a large ventilating hole in the top of his headgear a place of easy entry.

In the midst of our excitement there came three blasts from the steamer's siren, and again three blasts, and yet again a third time. What was afoot? Had they decided to put out to sea? Were we all wanted aboard? Meanwhile neither wind nor rain showed signs of abatement. We thought rapidly, and came to the conclusion that two months was rather *too* long to wait for the next steamer. We must race for it, and we did! Before we had gone a dozen yards our tropical clothing was drenched through and through. Paths that half an hour previously were baked dry were now ankle-deep in water and mud. Once on the quay we could see for ourselves what was afoot. Hundreds of yards from the steamer one of the lighters was gaily drifting out to sea, and speeding after it in hot haste was the motor-launch that was to take us back to the ship.

A few hours later, when we weighed anchor, the Hermit Isles were once more basking in sunshine, and the beautiful green of the coral reef stood out against the calm blue sea. That evening saw the last of our fourteen happy months beneath the Southern Cross, for we were now once more in the Northern Hemisphere.

Yap in the Carolines

For a day or so after leaving Maron our ship slipped along over a mirror-like Equatorial sea, and then our horizon changed, for the island of Yap or Uap* hove in sight. This island was purchased by Germany from Spain during the Spanish-American War; it is little more than a cable and wireless station, but there are about six thousand Natives on the island, and the Franciscan monks have a mission station there. At one time there were coco-nut plantations, but some pest had completely wiped them out. There was thus no copra to collect, and our stay was confined to the delivery of the mail and a few stores into the launch which came alongside. This was disappointing, for the Natives on the launch looked particular interesting and attractive. They are immeasurably superior to those of New Guinea, and as light-skinned as the Tongans or Samoans. They are quite charming in appearance, with their long fuzzy hair done up at the back with a big wooden comb like a jews' harp. Of clothing they have next to none, for wise men that they are they will not be bluffed into wearing unnecessary garments, not even lava-lavas. A narrow belt which passes between the legs and round the body answers the purpose of a fig leaf, and what more do they want?

It was quite a joy to note the smart way in which they

* Now under mandate to Japan.

handled the cargo, and saw what was wanted without explanation. Unfortunately their numbers are not on the increase.

Among the six thousand Natives on Yap there are no less than seven castes, the lowest two of which are slaves. About twenty out of the hundred-and-twenty villages are inhabited by these slaves. They are easily spotted from the fact that they are not permitted to wear a comb in their hair! This slavery is tolerated, for with the removal of the power of the master to punish the slave it is no longer a very serious matter. Before the coming of the European the masters wielded the power of life and death, and the slaves were slaves indeed. Another factor that is affecting the caste system is money. Wealth is beginning to override the superiority of the individual of one tribe over those of another.

Manila, Capital of the Philippines

Looking back it seemed an endless voyage from Yap to Manila. But in reality it did not take so many days, slow as our vessel was; and then had we not the excitement of the surreptitious typhoon that we knew to be ahead of us, and might it not turn back upon its course, as so often happens, and even yet overwhelm us?

For the best part of two days before we came to Manila we were steaming among the three thousand islands that compose the Philippine group. Magnificent peaks are there, for the most part richly clad in verdure of varying hues and timbered with dense forests even to the rocky edge of the shore. The heat by day and by night was equally dispiriting, damp, and exhausting, and the fact that one's baggage and wearing apparel turned mouldy unless a strict watch was kept upon it did not add to our peace of mind. By night the lightning played incessantly, and balked our eagerness to observe the Big Bear, whilst by day we could but sit and read on deck, go down to meals, and sit and read once more. For nearly four weeks we had steered our course by the sun and stars, but now our way was well marked by the excellent American lighthouses, and late one evening the red-and-white light of the naval station flashed ahead of us and Manila would be but an hour's steam beyond that.

At break of day the *Coblenz* crept from the shelter of broad Manila Bay into the harbour, a spacious anchorage protected by a mile-long breakwater. From the deck the scene was a fascinating one. The pink clouds of morning cast their reflections in the still waters of this haven where a multitude of vessels lay at anchor. There were the great modern Blue Funnel cargo boat, the trim American and Chinese cruisers and an antiquated coaster that had been badly battered by a recent typhoon at Angaur, and a host of other craft of all sizes. Hither and thither raced pinnaces and tenders, these last bearing gangs of chattering Philippinos clothed and capped in the greatest collection of oddments imaginable. Beyond lay the city of Manila, with its wharves enshrouded in fog, only the factory chimneys sticking out above it, and these busily adding to the murk, whilst across the breakwater some fishing boats moved slowly to and fro over the mirror-like waters of the bay, their quaint sails tinged by the light of the rising sun, and then they vanished behind a curtain of haze.

Soon our vessel was surrounded by curious-looking lighters, built high in bow and stern, painted in singular designs of red and white upon a blue ground, their holds covered with semicircular screens of dried palm fronds to keep out sun and rain, and under these the boatmen's families carried on their not too clean *ménage*.

For centuries Manila has been the centre of vicissitudes, the intriguing ground of bad Governments, and a hotbed of pestilence; what more would one expect from the capital city of three thousand treasure islands?

And whilst we were leaning over the side of our steamer dreaming of old-time galleons and gold and silks, pirates and treasure trove, who should come aboard but an army of most exacting Customs officials, and a most matter-of-fact Yankee doctor in khaki and gaiters! He did not feel our pulses or even suggest that we should put our tongues out at him, much as we felt inclined to do so; but the excise officers made up for any leniency on his part.

Soon afterwards we were speeding ashore in a launch, threading our way between tugs and sampans up the crowded Pasig River, whose banks were lined by craft, houses, and battlements, a bewildering jumble of modernity and medievalism. Indeed, the riddle of Manila is a difficult one to solve; it was impossible to do so in the few hours we were allowed ashore, and we were so astounded by the many strange sights and peoples that suddenly surrounded us that the memory of the place remains like a dream which one cannot explain on account of its quaint complexity and unreasonableness.

The first street we walked down seemed rational enough, but, after passing an imposing modern fire station with the brigade horses standing ready in their stalls for an immediate call, we turned into a thoroughfare lined with cubicles on either hand. Each of these cubicles represented a shop, and each shop was offering for sale identically similar wares. There would be a dozen shops with striped cottons for sale, and opposite another dozen where one would see things still *more* likely to please the feminine mind. In all of these sewing machines were busy, and the Philippino ladies, with their bare arms and curious short gauze sleeves sticking out like fairies' wings, chatted and gossiped over their purchases. Up the centre of the sun-baked street came processions of two-wheeled carts, drawn by heavy-footed water buffaloes, their dark hairless skins gleaming in the sunshine and their great curved horns swaying to and fro as they were guided by shouting coolies who pulled at a rope running through the poor beast's nose. These animals would seem to be the soul of Manila; you see them everywhere, patiently plodding along with their driver, in his queer pointed straw hat, perched on the summit of a towering load.

Manila is intersected by many narrow canals and rivers, at all times crowded with sampans and barges, and here and there you will see a group of water buffaloes enjoying a wallow in the muddy water, totally immersed except for their nostrils and a small portion of their backs.

Unfortunately our time was too limited to enable us to visit a cigar factory. We passed any number, for cigars and hemp form the chief exports of the American colony. It was some time before we could discover the European quarter of the city where Stan had calls to pay, and as we had nothing but English money on us we had to walk everywhere in spite of the tempting tramcars and buggies. The heat was terrific, but there was nothing for it but to tramp the winding narrow streets and dodge the hurrying trams and carriers. These carriers surprised us more than anything in Manila, but they are as essential to everyday life there as they are in China and Japan. This man—or rather a pretence at a man, for he is usually nearly a skeleton and what flesh does cover his bones is muscle, but muscle so overworked and strained that it stands out like whipcord—is naked except for a loin cloth, a hat, and perhaps sandals. He staggers along always at a jog-trot, with a long bamboo pole across his shoulder, and suspended from each end of it is his load. This is just as heavy as he can bear, seldom less, and these coolie carriers labour and sweat day after day in terrific heat and rapidly wear themselves away in the prime of life.

In nearly every doorway squatted the proprietor of the shop or owner of the house nursing a fighting-cock and fondling it as if it had been his baby, or else the bird was made fast to the doorstep by a string tied around its leg. Suddenly we came across another relic of the olden days of Spanish occupation: an enormous church, green with age outside, and from the inside of which we were chased by a toothless harpy mumbling for alms; whilst on the pavement overlooking a large square and beneath the towering walls of the church was a promiscuous flower market, and señoritas buying posies from the mongrel, dark-skinned flower-sellers. From what we could see, there must have been a great deal of cross-breeding between Spaniard and Philippino in days gone by, and when we came to a big green playground where was a dense mass of these white-robed gentry, the mixture of races was still more apparent. So excitable was the cheering that we asked a passer-by what the amusement might be, as we could not see from the road owing to the crowd. "Playing catch ball with ladies," he told us. Thinking that the "ladies" must be very attractive to solicit such applause we were about to leap the fence to find out for ourselves, when at that moment the meeting broke up, and the white-clad multitude invaded the sunny street and spread across it with that dazzling effect only to be found in tropical crowds.

After visiting another ancient Catholic church, wherein we found few worshippers but a startling array of unheeded spittoons, we found ourselves in the more rustic quarter of the Native town. Here the huts stand much as they were before the Spanish occupation of many centuries ago. Built of bamboo and thatched with dried fronds from the nipa palm, they are raised from the ground on poles.

To-day the main street is traversed by a tramway and electric telegraph wires, whilst beneath the huts was a swamp of half floodwater and half cesspool refuse that was both unsightly and insanitary. At the best Manila is an awkward place to drain, being built on flat ground, and at this time of year is easily flooded by excessive rainfalls and swollen rivers. Only two days before we arrived there had been a particularly bad storm, and a resident told me he had had to wade to his business from his house in the European quarter up to his knees in water. Yet when we arrived there was no sign of rain having fallen for days, except in these roadside cesspools of the Native town.

From the upper rooms of these curious habitations women looked down upon us with their great dark soft eyes and wondrous tresses of long black hair drooping over their bare arms. In the street others passed clinking their clogs, stopping at the unglazed shop frontages to buy a minute particle of meat or vegetables that they carried away proudly on flat wickerwork trays.

At one time we were interested spectators outside a blacksmith's shop, where a water buffalo, strung up in a maze of ropes, canvas, and pulleys, was being shod by three Chinamen; and at regular intervals we came across the khaki uniform of the American policemen and a crowd of coolies around a water main. But in spite of this excellent fresh-water supply that the Americans have brought to the city, notices were not absent in the Native quarter pointing out that water should be boiled.

At the end of the town we came to a cleanly looking and busy market hall, but close to it was the biggest and most unsavoury swamp in which we beheld a young Philippino maiden bathing—but perhaps this was better than the muddy waters of the river close by with a drowned cat or dog and other offal as companions.

After a long walk back into the centre of the city, and after making several enquiries, we at last happened upon the principal street of Manila, and with an almost startling suddenness we found ourselves seated in an American café surrounded by gaily dressed ladies and business and military men. All of us came here to eat ices or drink tea, transact business, flirt, and gossip.

I was waiting for Stan to finish a call on a bookseller, and as I stood on the pavement a busy throng rolled up and down the street in tramcars, motor-cars, and buggies. The buggy ponies appeared to be well looked after, but we saw no horse in Manila without the cruel bearing-rein, a ridiculous torture in the awful heat, which the American authorities ought to have had the decency to prohibit.

There were many rich Natives in Manila whose plantations of rice or palm trees enable them to keep fine cars, and it is no uncommon sight to see a hatless and gauze-winged bevy

126 Foreshore at Maron a moment before the hurricane

127 The waterways were crowded with sampans and barges

128 The German Franciscan monk in his white robe

129 Rice fields in Japan

of Philippino ladies flash by in their automobile. Indeed, we were told that the fine American-made roads make motoring a rare pleasure in these islands, which are unsurpassed for the beauty of their mountains and lakes.

This part of the city of Manila and the private houses of the Europeans, and the parks and gardens across the river, might be taken to include the second town. But there is a third and far more interesting section of this bewildering capital, and to the ancient walled city of the period of Spanish conquest we now went by way of a bridge over the Pasig River. It was strange, indeed, to walk under these venerable walls, green with the moist heat of three hundred years, and to find oneself in the centre of a typical Spanish town, coming as we had so recently from larger cities not a quarter of the age of this, and from savage islands where the best house is built of wood. Within the circumference of the thick two-mile wall one might be in Spain, with its buildings of large entrance-ways and grilled windows, its gay squares and enormous churches, which at midday were all unfortunately closed, and its streets all bearing Spanish names. But when an American gentleman, seated on a window-sill, told us in a drawl that he "guessed the priests had gone to tiffin," and when we gazed at the lanky policemen in khaki standing at street-corners, we "*guessed*" the place was a riddle, and after hurrying along the top of the wall we dashed back to the wharf. As we hastened back through the narrow streets of the Native quarter we noticed that all the goods were kept in glass cases in the shops which had no glass frontages. This precaution kept the stock better protected against mildew and damp.

On our way across the harbour to board the *Coblenz* we passed close to two large vessels that belong to the Quartermaster Department of the United States Army. A vessel of this class comes out from America every month or so with fresh troops and stores, takes invalids home, and calls at the China coastal ports and Japan.

Manila, we are told, is a place of unlimited credit, so

much so that a great many people cannot return home if they want to; it would seem to be a case of stay or *pay*! The dollar was the standard coin, and they would not look at English silver money except at a low exchange.

There remains but to add a brief comment on the Americans as colonizers. Their task has been no easy one. Merely to maintain order in the outlying parts has proved a serious undertaking, and one which even now they would not pretend to have completed. The problem they have to face is not one that can be solved in a day, or even in a single generation, for they cannot absorb the Philippino population as they are accustomed in America to absorb the alien population of Europe. Again, the impress of three hundred years of Spanish civilization is not hurriedly effaced. The Americans have poured out money lavishly: roads have been built, railways constructed, miracles performed in sanitation and the prevention of disease, everything modernized and abreast of American standards except—the people themselves. As in a palimpsest the earlier writings continually show through, so with the Philippines the hallmark of Spain is wellnigh indelible.

The dilapidated Catholic churches and the absorption of the populace in cock-fighting are the two things that stand out most in our minds; and this despite the millions that America has spent and is spending on the improvement and the efficient government of the Philippine Islands.

We steamed out of Manila Bay at sunset, threading our way among a fishing fleet whose picturesque square-cut sails flapped to and fro in a listless breeze. So past the Corregidor, the Gibraltar of the East, an island that guards the broad bay of thirty miles.

The heights of Corregidor bristle with armaments of the most modern kind; the fairway is mined, and the whole place, besides being impregnable, carried sufficient supplies of food, ammunition, and water to shelter fifteen thousand Americans and Europeans for ten years. At least this is what an American told us as our ship passed by! Our glasses enabled us to admit that this *might* be possible, and that it *might* take the Japanese guns—for the Japanese are admitted to be the next conquerors of Manila—a long time to subdue the island fort. But the most likely thing for the Japanese to do would be to turn their attention upon Corregidor last of all and reduce the stronghold from the superior heights of the main island.

Between Two Typhoons to Hong Kong

Our boat was a full one on our departure from Manila. There was the German planter from New Guinea in white, the German naval stoker in white and low neck; there was the German Franciscan monk in his white robe and pith helmet; and besides these there were an American automobile agent, a Norwegian serving in the Manila police, an Indian, and a young medical student whose father was American and his mother a Mexican. Then there were ourselves, *not* pure-blooded Englishmen, for we can boast of Italian, French, and Flemish ancestors between us; and to finish, the Russian lady who sat at a separate table and her mysterious son, who remained in his cabin when we were in port with a Mongolian quarter-master guarding his door! We found out afterwards that he was "wanted" in Russia, and had been extradited from Rabaul. We were told his crime was forgery.

So much for our two days and a half of voyage to Hong Kong, which passed pleasantly enough but for a heavy swell caused by the preceding typhoon, and no sooner were we landed at Victoria than we heard that another typhoon was following us from Manila, and they were making ready to receive it in the harbour; but unhappily, like the serpent, it doubled back on its tracks and we saw it not. Hong Kong was greatly relieved though, and the mail-boats that, thanks to wireless, had been kept informed of the direction of the storm, now all steamed into the harbour together and gave the postal authorities an extra-busy day.

The sea passage between Manila and Hong Kong is admittedly the worst in the China Seas. The Philippine coast breeds the typhoons that sweep in any direction at any moment in season; so we were particularly fortunate in escaping as we did.

We came to anchor overnight, and we awoke when it was still dark with an objectionably musky smell in our nostrils. We knew it at once to be the same as we had smelt so often in Chinese embroideries and other goods, and this unpleasant scent of the East seemed to be sweeping off the coast from the vast continent of China—the stench of the heat of day being expelled by the cooling nocturnal breezes.

We awoke again with the break of dawn and hurried on deck to obtain a view of this new world that lay about us. Our vessel was moored at the wharves on the Kowloon Peninsula, and all around us was a shouting, struggling army of coolies unloading gigantic baulks of timber from adjacent ships. In the harbour lay a whole fleet of huge cargo and passenger ships and vessels of war, and in and out among them sampans and junks wriggled their aimless course, propelled both by their strange quilt-like brown sails and by the united and untiring efforts of a trousered crew of skinny men, women, and children, who swung backwards and forwards to the long side-thrust oars.

Beyond this mass of shipping, for which the port of Hong Kong headed the tonnage list of the entire world, lay the reddish-coloured hills of the mainland, and 1,840 feet above our heads towered the splendid Peak, lightly capped in clouds, the large buildings on its summit looking like real castles in the air, and quite as inaccessible to this slaving world below!

The hotel runners were early on board, and to one of these we entrusted our luggage. They were rapidly followed by money-changers and vendors of post-cards, buttons, and wickerwork chairs.

Since we left Home we had been in some warm corners: 107° in the shade at Melbourne was bad enough, but then the heat was dry; 90° in the shade at Hong Kong is about twice as bad, owing to the excessive humidity of the air, and a good test of the heat when we landed at Victoria from the Kowloon ferry is obtained from the fact that Stiller, our New Guinea planter friend, who has spent many years practically *on* the Equator, had his cotton coat and shirt wringing with perspiration at 9 *a.m.*!

The first sight of the city of Victoria, or Hong Kong as it is more commonly known, as one approaches from Kowloon, is somewhat disappointing. Rows of shabby-looking houses line the water's edge, and rise one above the other in tiers of curiously arcaded verandas high up the precipitous sides of the Peak.

But, once on land, what a revelation! It is like the lifting of a dingy drop-scene before a tableau of the brightest staging. We were walking down the centre of a spotlessly kept street, tall and imposing buildings rose on either hand, and in the shadow that they cast staggered a jostling throng of coolie carriers shouting under superhuman loads. Bobbing along over the heads of the crowd came a pretty European woman in her chair, the poles of which rested on the shoulders of four coolies in uniform; or else at a more rapid pace came an official in his rickshaw, pulled and pushed by the swiftest runners.

Everywhere one sees Chinese characters. The streets are named in both languages, and farther on is a glimpse of a square, all green with foliage and gay with sunshine. Now and again, looking upwards, you see a house veritably in the clouds far, far above; that is a shoulder of the Peak. Up there the air is cool! No wonder the streets of Hong Kong are clean; you can be there for days and never see a horse. We were lucky; we saw *one*. The beast of burden is the Chinaman, and he is so cheap to keep and so numerous that it is not necessary to bother further. He will carry on his bamboo pole, or rather slung from it in baskets, earth and stones, cocks and ducks, vegetables, and in fact *anything* that he can manage single-handed; whilst, with a mate at the other end of the pole, we saw them stagger down the street carrying blocks of ice, heavy pieces of furniture, and iron safes. The load must be just not *too* heavy to lift, and off they go with it at a jog-trot. A Chinaman will live on a few cash a day: a cash fluctuates in value between an equivalent of 100th to 110th part of a cent, and 100 cents equal a dollar, or at the then rate of exchange, which was a low one, 2s.! No wonder these hoards of carriers look emaciated, and from the burdens they carry no wonder their faces wear a contorted and pinched look, and no wonder their lives at the game are short. What is more, it is no uncommon sight in Hong Kong to see spare-looking women carrying loads almost as heavy as those of the men; these, of course, have not had their feet bound. Women whose feet have been thus ill treated are free from burden carrying, for even without a load they can scarcely keep their balance, and have the appearance of walking on stilts.

There are some tram routes running through the streets of Hong Kong, but for the most part it might be called the City of Voices and Footsteps, and the absence of roar, the strange hush only broken by a murmur of distant shouting, comes as a delightful fascination after the racket of Sydney and the bustle of tramcars and buggies in Manila. Yet to a stranger there is something horrible in the sight of this patient, long sufferance, and dogged determination of these slavish beasts of burden. But for a resident in Hong Kong it is as natural to loll behind these sweating backs that are occasionally mopped with a towel carried for the purpose as it is for us in London to hop into a taxicab; to them the coolie is nothing more than a piece of machinery.

The hire of a rickshaw or chair was about 20 to 25 cents, or about 6d., an hour! The terror of the coolie in Hong Kong are the tall, handsome, and turbanned Sikh policemen, who, according to all accounts, are justly hated. They lend an additionally picturesque appearance to the staging of this semi-Oriental, semi-Occidental island city.

Mr. Joslyn and Mr. Pearce gave us a most cordial welcome, and the last-named gentleman took us up to his home on the summit of the Peak for afternoon tea. Hong Kong, according to some, is a homeless place from a bachelor's point of view, but upon the beautiful steep slopes and the numerous minor summits of the island that cluster immediately around the Peak are scores of pretty home-like residences, of which our host's was one. It is approached by a cable tramway that climbs almost precipitously to a fine hotel near the summit —a veritable gold mine, this building—and as soon as you are a few hundred feet above the murk of the city the air, though still not perfect, is a very joy to breathe, and one ceases to perspire even when sitting still!

From the top we sauntered along a path that followed the contours of the rich green slopes, and from here were most gorgeous views over a sea that is broken up into lagoons by the countless islands that form the Hong Kong group. In the distance were the peaked hills of the mainland coast, whilst at our feet nestled fishing villages and on the sheen of the waters the dark sails of innumerable Chinese boats.

Along our path the white-clad Europeans came and went bobbing in their chairs, and from time to time a party of pale-faced children passed in charge of their amahs.

So with the setting sun we sipped our tea and puffed at cigarettes with our host and hostess on a pretty lawn before their house; we overlooked this beautiful panorama of sea and isle, and watched the great ships creep like ants along the waterways dazzling with the evening glow.

Mr. Pearce's house was situated so close to the hillside that his little son, breaking through a slender fence, fell backwards, and would have gone many yards before the low green bushes stopped his fall had not Stan caught at him in time!

We returned to the city by tramway, and in darkness the effect of dropping down upon those thousands of lights from such an altitude was a most uncanny experience. Late as it was, we went straight to the N.D.L. offices and booked a cabin for Kobe (Japan) by the *Gneisenau.*

The following morning we were speeding along in rickshaws to Happy Valley, the most beautiful cemetery in the world. Here, midst the flowers and pine trees and murmuring streams, are many sad testimonies to the deadliness of the climate only a few years ago. Such diseases as dysentery, cholera, plague, fever, and smallpox were rife. Things have changed for the better now in Hong Kong, but still many evils remain.

A few days later we were looking down upon the muddy waters of the Yellow Sea—"China going to waste," as someone called it. Pigtails and trees have all been shorn off. There is nothing to keep the soil from being washed away during heavy rain, so away it comes down the great rivers like the Yangste and out into this desolate ocean.

Tsingtau

Of the many thousand tourists who visit the Far East, comparatively few find their way to the German port of Tsingtau.* To the conventional globe-trotter it has fewer attractions to offer than most places in that part of the world; but to the student of town-planning and development there could hardly be a more interesting example, for what was a fishing village a few years ago was now the sixth most important Chinese coastal port.

We had heard many glowing accounts of Tsingtau during our journey through the German possessions in the Pacific; we had heard of the countless millions that had been lavishly spent upon this youngest of the German Colonies; we had heard it referred to as an object-lesson to China and to the Chinese—a proof of how a lifeless junk anchorage could be transformed in a few years into a flourishing trade centre, and an indication of the results that could be achieved by a

* Now once again a part of China.

good harbour and a single line of railway under efficient management.

We must confess that Tsingtau answered all our expectations, save that the mixed styles of architecture and the presence of much new bricks and mortar gave an unfinished impression that was not beautiful. The general planning of the town was typically German: broad avenues planted with trees, and magnificent Government buildings were to be seen in every direction; everything had been thought out, and the design had evidently been for a city that would rank in size with Shanghai.

Apart from the military (an ever-changing population) there were already nearly two thousand European and over forty thousand Chinese residents. In addition, Tsingtau was increasingly used as a health resort, for its climate is of the best, and its location near the sea and in the midst of wooded hills makes it distinctly attractive.

We were fortunate enough to be armed with an introduction to Mr. Ohlmer, the Commissioner of Customs, and our visit to him is a memory that will not easily be effaced. From him we learned of the progress that had been made throughout the whole province of Shantung, upon which the prosperity of Tsingtau depends.

Shantung is not a rich province as compared with others in China. Until 1905 the export trade had been the weak point. By 1913, when we were there, straw-braid, ground nuts, vegetable oil, silk, bristles, cotton, etc.—much of it formerly shipped from other ports—were being exported from Tsingtau in considerable quantities.

The imports, thanks to a very wise arrangement by which the Chinese Customs House was located at Tsingtau, had increased materially. Under this scheme there was free trade with the hinterland and effective control of the entire shipping in the Kiao-Chau Customs district.

The province of Shantung has great possibilities in the way of coal and iron, and several large German mining companies were at work, with a capital running into many million marks.

In an adjoining room the Commissioner had a complete museum, not of antiquities, but of the goods imported to and exported from the province. At a glance one saw what goods were imported from America, what from Germany, and what from England, and similarly what was purchased by those countries. In many cases the actual prices were given.

The importance of such an object-lesson to the local trader or the foreign representative can hardly be over-estimated.

From the foregoing it will be seen that Tsingtau was of vast importance to Germany other than as a naval station. The port, it must be remembered, is directly connected by rail with Tientsin and the Siberian Railway. Many steamship lines called regularly, though the North-German Lloyd was the only European line running direct passenger boats from the China ports to Europe. By the P. & O. Co. it was necessary to change steamers at Colombo.

It is of interest to note that Yuan Shih-K'ai, the famous President of China, established his career as Governor of Shantung, and the province has him to thank for the founding of the first college at Tsinanfu in 1901. To-day there are many modern schools, because the craving for foreign learning pervades all classes.

To those who have seen Tsingtau in the making, it may come as a regret that the experiment should not be completed, but enough has been done to teach the Chinese many lessons. It will be interesting to watch to what extent they profit by them.

A Chinese town in which everything possible has been done in the way of sanitation, in which the streets are lighted by electricity and are kept scrupulously clean, in which there is a plentiful supply of pure water, a model slaughter-house, cold storage rooms, and a properly supervised market will be a novelty. If the Chinese are wise they will make the most of it.

Two Young Men See the World

JAPAN

✣

YUKO: A REMINISCENCE

("Tenshi-Sama go-shimpai." The Son of Heaven augustly sorrows. . . .

There is a young girl, a serving-maid, named Yuko, a samurai name of other days, signifying "valiant." Forty millions are sorrowing, but she more than all the rest.

In the night Yuko asks herself questions: "What can I give that the sorrow of the August may cease?" "Thyself," respond voices without sound.

She resolves to take her life in order that "Tenshi-Sama" may grieve no more, and journeys by train to Kyoto for that purpose.)

Dawn breaks; and Yuko rises to make obeisance to the Sun. Very sweet the day is; all distances, blue-toned with drowsy vapours of spring, are good to look upon. She sees the loveliness of the land as her fathers saw it, but as no Western eyes can see it, save in the weird, queer charm of the old Japanese picture-books. She feels the delight of life, but dreams not at all of the possible future preciousness of that life for herself. No sorrow follows the thought that after her passing the world will remain as beautiful as before. No Buddhist melancholy weighs upon her: she trusts herself utterly to the ancient gods. They smile upon her from the dusk of their holy groves, from their immemorial shrines upon the backward fleeing hills. . . . For her the future holds no blackness. Always she will see the rising of the holy Sun above the peaks, the smile of the Lady-Moon upon the waters, the eternal magic of the Seasons. She will haunt the places of beauty, beyond the folding of the mists, in the sleep of the cedar-shadows, through circling of innumerable years. She will know a subtler life, in the faint winds that stir the snow of the flowers of the cherry, in the laughter of playing waters, in every happy whisper of the vast green silences. But first she will greet her kindred, somewhere in shadowy halls awaiting her coming to say to her: "*Thou hast done well, like a daughter of samurai. Enter, child! because of thee, to-night we sup with the Gods!*"

Out of the East, by LAFCADIO HEARN

Chapter XV

OUR EXPERIENCES IN JAPAN

SO much has been written about Japan that we feel diffident about adding to its bibliography. But perhaps a few of our experiences ought to be recorded here to complete the title of our book, and for the fact that being nearly at an end of our money we were compelled to see this land of "The Origin of the Sun" in a way unusual to most European visitors. We found ourselves forced to abandon the methods of the conventional tourist who patronizes European hotels and is conducted from place to place in luxury, and take the way of the unconventional man who prefers to leave the beaten tracks and wander whither the spirit moves him, putting up at wayside inns and living as far as possible as a Japanese traveller would live.

From Tsingtau the crossing of the Hwang-Hai (Yellow Sea) was uncomfortably rough, and the *Gneisenau* lifted her stern to the angry seas. Our cabin, which was our principal refuge during this time, was directly over the propellers, and never before had we had such a tossing or suffered more from vibration! So that it was with relief that we at last made the narrow entrance to that fascinating water, the Inland Sea of Japan at Shimonoseki, and steamed along its entire length to Kobe one exquisite day at the end of September.

It is useless to describe such "a thing of beauty" as this inland sea; its innumerable islets with their green wooded slopes and rocky shores, picturesque waterside temples, townships, and fishing vessels are beyond compare. Many of us have seen Japanese prints and wondered at their quaintness, expostulated at their "impossibility"; but these artists have exaggerated neither in design nor colour; their countryside is remarkable for its uncommon perspectives and rich beauty of the darker hues, often relieved quite unexpectedly by a splash of brilliant vermilion, gold, white, or pink.

Stan was fortunate in having at Kobe, where we disembarked, an old friend, "D.H.J," an Englishman who spoke Japanese with the fluency of a Native. He it was who kindly undertook to travel with us for a few days and put us wise about the country and its habits.

Our first short journey was to Osaka by tram, where we found our friend and future guide in his office. He was a man of many parts, whose life had been spent in the mind-broadening arts of travel and adventure. He had been a sledge-driver in Alaska, a Chinese compound manager on the Rand, a writer of books in the sweet atmosphere of Switzerland, and war correspondent during the bloodshed around Port Arthur.

Osaka is the second largest city in Japan and almost of greater commercial importance than Tokyo itself. At the time of our visit its population was estimated at one and a quarter million. Here we found ourselves rubbing shoulders with a real Japanese crowd for the first time, and I must admit that I would rather find myself surrounded by these amiable people than the cut-throat-looking population of parts of Hong Kong or Shanghai.

We had heard a great deal in Australia and New Zealand and the South Sea Islands about the "Yellow Peril." In those countries the Japanese invasion was imminent in the minds of many, and the Japanese settler or the business man travelling for orders was a thoroughly suspected person. On every hand we were told that the Japanese merchant was not to be trusted, his word was not his bond, whereas the Chinaman never broke either, that the Chinaman was the man with whom to do a deal! Even "D.H.J." did not dispute this opinion, so there may have been something "in it"; but a nation that has made such a rapid advance as Japan has done in recent years is naturally feared by her competitors in trade.* Be that as it

* Mr. Walter Tyndale deals with this subject in a very just and amusing way in his excellent book *Japan and the Japanese*. Methuen, 1910, pp. 204, 299–304.

may, we met with no discourtesy of any kind whilst we were in their country; the further we got from the beaten track the more "distinguished strangers" we became and the more polite they became, despite our inability to speak their language.

It must not be imagined that the Japanese go about in the gaily coloured garments one would suppose from the feasts of Eastern colour our theatre managers provide: the contrary is the rule. The streets are thronged by very drably clothed crowds, but their appearance is not lacking in amusement to the Westerner. The women, in nearly every case, keep to the quiet modesty of their national costume, but many men are so attired as to make it difficult to refrain from laughing in their faces when they mix the sartorial fashions of East and West in the hopeless way they do. Imagine a top-hat, frock-coat, Japanese kimono, and yellow shoes; or Native clogs combined with a smart Western toilet and straw hat, for example! Many people seemed over-dressed, especially the women, but it was no uncommon sight to see them suckling their children on the doorsteps of their shops in the principal streets of the large cities, or labourers wearing nothing but sandals, a hat, and strip of calico between their buttocks, carrying on their daily work on the large new concrete buildings that were springing up in every direction. The most gorgeously dressed women we saw were those unfortunates, sitting like the wax models of some big modiste's establishment in the brightly lit open-sided rooms of the great Yoshiwara at Asakusa, in Tokyo, or the actresses at the theatre. But the prettiest costume of all that I have seen was worn by a lady from Nippon strolling along Piccadilly one sunny winter morning!

Electric lighting is made full use of in towns and villages, and the city streets are well served with electric tramcars, and darkened overhead by a maze of telephone and telegraph wires. Another first impression we obtained was the quaint charm of the very small children and young maidens; they gave a jolly atmosphere to the otherwise rather drab side-walks and ill-ordered streets, where large modern buildings stood side by side with old-style shops. Beauty of countenance seems to decrease rapidly with the advance of age both in men and in women; they all seem to look very much alike, but some of my Japanese friends tell me that they think we Europeans look all alike also, so on that point we can shake hands!

It did not take long, in spite of the wide choice at our disposal, to decide on our first objective in Japan, and this was the Amanohashidate Peninsula on the north coast in Wakasa Bay, one of the three "sights" of this fascinating land.

It seemed to us an age since we had travelled by train; it was, in fact, but six weeks ago that we had thus come from "Chilworth" to Sydney to board the *Coblenz*. Now, as we puffed along in our Japanese coach through new and interesting scenes upon our journey northwards to Umi-Maizuru, we felt once again how much there was to be said for train travelling as a means of locomotion. Japanese trains do not hurry, but they keep to schedule; the coaches (second class) are arranged similarly to those in New Zealand, with the seats running lengthwise and corridor between. The Japanese traveller invariably takes off his clogs or boots and folds his legs under him on the seat in that inimitable way which is the envy of all foreign visitors; thus there is no apologizing for treading on his toes, though sometimes, when leaving the compartment, you do trip up over his clogs or his basket of very evil-smelling vegetables that he is taking as a gift to his friends. When such a misfortune befalls you, you bow low and you receive in return such a charming bow, a smile, and a hissing noise through the teeth that at first you are not quite sure whether you are being chided or excused; the hiss is what you must go by, *not* the smile. The hiss, which is performed by a deep inhalation, is the sign of respect and veneration in Japan, but I am told the more a Japanese smiles at you the more angry he is becoming: so when he smiles and hisses together when you trip over his belongings, you can translate his meaning pretty

130 We abandoned the methods of the conventional tourist

131 Japanese village on the shores of Lake Biwa

132 Sacred Tortoises at a Japanese Temple

133 Our ablutions next morning took place at a window overlooking the lake.

accurately thus: "Granted; but why don't you look where you are going!"

Curious as they are about the appearance and comings and goings of all foreigners, in the railway train the Japanese will often turn their backs on you, preferring to gaze at the passing scenery out of their own window in their comfortable squatting posture. This, on a long journey, is a relief from the study of the physiognomy of one's *vis-à-vis* that is denied the European whose heels he has long since forgotten to use as cushions to sit upon! At the end of each coach is a lavatory which is unlike anything of its kind that I have seen in Europe, Africa, or Australasia, but similar to what one finds in every Japanese inn, just a simple hole in the floor with an efficient porcelain surround.

We noticed as we stopped at the wayside stations that these were all named in English letters as well as Japanese, and many of the notices also; this was, we thought, very considerate of the authorities, and an excellent way of assisting the foreign traveller. "D.H.J." insisted on our giving our sandwiches, with which his wife had thoughtfully provided us on leaving Kobe, to some Japanese kiddies in our coach; and whilst they were soon busily engaged in munching them and peering at us with their large dark eyes over the tops of the crusts, our friend bought three boxes of *bentō* from a refreshment room at one of our stopping places. *Bentō* means a luncheon and it was to prove our first introduction to Japanese food and *chopsticks*! Out of a clean white wooden box about the size of a small strawberry punnet came a meal as neatly packed, as carefully conceived, and as appetizing in appearance as one could wish to see. Here was warm boiled rice pressed tightly in the bottom of the box, enough in itself for a meal, and often arranged in sandwich form with seaweed in the place of bread. Above one found a whole collection of dainties to help down the rice: these consisted of curious tasty beans, pieces of chicken, cooked and raw fish, and strange roots of plants and sometimes ginger. In a sealed envelope bearing a charming design were to be found the chopsticks, still in one piece, proof of their not having been used before, but easily broken asunder at one end. Stan and I were naturally modest about making our début as eaters with chopsticks in a public railway carriage, but the kindly instruction of "D.H.J." and the friendly amusement of our fellow passengers quickly put us at our ease, and although the swaying motion of the train did not assist us, we managed this most intricate task fairly satisfactorily. If it recalled to us the helplessness of our infant days, the tea-set that contained the liquid refreshment of our meal did even more so. In England we think nothing of paying 4d. for a pot of tea; the usual charge on the Japanese railways was 1d. (5 sen), and at this price teapot and cup were thrown in! So fascinating were these little utensils that it seemed a pity to throw them away as most people did, either out of the windows or under the seats. We wanted to keep all of them as mementoes for our friends, but our luggage being already greatly overburdened we only retained one or two. I shall have more to say about Japanese tea later, but by now our train had arrived at Umi-Maizuru, and we were soon seeking out the little steamer that was to take us across the head of Wakasa Bay to Miyazu, where we were to sleep the night in our first Japanese inn.

Amanohashidate

Being a small boat, of course the sea was rough, and we, in spite of our thousands of miles of ocean travel, were unwell. But in about two hours we were ashore again, and traversing the rather dark village streets of Miyazu. Here we were in real Japan—anyhow as far as buildings were concerned—and "D.H.J." was asking the way of two children who, lantern in hand, led us to the picturesque Seiki Hotel. On clapping our hands a "né-san" (waitress) came shuffling along on her straw sandals to slide open the door for us, but before entering we had to sit on the threshold and remove our boots. After choosing a pair of sandals from a large collection in the passage, the né-san shuffled off upstairs with our knapsacks, whilst we all shuffled after her. To balance a Japanese sandal on your foot when its only attachment is a thong between your big and second toes, is almost as great an achievement as eating with chopsticks, and as we went upstairs to our rooms Stan and I kept parting company with our footwear, which more often than not went rolling down to the bottom just as we reached the top step! "D.H.J." laughed immoderately at our discomfort, and the né-sans, now collecting from all parts of the inn, hissed and bowed excitedly.

In these days of cinemas and excellent Press photographs most people know what a Japanese house looks like, and they know it is built of wood, the inside walls of paper or matting stretched on a wooden framework, and the passage-ways mostly of wood; but what most folk do not know, perhaps, is that the floors of the rooms are composed of mats. These mats are not like those we import into the West. They are made of finely woven rush with a uniform surface measurement of two or three square yards, and underneath they are padded to some depth with compressed hay or straw, so that when you sit on the floor, which is the Japanese chair, even if you do so suddenly or ungracefully, as we did, you do not hurt yourself. To look at and walk upon, these *tatami* resemble the even surface of an ordinary floor, and the rooms are described not as large or small rooms, but by the number of mats they contain—a five- or six-mat room.

Our né-san drew aside a sliding paper wall, switched on the electric light, and instantly a spacious apartment was revealed to us, exquisitely empty and shining with spotless cleanliness. The only furniture consisted of four elbow rests beside which were four cushions disposed about the centre of the room; a charcoal brazier and smoking utensils stood near by the rice bowl on its little stand. In a central alcove hung the only mural decoration, a beautiful kakemono, beneath which on a low lacquer stand was a china group of a geisha picking wax out of a red god's ear, and a simple vase containing two or three blooms of the national flower—the chrysanthemum. Beside a sliding paper-covered window that gave access to a balcony overlooking the bay was another vase of three or four pretty blossoms, standing on a little low lacquer table upon which our evening meal was soon to be served. Near a second window a few low box-like cupboards contained our bedding; the tea-set, large brazier, and kettle completed the furnishing of our eight-mat room, the woodwork of which was scrupulously finished and polished.

The maids had withdrawn—after some conversation with "D.H.J."—and we divested ourselves of our coats, collars, and trousers, but before this operation was over they returned with kimonos and our landlord's presents, which consisted of a fan, a pretty towel, or some such knick-knack done up in a daintily printed paper wrapper. This was the response to "D.H.J.'s" gift of *chadai* or tea-money, which varies in accordance with your status and the amount of attention you expect.

The charges at Japanese inns are very moderate, and are arranged to suit all purses. The innkeeper would be in a poor way if his charges were not supplemented by tea-money, given at the beginning or end of the visit, and as many people like to be thought of more importance than they are the landlord does not fare so badly! A European who visits a Japanese inn is a distinguished guest, whether he feels it or not, and his gift must be according to his status. But the ceremony is not over with the presentation of the tea-money, for the little maid to whom you make the gift, after much bowing and scraping, returns with a formidable document which is the official receipt for the *chadai*. In our case the amount was rather substantial, and the landlord himself followed swiftly on the heels of his domestic. Crossing the threshold of our room he dropped on his knees and, placing his hands on the floor so that his forefingers and thumbs formed a triangle, he bent forward in a low respectful bow until his nose touched the matting bounded by his fingers, then slowly straightening his body again he made the curious hissing noise between his teeth. He repeated this salutation three or four times, not a flicker of a smile crossing his face, and as he rose to his feet and backed bowing from the room we inclined our heads and hissed in return. All this went on while we were still in a state of *déshabillé*, but now we donned our kimonos and the né-san conducted us downstairs for our evening bath without which no self-respecting Japanese will conclude his day.

We had heard something about this ancient custom from "D.H.J." Apparently the Japanese knew all about "tubs" long before the West was awake to their necessity, and recently it was still the custom, in remote country places in the south, for the townsmen and villagers to bring their bathtubs out into the street before their dwellings every evening, fill them with nearly boiling water, and discuss the current gossip of the day with their neighbours as they disported themselves with their wives and children and guests in these steaming vats of liquid. To modern Western eyes this would be an even more startling revelation than the first sight of a Native African woman at home in her kraal, or one's first impression of the beauty chorus at the Casino de Paris, for a Japanese sees no immodesty in appearing entirely nude in his or her bath, even when taken in the public highway, so that loin cloth or bejewelled cache-sex are unnecessary. But in these days, such is the rapid assimilation of Western civilization in Japan that the outside tub bath is nearly a thing of the past, but not so their national conception of modesty. The bathroom in which we found ourselves was very different from anything of its kind that we have in the West; the bath was of wood and let into the floor, under which presumably was a charcoal furnace to heat the water; you soap and rinse yourself standing on the floor, a dipper always being at hand in place of a sponge, and no one would contemplate being so dirty as to get into the bath until he had made himself clean.

We were nearly ready to plunge into the steaming water

when the paper wall was slid aside and a charming né-san appeared with towels, and our embarrassment was considerably increased when she insisted on scrubbing our backs—a pleasing indignity we had not suffered since the days of our infancy! But there is no privacy in Japan; to us this was rather alarming, but the Japanese think nothing of it, and are surprised that anyone should see anything unusual or immodest about it. Certainly no one seems one penny the worse, and it serves to show how much these things are a matter of convention, for there are times when the Japanese are scandalized by what *we* think is an ordinary action!

After a good soak in the hot bath and a cold sponge down from a tank of cold water which is generally to be found handy, we preferred to dry ourselves on our own towels to those provided by our hotel, which were no bigger than a large handkerchief.

The maid remained with us until we were ready to return to our bedroom, where, clad in little else than a kimono which left our chests, arms, and legs bare, we awaited the coming of our evening meal and practised sitting cross-legged on our floor cushions. Presently a commotion, tittering, and shuffling of feet in the passage announced the arrival of our supper. We each had a tray on which were several little bowls of various delicacies, and two larger bowls, one full of hot soup, the other empty but to be filled later from the enormous rice-bowl which was in charge of one of the attendants. The meal went off pleasantly enough. We were getting more *au fait* with our chopsticks, and were amused by "D.H.J.'s" conversation with the né-sans and their answering prattle. They sit on the floor opposite the guest during the entire meal, and their duties are to keep his rice-bowl and teacup filled, amuse him and be amused by him, and attend to his every command.

We learned that it was necessary to sleep with our valuables under our pillows, and the windows shut and shuttered, owing to the common prevalence of robbers, and later on when the shutters were drawn and bolted for the night the noise made by our attendants was such that we might have been prisoners being locked in their cells. When the meal had been cleared away it was a problem to know what to do, for one feels very absurd sitting on a cushion in the centre of the floor of an empty room. Writing, in that position, was impossible, nor had one any enthusiasm for reading. As a result we generally turned in early, and when we were ready to do so we just clapped our hands: the sliding panel on one side or the other of our room immediately slipped open and the little né-san arrived with something which might be described as a cross between a mattress and a piece of felt. This she carefully laid on the floor, together with a pillow cylindrical in shape and about as hard as a piece of wood. We looked at the pillow in amazement, for no one could ever sleep with their head upon it. But the Japanese use it to support the neck. It would never do for a Japanese lady to put her head on a pillow, for her coiffure is generally so elaborately done that it is intended to last for a week or more! To the surprise of our né-san we discarded the pillows she had brought, and seized the cushions upon which we had been sitting and which she was about to remove to the cupboards at the end of the room.

By way of covering we were supplied with a wadded garment—*O-yogi**—like a kimono and fitted with sleeves. Stan and I thought, naturally enough, that these sleeves were meant to put one's arms in, so as we lay on our backs we proceeded to thrust our arms through the sleeves and draw the garment over us, much like putting on a greatcoat hind-side before! When "D.H.J." and the maids burst out laughing we realized that we had made fools of ourselves once more, and they explained the correct way to use the arms of our covering was to tuck them under us to keep the small part of our backs warm. It was a thousand pities that the rule of the house would not allow us to sleep with our shutters open, for as we stepped out onto the balcony for a few moments the view that was revealed to us filled us with admiration. It would

* Winter = *Ō-yogi*; summer = *Ko-yogi*.

be hard to imagine a more perfect Japanese picture. Immediately below us the land-locked bay was spread out like an immense carpet of dazzling silver bordered by the blue-black surrounding hills at the foot of which twinkled here and there the orange lights of waterside villages. Near by a grotesque pine tree cast weird shadows upon adjacent tile-roofed Native houses, and a sampan, moored to the embankment of rough stones, swung gently this way and that to the lapping murmur of the little moonlit waves. It was to this whispering music of water, still audible though the shutters were now closed, that we lay down to sleep for the first time in a *real* Japanese bed!

A Japanese inn is one of the cleanest places imaginable, for there is precious little in it to get dirty, and as I have said before you take off your boots before you enter. Moreover, twice a year is the *Ō-Sōji*, or Great Cleaning, when every house in Japan, if of Native construction, is practically dismantled, cleaned, and put together again by order of the Government! This takes place in the spring and in October, and on more than one occasion we witnessed our hostess and her assistants busy taking down the wood and paper walls or *shōji*, fixing new paper on them, and washing the woodwork, and so on. But in spite of all this cleanliness, personal and domestic, Japanese bedding is invariably at fault, due no doubt to the fact that each guest shares the matresses and kimono in turn, and it seems unlikely that these are cleaned more often than the other furniture of the inn. Again, the *tatami*, or thick rush mats that comprise the floor, form excellent hiding places for unpleasant insects, and although such creatures are not supposed to exist in polite society our experience of eighteen months' travel points to the fact that there are few parts of the world that are absolutely immune from parasites, and in particular fleas, and they were the only real source of discomfort of which we had to complain in Japan. These and similar disgusting pests can spoil the traveller's enjoyment so completely, from a moral and physical point of view, that it might help others to mention here oil or essence of pennyroyal which, smeared lightly over the body before retiring for the night, will keep most insects at bay. It has a very pungent scent which is unpleasant to many people, but there are much worse smells to be encountered on a journey such as ours!

We were awakened next morning by the ghastly racket of opening the shutters, a typically Japanese noise. The *shōji* behind them were also drawn aside, and a glorious view was revealed to our still sleepy eyes. Such reflections of white sails and pine-clad mountain slopes on the shining surface of the bay; such golden tones of sunshine! And all seen from the floor-level of our room where we lounged on our quilts! After feasting our eyes on this charming scene in the contemplative manner of the born Oriental, we shuffled off in our kimonos and straw sandals to the passage, where, at a long open window, a row of brass basins were suspended outside on a shelf of battens. Here in the warm morning sunshine we proceeded with our toilet. Stripped to the waist, we leant out of the window and splashed about in the basins, whilst the né-san, going about her household duties, criticized our anatomy from the opposite wing of the building. Below us was the little garden of miniature rocks, ponds, plants, and stone lanterns without which no hotel courtyard is complete, and on this exquisite example of Eastern art we, together with our fellow guests, spat out our tooth water and emptied the soapy contents of our wash basins. Then back to our room, back to the beautiful view of lake and mountain, the blaze of sunshine and breakfast! This meal is almost identical with all other repasts, rice being the foundation for one's day's work, whilst raw or cooked fish, fish soup, chestnuts, sweet potatoes, salt and sour beans all help it down, and sips of hot bitter green tea complete the menu. We found ourselves unable to consume more than two bowls of rice at any meal, and even that with difficulty, whereas a Japanese would have his bowl replenished four or five times.

We were soon on the tramp to Amanohashidate, around the wooded shores of an inlet of the bay. Although this was a very much longer way of arriving at our destination than going by water, we enjoyed the walk immensely, for many weeks had elapsed since we had been able to stretch our legs in a steady swing for two or three hours. At Monju, where there is a most picturesque Native inn, we took a sampan across the narrow piece of water that separated us from this curious two-mile-long strip of land, only about 200 yards wide, which is known as the Amanohashidate Peninsula, and counts among the "three sights" of Japan.

The sun had been shining brilliantly, but now a cool breeze and the shadow of countless weather-beaten fir trees which lined our way made walking a real delight. At short intervals we passed quaint temples, with their stone lanterns and *torii*, and pretty tea-houses with gardens at the water's edge where pleasure seekers come to bathe in summer time; and now and then we met a fisherman clad in a queer-looking raincoat made of reeds and a large round hat of coarse straw. When at last we arrived at the end of the peninsula we quenched our thirst with citronade at a refreshment house before starting the climb up the hill to Narai. The ascent was steep, hot, and exhausting, but it did not take us long to arrive at the celebrated viewpoint. Here we admired this wonderful panorama in the true Japanese fashion by standing on a stone bench with our backs to the view, and, bending down, looking at it upside down from between our legs! Whilst we were busy with our *bentō* and green tea supplied at the tea-house near by, we were delighted by the arrival of a Japanese picnic party of ladies and gentlemen who appeared to be more overcome by the arduous climb than we had been. Imagine our astonishment when both sexes started stripping to the waist and had a good rub down with the sweat towels which are an important item in the equipment of every Japanese tourist. They showed not the least embarrassment at our presence, nor did the ladies take any precautions to retire behind the trees!

After they had cooled down they in their turn began an examination of this unique view. One gentleman was very annoyed because, as he said, he could "see nothing in the view" between his legs. He girded his kimono up to his buttocks, but kept getting trees and people in his line of vision instead of the much desired two-mile-long peninsula, which at this height up the mountain side resembled the tail of an enormous lion stretched across the calm shining waters of the bay.

We climbed the hill still higher to visit the ancient temple, and after ascending what seemed to us an endless flight of steps we had a long talk with the shrivelled priest who warmed his hands over a fire-box and puffed at his diminutive pipe intermittently. He told us—with his tongue in his cheek—that the only difference between Buddhists and Shintoists, the two principal religious sects in Japan, was that the priests of the former received offerings of vegetables and the Shintoists received presents of fishes! He might have given us a little more enlightenment had he pointed out that Shintoism stresses reverence for and worship of ancestors, and Buddhism faith in a future state of happiness.

That evening we returned to Mizazu by sampan, across the darkening waters of the bay. This craft is propelled by means of an oar over the stern which causes the boat to rock unpleasantly. We had an hour's run for 40 sen (not quite 1s.), but our old boatman made a special bargain with "D.H.J." on the understanding that *he* "squeezed" an extra 10 sen out of us "foreigners" at the end of the trip! This was our first experience of the famous Oriental "squeeze."

The "Rats" of Nara

In a strange foreign land like Japan we were particularly fortunate in having a friend like "D.H.J." to act as interpreter for us; so many people lose the joy of travel by being unable to speak or understand the language of the country in which they find themselves, and in this way many misapprehensions have been circulated, especially concerning those nations whose ideas differ so widely from our own. Thus we were eager to see all we could of Japanese life and scenery in the few days "D.H.J." could devote to us. So the following morning we pressed through to Nara, the ancient capital of Nippon, having two or three hours in Kyoto on the way. It rained solidly all day long, and we had a good view of the way in which townsfolk and country people dress to meet the deluge, which is often very severe. Clogs built high off the ground came into evidence, and one wondered how the wearer could possibly walk in them, much less hop in and out of tramcars. The reed coats and wide straw hats were interesting to those who have relied on mackintoshes all their lives, whilst the immense umbrellas of oiled paper, generally painted a dull brown and decorated with the name of the owner in big black letters, were exceedingly practical. One wondered how their owners would pack them away when they mounted a tramcar, but this also was easily done, for a Japanese umbrella is held when shut by a loop in the top where ours have a ferrule, and the ends of the ribs fold compactly round the handle, and being pointed downwards they do not sag outwards and catch in baskets and handbags as ours do in the West.

That night found us guests in another Japanese inn, not quite so fascinating as the Seiki at Mizazu, but the né-sans who attended us at the evening meal were much more full of fun, and one of them amused us very much by singing "Gory, gory, A-e-ooia!" The Japanese find it very difficult to pronounce the English letter *l*. That evening also conversation turned to robbers and rats; we were told that these unpleasant rodents often amused themselves at night by running over the sleeping guests as they lay on the floor. Eventually bedtime came, our room was converted into two as if by magic, by the sliding into place of two or three *shōji*, and we were soon sound asleep. Some time later I was rudely awakened by a terrific thud which seemed to come from the adjoining room where "D.H.J." was sleeping alone. Suspecting a visit from the robbers we had heard so much about, I quickly aroused Stan, who was in charge of our electric torch. I should mention here that Japanese robbers have a nasty way of seizing their sleeping victims by the ankles, so that it is impossible for them to jump up onto their feet from the recumbent position—an accomplishment of ju-jitsu in which "D.H.J." was very proficient. We listened a moment but could hear no sound; fearing some misfortune had befallen our friend we called out to him, and were relieved to hear him reply that he was quite all right, but that he had been aroused by what he thought was a rat nibbling at his feet! He recommended us to go to sleep again, and with this assurance we were soon dreaming of far-off lands. It may have been an hour later, perhaps a little less, when Stan and I woke up suddenly and simultaneously struggled to our feet at the sound of two more terrific thuds. We again called to "D.H.J." and asked what was the matter. He said he *suspected* robbers this time, as someone *seemed* to be trying to get at his feet, and he saw the *shōji* at the other side of his room had moved a little! He told us to stand by where we were, whilst he made a tour of inspection of his room and the passage. If he called we were to dash to his assistance with what weapons we had—we only had our fists! After what seemed to us an interminable time, "D.H.J." returned to his room and spoke to us through the paper *shōji*, telling us he could find nothing amiss, and we had better return once more to our beds and forget all about it. Most probably, he added, he had been disturbed by rats.

Next morning, when we met at the row of brass wash-basins in the passage, he gave us an amusing and detailed account of what had actually taken place during the night. On both occasions he had been aroused by a tickling sensation on the soles of his feet, and twice he had leapt up in the way he had been taught at a ju-jitsu school when he was a boy. The first time, thinking he had been disturbed by a rat, he did not trouble to make a thorough investigation of his room, but on the second occasion he saw a dim light shining through the slightly opened *shōji.* When he went to investigate he found the two women who had waited on us that evening squatting on their heels and convulsed with suppressed laughter. He asked them what they meant by disturbing his slumbers and tickling his feet in this unseemly manner. They answered in a profound whisper that they much regretted breaking in upon the honourable slumber of his excellency their guest; their desire was really to communicate with the honourable foreigners his friends, but as we could not speak Japanese they had taken the liberty of awakening our interpreter. Thinking we might feel frightened after the dreadful stories we had heard during the evening they wished to offer us their company for the remainder of the night! But "D.H.J." knew that we preferred to sleep alone, and ordered the né-sans away, and not wishing to let us know what was afoot he came back and told us that he must have been awakened by rats! The rats of Nara, therefore, will remain ever green in our memories, and longer perhaps than the sacred deer that ornament the parks of the shrines and temples, and are so tame that they feed from the hand of enchanted visitors.

The greater part of the following day we spent sightseeing in Nara, which is certainly one of the most picturesque spots in all Japan, and was the seat of Imperial Government from A.D. 710 to 794.

At the end of such a lengthy volume as this, it is impossible to give an adequate description of the scenery and places of interest in this astounding country; all we can do is to mention where we went, as a guide for future travellers who happen to read these lines and refer to those less frequented places which appealed to us as worthy of special mention. Nara, then, is a place, like Nikkō, which we visited later, where the Japanese temple is to be seen in all its grandeur. Here the great Shinto temple of Kasuga, founded in 768, is a glorious example of the Japanese religious spirit. Approached by lines of some three thousand stone or bronze lanterns called *Toro*, and surrounded by magnificent lofty cryptomerias, it is in itself a sight worth coming many hundreds of miles to see. Then there is the Tōdai temple, founded in 728, which contains the famous Nara-no-Daibutsu, the colossal image of Buddha completed in 757*; some idea of the size of this statue may be realized by the following figures: height, 53 feet 6 inches; length of face, 16 feet; length of finger, 4 feet; and circumference of the lotus leaf behind the head, 69 feet. There are many other temples of equal interest and charm, and these, with the park-lands and Imperial Museum, make Nara one of the most attractive towns in Japan.

Later that day we took train to Otsu, on the shores of Lake Biwa, the largest lake in the country, thirty-eight miles in circumference and some thirteen miles across; it has been likened to Lake Constance in Switzerland for its serene beauty. Otsu is quite a large town of about forty thousand inhabitants, and here we slept the night.

No adventures befell us worth recording, and the next morning we were crossing Lake Biwa in a little steamer, and arrived in due course at Hikone on its eastern shore. From the castle grounds, which have been turned into a public garden, there is a wonderful view over the lake and surrounding hills, whilst the castle itself is of particular interest to the foreigner, for it belonged to the celebrated daimyō named Ii Kamon-no-Kami, who was assassinated at the Sakurada Gate of Tokyo in 1860 because of his supposed desire to open the country to foreign intercourse.

From Hikone we took train back to Otsu, and here we boarded a barge-like boat on the Biwa Canal, and were soon dropping downstream towards Kyoto with thirty jovial Japanese students who sang *John Brown's Body* and *God*

* The image was begun in 746, completed in 757. The original Buddha was injured by fire and also the one that took its place. The present one was erected in the sixteenth century.

Save the King for our special delectation. The canal passes through many tunnels, and the banks are covered with cherry and maple trees; the leaves of the latter were just beginning to turn, and made vivid splashes of colour here and there. The hours thus spent in the descent to Kyoto passed pleasantly enough, our fellow passengers being eager in their questions about England; our only regret was that we could not reply with a Japanese song, but we applauded theirs with shouts of "Banzai!" which means "Ten thousand years," and is the national cry which expresses congratulation. When we parted from them we bowed low and hissed and said "Sayonara" ("Good-bye"), which seemed to amuse them very much. As we made off to the railway station to take train back to Kobe we were "honoured" by yet another round of *John Brown's Body*, which floated over the still waters of the canal, and faded away as the distance increased between us and our cheery companions of the barge.

From Miyajima to Atami

That night it was a joy to creep between the cool sheets of a European bed under the hospitable roof of "D.H.J.'s" house at Kobe. That was the end of his chaperonage, and the next day we parted from him with regret, for he had to return to work. We set out on a dash to Miyajima, some hundred miles distant, which is the station where one descends to take boat for the delightful island of Itsukushima, another of the three famous sights of Japan.

Of the many beautiful temples in Japan here is to be found the gem of them all perhaps. It is a Shinto temple called Itsukushima, and our guide book informed us that it was "dedicated to the Goddesses of Ichikishima-hime, Tagori-hime, and Tagitsu-hime," the three Graces of Nippon maybe. This was the first time that we found ourselves entirely alone in Japan, and thanks to the few words "D.H.J." had taught us and his other instructions in etiquette, we found we got on quite all right. Nevertheless we had made arrangements with the Welcome Society of Japan (a most excellent institution) at Kobe to provide us with a student guide, who was to travel with us during the remainder of our stay in the country. But here at Miyajima we were alone, and being experienced travellers by this time we greatly enjoyed the regained freedom of being our own boss.

We had, alas! no time to explore the island of Itsukushima in detail, an island paradise from all accounts, but we were spellbound by the beauty of the temple. Built on the shore of the island, it appears at high tide to be floating on the sea. About 170 yards from the temple, and apparently well out in the sea, stands the "Great Gateway" or Ōtōrii, the uprights of which are 44 feet high and its cross-beams 78 feet wide. No Shinto temple is complete without its *tōri* or gateway; you see them everywhere in Japan; they are as conspicuous in the landscape as our own church spires and towers are at Home. The Ōtōrii at Itsukushima is perhaps unique, and its setting undoubtedly so. At high tide or low tide, by moonlight or in the full glare of the sun, it makes a fascinating picture which words can hardly describe. All around the little bay in which it stands are pine-clad hills, and quaint rooftops peep out from the tangle of branches. Along the foreshore moss-covered stone lanterns, sacred deer, and long-legged cranes complete the detail of this charming scene so Japanese in every essential. Near by on a hill is the Senjōjiki, or "Hall of One Thousand Mats," constructed in 1582, and here at the time of our visit was an enormous collection of objects that looked like ping-pong bats inscribed in Native writing with prayers for those who were killed or had fought in the Russo-Japanese War.

Of Yokohama and Tokyo, whither we went next in company with our student guide Ken (which was not his real name, by the way), I propose to say little or nothing: other writers have told about them at length. Of course we saw all the principal sights in each, and Stan was exceedingly occupied with business calls.

We were very fortunate in the discovery of a most comfortable Native hotel with moderate prices in Tokyo which we made our headquarters for a week or so, and came back to it from time to time after visiting Yokohama, Nikkō, and the Hakone district.

Ken was not a success from the start. He was rather morose, and seemed to get a swollen head from the fact that he was acting as interpreter to two "honourable foreigners." He knew a little English, and of course wanted to learn more, and he wasted much of our time and patience, I fear, pestering us with questions. We, on the other hand, found that we were quite capable of looking after ourselves, especially in Yokohama and Tokyo, where English is pretty generally known, and we were resentful with ourselves for having so foolishly blundered into this contract with the Welcome Society. We had to pay Ken's expenses as well as our own; we had taken him on for so many days, and he was adamant on working out his contract.

The crisis arose when we took him on a few days' walking tour in the Hakone district after ten days of strenuous sightseeing and business in Tokyo. We had visited Miyanoshita, a charming spot at the head of the Itzu Peninsula, some 1,000 feet above sea-level, and famous for its exquisite scenery and hot springs. From here we were making for Hakone some seven miles farther on and 1,000 feet higher. Our tempers were a little ruffled by the fact that after the glorious sunny days in Tokyo the weather had now changed; a thick mist had descended on the hills and threatened to obscure our eagerly anticipated view of the reflection of Mount Fuji in the lake of Ashi-no-ko. In the mist we thought we had lost our way, and we asked Ken to request a passing Japanese pilgrim if we were on the right track. This conversation lasted five minutes, lasted ten, and went on for even another ten. Stan and I were becoming exasperated; we were already late, and were beginning to wonder if we should not be cut off by darkness before our destination was reached. At last we shouted to him, "Come along, Ken, we can't wait any longer," and with that turned on our heels and left him. Some minutes later he came panting up the hill after us, and when we asked him if our direction was correct he replied that he had not arrived at that part of the conversation with his "honourable" compatriot before he was forced by our withdrawal to leave him! In Japanese I am told there are different kinds of language in which to address different grades of society, and the greater the importance of the person spoken to the more often does one bow and hiss, and the more flowery does one's language become. The health of the entire family has to be enquired into, and perhaps the history of the family's ancestors also, if one would be really polite, and if you happen to be escorting "honourable foreigners" then of course their history has to be added to the catalogue.

We also found that Ken's company in the evening was too much of a strain, after having him in tow all day, in spite of the fact that he presented me with a wonderful game of "solitaire," which we played assiduously every evening until we were sick and tired of it! Hakone proved a great disappointment to us; the mist did not clear, but the shops proved attractive, and we solaced our grief at not seeing Fuji's reflected glory in the lake by buying some of those exquisite little inlaid boxes and sandalwood trinkets that the Japanese make with such taste and skill. We pressed on then over the Jikkokutōge Pass to Atami, where we came to the railway and the sea coast again; from the top of the pass, which is noted for its view, we saw nothing but mist, and this so upset our nerves that we decided to play an un-English trick on poor Ken, and whilst we sent him on some trifling errand we intended to slip off to the station and board the first train back to Tokyo! However, it was some little time before we discovered the station, and just as we were about to enter to book our tickets who should we meet in the doorway but the inevitable

Ken, who had gone there to buy a paper! So there was nothing for it but to make up our minds to "see" Atami under his escort and put up there for the night. As it happened it provided us with an interesting experience, for after supper, as we were sitting in our room trying to talk to the né-sans and playing disinterestedly at solitaire, we heard a weird cry in the street, and Ken informed us that it was the blind masseur passing by and would we like to be massaged?

Stan thought he would like to try, for we had heard a good deal about the excellent skill of these blind manipulators to whom the trade is reserved in Japan. So while he lay on his mattress quilts in a semi-nude condition, grunting and groaning to the masseur's touch, and the né-sans examined his undergarments and his anatomy, Ken and I continued with our solitaire, until filled with the healthy drowsiness brought about by exercise in the open air my chin dropped to my chest and I fell asleep, squatting there on my cushion, fantastic in my Eastern dress, just like a living effigy of some wayside Buddha.

The scenery along the coast of Atami is grotesque in the extreme. Rocks and fir trees seem to fall in a fantastic jumble into the sea, and there are many wonderful surprises to delight the eye as one walks along this rugged coast. There is also a hot geyser and splendid natural hot sulphur baths here which we enjoyed immensely. On our return to Tokyo that evening we decided that we must get rid of Ken at all costs. It was easy to invent some little fib after the examination of our letters which awaited us at the post office. Incidentally there was one from some friends inviting us to spend a few days with them in Yokohama before we sailed for home. Our time was already getting very short, so we explained to Ken very politely, but very firmly, that his services were no longer required, as we could not take him with us to Yokohama, and next day we had the satisfaction of seeing him off in the train for Kobe after we had generously bought him a second class ticket!

Nikkō

We had already learnt that an Oriental is not unlike a typhoon —he comes back when you think he has departed; my friend the son of the Samoan Chief Asi had the same characteristic; so we decided to leave early next morning for that most holy town called Nikkō, and thus place as great a distance as possible between Ken and ourselves. Our spirits revived with his absence, and it was remarkable how well we got on on our own.

Nikkō is considered the most beautiful place in all Japan for scenery, construction of its temples, and the artistic treasures they contain. Throughout the world one finds that the ecclesiastic generally selects the most beautiful of Nature's handiwork as a background for his place of worship. Here at Nikkō are the burial-places of the First and Third Shoguns of the Tokugawa line of the seventeenth century, and the common saying is: "Nikkō wo minakere ba kekkō to iuna," or "Don't use the word *kekkō* (splendid) until you have seen Nikkō."

The little town is approached by long avenues of giant cryptomerias that stretch for miles across the surrounding country; they were planted by the daimyōs of Japan in the seventeenth century, and it would be hard to conceive a more imposing Pilgrims' Way, for hither come thousands of pilgrims every year to pray at the shrines of their national heroes, and on the lofty summits of the mountains that surround this enchanting place which is naturally, as well as ecclesiastically, divine. A great number of these pilgrims come from the most distant villages of Japan. They are elected and their expenses paid by their fellow villagers, and they pray for their village and its inhabitants at each shrine they come to on their pilgrimage. These pilgrims journey as economically as they can, largely on foot; but the distances they have to traverse are great, so that the train and the rickshaw are often employed. When they return to their villages the pilgrims tell of all they have seen on their travels, and the Japanese being a very observant person sees much more in the course of his journey than temples and shrines. In this way the people, even in remote districts, are very well informed about what their country looks like and what is going on in it; and immense numbers travel long distances in spring and autumn to see the famous beauty-spots where plum and cherry bloom and russet maple leaves gleam in their greatest profusion. When we alighted from the train at Nikkō Station we did not wait to bother about our luggage, for the simple reason that we had none! We swung our knapsacks onto our shoulders and tramped off like a couple of pilgrims up the long street, lined with humble inns and shops, that led to the Kanaya Hotel. Needless to say we did not enter here, but pushed on over a bridge, and turning to the left soon found ourselves before a decent-looking inn, surrounded by giant pine trees and the swift-flowing Daiya Gawa rushing over its rocky bed beside the road. Night had already fallen, and we saw little of the beautiful scene that lay hidden in deep shadows around us.

We were received with the usual cordiality at the inn, and it was not long before the whispering waters of the Daiya Gawa were soothing us to sleep as they sped by beneath our window.

When we had been aroused next morning at an early hour by the customary racket of opening shutters and *shōji*, the sun was already high enough to flood our side of the narrow valley with its welcome rays, whilst opposite the dark wooded hill-side was veiled in a rising mist shot with shafts of sunlight. The Daiya Gawa sparkled and spumed at our feet, and not a stone's throw away to our left, lit by the full brilliance of the morning light, was the sacred and costly red lacquer bridge reserved for the use of the Emperor alone!

That evening, as we were balancing our mouthfuls of rice on the tips of our chopsticks, and sipping the green tea from our dainty cups, we managed to make a joke at which our né-san laughed right merrily. We pointed at everything and said:

"Kekkō, kekkō!" for had we not seen that day nearly all the glories of Nikkō? The mausoleum of the famous Ieyasu, the founder of the Tokugawa line of Shoguns and creator of Tokyo's greatness, and that of his grandson Iyemitsu, the third Shogun suppressor of Christianity, are among the most famous examples of Japanese art.

These two shrines cover an immense deal of ground on the hillside, and one mounts from one courtyard to another up flights of steps green with the moss of ages and overhung with cryptomerias and pine trees. Every building is ornamented and richly carved with panels of birds, animals, and flowers painted in vivid hues among which vermilion, green, silver, and gold predominate: a brilliant picture with its dark background of ancient lichen-covered trees. Among these carvings are to be found the world-renowned Three Monkeys of Nikkō, depicting "Hear no evil; Say no evil; See no evil."

The entrance-way to the tomb of Ieyasu is called Higurashi-mon, or "The Gate where One can Pass the Day," from the fact that many pilgrims spend the whole day gazing upon this wonder of human achievement. Part of the shrine of Iyemitsu consists of two superb red lacquer halls wonderfully constructed, and the "Gate of Chinese Wood" inlaid with other woods is another remarkable piece of skilled craftsmanship.

All these buildings contain a wealth of objects of art, both Japanese and foreign, that are beyond description, and together with the Fine Art Exhibition of Nikkō make a great feast of exquisite things worth going miles to see. Indeed, it is hard to say which is the finer, the display of Nature's magnificent cascades, mountains, and woods or the gems of Man's creative art that are to be found here. So much has been written about Nikkō that we will only say that it is indeed *kekkō*.

Chuzenji and Yumoto

The village and lake of Chuzenji are eight miles away, and thither we set out next day on foot. An early frost made the air crisp, and an excellent morning for a good brisk walk up the fascinating valley of the Daiya Gawa, past the refining factory of the famous Ashio Copper Mine, the largest in the Far East, and thence up a winding rock-strewn gorge with dashing cascades where the autumnal foliage of the maple trees gleamed from their surround of pines, or hung grotesquely from a rocky crevice, their lacquered boughs aflame in a sea of azure sky. Now and then a peasant passed us; here and there a tea-house greeted us, gay with pilgrims' flags. Great mountains looked down upon us, tempting us to scale their summits like all the pilgrims who came this way to climb and pray, rest and return to bathe the weary body in Chuzenji's icy waters which now broke upon our view through the border of a wood. Here the great cataract of Kegon-no-taki crashes over a precipitous rock to fall 400 feet into an inky pool below. Chuzenji reminded us very much of some Alpine villages in Switzerland, except, of course, the architecture of the villas dotted about its shores was entirely different.

We found our scanty raiment distinctly chilly that evening as we sat in our room which overlooked the lake, and tried to keep ourselves warm before the fire-box of smouldering charcoal which serves as a fire in all Japanese apartments. We were now about 4,500 feet above sea-level, and how the people managed to keep warm in their frail houses during the intense cold of their winter is a problem that we were never able to solve. Our ablutions next morning took place at a window overlooking the lake. It was a fascinating but very chilly proceeding, over which we hurried as much as possible, so after breakfast we made haste to take the road again.

Yumoto lies some seven miles from Chuzenji, and about 500 feet higher. The way there is again very beautiful, and many fine waterfalls are to be seen, beside which it is the custom to rest and contemplate. Yumoto is celebrated for its warm sulphur baths, in which we spent most of our evening, and a very pretty lake, not nearly so large as the one we had left, called Yunoumi. As we approached the village the steam rising from the hot spring gave one the impression that some of the houses were on fire. Our little inn seemed much more homely than our last at Chuzenji, and from our window we again had a glorious prospect of the lake surrounded by its wooded hills and over-topping all the great rounded shoulders of Nantaisan, the mountain of the pilgrims which had been a dominating partner in our journey all the way from Nikkō.

The day being yet young when we arrived at Yumoto, we decided to push on after a plunge in the natural hot baths and some food at the inn, and endeavour to reach the summit of the Konsei-toge Pass some 7,000 feet above sea-level, and view the sunset from there. This was the turning-point of our travels. From now onwards our faces were to be turned really homewards. This was our "farthest East"; we had been wandering for just sixteen months.

We could not find out exactly how far we had to go to reach the summit of the pass, nor was our map any too good. The mountain track we followed was rough but picturesque in the extreme, the climbing hard work, and streams often flooded our way. Unfortunately darkness overtook us before we arrived at the top, and we thought that a good hot sulphur bath was better than sleeping out among those wet rocks all night! So, after shaking hands and congratulating each other that the greater part of our World Tour was an accomplished fact, we started back at as smart a pace as we could maintain. It soon became so dark that we fixed a handkerchief on Stan's arm, so that I could follow him as he groped his way over slippery boulders and through slimy bogs. How we did not lose ourselves I do not know: our way was so ill defined in places that we had to light matches to find our next footholds, and only those who have travelled a boulder-strewn track of this nature for the first time can realize what a trying ordeal it can be, especially on a pitch-dark night. However, we did get back at last to our inn, and after another glorious bathe and some more raw fish, rice, and bamboo soup we called for our bedding early and were soon soundly asleep.

Fifteen miles mostly downhill back to Nikkō was our programme for the following day. By lunch time we had reached Chuzenji; it had been a beautiful morning, sunshine and rain bringing out to perfection the high lights and deep shadows of mountain and vale, of cloud forms, and swirl of rushing streams. At the tea-house on the border of the wood separating the calm waters of Chuzenji Lake from the 400-foot plunge of Kegon-no-taki we stopped to rest, contemplate, and eat. Having consumed our *bentō* I was just refreshing myself with the watery juice of a Japanese pear, and as I spat out the gritty, fibrous flesh my eye fell upon something sparkling in a sudden glimpse of sunshine that lit up a red lacquer stool standing by the bole of a maple tree. Feeling curious I approached the object, which at a distance looked like a small dog stretching himself after a heavy sleep. With rump on high, back hollowed, and head raised, he yawned seraphically, disclosing his shining teeth and broad dull tongue. When I got up to him I saw he was no dog at all, but a household god—a dragon, about the size of a well-grown pup. It was made of pieces of ore from the copper mine at Ashio, and its wet coat of mineral quartz gleamed in the sunlight as if studded with precious stones. I fell in love with this amusing creature at once, and indicated to the shrivelled old woman who served our tea that I would like to buy it. I held up two fingers and she hissed; I produced a two-yen piece (about 4s.) and the old lady was delighted. But I was not so well pleased with my purchase when we came at last to Nikkō that evening, for it weighed close on ten pounds, an unwelcome addition to my pack; but it remains, nevertheless, one of my most treasured mementoes of the valley of the Daiya Gawa.

Only a very few days now remained before our departure from Yokohama on board the *Kleist* for Home. Most of these were spent with friends who had a pleasant European house overlooking the great port. One day we went to Haneda where is the large temple of the Fox God, to enter which one has to pass under an amazingly long tunnel of *torii* of all sizes, and so closely packed together that it is impossible to pass between their uprights. Large ones straddled over smaller ones; some were quite plain and others lavishly lacquered or carved; all were offerings of thanks from rich and poor for the Fox God's answers to their earnest prayers.

At the village we became the eager purchasers of curious lanterns made out of the skin of a kind of globe fish. These creatures have sharp spines on their skins to keep off their enemies, and are furnished with strong horny mandibles with which they crush the shells of the mussels upon which they feed. When they wish to rise to the surface to breathe they inflate their skins to the shape of a sphere. Their insides are considered a great delicacy by Japanese epicures, and when empty their captors stuff the skins with rice husks until they are stretched to their full globe-like capacity. They are then hung in the sun to dry, a wooden ring is fixed to the top of the back which is fitted with a wire handle and candle holder, and this very remarkable and efficient lantern is ready for service on bicycles or in drawing-rooms for many a year to come.

Perhaps the most lasting memory one retains after a visit to Japan is the beautiful things one sees in the shops. Above all else these people are artists, every inhabitant can see beauty in Nature; a leaf, a flower, an insect, a rock or the sea bring infinite delight to these intelligent people, and everything they touch, be it cheap or expensive, is turned into an object to charm the eye. From printed sweat towel to elaborately embroidered kimono, from picture postcard to matchless kakemono, from inlaid trinket box in beech or sandalwood to the magnificence of a large lacquered screen, from a common tea-cup to their glorious masterpieces in porcelain or cloisonné, these craftsmen bring beauty of form, brilliance of design and coloration to perfection. In bronze and paper it is the same. "The impossible flies before patience and toil," they say, and how well they believe in this aphorism is shown by the efficiency of the country, which has been thrown open to foreign intercourse for barely seventy years, and by the intellectual keenness of the rising generation.

Much of Japan's greatness to-day has been due perhaps to this love of beautiful things, to the deep religious regard of its people for their ancestors, and for the devotion of the Japanese mother to her family. Mr. Arthur Lloyd, writing in his very interesting book *Everyday Japan*, says: "Everything in a Japanese household turns on the mother, and if Japan has astonished the world by its virtues and powers the whole credit is due to the mothers who understand so well how to do their duties." It would be hard to find a better acquainted witness of Japanese life than Mr. Lloyd, who has spent twenty-five years in Japan in daily contact with all ranks of society.

Homeward Bound

And now we also were really "Going Home." Home is a magic word, a wonderful thought, with all those who live abroad. How often had we talked and planned on tropic starlit nights in Africa, midst the falling poplar leaves of the Canterbury Plains, and the sweltering midday darkness of rubber plantations in the Bismarck Archipelago, and here in this eastern Empire—talked and planned of Home and what we should do and when we should go there! Too few people realize what England means to those of her countrymen, and especially the women, who are forced to live so far away; and there are many who have never seen the land of their fathers, but whose love of that land is none the less keen. Even the silent, broad-shouldered, horny-handed bush whacker becomes eloquent when we talk about Home, and many a "remittance man" will stay his drinking bout and a wistful look will come into his bloodshot eye. As our boat threaded its way among the multitude of islets of this incomparable inland sea we became imbued with this same longing for the

Homeland, a sensation so difficult to describe. The glory of autumn was tinting all the coast-line, and at sundown the sky was aflame and the sea a shining and glittering expanse of mingling hues which gradually faded into darkness, leaving only the Eastern crescent moon and her escort of twinkling stars.

At Nagasaki we were surprised to find that the coaling was done by a swarm of women, who crept up and down the gangways with baskets of fuel on their shoulders like a myriad ants about their nest. A great and totally unexpected pageant, which seemed as if it had been staged for our special benefit, greeted us the following afternoon as we were setting out on our thousand-mile journey to Hong Kong. What must have been the entire Japanese fleet, stretched out in line ahead, steamed past us within hailing distance that radiant afternoon. Unit after unit they went majestically on their way, over one hundred strong, from battleship to supply ship, submarines and all. It was sunset when the last dark hulls of these heroes of Tsu-shima appeared on the Western horizon, another blazing sunset of red and gold and green and yellow, all the favourite colours of Old Japan. Whilst turning to glance over the stern of our ship all we could see was a veil of smoke, which, lifted here and there by the evening breeze, revealed patches of sepia and purple, the last and fast-disappearing islands of Nippon, "Origin of the Sun," as great in the romantic history of her past as in the revolutionary progress of her modern life.

. . . . .

Three incidents surprised us during the few hours we tarried at Hong Kong. The first of these was to see a Chinese family in a sampan fishing with a kind of butterfly net on the end of a long bamboo at the bilge hole of a liner. As soon as they caught some solid waste from the great ship, the net was lowered hastily, and its contents grabbed and eaten without so much as looking to see what it was. Then a tin-can would be dipped into the filthy water of the harbour, and the liquid gulped down with evident relish. A tub of live crabs without their shells, live fish being cut up with axes, and Oriental shoppers trotting along with the entrails of a rabbit or chicken dangling from a skewer were not very pleasant sights in the Native fish market. But these unpleasant memories were counteracted when I entered the post office to collect my mail and was told by the clerk that His Excellency the Acting Governor wished to be informed at once of my arrival! This resulted in a very pleasant evening spent on the veranda of Government House, with a superb view of a myriad lights twinkling in the dark abyss below, a distinguished and genial host on one side and a cooling drink on the other. But fortunately no one knew that I was too poor to hire a rickshaw to take me there, except perhaps the great Sikh sentries at the entrance gates who seemed to turn to pillars of chocolate as I slipped on foot between their massive forms.

We will only mention the names of Singapore, Penang, Colombo, Aden, and Suez as a few of the stepping-stones to our homeward journey. We did the classical dash to Cairo, whilst our boat was making her way through the Canal, and we had a delicious lunch at the Mena House Hotel. Long shall we remember the exquisite taste of the freshly culled dates, and the story of a French traveller who was of our party who asked us if we had ever noticed that there was a little *o* on every date stone. He told us there was a legend that when the Virgin was journeying through Egypt she ate some dates and cried "*O quel fruit délicieux!*" Ever after date stones have borne this imprint of the Virgin's lips when she exclaimed "Oh!" We rode camels for the first time on our travels around the Pyramid and the Sphinx; we visited bazaars and mosques, and slept for a few hours uncomfortably in a bed on legs. Port Said we were glad to leave to its heat and undesirable population, and when we arrived in the course of time at Naples it was midnight and pouring with rain. Next morning the Bay of Naples left us cold, and even Vesuvius did not impress us, but Genoa seemed an historic place, for here we were to part company after so many months of adventure together. Stan remained with the boat until it arrived at Southampton, calling at Algiers and Gibraltar on the way, whilst I went overland to Paris and London.

One dark December morning, just before Christmas, I was walking around the Whitestone Pond on Hampstead Heath. The stars were beginning to pale, the eastern horizon to brighten, the dome of St. Paul's was a dark smudge down in the plain of the Thames. My companion was growling at the steward, no doubt, bringing him his cup of morning tea, somewhere where the great stars of Africa wink across the narrow sea. After waiting like what seemed to me an interminable time a clock struck seven. I moved off along a road gaily lit with lamps; I came to a house—the milkman was leaving as I entered the gate. A light shone from the basement. I rang the bell, and after a slight delay, during which my heart gave great thumps within me, the door opened and I hurled myself into my old Nanna's arms: "Home!" How *good* it is!

Index

Index

Index

Index